THE [illegible])K SERIES:

Lenses and Lens Systems

Joseph D. Cooper and Joseph C. Abbott

AMPHOTO
American Photographic Book Publishing Co., Inc.
Garden City, New York

NOTE FROM THE PUBLISHER

The Nikon Handbook Series was previously published as *The Nikon Nikkormat Handbook*. The series was compiled from *The Nikon Nikkormat Handbook* and the supplements that were used to update it. As the series goes to press, it contains the latest available information on Nikon equipment.

ACKNOWLEDGEMENT

Grateful acknowledgement is hereby made to Mark Iocolano for his assistance in preparing this work for publication.

Library of Congress Cataloging in Publication Data

Cooper, Joseph David, 1917-1975.
Lenses and lens systems.

(The Nikon handbook series)
Includes index.
1. Lenses, Photographic. I. Abbott, Joseph C., joint author. II. Title. III. Series.
TR270.C66 1979 771.3'1 79-9833

ISBN 0-8174-2488-1 (hardbound)
ISBN 0-8174-2160-2 (softbound)

Manufactured in the United States of America

Contents

Introduction

This volume of the Nikon Handbook Series discusses all of the Nikkor lenses. Chapter 1, "Nikkor Lenses: Introduction," presents a general overview of the features and design considerations of lenses in general, and Nikkor lenses in particular. Chapter 2, "Nikkor Lenses: General Range," discusses the lenses most commonly used for general photography—from wide-angle through telephoto. The final chapter, "Nikkor Lens Guide: Special Lenses," deals with such lenses as the fisheyes, zooms, perspective control (PC), 45mm GN-Auto Nikkor, close-up lenses, and the El-Nikkor enlarging lenses used for close-up photography. Lens Data Sheets, detailed descriptions of each of the Nikkor lenses, follow each of the final two chapters.

This compact, seven-volume edition of the Nikon Handbook Series constitutes a significant revision of the original two-volume loose-leaf edition by the late Joseph D. Cooper. The present work is not a condensation; all of the material of the original Nikon-Nikkormat Handbook, including loose-leaf supplements volumes one and two, is presented here. Additional material on the latest Nikon equipment has been collected especially for this edition. The original text, containing references to material and techniques, has been thoroughly revised to reflect current developments.

Insofar as possible, material has been organized so as to separate descriptions of equipment from explanations of usage. In the book on cameras, for example, Chapter 2 is the basic reference source on individual cameras and their features. The handling of cameras is treated in the following chapter.

As a systems reference guide, this handbook is also designed to serve photographers (and photographic dealers) in discovering new applications and information about equipment they do not have but may want to procure. It includes historical information: the evolution of the entire Nikon camera line, beginning with the rangefinder models; characteristics of discontinued lenses for the Nikon reflex cameras; and operating information on important discontinued accessories.

In addition to being a technical reference source, the Nikon Handbook Series has been designed as a general guide to photography with the 35mm single-lens reflex camera and its lenses, accessories, films, and other materials. For example, the chapters on exposure, artificial lighting, closeups, motorized photography, underwater photography, special effects, and other subjects are fairly complete coverages of principles and methods going far beyond the use of Nikon equipment alone.

CHAPTER 1

Nikkor Lenses: Introduction

Nikkor lenses are made by Nippon Kogaku, one of the several manufacturers in Japan that make their own optical glass and completely assemble the entire lens in its mount for attachment to their own cameras. Even the glass crucibles, with their own platinum liners, are made in the factory.

Many different Nikkor lenses have been designed to satisfy almost every conceivable need of the photographer. Lenses for general use range from the 13mm extreme wide-angle to the 2000mm mirror-reflex telephoto. Special-purpose lenses include the fisheyes; the 55mm, 105mm, and 200mm Micro-Nikkors; the 28mm and 35mm perspective control PC-Nikkors; the 200mm Medical-Nikkor with built-in ring light electronic flash for special closeup uses, and a variety of zoom lenses incorporating focal lengths from wide-angle to super-telephoto. All are covered in succeeding chapters.

The present chapter is concerned with lens characteristics in general as well as design and mechanical features of Nikkor lenses in particular. It presents certain optical concepts common to all lenses. From a practical standpoint, this chapter offers some general criteria for selection of lenses based on the needs of the user.

LENS PRODUCTION IN BRIEF

The attributes of a fine lens most sought out include the quality called sharpness, which combines fine image resolution, color correction, and optical contrast; consistently good performance over the entire image area (or most of it); and maximum freedom from optical aberrations. In part, such quality is achieved through the formulation of good optical design, including the selection of ideal combinations of optical glass, superior manufacturing processes, and rigid testing of each lens.

The widest range of optical glass—more than 200 types—is now available to meet demanding design specifications. New types of optical glass have been playing a significant role in lens making including rare earths such as lanthanum and thorium. These new types of material have brought about substantial improvements in the quality and performance of Nikkor lenses and a reduction in production cost.

To put all this into perspective, this section gives a brief summary of lens manufacturing by Nippon Kogaku.

First, raw materials are cooked in a crucible. They are heated to around 1500° C. Then the mixture is either cooled in the crucible until it hardens or is cast according to its usage. The solid mixture hardened in the crucible is broken into lumps. Each lump of glass is rigidly inspected against undesirable bubbles, stria, and nontransparent elements.

After inspection, the glass is heated again until it softens sufficiently to allow for molding into rough blocks. It is then either cut and/or pressed and annealed by cooling slowly for days or weeks. From this process, discs of the right size for a particular lens element emerge. Before the next process, each glass is rigidly inspected to make sure it is completely suitable for use as a lens. In the grinding-polishing stage, the lens surface is ground by fine meshed sand (such as carborundum or corundum) to obtain roughly the specified curvature.

Next, the surface is polished with cerium oxide to obtain finer curvature, texture, and transparency. To make sure that the polished lens will have its optical axis in the center, extraneous marginal edges are ground off. Then, a thin low-refractive layer coating is applied to the glass surface by the vacuum depositing method to minimize surface reflections.

At the end of a complex sequence of operations, optical glass is produced that is *virtually* bubble-free, although complete elimination of bubbles is said to be an impossible achievement. The ground and polished lenses are then brought into a further complex of precision mechanical operations. The lens elements must be precisely seated in the lens barrel to tolerances that would impress a fine watchmaker. The separate lens elements must be aligned at meticulously precise distances from each other with their optical axes centered. The lens mount itself must be milled so that it will fit precisely into the camera mount to assure accurate alignment of the aerial image with the film plane.

The result of this combination of optical and mechanical precision is maximum distortion-free performance. Nikkor lenses provide maximum corner-to-corner sharpness without vignetting, even at full aperture. Color correction is notably outstanding. This is as important in black-and-white photography for sharp image definition as it is in color photography.

Nikkor lenses are in black mounts made of special aluminum alloys, with phosphor-bronze at points of wear to

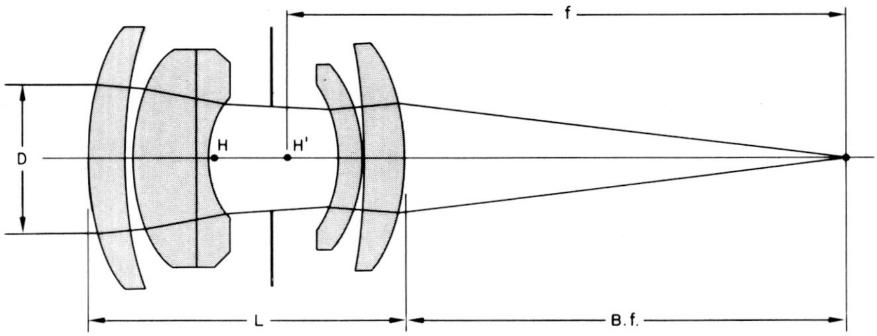

f = focal length
L = lens length
D = aperture

H & H' = principal points
B.f. = back focal length

This form of schematic is used in this book to designate the specific dimensional attributes (the "optical formula") of each lens, as shown in the abbreviation key below the schematic.

maintain continued precise alignment. These mounts average 50 per cent lighter in weight than earlier lenses, thus freeing the user of undue strain when working for long periods. Further, each black-mount lens features oversized white numerals for maximum visibility.

In addition to performance and precision tests, the completed lenses are given a series of tests for vibration, heat resistance, and sub-zero temperature, and then put through various torture tests. Only lenses that have fulfilled rigid lens standards can bear the company's guarantee of quality and leave the plant.

OPTICAL TERMS

Several technical terms are described here briefly. They have a general bearing on subsequent explanations and discussions.

Focal Length

The focal length is the factor that determines the size of the image reproduced on the film, the angle of coverage of the area of the subject to be photographed, the brightness of the image on the film plane, the depth of field, etc. The light rays that come from a point at infinity run parallel along the optical axis of the lens to converge at a point called the "focal point" after passing through the lens. The distance from the rear surface of the last element to the focal point in the lens system is referred to as the "back focus" and is not, in the strict sense of the word, the focal length. Focal length is the distance from the principal point to the focal point. There are principal points (H and H′) and focal points (F and F′) both on the object and image size of each lens.

In most camera lenses, the principal point does not coincide with the center of the lens system, especially in a telephoto or retrofocus lens where it is distant from the center. Some special lenses are designed so that their principal points cross: The first point is located on the image side and the second point on the object side.

Speed and f/number of Lens

The amount of light entering the camera through the lens is important for exposure control purposes. It is quantified uniformly and interchangeably for all lenses through use of a standard series of mathematical representations of relative lens apertures.

The maximum aperture of the lens is found by dividing the diameter (D) of the lens by its focal length (f). Thus, if the lens is 25mm in diameter and the focal length 50mm, the relative aperture of the lens, as engraved on its mount, would be 1:2 (which is the same as 25:50mm or D/f referred to as the aperture ratio or as the relative aperture). If the optical diameter of a lens is 25mm and its focal length is 100mm, the relative aperture would then be 1:4 (the ratio of 25 to 100mm).

These ratios are sometimes called *f*/numbers, commonly expressed as *f*/2 and *f*/4 in the examples cited above, or as 1:2, 1:4, etc., and engraved on the ring around the front lens element as such. These *f*/numbers bear a very definite relationship to each other. The ratios of the squares of the *f*/numbers tell you the relative amounts of light transmitted through the lens. For example, assuming that light conditions remain constant, it is easily discovered that *f*/8 admits only 1/16 of the light as *f*/2. This is calculated by squaring 2 and 8, which is 4 and 64, respectively, and which reduce to the ratio of 1:16.

METRIC CONVERSION TABLE

For use in formula computation and with depth-of-field tables.

Inches to Metric		Metric to Inches	
1/8 in.	0.32 cm.	0.5 cm.	3/16 in.
1/4 in.	0.64 cm.	1 cm.	3/8 in.
1/2 in.	1.27 cm.	2 cm.	13/16 in.
1 in.	2.54 cm.	3 cm.	1-3/16 in.
2 in.	5.08 cm.	4 cm.	1-9/16 in.
3 in.	7.62 cm.	5 cm.	1-15/16 in.
4 in.	10.2 cm.	6 cm.	2 3/8 in.
5 in.	12.7 cm.	7 cm.	2 3/4 in.
6 in.	15.2 cm.	8 cm.	3 1/8 in.
7 in.	17.8 cm.	9 cm.	3 1/2 in.
8 in.	20.3 cm.	10 cm.	3-15/16 in.
9 in.	22.9 cm.	12 cm.	4 3/4 in.
10 in.	25.4 cm.	15 cm.	5 7/8 in.
11 in.	27.9 cm.	20 cm.	7 7/8 in.
1 ft.	30.5 cm.	25 cm.	9-13/16 in.
2 ft.	61.0 cm.	30 cm.	11 3/4 in.
3 ft.	91.4 cm.	40 cm.	15 3/4 in.
4 ft.	1.22 m.	50 cm.	19 3/4 in.
5 ft.	1.52 m.	60 cm.	23 5/8 in.
6 ft.	1.83 m.	80 cm.	31 1/2 in.
7 ft.	2.13 m.	1 m.	39 1/2 in.
8 ft.	2.44 m.	1.5 m.	4 ft. 11 in.
9 ft.	2.74 m.	2 m.	6 ft. 7 in.
10 ft.	3.06 m.	2.5 m.	8 ft. 3 in.
15 ft.	4.57 m.	3 m.	9 ft. 10 in.
20 ft.	6.10 m.	4 m.	13 ft. 2 in.
30 ft.	9.14 m.	5 m.	16 ft. 5 in.
40 ft.	12.20 m.	10 m.	33 ft. 0 in.
50 ft.	15.24 m.	15 m.	49 ft. 2 in.
100 ft.	30.48 m.	20 m.	66 ft. 0 in.

An easy rule of thumb in converting inches to centimeters is simply to multiply by 2 1/2. For exactness multiply by 2.54. Conversely to convert centimeters to inches divide by 2 1/2 or 2.54.

The *f*/numbers are also called *f*/stops. Sometimes the term *stopping down* is used to mean that a smaller lens aperture is selected. Smaller lens apertures have larger *f*/numbers whereas larger apertures have smaller *f*/numbers. Stopping down is done mainly to achieve a greater depth of field or area of acceptable focus in the photo while the shutter-speed adjustment is used mainly to regulate the amount of light. Often, the lens must be *opened* wider to allow more light to enter the camera when lighting conditions are inadequate for good picture taking or to achieve a shallower depth of field for particular pictorial reasons.

When the photographer has a choice of Nikkor lenses of the same focal length—hence a constant—the larger the aperture (D), the greater the aperture ratio (d/f or D:f), and the greater the amount of light transmitted at maximum aperture. For exposure control purposes, the same *f*/number on any lens of any focal length transmits the same image brilliance.

Each lens (other than special mirror-reflex lenses) is equipped with an iris diaphragm—an internal aperture control that is regulated by turning the lens aperture ring. As the opening of the diaphragm is made larger or smaller, the aperture ratio changes correspondingly, thereby allowing more or less light to enter the camera, both for exposure control and depth-of-field control. The *f*/numbers are marked progressively so that each consecutive marking or "stop" denotes a halving of the next larger aperture (next smaller number) and a doubling of the next smaller aperture (next larger number) in the sequence 1, 1.4, 2, 2.8, 4, 5.6, 8, 11, 16, 22, 32, 45, and 64, to the extent applicable to a given lens. An image exposed at *f*/4 will be half as brilliant as one at *f*/2.8 and twice as brilliant as one at *f*/5.6, assuming the same shutter speed is used.

F NO. 1/2 STOP INTERVALS		1.2		1.7		2.4		3.4		4.8		6.7		9.5		13.5		19		27		38		54	
F NO.	1		1.4		2		2.8		4		5.6		8		11		16		22		32		45		64
F NO. 1/3 STOP INTERVALS		1.1 1.3		1.6 1.8		2.2 2.5		3.2 3.6		4.5 5		6.4 7.1		9 10		13 14		18 20		25 29		36 40		51 57	

Fractional *f*/stops. Not indicated on lens scales.

With the Reflex-Nikkor (mirror) lenses, the aperture ratio cannot be computed or expressed in this way, because the cross-section of light bundles entering it is doughnut-shaped, except at the nodal point. The equivalent *f*/value is calculated by comparing the effective ring area of the mirror that corresponds to the disc-shaped opening area of the ordinary lens. The Reflex-Nikkor lenses do not have an adjustable iris diaphragm

The *f*/value assigned to a lens is calculated for the infinity setting. When the lens is focused for closer objects, its distance from the film plane is lengthened. Hence, the relative aperture decreases in its ability to transmit light and theoretically should be represented by a larger *f*/number. In practice, this is ignored with ordinary lens extensions within their normal focusing ranges. It is only when lens extensions are extreme that it becomes necessary to recalculate *f*/values. This is done, for example when using the extremely close focusing Micro-Nikkor lens or when using other lenses with extension tubes or bellows

In the accompanying table of fractional *f*/stops the standard series of *f*/numbers is shown in the middle line Above it is shown a series of half-stops, and in the bottom line is shown a series of one-third stops. Each half-stop represents a factor of 1.4 times the amount of light transmitted by the smaller adjacent stop. Each one-third stop represents a factor of 1.26.

Another purpose of stopping down is to achieve optimum performance. Although some lenses are designed for such performance at full aperture, most lenses yield the most even illumination and provide correction for at least some optical edge distortions or aberrations when they are stopped down two or three full settings. For example, an *f*/1.4 lens might ideally be used at *f*/4, although there are occasions when the reserve powers of the lens at full aperture must be used, such as when lighting is poor.

For any given light situation and scene, various combinations of *f*/numbers and shutter speeds will yield the same total amount of light transmitted through the lens. Each combination of equivalent *f*/numbers and shutter speeds is called a "light value" or "exposure value," and provides the photographer with the flexibility of being able to use several different lens openings and shutter speeds in the correct combination while maintaining exposure equivalence.

Light passing through the lens is reduced slightly by absorption and reflection occurring within the lens elements and on their surfaces. The *f*/numbers indicate the amount of light striking the outer lens surface. T/stops (transmission-stops) indicate the amount of light actually passing through the lens. Therefore, T/stops are a more accurate indication of the light that reaches and exposes the film.

T/stop numbers are always larger than the corresponding *f*/numbers of the same lens. Differences in exposure and depth-of-field values derived from T/stops and from *f*/numbers are virtually negligible in practice. *T/stops are not used in this book.*

Picture Angle (Angle of View)

The picture angle or angle of view of a lens is the angle at the image side principal point subtended by the diagonal (43.2mm)—or sometimes, by the horizontal or vertical—measurement of the picture frame (24mm × 36mm) when the lens is focused on infinity (see diagram). When the lens is moved forward to focus on closer objects, the picture angle decreases. In most cases, lenses designed for 35mm cameras do not cover a format larger than 24mm × 36mm, unless specially designed.

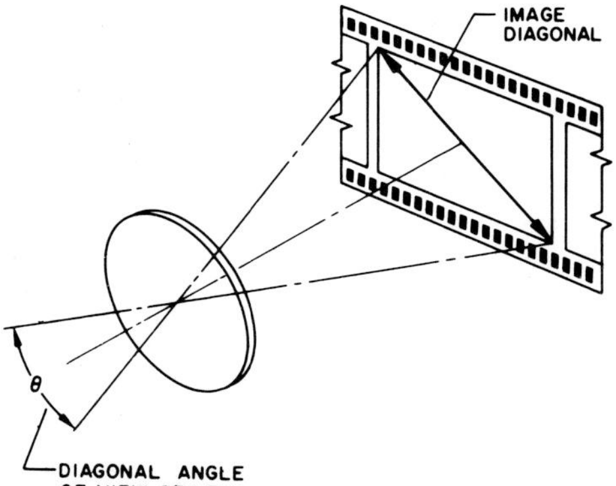

Maximum acceptance angle of lens. The picture angle of a lens is computed with the lens focused at infinity. Image quality tends to fall off outside the circle of which diameter serves as diagonal.

A "normal" or "standard" lens has a focal length that approximates the length of the diagonal of the image or film frame. Customarily, any lens in the range of 45mm to 58mm is regarded as a standard lens for 35mm photography. The 50mm lens, used extensively as a normal lens, has a viewing angle of 46 degrees, which corresponds closely to the viewing angle of the human eye. Lenses in the "normal" category are furnished as original equipment for general-purpose photography. Lenses with a shorter or longer focal length are available for particular problems of image coverage.

Lenses of longer focal length than those in the "normal" or "standard" group are popularly referred to as telephoto lenses because they bring images in closer. In a strictly technical sense, telephoto lenses are of special design, being shorter in actual physical length than lenses of equivalent focal length that are merely long focal-length lenses.

Lenses of shorter focal length than those in the normal group are referred to as wide-angle lenses, covering viewing or picture angles wider than about 60 degrees.

The focal length of each lens is engraved on the lens mount in conspicuous white letters such as f=50mm (which is the same as 5cm in the metric system), f=135mm (or 13.5cm), and so on.

Object Distance, Image Distance, and Reproduction Ratio

The object distance is defined as the distance from the first principal plane of the lens to the focused object plane; the image distance is the distance from the second principal plane of the lens to the image plane on the film. The distance engraved on the lens barrel, however, does not represent the object distance, but rather the distance from the object to the image plane: the sum of the object and image distances, plus the distance between the first and second principal planes.

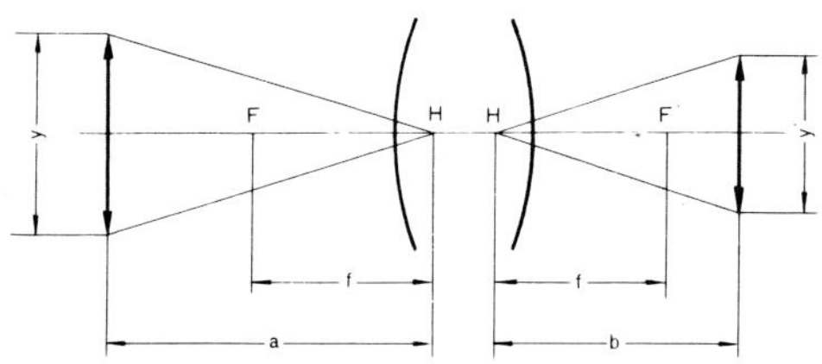

Object distance, image distance, and reproduction (image) ratio.

The following relationship is established between the focal length of the lens (F), object distance (a) and image distance (b):

$$1/a + 1/b = 1/F$$

The reproduction ratio of magnification (B)—the proportion of the image (Y′) to that of the object size (Y)—is equal to the ratio of the image to object distance, as shown by:

$$B = \frac{Y'}{Y} = \frac{b}{a}$$

Thus, the following relations are obtained:

$$a = F\left(1 + \frac{1}{B}\right)$$

$$b = F\,(1 + B)$$

Flange Focal Distance

The flange focal distance (FFD), sometimes called the "flange back," is the distance from the mechanical rear end surface of the lens mount to the focal plane of the lens. Thus, the FFD determines the position of a lens properly seated in the camera mount, depending on the mechanical design of the camera (46.5mm in the Nikon and the Nikkormat cameras). The FFD is one of the important elements for consideration in assembling, fitting and testing of a lens.

DEPTH OF FIELD: THEORY

Theoretically, the image is at its sharpest focus only in a single plane, that is, at a given distance from the camera lens (which must be set for that distance). As a practical matter, what governs is how sharp the image appears when it is enlarged onto paper to make a print or projected onto a viewing screen if it is a color transparency. Instead of a *single plane of sharp focus,* what is seen is a *zone of sharp focus* that extends in front of and behind the plane of sharpest focus. This zone of relative sharpness is called depth of field. Beyond this zone, coming in toward the foreground and receding toward the background, image areas become noticeably less sharp.

Optical Factors Governing Depth of Field

The photographic image is formed by rays of light coming from a subject, gathered by the lens, and projected onto the image plane. Before the light rays come together in a plane of sharp focus, they are in a state of "confusion" in which no sharpness of image can be discerned. When the light rays converge at the image plane, what seems to the eye alone as sharpness formed by points of light can be seen, under sufficient magnification, to be circles of light. Each is a circle of confusion of light rays that cannot be made to come together at precisely the same image plane. The circle is at its smallest diameter at the plane of sharpest focus. The circle widens in front of and behind the plane of sharpest focus.

Beyond certain near and far limits on either side of the plane of sharpest focus, the circles become so wide as to cause a blurring of the image. The near and far limits of acceptable sharpness at the image plane constitute the depth of focus. This varies with the same lens under different conditions and combinations of conditions. The range of sharpness at the image plane is analogous to the observed depth of field of the object or subject area.

The circle of confusion is made smaller—and hence depth of field is recorded as greater—as the diaphragm opening is decreased. The smaller the aperture (large f/numbers), the narrower are the shafts of light reaching the film. The converse—effect of widening the aperture—is also true.

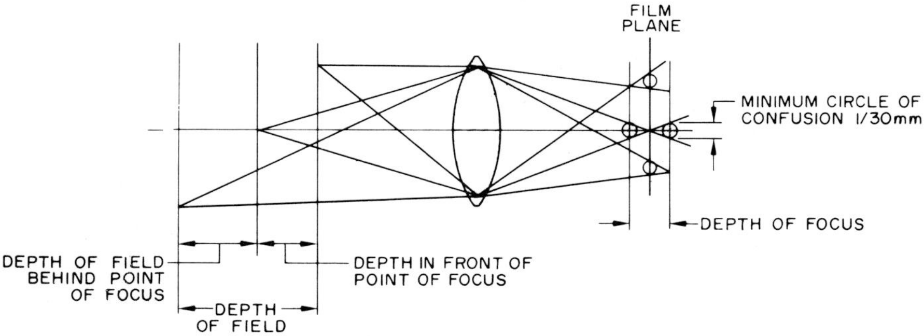

Depth of field (optical diagram).

Diffraction Effect Caused by Diaphragm

Since the diameter of the circle of confusion grows smaller, with correspondingly greater depth of field, as smaller lens apertures are used, one might think the best rule is to shoot at the smallest aperture consistent with available light and shutter-speed requirements of the subject. In fact, in the history of photography, there used to be an "*f*/64 school" of picture taking. Actually, an offsetting factor—the diffraction disc—causes an overall softening and degradation of image at very small apertures.

The diffraction disc consists of a series of light rings of diminishing intensity surrounding the circle of confusion. These rings result from light diffractions that are due to interference of light wave motions. Hence, even if circles of confusion could be eliminated through lens correction, physical resolving power of a lens would be limited by the phenomenon of the diffraction disc.

As the lens opening is widened (smaller *f*/numbers), the diffraction disc becomes smaller. This benefit is offset by a wider circle of confusion. In other words, for any given advantage, you must accept some disadvantage as a trade-off. This explains why, for most lenses, an aperture less than maximum is recommended for optimum optical performance, unless special conditions call for use of the maximum. As a general rule, an aperture smaller than *f*/16 should be avoided unless greater depth of field is more important than image sharpness. Size and contrast of image details are a factor in favor of even smaller apertures. Hence, when depth of field is so badly needed in making close-up pictures of three-dimensional objects, the use of the smallest apertures is warranted.

Perceptual Aspects

Another practical consideration stems from limits of visual perception of the human eye. Any point that measures less than 1/100 inch in diameter when viewed at a distance of 10 inches (thereby subtending 2 minutes of arc or less) will appear sharp. An image point larger than 1/100 inch will appear blurred. Hence, the degree of enlargement of the negative must be taken into account in

Hyperfocal Distances of Wide-Angle and Normal Lenses

(Unit: meter)

f-number / Focal Length	1.4	2	2.8	4	5.6	8	11	16
20mm	–	–	–	3.2	2.3	1.7	1.2	0.9
24mm	–	–	6.3	4.4	3.1	2.2	1.6	1.2
28mm	–	12.4	8.8	6.2	4.4	3.2	2.3	1.6
35mm	27.9	19.6	14.0	9.8	7.0	5.0	3.6	2.5
45mm	–	–	23.3	16.3	11.6	8.2	5.8	4.2
50mm	57.2	40.1	28.4	20.1	14.2	10.1	7.2	5.1

relation to viewing distance. For example, an exhibition print intended for viewing from afar can be of greater magnification than a print that is to be viewed at close quarters. For hand-held viewing, the limit of magnification for depth-of-field purposes depending on negative quality is from about 8× upward, assuming a comfortable viewing distance of about 13 inches (approximate length of print diagonal). While visual sharpness can be maintained at even greater magnifications, perceived depth of field will diminish accordingly. Smaller lens apertures permit greater enlargement due to narrowing of the shafts of light that come to a focus in a circle of confusion at the image plane.

Calculating of Depth of Field

The depth of field for the front (nearer to the lens) and rear (farther from the lens) depths is calculated by the following equations:

$$\text{Front (nearer) depth} = \frac{d.f.a^2}{F^2 + f.a}$$

$$\text{Rear (farther) depth} = \frac{d.f.a^2}{F - d.f.a}$$

When f = *f*/number

F = focal length of lens

a = distance of the object focused

d = permissible diameter of circle of confusion

LENS DESIGN FACTORS

For any given lens design, the aim of the optical engineer is optimum performance, which means that some ideal aims must be sacrificed in order to satisfy other optical requirements. In other words, since there can be no "perfect" lenses, compromises must be made in favor of the most important priorities. The considerations may also include economic feasibility. In this light one can perceive the optical gamesmanship involved in producing a new lens design or improving on older designs and manufacturing processes.

Type of Lens

To correct aberrations within proper limits, the photographic lens should consist of at least three components. Among an unlimited number of combinations of different glass types and curvatures, only a few are considered suited to correct aberrations. Within a wide range of focal lengths and apertures, lenses are grouped into several types. Some are named after their inventor (e.g., Petzval type), others after the number of elements comprising the lens (e.g. Triplet), or after an

TYPICAL TELEPHOTO DESIGN: principal points in front of lens with negative rear element to shorten length of lens.

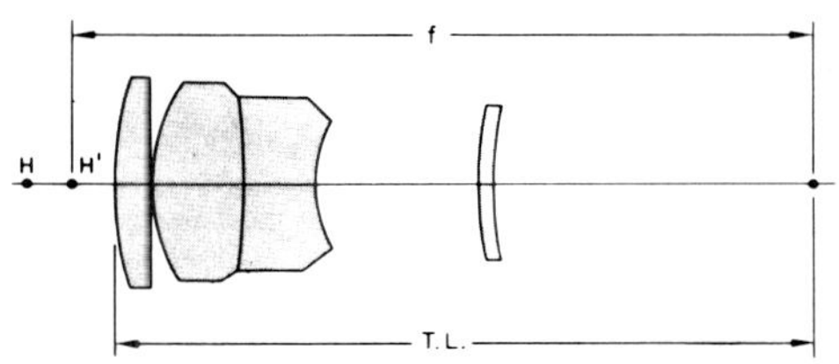

TL = distance from front of lens to focal plane
f = focal plane
telephoto ratio =
$\frac{TL}{f} < 1$ = telephoto type lens
(not long focus)

TYPICAL RETROFOCUS DESIGN

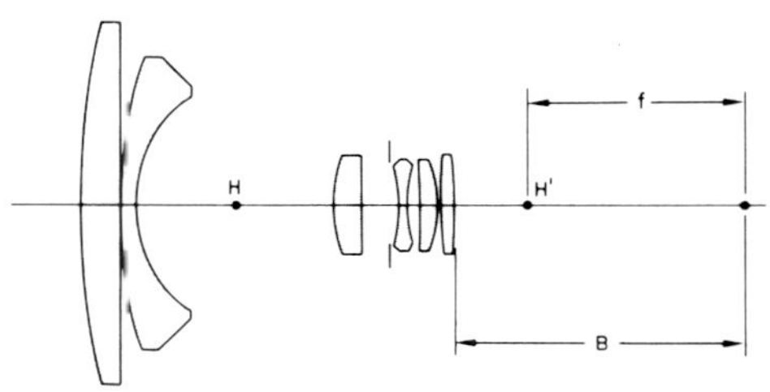

B = distance from back of lens to focal plane
f = focal length
f < B = retrofocus type

established brand name of a particular type of lens.

Some types of lenses have to be designed within certain restrictions. In a telephoto lens, for example, the distance from the outermost lens surface to the focal plane is designed to be physically shorter than the focal length (the distance between the second principal point H′ and the focal plane F′). Many long-focus lenses now on the market are telephotos and feature this formula.

To further reduce the length of a lens barrel, it is now common practice to combine a reflecting mirror surface and the lens elements as in the Reflex-Nikkor lenses (called "catadioptric").

Lenses for the SLR camera must have a certain clearance between the lens and the focal plane. The back clearance of wide-angle lenses of conventional design is too small to allow the movement of the reflex-mirror. In such a case, a "retrofocus" type lens is the answer. Its physical back focal distance is greater than the optical focal length. This type of lens design is advantageously applied to wide-angle lenses for use with the SLR. The retrofocus lens is also called the "inverted telephoto."

Resolution of Photographic Lenses

Sometimes the calculation results of the lens aberrations (discussed below) are utilized as a criterion to determine the picture quality of photographic lenses. However, it is known among lens designers that there are many other factors that have to be taken into consideration in evaluating optical performance. Judgment based solely on the calculation results is often erroneous, especially in designing lenses of large apertures.

The quality of a lens may be accurately described in terms of resolution or its ability to separate the lines of different thicknesses precisely marked on a test chart. Hence, the more lines a lens can record separately, the higher its resolution or resolving power. This resolution involves the diffraction of light that affects the sharpness of the image as the lens is stopped down to a smaller aperture. It is regarded as a reliable criterion for judging the quality of a lens.

In *comparing* lenses, however, resolution tests present a number of problems that raise questions as to their usefulness. The results of a test may differ if it is conducted by different people at different times. Measurement and determination of the resolving power are governed by numerous factors:

1. Form or shape of testing marks.
2. Contrast of marks shown on the test chart.
3. Illumination of the test chart.
4. Whether the test mark images are observed in the air or projected on a screen or photographed.
5. Criteria used to distinguish resolved test mark from the unresolved test mark. mark.
6. Sight of inspector who judges the focused plane.
7. *f*/stop of lens chosen for the test.
8. Reproduction ratio of image for the test.
9. Tolerance limit for determining resolution.
10. Sharpest image plane chosen.
11. Fineness of emulsion grain of the film used in test.
12. Thickness of film emulsion layer.
13. Length of exposure time in photographing the test chart.
14. Method of developing film negative.
15. Actual position of film plane on the camera used.

And that is why lens makers have their own standards for each of the above points. Manufacturers conduct analytical tests not only on their own lenses but lenses of other manufacturers for the purpose of comparison. Reputable manufacturers usually do not release the outcome of such tests because, as mentioned

Optical aberrations and effects of stopping down the lens aperture.
Since a lens cannot be completely free of all aberrations, it is properly corrected only in terms of its main purpose.

ABERRATIONS	EFFECT OF STOPPING DOWN THE APERTURE	
Spherical aberration When light rays from an object point on the axis of a lens or mirrored surface pass through or are reflected, the rays at various circular zones of the surface around the axis become focused at different points along the axis. This defect is the "spherical aberration" which blurs the image at the picture center.	By stopping down the aperture, the aberration will be greatly lessened, but this may cause displacement of focus.	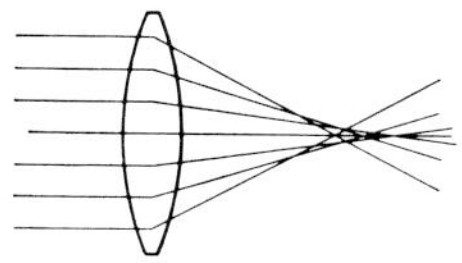
Coma The images produced from an object point off the axis, after passing through or being reflected on the different zones of a lens or a mirror, will vary in size and be superpositioned at the focus, resulting in an unsymmetrical image blur. This aberration arising from a variation in size is referred to as a "coma."	Improved by stopping down the aperture. The coma is determined by the location of the aperture diaphragm.	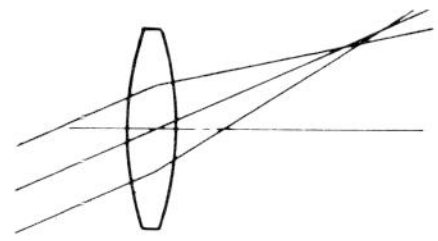
Astigmatism Even in a narrow pencil of light, object points off axis are imaged as two sharp lines at right angles to each other and at different locations. This defect is called "astigmatism." The line foci corresponding to object points distributed in a plane normal to the axis are located on two curved meridional and sagittal surfaces.	Cannot be improved by stopping down the aperture. The location of aperture diaphragm has an influence on the degree of astigmatism.	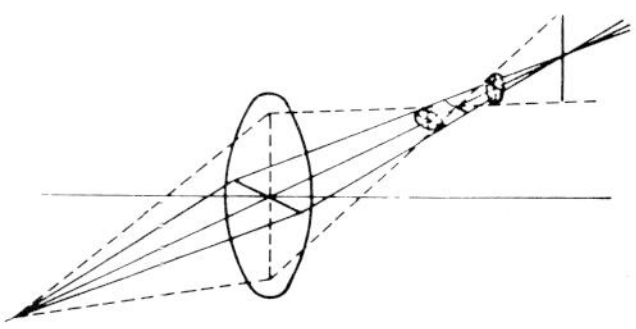
Curvature of image field In general, this surface is a curved one, conjugate to a plane in object surface. If the image is to be projected on a plane (photographic film or paper), it will be impossible to simultaneously obtain a sharp image of the entire object plane. This is true when the astigmatism is eliminated, that is, the two astigmatic surfaces are brought into coincidence on a common surface.	Same as above.	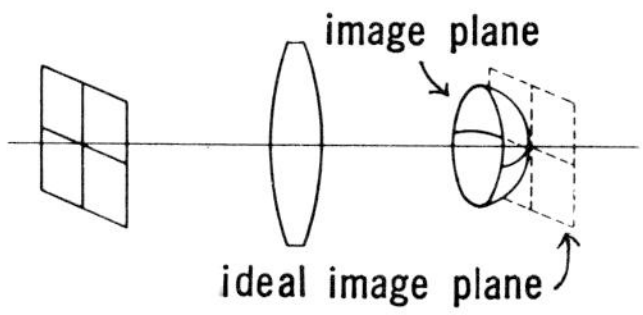
Distortion If the image magnification is not the same over the entire image field but varies radially outward from the center, the resultant shape of the image will be distorted. If magnification increases outward, a square object is imaged in the shape of a pincushion. If it decreases, the image of square has laterally bulging sides and the distortion is said to be 'barrel-shaped.'	Cannot be improved by stopping down the aperture. Distortion is determined by the location of aperture diaphragm.	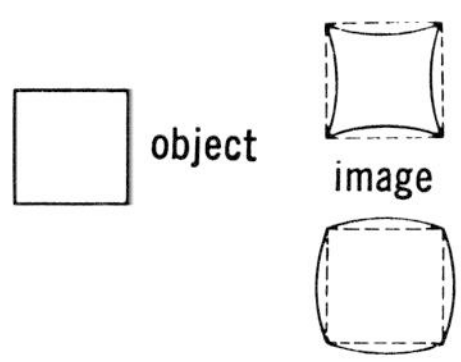
Chromatic aberrations Since the refraction of any optical glass depends on the wave length or color of the light, all properties of a lens will vary with wave length. The change in focal length of the lens and the location of its image plane lead to defects called "chromatic aberrations." Longitudinal chromatism is a variation in location of the image plane with change in wave length. It produces the image point surrounded by different colors which result in a blurred image in black-and-white pictures. Lateral chromatism is a variation in image size or magnification with wave length. This aberration does not appear at axial image points but toward the surrounding area, proportional to the distance from the center of the image field.	Cannot be improved by stopping down. For correction, a lens system consisting of at least a pair of compensating lenses is required. These lenses are made of different types of glass in respect to their refractive index and color dispersion.	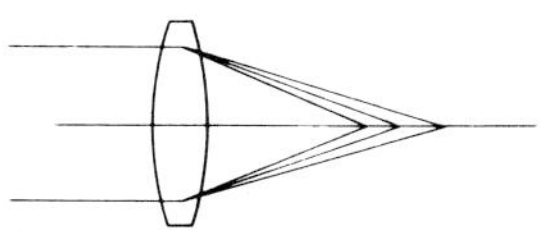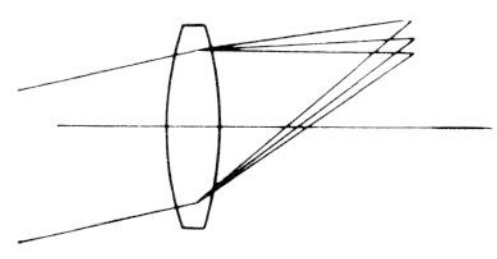

earlier, each lens maker has his own standards and the standards of one manufacturer may not be acceptable to others.

The quantitative expression of resolving power, however, does not necessarily determine the quality of the actual picture taken. Other factors must be considered when determining the quality of the lens image. Some have not yet been calculated or are beyond scientific measurement.

Nikkor lenses are tested on the basis of resolution as well as the qualitative faculty of reproducing not only circular dots, lines, concentric circles, and so forth, but three-dimensional subjects as well. Tests are also conducted to ascertain the "Modulation Transfer (Response) Function" of a lens, which expresses the optical contrast transfer characteristic of a lens in relation to resolution.

Focus Distance and Resolution

Lenses for 35mm cameras are corrected primarily for "infinity" distance. They perform most satisfactorily at distances ranging from a few feet to infinity within normal focusing ranges. Therefore, with some exceptions, they are not suitable for extreme close-up work. To meet the special requirements of performance at near-focus ranges, Nippon Kogaku produces close-up lenses such as **the Micro-Nikkor 55mm *f*/3.5, the Micro-Nikkor 105mm *f*/4, the Micro-Nikkor 200mm *f*/4 IF, and Medical-Nikkor 200mm *f*/5.6. They are designed to provide excellent definition as well as to correct distortion at close distances. The 50mm *f*/1.8 and *f*/2 Nikkors are also recommended for the same purpose.**

An original approach has been used to overcome image deterioration at closest focusing distances when using high-speed wide-angle lenses of retrofocus design. In 1967, Nikon introduced the 24mm *f*/2.8 lens incorporating rear elements that shift automatically for image correction during focusing, governed by distance. This "floating element" design has been incorporated into the 28mm *f*/2 Nikkor-N Auto and 35mm *f*/1.4 Nikkor-N Auto lenses. Image quality is thereby maintained throughout the entire focusing range from 1 ft. (0.3 meters) to infinity.

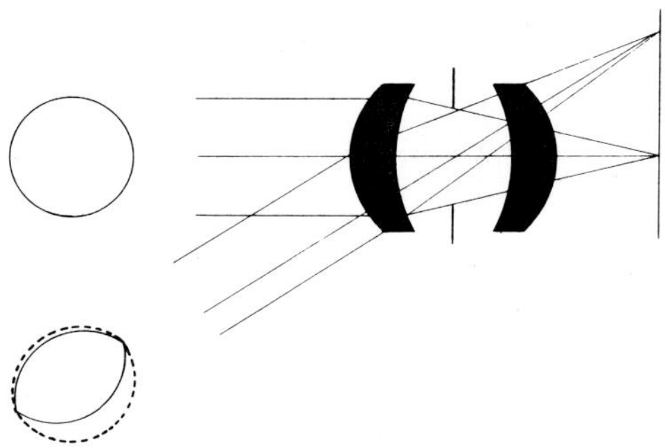

With extreme wide-angle lenses image content near edge tends to assume elliptical form due to greater travel of light rays. See caption and illustrations on facing page.

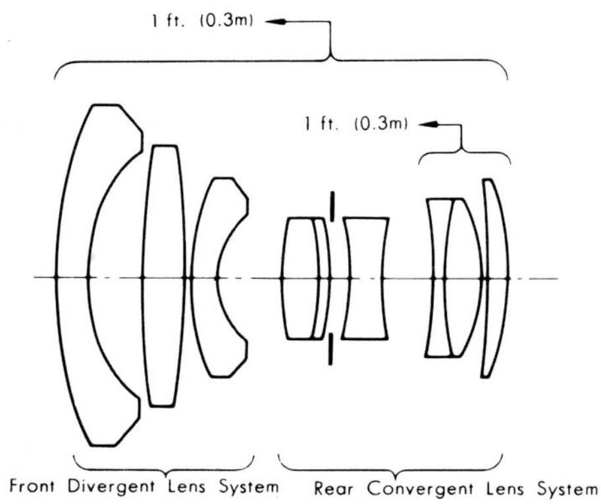

"Floating Elements" Correction System provides automatic correction for image quality at close range. This system is used, for example, with the 24mm *f*/2.8, the 28mm *f*/2, and the 35mm *f*/1.4 Nikkor Auto lenses. Above is a schematic for the 24mm *f*/2.8 lens.

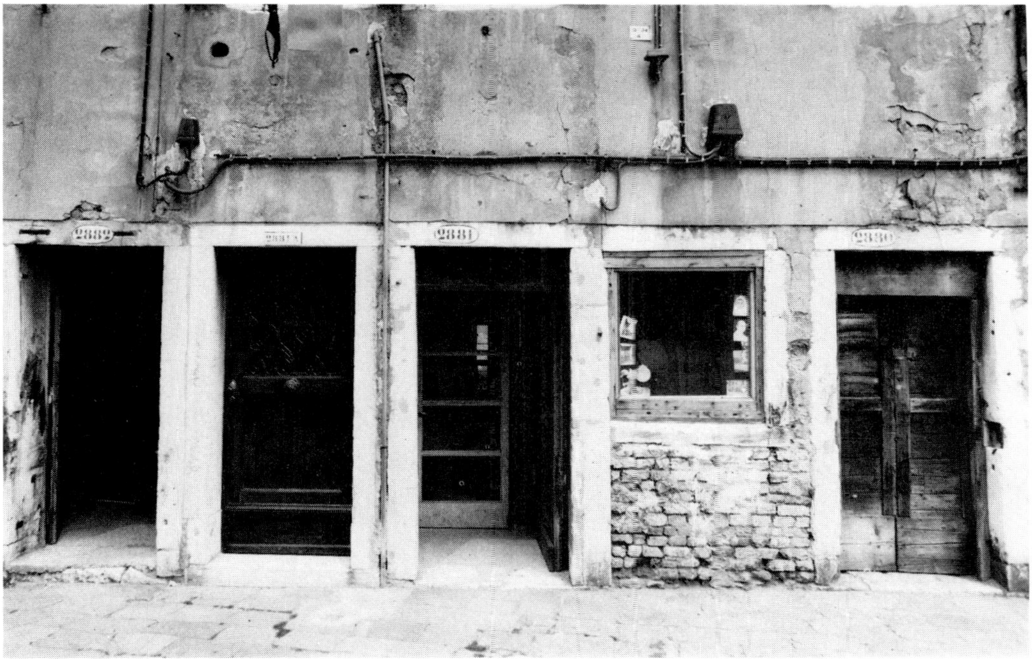

Extreme wide-angle lenses render peripheral objects in an apparently distorted manner as shown in the diagram on the preceding page. A circle located near the edge tends to be rendered in an elliptical or ovoid configuration, due to the fact that the rays of light have to travel a greater distance to the most extreme end than to points closer to the center of the image area. Additional effects, as an adaptation of this concept, are that wide-angle lenses see to the sides in a manner not possible with longer focal-length lenses. In the accompanying examples, the wide-angle picture (above) shows the insides of the door jambs; the other (below), made with an 80–200mm zoom near its shortest focal length, does not. Photos by J. D. Cooper.

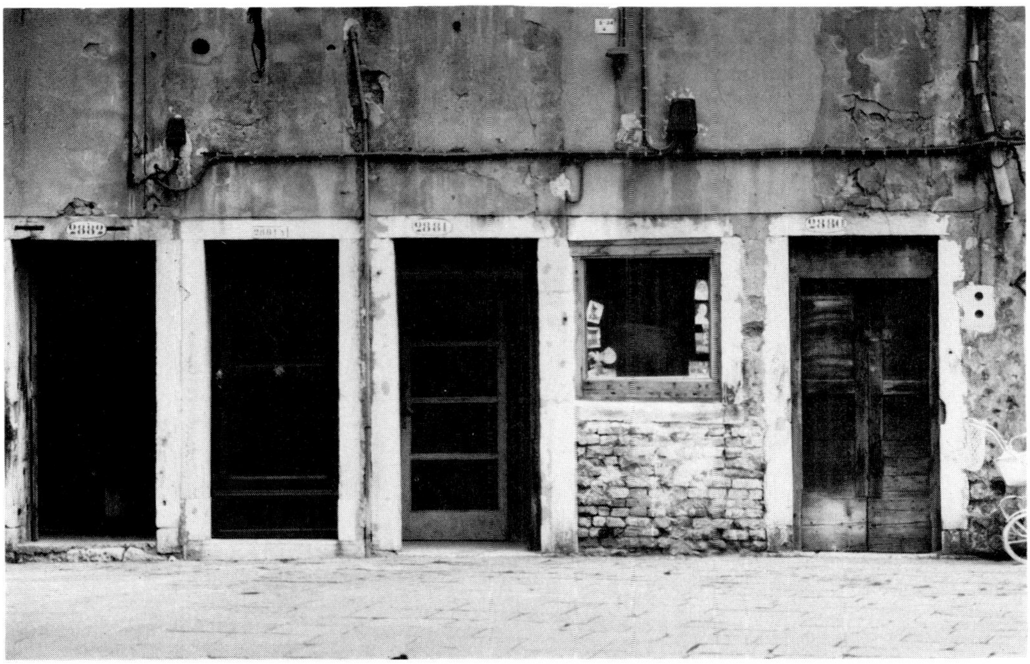

Aberrations of Lenses

It is essential that the photographic lens provide sharp, correctly formed images on the film plane. For this purpose, the lens must be capable of gathering light rays originating at every point on the object plane and reproducing them precisely on the film plane. A perfect lens would reproduce the exact shape of the object as the photographic image in perfect focus and definition over the whole picture field.

In practice, however, it is not possible to attain such an ideal result: The light rays in each bundle that are scattered near the ideal point are generally referred to as "aberrations of the lens."

For the convenience of designing the lens, aberrations are classified into chromatic aberrations, spherical aberrations, coma, astigmatism, curvature of image field, and distortion. These are diagrammed in the accompanying chart. No lens can be completely free from these aberrations. The performance of a lens is primarily determined by the residual amounts of various aberrations. A lens is designated as being "correct" when its aberrations are properly corrected to fulfill the particular purpose of the lens.

Optimum *f*/number of Lens

Theoretically, the larger the aperture of a lens, the higher the resolution, but, in practice, most photographic lenses do not give full sharpness at their maximum opening because of residual aberrations. This is because, in lens designing, the larger the aperture, the more difficult it is to correct the aberrations. Therefore, if the *sharpest* image is to be attained with a particular lens, the lens should be used at its optimum *f*/number, that is, generally, stopped down two or three stops from the maximum opening.

Flare and Ghost

Light falling on a lens surface may sometimes cause "flare," which reduces image contrast and fogs the picture to some degree. Such flare cannot be avoided in some large aperture lens systems containing a series of lens elements. An intense light in the picture angle of the lens will be prominently reflected on the inside surfaces of the lens elements while passing through the lens system. This will produce not only serious flare but will also yield a strange, bright light, called a "ghost," at unexpected positions in the picture.

These phenomena, when caused by light reflection on the internal surfaces or edges of the lens barrel or a filter frame, can be prevented to a certain extent with a lens hood. Thus, taking pictures "against the light" should be avoided as much as possible, except when particular lighting effects are desired. Pioneering the field of high-speed (large-aperture) lenses, Nikon has produced lenses that keep these defects at the lowest possible levels.

Lens Coating

Glass surfaces in contact with the air will reflect as much as 4 to 5 percent of the light striking them. Hence, when light passes through a number of glass surfaces, a good amount of the light will inevitably be lost by reflection before it reaches the film plane.

This will result in reduced transmission of light and is liable to produce flare, thus reducing the contrast of the picture. As the number of air-to-glass surfaces in the lens system is increased, the effect of the reflection becomes more pronounced. "Lens coating" is designed to reduce such detrimental reflections to about 1 percent or less. Today, the surfaces of all photographic lenses are coated. When the lens is coated, the surfaces are covered with a thin single layer or multiple layers of one or more substances with varied refractive indices, each smaller than that of the glass. The thickness of the layer—one-fourth of the wave length of light—varies according to the type or usage of the lens.

According to the type of coating, the coated lens presents blue, green, magenta or amber tints. The layers of coating, besides preventing surface reflections, help protect the surface of the lens because of their stable chemical properties. The effects of coating a lens are: (a) reduction of flare and improvement of image contrast and clarity; (b) increase in light transmission; (c) better color balance through improved spectral transmission characteristics; and (d) minimization of ghost images from reflection.

In the past, with relatively simple lens designs, it was sufficient to coat each lens element with a single layer of magnesium fluoride. In modern lenses with numerous elements and a variety of glasses with low refractive indices and extraordinary dispersion characteristics, the practice of imposing multiple layers of coating on lens surfaces has developed.

The Nikon factory first began to use multiple-layer coating in 1969 on selected elements of the wide-aperture standard 55mm *f*/1.2 Nikkor-S Auto lens. Thereafter, as a matter of continuing product improvement, the factory extended multiple coating to other lenses. This is done selectively, for not all lenses and not all components of a lens can benefit from multiple (as opposed to single) coating. The decisions for multiple coating are computer-assisted. As spectral transmission characteristics can be controlled through the use of different chemical coatings, the desired performance (or ideal color index) considerations of a lens can be fed into a computer that will print out the best-suited type of coating to use, element by element.

A second type of coating, used with special-purpose lenses such as the Ultra-Micro-Nikkor, which has application in extreme image reduction, is highly selective in almost completely reducing the reflections from a surface of a specific wave length.

In the future, multiple coating will be used increasingly on a selective basis where beneficial. Multi-coating can mean lighter, smaller lenses since it is now possible to reduce the element size needed to obtain the speed necessary with many lens formulas. It can be applied to mirror lenses to achieve close to 100 percent reflectance for truly significant increases in speed. The hardness and stability of multi-coated lenses is at least equal to that of single-coated lenses.

Use of "Foreign" Optics

Independently manufactured lenses are available for use with Nikon and Nikkormat camera bodies as well as for use as front lens attachments. These include prime lenses, dioptric lens attachments for close-up work, and "tele-converters" to increase focal lengths of prime lenses. Also, various brands of filters are available. Inasmuch as many of these "foreign" optics can be purchased at what appear to be bargain prices, the question often arises as to whether they are of a quality that at least matches that of a related Nikon/Nikkor product.

The advances of recent years in optical technology are widely shared among optical designers and engineers. Notwithstanding the fact that Nippon Kogaku has pioneered many optical innovations, it must also be noted that other manufacturers are capable of producing lenses and filters of a high quality. On the other hand, some manufacturers produce items that do not meet the same standards of acceptance as are required by Nippon Kogaku although they are physically compatible with Nikon equipment.

The differences might lie either in the optical or mechanical components of the lens assembly or both. Qualitative differences might lie in the precision spacing of lens elements; the correctness of alignment with the optical axis; the materials of which the lens barrel and mount are made; the dimensional precision of the bayonet lens mount; and the precision linkage of the automatic diaphragm and exposure meter couplings of the lens assembly to the corresponding controls of the Nikon/Nikkormat camera bodies, among others. With special concern for the last point, minor differences in cam configuration or in spring tension could affect accuracy of function. Even where independent brands are made to meet high standards, the ability to establish precise physical linkage to camera controls is affected by the fact that a single lens must be capable of adaptation to different camera systems by changing the lens mount itself. For this reason some independent lens brands are made as total assemblies including lens mount and linkages to exposure-meter and shutter controls.

The problem for the buyer is to be able to recognize high quality in an independent lens. In this he is at a disadvantage unless he uses the particular lens on his own camera in a test trial. Even so, he may not know whether the smooth rotation of the lens mount is due to precision meshing of the parts or to an expedient packing of the parts with grease. To some extent the buyer will have to rely on a combination of factors, including the reputation given to the lens make, the cost of the lens, the feel of the lens as it is operated on the camera, and the claims of the manufacturer as to quality controls and testing procedures.

Much the same can be said about quality of front lens attachments. Filters must be ground to optically flat standards; their spectral-pass characteristics must be standardized and known; their surfaces should be anti-reflection coated; and their screw-thread mounts should be made of fine metal and precision-machined. Supplementary close-up lenses must be ground to assure that their optical centers lie on the same axes as those of the prime lenses to which they are to be attached, while also satisfying other quality standards such as those required for filters.

Compatibility factors must be taken into account when choosing a lens. For most efficient operation, particularly under stress conditions, it is desirable that focusing and diaphragm control rings turn in the same direction and that they are located in the same relative positions on the lens barrel as on other lenses in the system. Also, exposure factors for influence of the finder screen should be given; otherwise, they must be determined by trial and error.

Independently made teleconverters are sold as an inexpensive means of extending focal lengths of prime lenses by the stated factor, usually 2× or 3×. However, the converters also diminish light transmitted by the same factors. Thus, when the teleconverters are used, the effective aperture is two or three stops below that indicated on the lens aperture ring. Image quality is also degraded, making it necessary to stop down at least one or two stops in order to achieve reasonable image quality.

The Nikon Teleconverters TC-1 and TC-2 (non-AI) and TC-200 and TC-300 (AI) all produce a 2× magnification and result in a two *f*/stop transmission loss. However, they are specially designed for optimum results when used with certain Nikkor lenses. The Teleconverter TC-14 produces a 1.4× magnification and results in an only one *f*/stop transmission loss. It is designed for use with longer focal length AI-Nikkors.

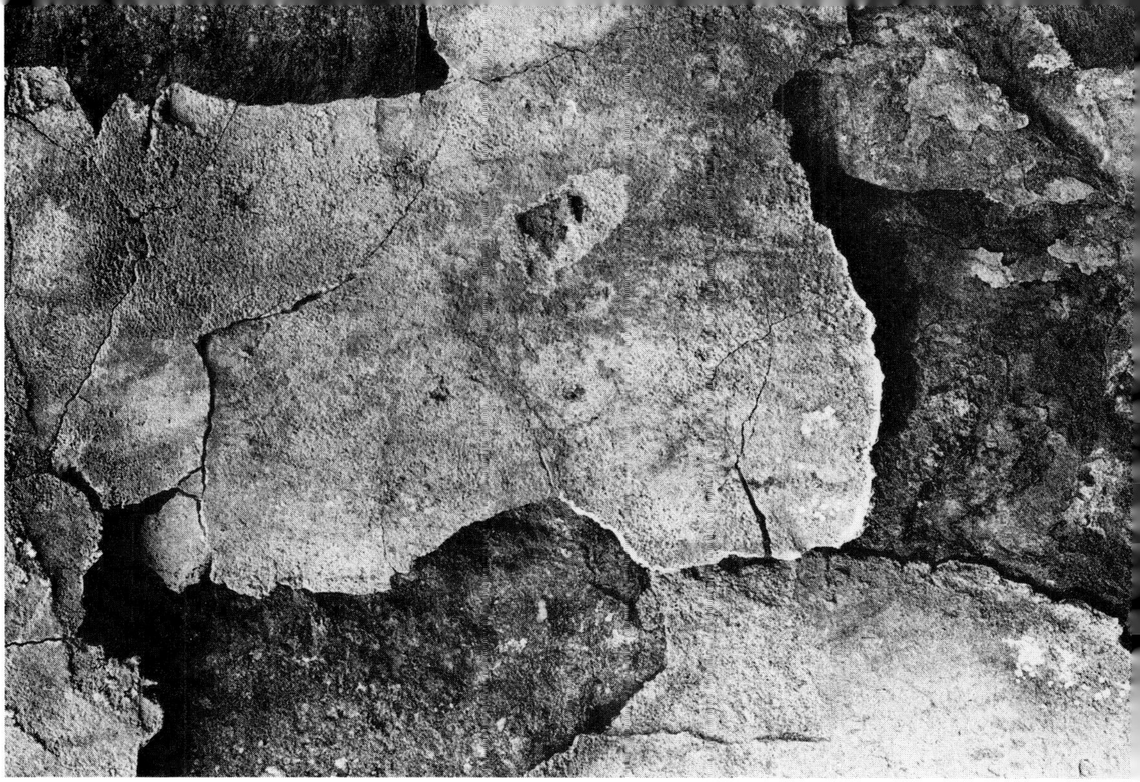

George Harvan

Abstract Rock Design. Nikkor lenses yield unusually sharp and finely resolved images. The 55mm Micro-Nikkor yields unusually fine results at close-working distances limited more by capabilities of films and papers than by optical potential. H and W Control Film.

Certain "pictorial aberrations" represent normal optical performance, for example, rendition of point-light sources or reflections as out-of-focus images. General principle is that these take on shape of lens diaphragm. Round circles indicate aperture was wide open or nearly so. Trades Union Council leader George Woodcock. 400mm lens.

Ian Bradshaw

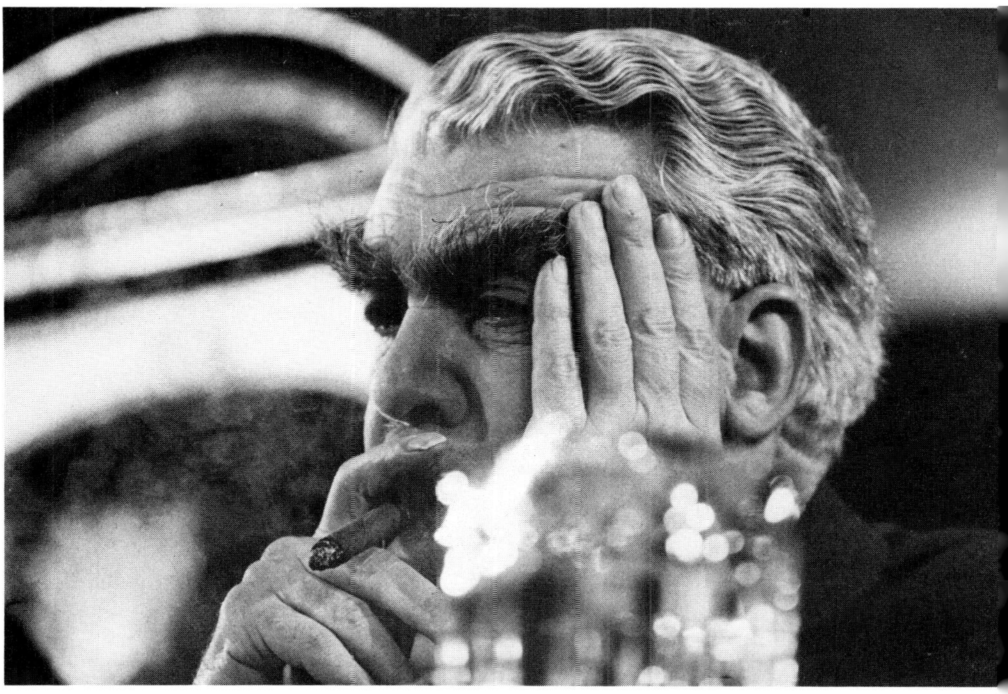

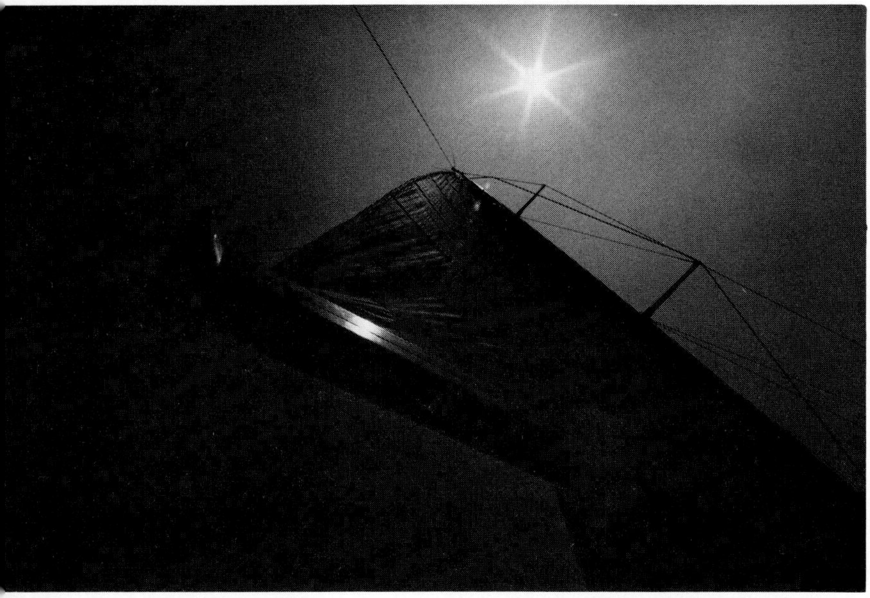

Douglas T. Mesney

Star-spurred rendition of sun is caused by stopping down lens to point where diaphragm lets minute amounts of light leak through as "diffraction spokes." 22mm *f*/11 lens at 1/125 sec. with red filter.

Ian Bradshaw

Countless diffraction spokes caused by reflections from brilliant water peaks indicate that 200mm *f*/4 lens was stopped down to *f*/11 or more.

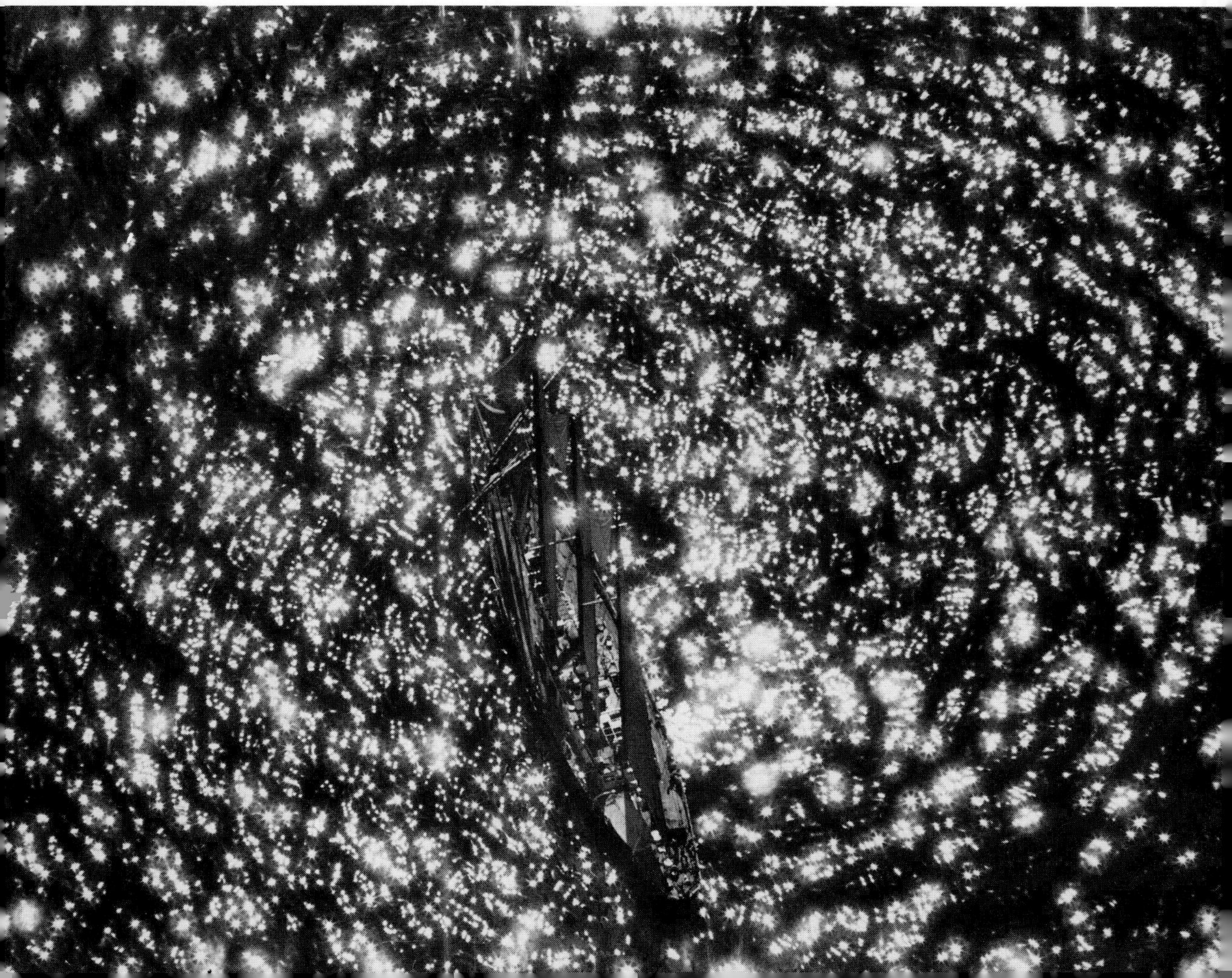

John Minihan

The diaphragm is at an intermediate position as indicated by hexagonal form of out-of-focus spots. Some Nikkor lenses will have diaphragm configurations that yield round spots when stopped down. The latest lens coatings tend to minimize such so-called "ghost" images but will not necessarily eliminate them entirely. Sometimes a ghost or two will contribute positively to the creative effect of the shot. Indoor tungsten illumination at the Lyceum, London. 135mm $f/4$ lens at 1/60 sec.

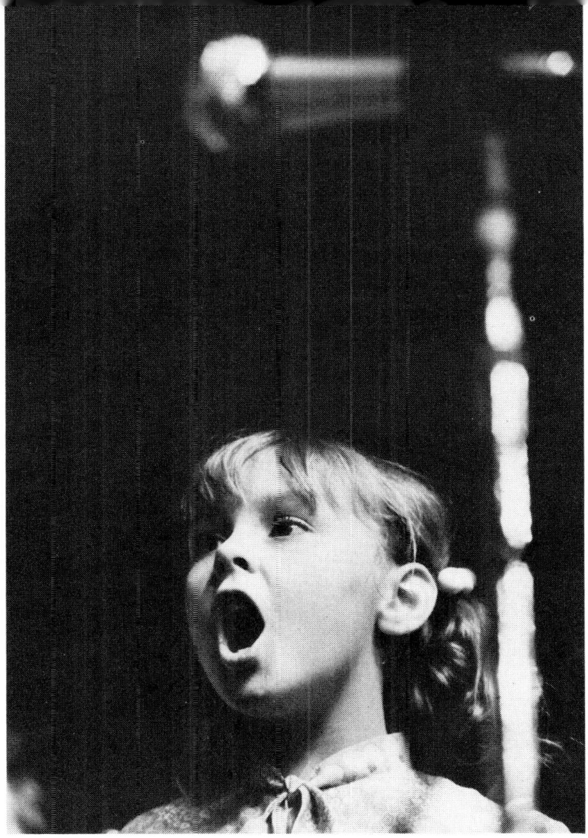

Chris Smith

The Rowers. Lens afficionados will recognize use of mirror-reflex lens, in this case 500mm $f/8$ Reflex-Nikkor. The clue is doughnut-shaped, out-of-focus highlight points in background which form interesting pattern. Many of foreground and middle-ground reflection points are beginning to expand into doughnut forms. Extreme compression of rowers is perspective effect known as "pancaking" characteristic of distant scenes magnified by long lenses. Shallow depth of field also characteristic.

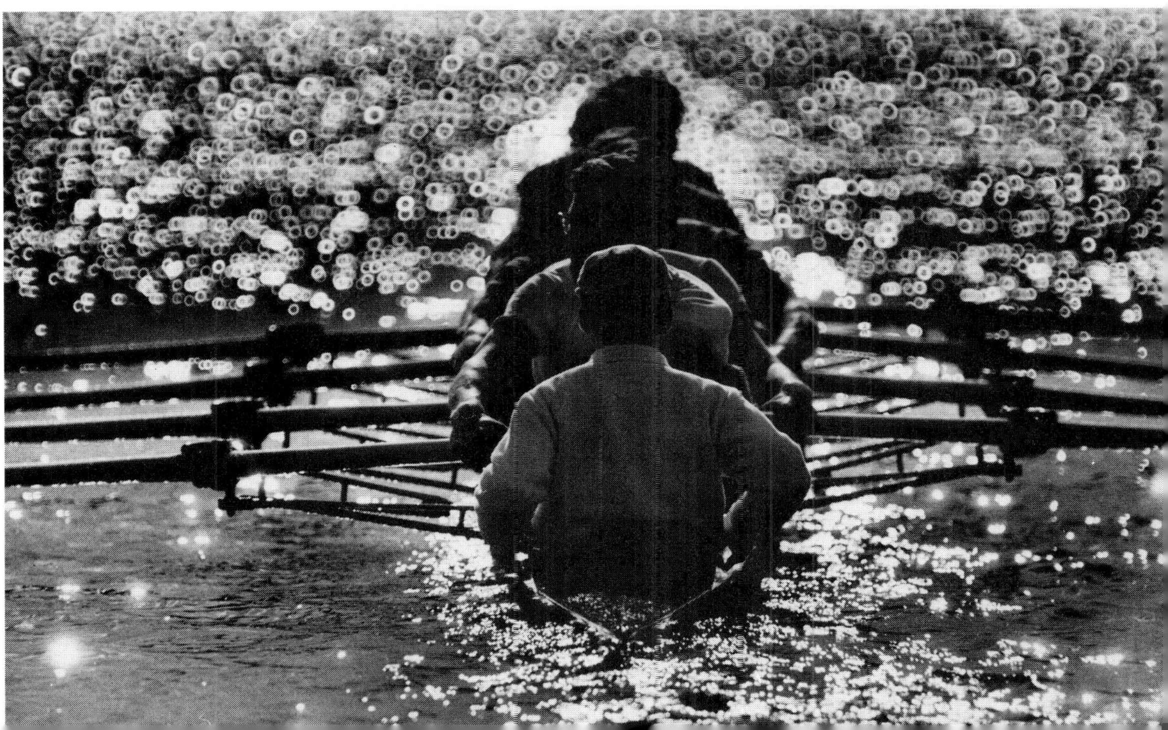

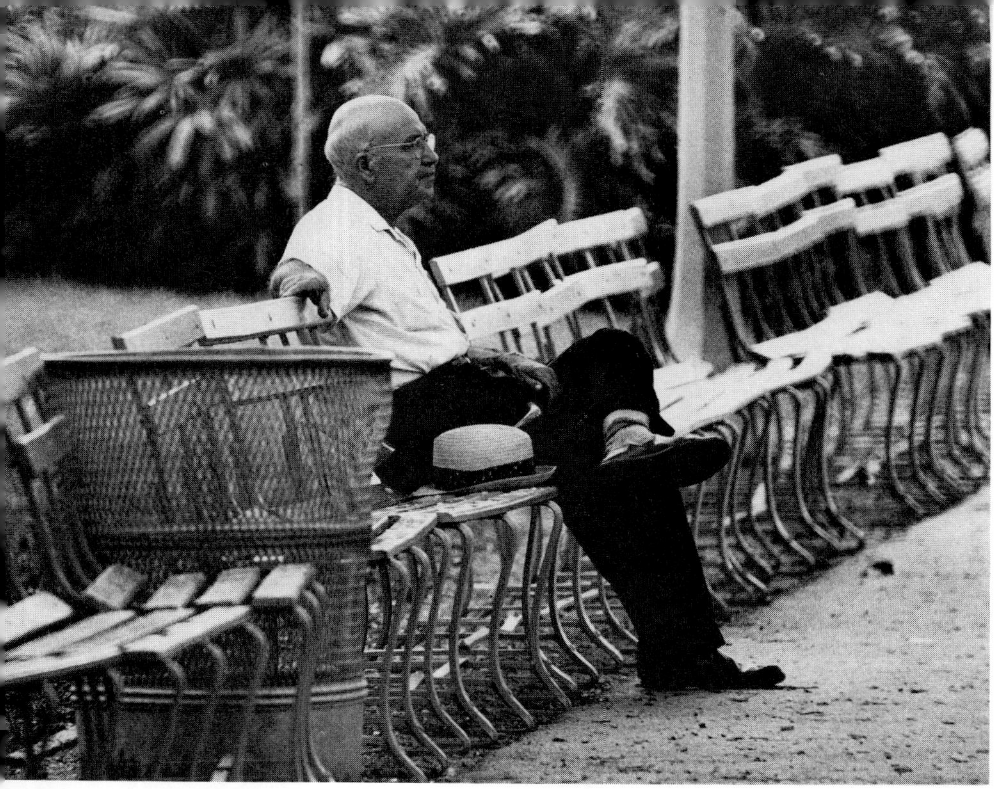

Al Satterwhite

Retired gentleman on row of park benches is at point or place of sharpest focus recorded with 500mm *f*/8 Reflex-Nikkor. Line forms break apart when out of focus; become double images in parallel. This may be seen in the legs of the benches toward the rear and in the branches of the background, but tips of branches tend to go doughnut. Kodak Tri-X.

Joseph D. Cooper

Trans-illuminated roof of pavillion at Naples formed convenient target to bring out characteristics of extreme wide-angle lenses. At left, concentric circles are perfectly round. At right, interesting geometric form obtained by shifting position and shooting angle; note elongation of circles now at edge of picture. This is a characteristic of extreme wide-angle lenses, explained in this chapter and is not to be regarded as inadequate performance. Otherwise, the 24mm *f*/2.8 lens yields corner-to-corner sharpness to an unusual degree.

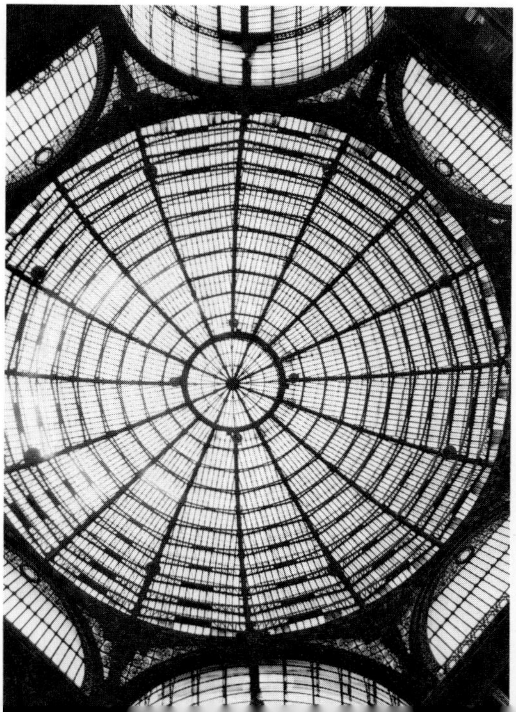

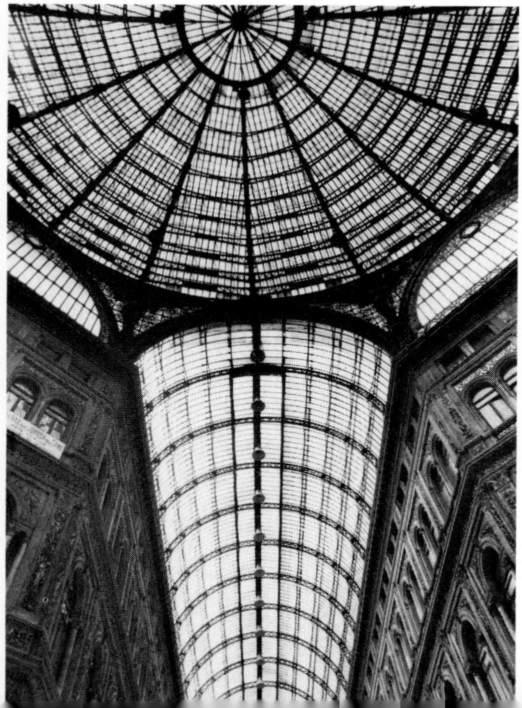

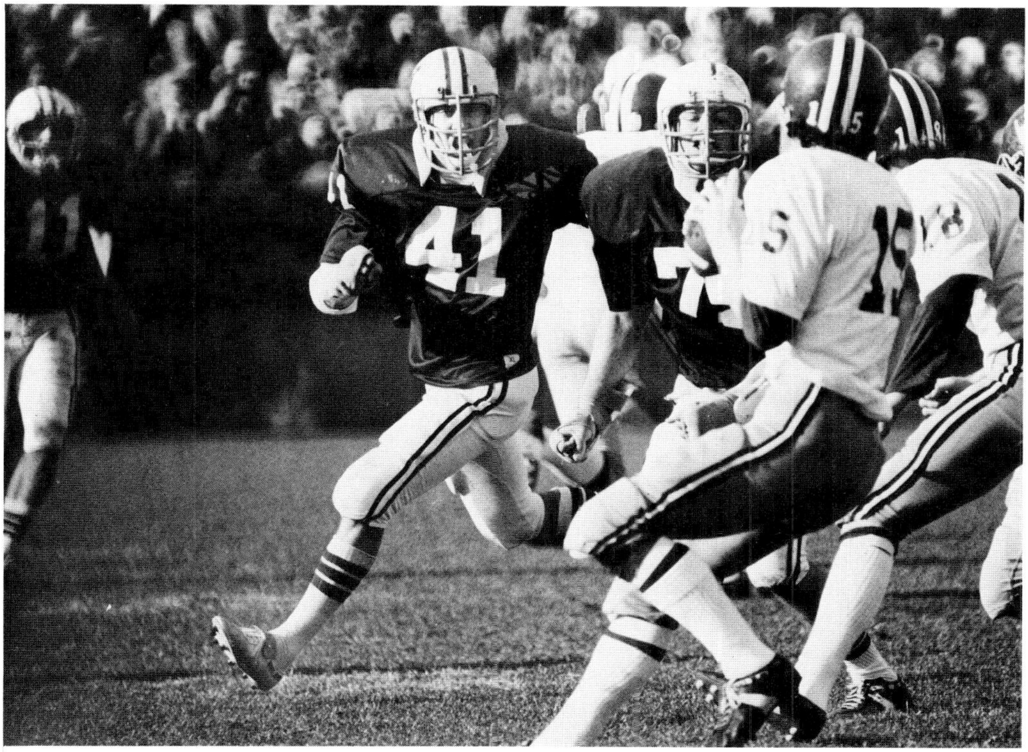

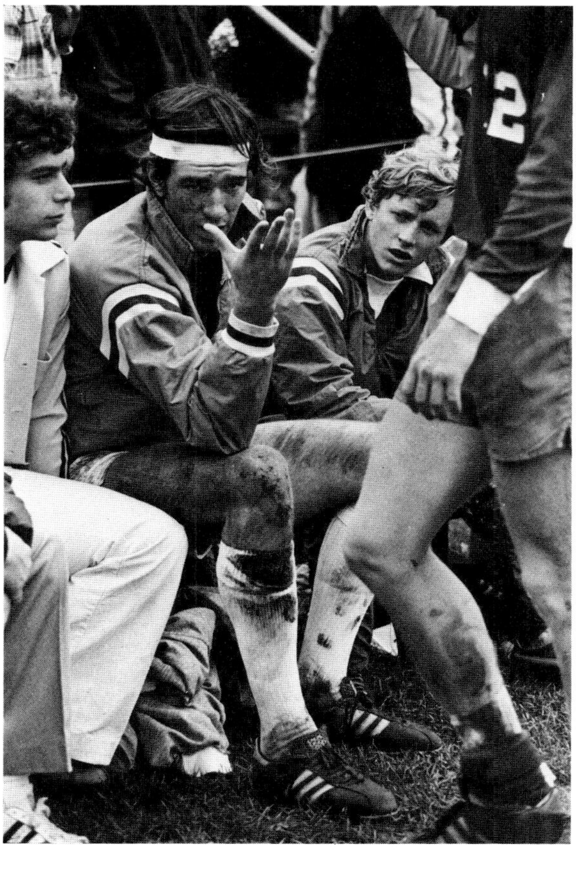

J. D. Levine

Photographers covering sports rely heavily on telephoto lenses. The 500mm Reflex-Nikkor (above) provides enough "reach" to enable Levine to photograph from the end zone rather than the sideline. Note the characteristic shapes of the out-of-focus background objects. (Below) The 300mm *f*/4.5 Nikkor captured action on the bench.

MECHANICAL FEATURES OF LENSES

While the term "lens" has traditionally meant one or more glass elements in a single configuration within a lens barrel, this has been superseded in fact by technological advances. Today, the lens is a combination of optical and mechanical features as described below, each of which makes an important contribution.

Automatic Diaphragm

The automatic diaphragm remains fully open except at exposure time. By depressing the shutter-release button, the diaphragm automatically closes down to the pre-selected *f*/stop. It returns to the maximum aperture opening instantly after the shutter action is completed. Nikkor lenses equipped with such an automatic diaphragm are designated as "Auto" lenses.

When the lens is removed from the camera, the diaphragm remains at the *f*/stop indicated on the scale, providing convenience for use with extension rings, bellows focusing attachments, and so forth.

Meter-Coupling Ridge

The lenses described in this book are the latest Nikkors, featuring automatic indexing (AI). Most automatic-diaphragm Nikkor lenses have a ridge, located at the lens mount, which engages the meter-coupling lever on the camera body to inform the camera's meter of the maximum aperture of the lens. Older Nikkors used a meter-coupling prong, located on the aperture ring of the lens, which engaged a pin protruding from the bodies of the older cameras. The newer lenses also have this prong so that they may be used on these older cameras.

Scales and Indicators

The *f*/stop markings on the diaphragm ring are equidistantly spaced. The use of intermediate settings is possible. Most lenses are equipped with a 52mm-diameter front thread to accept most lens front accessories, such as filters, close-up attachment lenses, and lens caps.

Most distance marks on the focusing ring are graduated in both feet and meters. However, some rings have only feet or meters. Instead of the usual numbered depth-of-field lines, Nikkor lenses have color-coded lines to correspond to the colors of the *f*/numbers engraved on the diaphragm scale.

The newer lenses (and older lenses adapted for AI use) have a secondary aperture scale immediately next to the lens mount. The numbers on this scale are visible in the viewfinders of certain cameras (F2A, F2AS, FM, and FE) via a prism-window which enables the user to look directly at the aperture set on the lens without removing his eye from the viewfinder.

Lens Mount

The rear section of the lens barrel that is mounted on the camera is usually referred to as the "lens mount." Nikkor lenses feature a three-tab bayonet lens mount.

This design enables any interchangeable F-mount Nikkor lens to be mounted to the camera rapidly and securely by a one-sixth counterclockwise turn after the *f*/number index dot on the lens barrel is aligned with the index on the front escutcheon of the camera body. With the *f*/number index dot at the top center position, the slot on the lens mount is joined to the spring-loaded coupling pin on the lens mount flange of the camera body. This also connects the automatic diaphragm with the shutter release and mirror mechanisms.

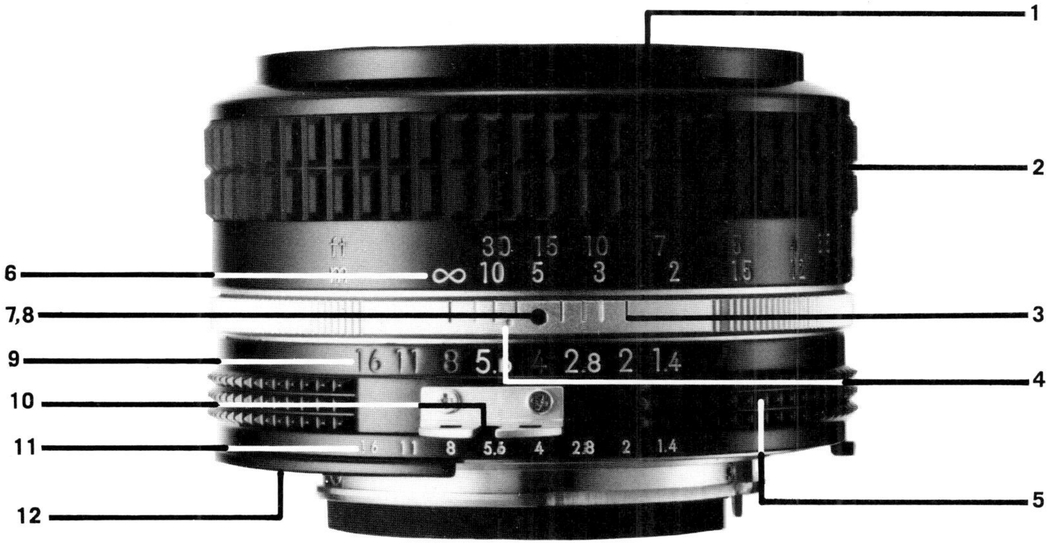

Mechanical Features of AI Lenses

1. Screw-in thread
2. Focusing ring
3. Depth-of-field scale
4. Infrared marking
5. Aperture-control ring
6. Distance scale
7. Distance index
8. Aperture index
9. Aperture scale
10. Meter-coupling prong
11. Secondary aperture scale
12. Meter coupling ridge

The mechanical features of Nikkor lenses are standard for easy operation and familiarity, whatever lens is in use. The features are indicated on the photograph above. The function of each lens is as follows:

Screw-in thread—accepts filter, lens hood, adapter ring, slide-copying adapter, or close-up lens. Comes in 52mm-diameter size on most Nikkor lenses;

Focusing ring—textured grip for quick and accurate focusing;

Depth-of-field scale—indicated by lines which are color-coded to match the color-coding of f/numbers on the aperture scale;

Infrared marking—corrects image plane displacement when using infrared film;

Aperture-control ring—presets the automatic aperture diaphragm;

Distance scale—calibrated in both meters and feet (except for a few Nikkor lenses which are marked in either meters or feet);

Distance index—for identification of focused distance;

Aperture index—for identification of selected lens aperture;

Aperture scale—has click-stops at each f/number, permits intermediate settings;

Meter-coupling prong—permits the use of the lens on older cameras lacking the AI facility; it engages the meter-coupling pin of these cameras to couple the lens diaphragm to the exposure-meter system;

Secondary aperture scale—visible through the viewfinder prism window of certain Nikons for direct readout of aperture setting;

Meter-coupling ridge—engages the meter-coupling lever to inform the camera's meter of the maximum aperture of the lens in use.

Angles of View of Full Range of Nikkor Lenses With the Exception of Fisheye Lenses

Focal Length	13	15	20	24	28	35	45	50	55	85	105	135
Diagonal	118°	110°	94°	84°	74°	62°	50°	46°	43°	28°30′	23°20′	18°
Horizontal	100° 20′	99°	83°	74°	64°	53°	42°	39°	36°10′	23°50′	19°30′	15°
Vertical	69° 40′	76°	61°	53°	45°	37°	29°	26°	24°40′	16°	13°	10°

Focal Length	180	200	250	300	400	500	600	800	1000	1200	2000
Diagonal	13°40′	12°20′	10°	8°10′	6°10′	5°	4°10′	3°	2°30′	2°	1°10′
Horizontal	11°30′	10°20′	8°10′	6°50′	5°10′	4°10′	3°30′	2°30′	2°	1°40′	1°
Vertical	7°40′	6°50′	5°30′	4°30′	3°30′	2°50′	2°20′	1°40′	1°20′	1°10′	0°40′

Angles of View of Most Nikkor Lenses

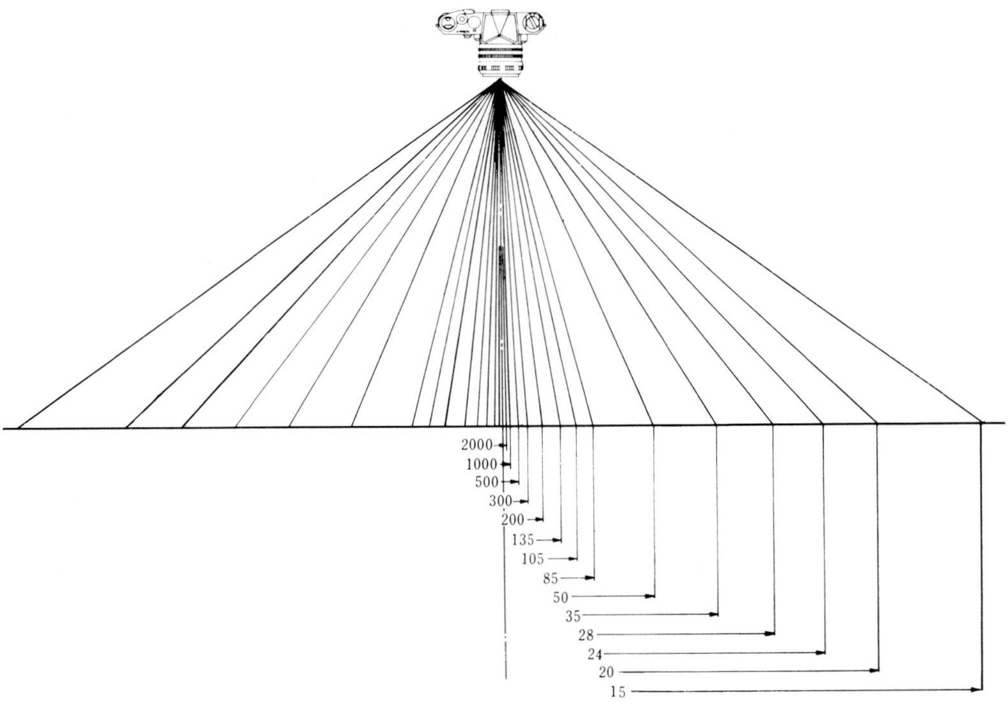

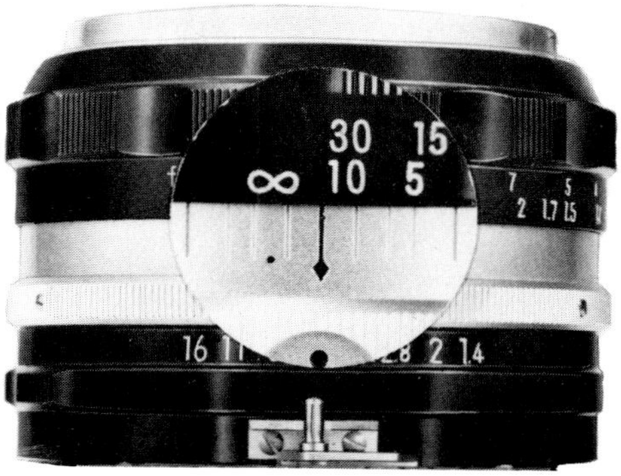

When infrared film is used, the plane of focus is not the same as with conventional films. Instead of the normal indexing mark on the top of the lens barrel—the long line with an arrow head at its bottom—used to point to the focusing scale of the lens, the selected distance on the scale is turned to match the small black dot to the left of the normal focusing index. Note that in the magnified inset the infinity mark appears opposite the black dot. The usual procedure is to focus visually on a subject and then to move the indicated distance opposite the black dot.

Maximum Aperture and Focal Length

A notation such as 1:1.4, or 1:2.5, or 1:2.8 on the front of the lens refers to the maximum lens aperture. It is the same as *f*/1.4, *f*/2.5, and *f*/2.8, as used throughout this book and is referred to variously as the *f*/stop, *f*/number, *f*/value, lens "speed," and relative lens aperture. Literally, it is the diameter of the maximum lens aperture divided by the focal length.

Infrared Markings

All Nikkor lenses except the Reflex-Nikkor lenses have a red dot or line near the black or white index provided for reading the distance scale on the focusing ring. When taking pictures with infrared film, a sharp image will be obtained by racking the lens out slightly after focusing on the image as seen by visible light.

This image plane displacement can be corrected by shifting the distance mark indicated on the black or white index to the red dot or the red line when the image is brought into sharp focus. The longer the focal length, the greater is the displacement or shift. In the normal or wide-angle lens, however, when the aperture is stopped down to *f*/8 or more, correction will not be necessary, as it is covered by the great depth of field at such a small aperture.

Serial Numbers

Each lens has its own serial number. It should be noted in one's inventory records in case of loss and to avoid confusion if the lens should be given out for repair. Occasionally, a lens of a given focal length and aperture will be changed optically. Knowledge of the serial number will identify whether the lens is of one formulation or another, as indicated on the lens data sheet, where pertinent.

LENS DESCRIPTIONS: DATA SHEETS

The directory chapters on Nikkor lenses include current Nikkor lenses designed for use with all Nikon and Nikkormat cameras and discontinued Nikkorex F cameras.

Discontinued F-mount lenses are covered in summary in an appendix to the relevant lens chapter. Also included are lenses originally designed for the Nikon S and SP rangefinder-type cameras, but usable with F-mount cameras in conjunction with the N-F Adapter.

For convenience, all current lenses are listed in order of focal length, beginning with the shortest and progressing to longer focal lengths. When lenses have the same focal length, but different maximum apertures, those with the widest apertures are listed first. Zoom lenses are listed in order of shortest of the zoom ranges for the several lenses.

The descriptive data for each lens, with some exceptions, consist of the following:

1. Summary of optical and mechanical features.
2. Narrative description of lens.
3. Optical formula of lens.
4. Photograph of the lens.
5. Diagram of the lens showing configuration of lens elements.
6. Miscellaneous performance data for lens selection purposes.
7. Depth-of-field table.

The exposure factors for use with some screens are not uniformly the same for Nikon F2A and F2AS cameras with particular lenses. Hence, data are provided for each type of Photomic finder/meter in the charts immediately preceding the first group of lens data sheets. The compensation may range from plus one-half *f*/stop to minus two *f*/stops. Make the compensation by lifting and turning the ASA film-speed index ring so that the compensatory mark appears opposite the film speed.

The exposure factors for use with some screens are not uniformly the same for F and F2 cameras with particular lenses. Hence, data are provided for each camera type with Photomic finder. The compensation may range from plus one-half *f*/stop to minus two *f*/stops. Make the compensation by lifting and turning the ASA film-speed index ring so that the compensatory mark appears opposite the film speed.

The optical diagrams shown in these preliminary pages are intended to show terminology and dimensional configurations typical of the diagrams included in the individual lens data groups.

A general schematic shows notations that are used in designating dimensions of specific lens attributes, including focal length, lens length, aperture, principal points, and back focal length.

Two other diagrams show typical telephoto and retrofocus wide-angle (inverted telephoto) designs.

The diagram of viewing angles shows the range of area coverage for lenses from 13mm through 2000mm, based on image diagonals.

Depth-of-field tables are based on use of a diameter of the circle of confusion of 1/30mm, except as noted herein, constituting a standard of acceptable sharpness. For the 55mm *f*/3.5 Micro-Nikkor, the circle of confusion used is 1/40mm. For the 200mm *f*/5.6 Medical-Nikkor, the circle of confusion used is 1/20mm.

The depth-of-field ranges shown in the tables, with the exception of the Medical-Nikkor lens, are measured in distances from the film plane to the front and rear limits of the depth of field. Therefore, the depth-of-field range obtained for lenses with same focal lengths but different lens design will differ slightly because the distance between the object-side and the image-side principal points will vary accordingly. The position of the film plane coincides with the top line of the serial number engraved on the top plate of the camera, a distance of 46.5mm from the lens-mount surface.

Approximate depths of field for distances not given in the tables can be obtained by interpolating from the two neighboring distances in the tables.

Depth-of-field tables for zoom lenses are not included. Approximations can be derived by reference to the lens tables of the nearest corresponding focal length.

GUIDE TO LENS SELECTION

The selection of lenses is influenced by personal picture-taking needs, interests, and patterns of work. What to buy is often governed by budget so that the photographer who can afford to add only one lens may need to make a clear cut choice between a wide-angle lens as opposed to a telephoto lens. More difficult decisions are made when selecting a wide-angle lens of a focal length of 24mm or one of 28mm, or a telephoto of 85mm as against one of 105mm. Then, too, should one purchase the 35mm $f/1.4$ or the 35mm $f/2$ lens and why?

We have just identified criteria of subject matter (wide-angle vs. telephoto), tight pictorial framing (focal length differences within category, such as 24mm vs. 28mm), and lighting conditions ($f/1.4$ vs. $f/2$). Other criteria for a single decision might include economics and unique optical properties. These are elaborated below. The uses of categories of lenses and of individual lenses are described in the several lens chapters.

Coverage of Image Area (Framing)

At a given working distance, a lens, ranging from wide-angle to telephoto, is selected to embrace a wide picture, to limit coverage to specific objects, or to bring in distant objects in magnified image size. Zoom lenses offer selective area coverage and image size at varying focal lengths, within near and far ranges of the particular lenses, without the necessity of physically changing working distances.

In black-and-white photography, precise framing within the film rectangle is not of prime importance, for there is always the latitude of cropping on the enlarger easel. This is true also in color printing. One can err, therefore, in these cases, on the side of a slightly shorter focal length or one can really use fewer lenses in view of darkroom flexibility.

When the main output is slides for projection or when a professional must use slides to show pictures to prospective clients, it becomes necessary to do the framing or cropping much more precisely at the moment of exposure. Some latitude for this can be gained through adjusting the shooting distance, but not always. Also, desired perspective effects may dictate that required area coverage be achieved using a lens of longer or shorter focal length.

Perspective Effects

Keep in mind the general rule that perspective effects are achieved by varying the distance between the subject and lens. At a given shooting distance the use of different focal lengths will not change the perspective effects—only the image size and area of coverage will change.

When particular perspective effects are desired, the factors to be considered are: how close can one be for foreground effects and how far away must one be for background effects? For the first, the focusing range of a wide-angle lens governs; for the second, the angle of view of a long-focus lens usually governs. There are, however, occasions when the choice might be wide-angle vs. normal or normal vs. long-focus.

Furthermore, selection of a lens may influence working distance. Since the wide-angle lenses permit working at close range, they tend to be used that way so the image details of the foreground can be brought out in larger scale. Similarly, long-focus lenses tend to be used at a distance in order to bring in sufficient coverage of relevant subject matter. Hence, perspective effects must be balanced against image area coverage.

For foreground emphasis, any lens permitting close-focusing (or with use of an extension ring or supplementary lens) can be used to photograph objects at close range, provided this permits adequate coverage in width. Hence, a wide-angle lens is often chosen to emphasize foregrounds, while also ensuring adequate width coverage. When longer focal lengths are used for near-focusing, they blur out backgrounds. Use of a low viewpoint with camera held level adds to foreground prominence.

For object separation in depth, also achieved by working close, generally any near-focusing lens can be used, but choice of focal length will be governed by the desired area coverage. Choice will tend toward wide-angle lenses, moderate or pronounced.

To achieve comparable size of objects in depth, adequate distance from the subject is necessary. Thereby, foreground prominence is reduced and objects are seen in increasingly relative proportion, especially as the objects are spaced at greater distances away from the lens. For suitable image magnification on film, telephoto lenses should be used.

Adverse Light Conditions

Whether or not light conditions are adverse is governed partly by film sensitivity. Hence, a relatively slow color film, ASA 25, might not be able to afford adequate exposure under some conditions with a maximum aperture of *f*/3.5 or *f*/2.8, but the same film used with a maximum aperture of *f*/1.4 might yield desired results under the same conditions.

Choose lenses with widest apertures for use under adverse light conditions or with relatively slow films, provided there is a choice in the same focal length. If necessary, use a lens of different focal length with a wider aperture, which will assure adequate exposure. Otherwise, use a faster film, if feasible.

Action Photography

Fast lenses, those with large maximum apertures, may be needed to accommodate a wide range of exposure conditions as well as faster shutter speeds. Consider wide-angle lenses with their great depths of field when action-movement is hard to follow. Zoom lenses, in combination with motor-driven rapid sequence equipment, are useful for fast-moving action situations.

Mechanical/Optical Features

Lenses may be selected for unique attributes. For example, the 55mm, 105mm, and 200mm Micro-Nikkors are widely used because of their ability to focus at distances ranging from inches to infinity. These lenses have been designed for optical correction at close-focusing ranges. Certain other lenses have been designed for improved corrections at all working distances through the use of "floating element" design. Hence, unique attributes of individual lenses, when desirable for the individual photographer, should be taken into account when selecting a lens.

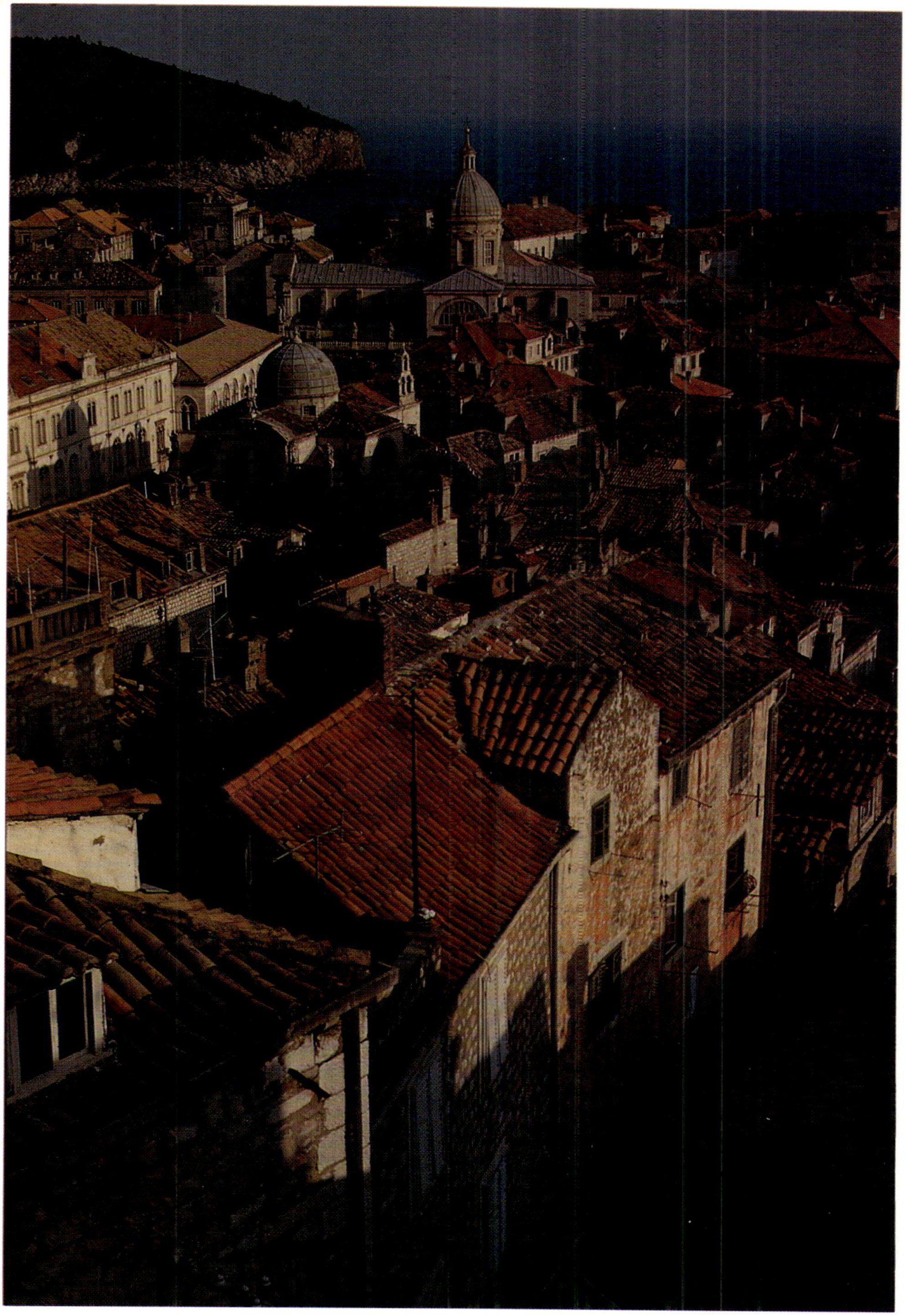

Tom Tracy

Rooftops of the seaside city of Dubrovnic, Yugoslavia, were photographed with a normal lens that afforded the depth of field required to keep both foreground and distant background in sharp focus.

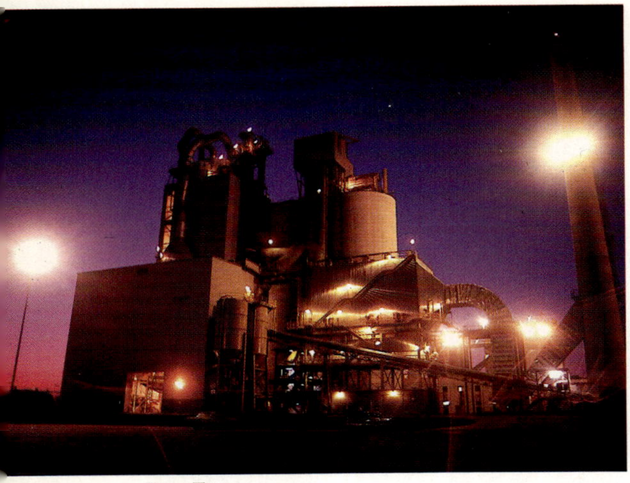

Tom Tracy

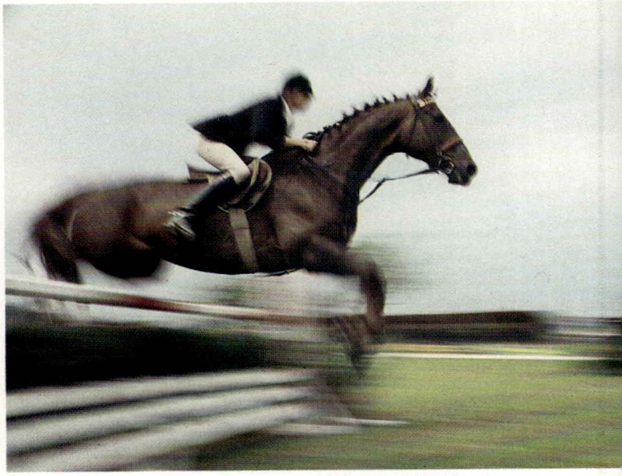

Michael Melford

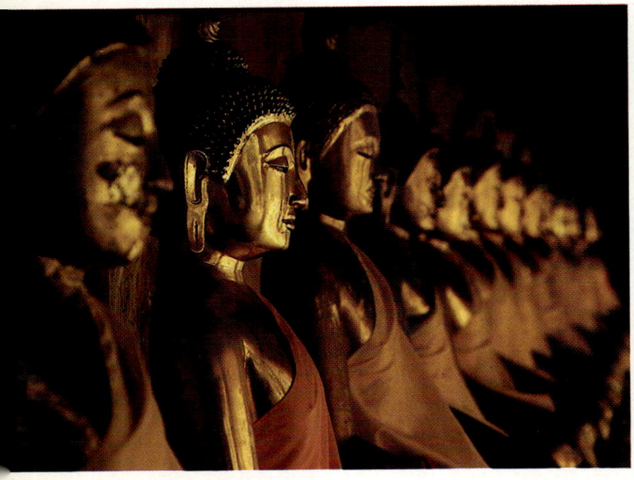

Tom Tracy

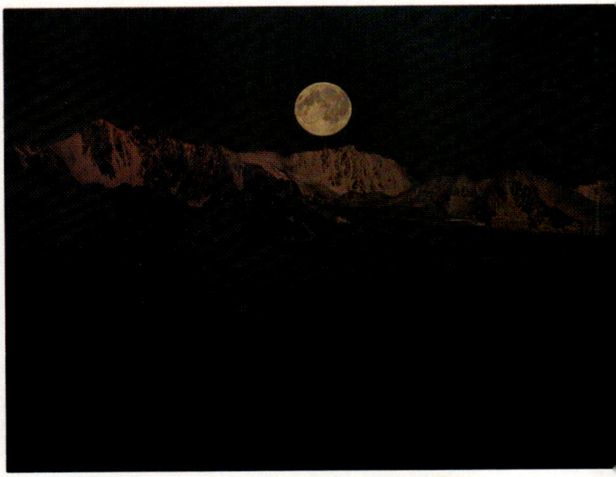

Tom Tracy

(Top left) Distortion caused by a very wide angle lens adds a final science-fictional touch to this night shot of a cement plant in Pennsylvania. Large spots of light and pinkish streaks were caused by the long exposure time. (Top right) The photographer used a fisheye lens and panned the camera, focusing on the horse's head, to create this impression of high speed and motion. (Bottom left) A moderate telephoto lens and an aperture wide enough to compensate for the low light level in this temple in Bangkok permitted the photographer to focus in on a single statue in this long row of golden Buddhas. (Bottom right) Use of a very long telephoto lens brought out details of the lunar surface in this shot of moonrise over mountain peaks near Valdez in Alaska.

Dan O'Neill

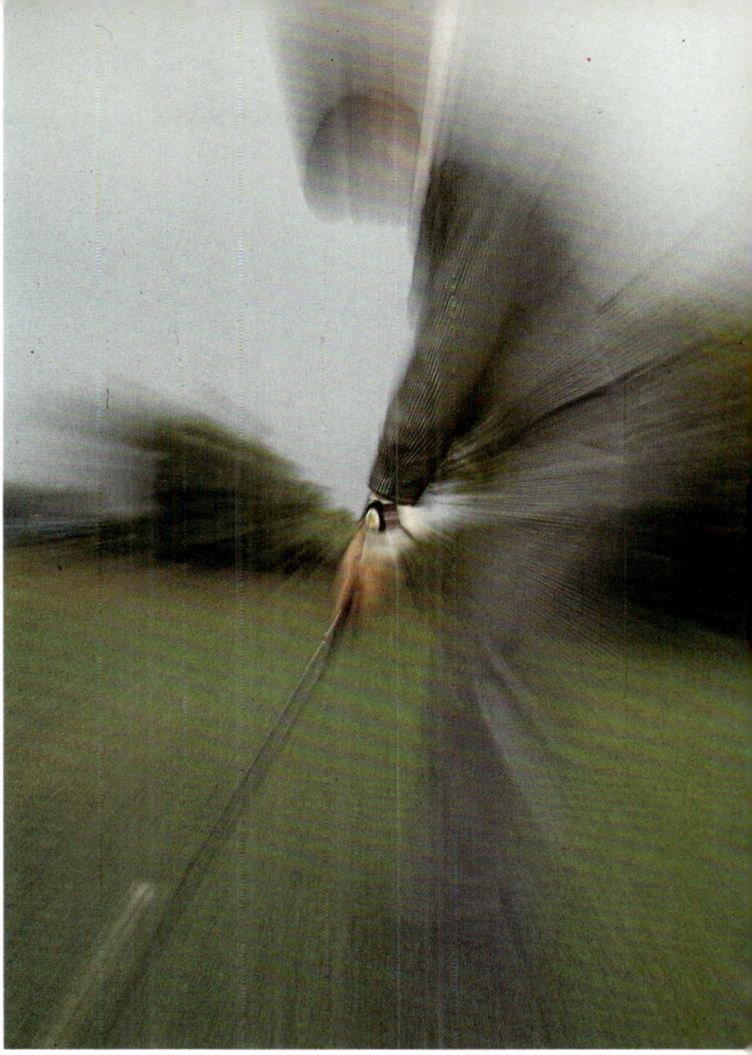

(Right) A zoom shot made with a 43-86mm lens gives the impression of full swing and carry-through, although the golfer is only preparing to hit the ball. (Below) These autumn maples in Oneonta, New York, were photographed in the light of early morning, which provided both the brilliant color and the soft light. The wide field of view provided by a 20mm lens allowed the photographer to maintain detail despite the surrounding fog.

Michael Melford

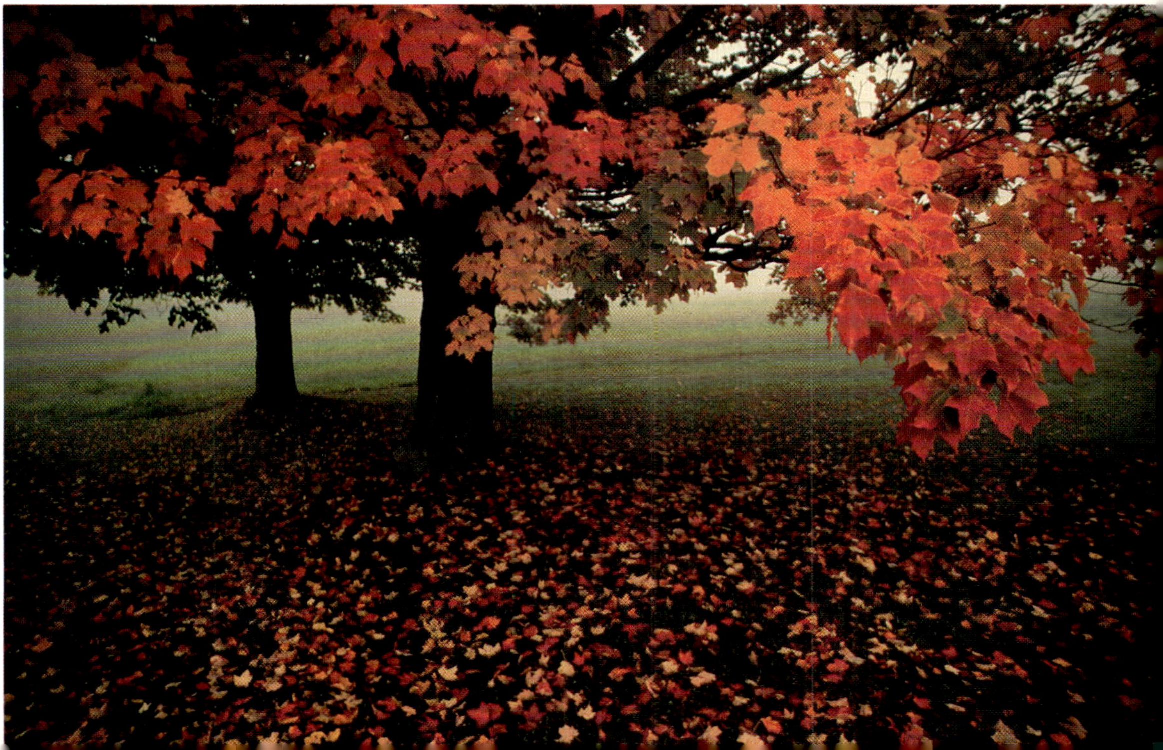

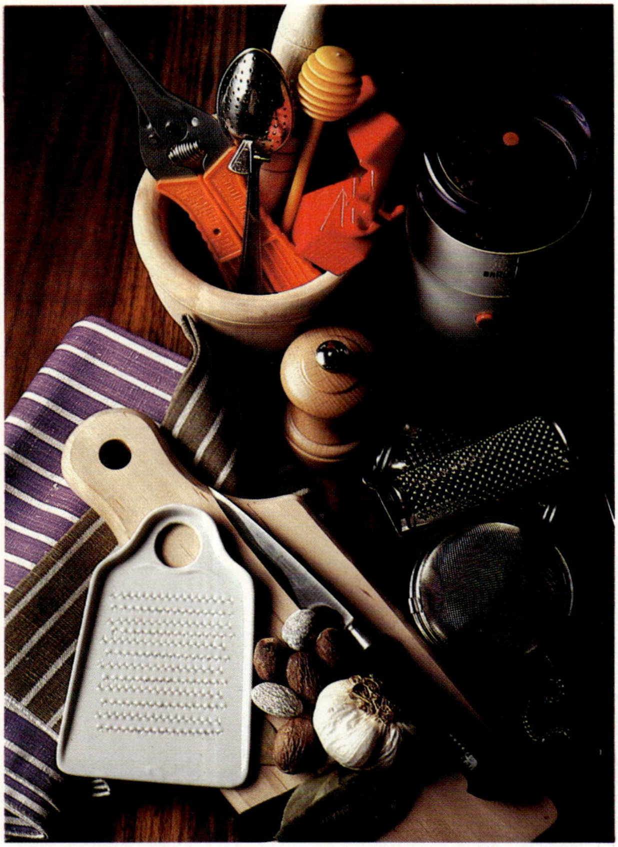

Tom Tracy

(Below) A normal lens captured this hang glider in flight, partly backlighted by the sun. A small aperture caused the diffraction spikes at the bottom edge of the wing, breaking the sun's light up into star-like fragments. (Left) The great depth of field offered by a wide-angle lens is ideal for product and tabletop photography. Detail was maintained in all the elements from foreground to background in this partial overhead shot of kitchen equipment.

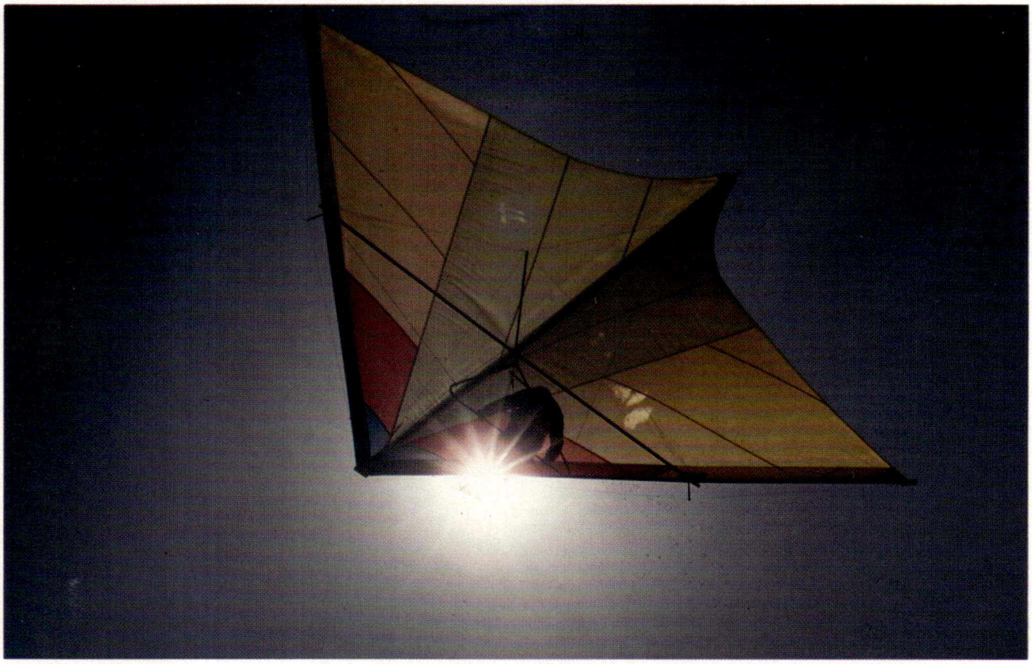

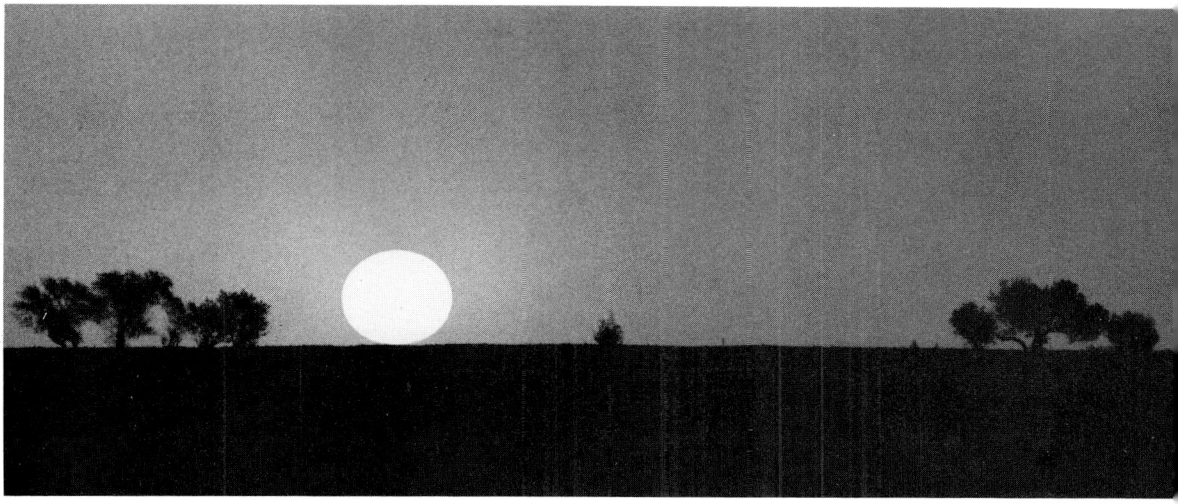

Winter Sunset, Transvaal. "Telephoto views of the setting sun have become a bit of a cliché," said Robertson. "I tried to stylize this picture by working for three tones: black, white and gray, and by using a medium long 300mm f/4.5 lens to make the sun a similar scale object to the silhouetted trees." A moment before or after and sun would not have been tangential with horizon line. Plus-X film developed in Acufine.

Struan Robertson

Seals and Cormorants, Cape Cross, Namibia. One of the largest seal rookeries in world. Heavy mist usually cuts power of near-tropical sun—good for seals, but challenging for picture-takers. 135mm lens. Plus-X film developed in Beutler developer.

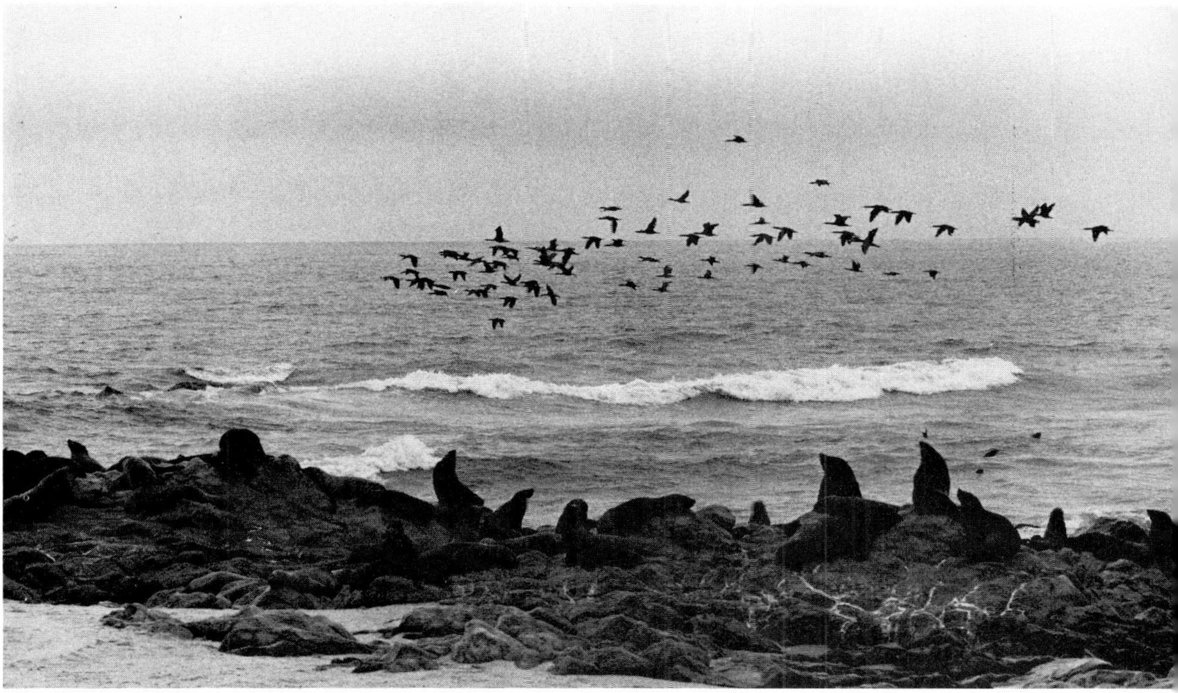

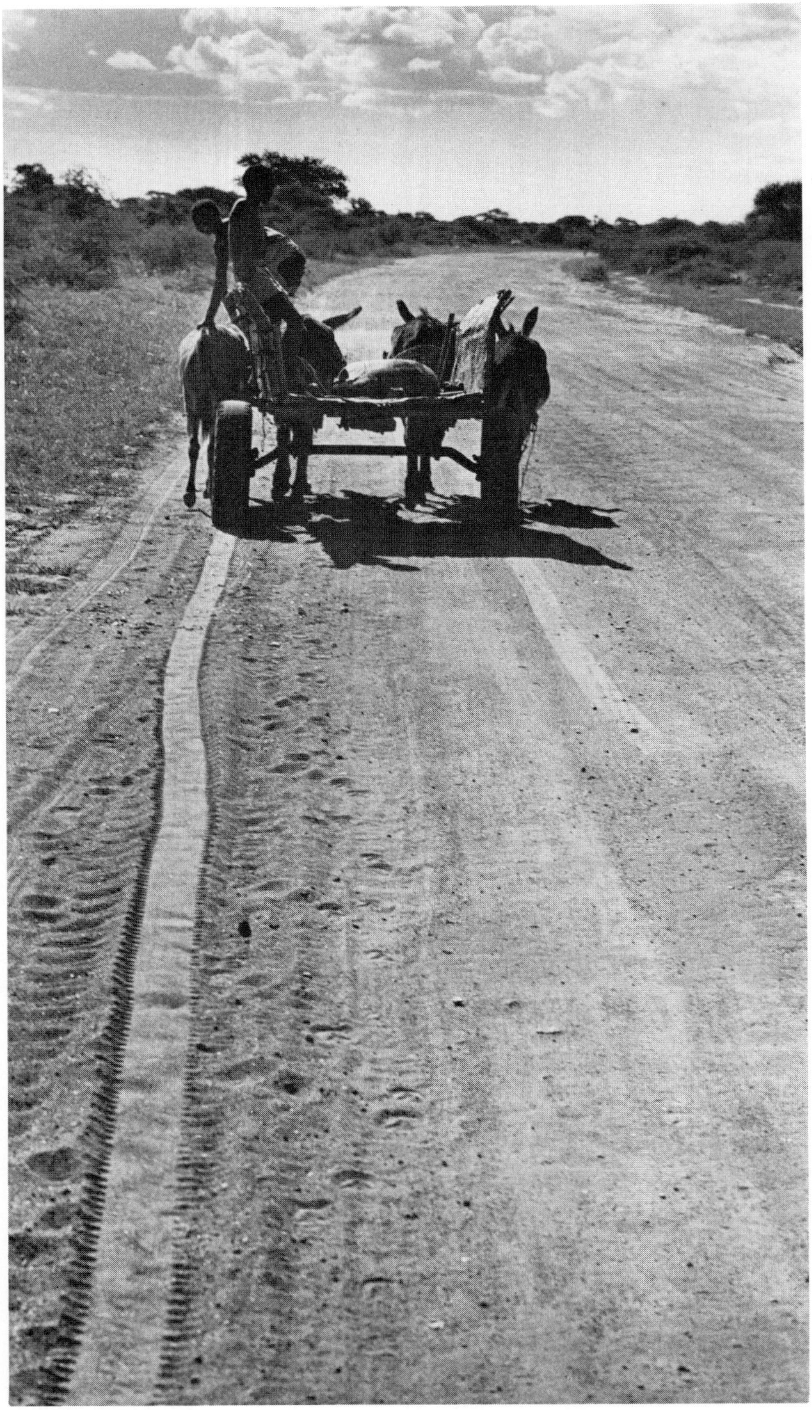

Struan Robertson

Donkey cart on road to Maun, Botswana. Even without technical data, one could tell this was made with moderately long lens. Clues are in gentle rate of perspective convergence of the tire track and absence of extreme background compression. 135mm f/2.8 lens used at high angle with the horizon well up the picture to emphasize the wheel tracks. Kodak Plus-X developed in Rodinal 1:75.

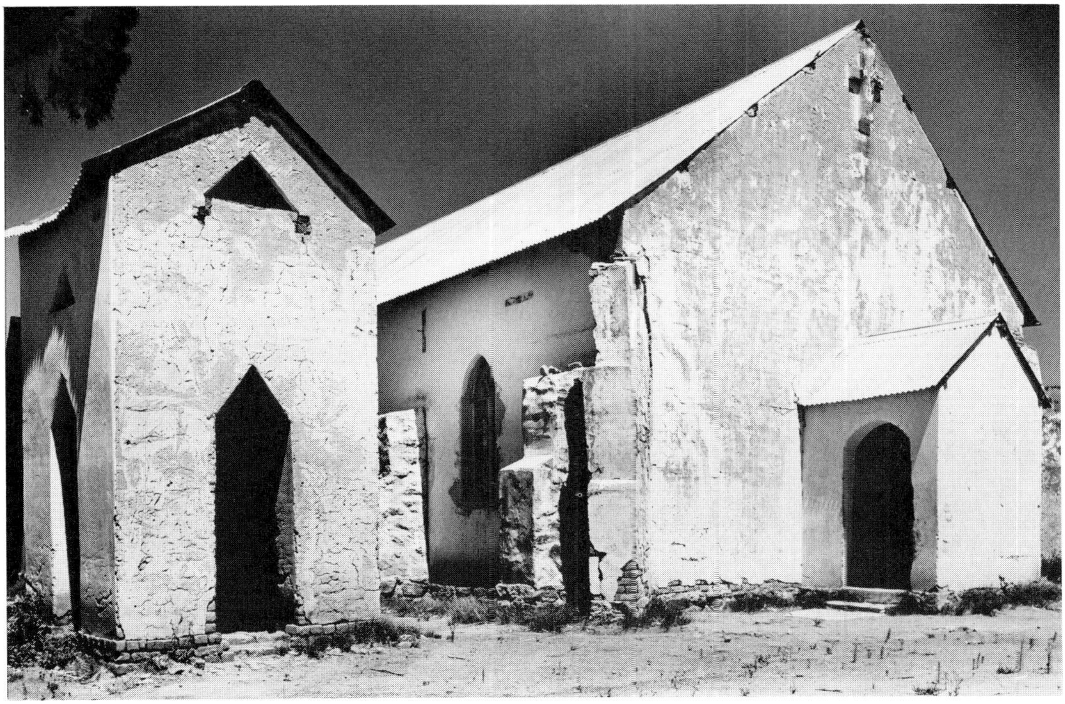

African church near Johannesburg. Example of big-camera quality with 35mm through care in exposure and development. Extremely fine Kodak Panatomic-X developed in Acufine which, although it does not give ultimate contour sharpness of Rodinal, yields very fine grain and tonal gradation. Made with PC-Nikkor to maintain vertical lines parallel. Wratten A filter to darken sky and bring out whiteness of plaster.

Struan Robertson

Basotho rider on the Sani Pass, South Africa. The Sani Pass separates Lesotho from South Africa. It is so steep that only 4-wheel drive cars are allowed on it. Said Robertson: "The rider was the lucky chance that changed a rather dull landscape into something better." 105mm f/2.5 lens afforded best relationship between foreground and background. f/11 at 1/500 sec. Plus-X, Rodinal 1:50 for 17 minutes at 60°F.

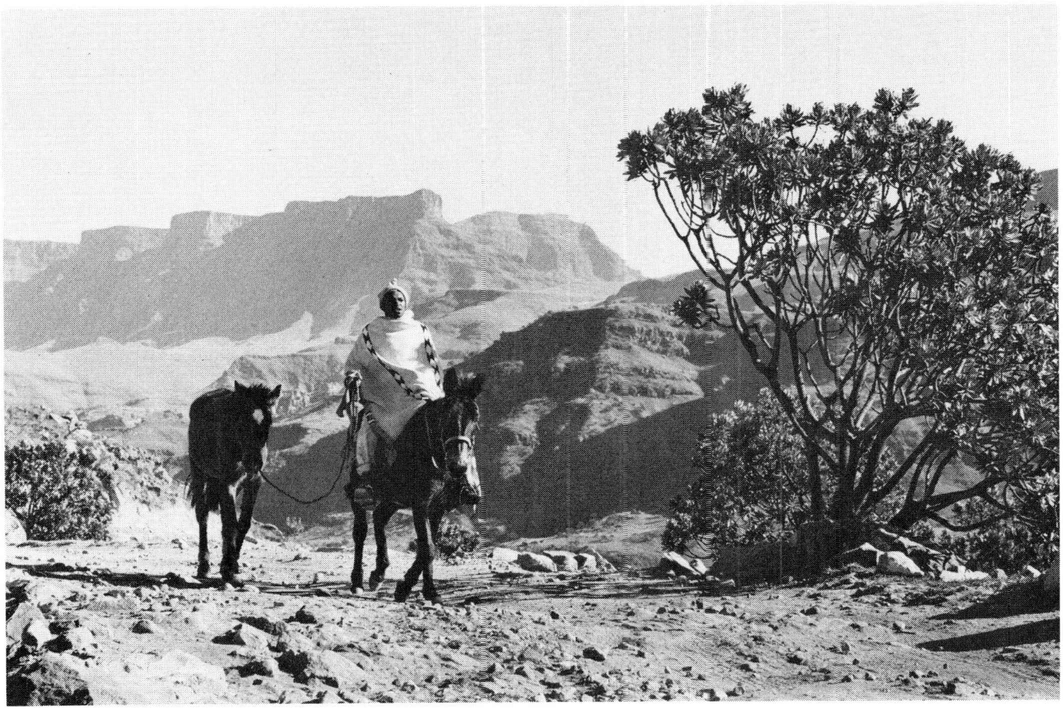

Struan Robertson

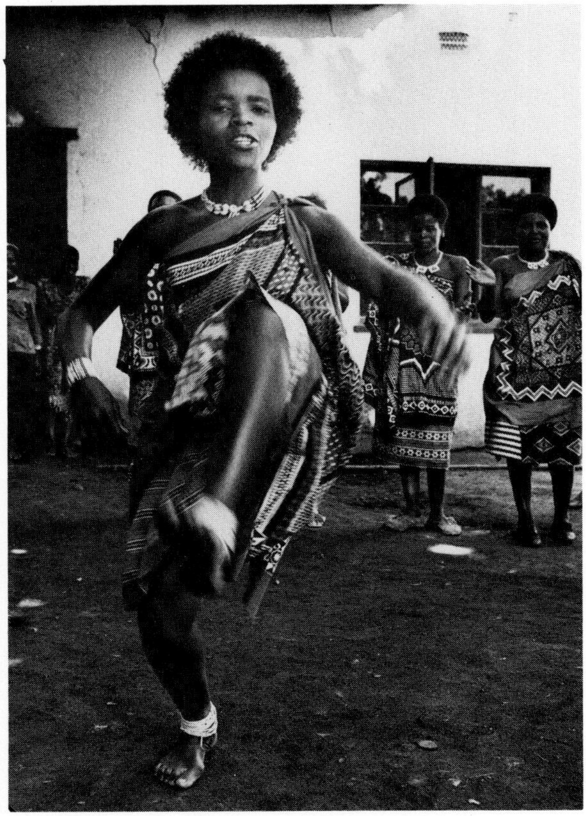

Swazi woman dancing. After having been photographed routinely inside their weaving factory, women asked to be photographed as group. At first they posed stiffly but then started singing and clapping and soon this woman did an extremely fiery dance photographed with 24mm lens at close range. 1/125 sec. Ilford FP4 film, Rodinal 1:75.

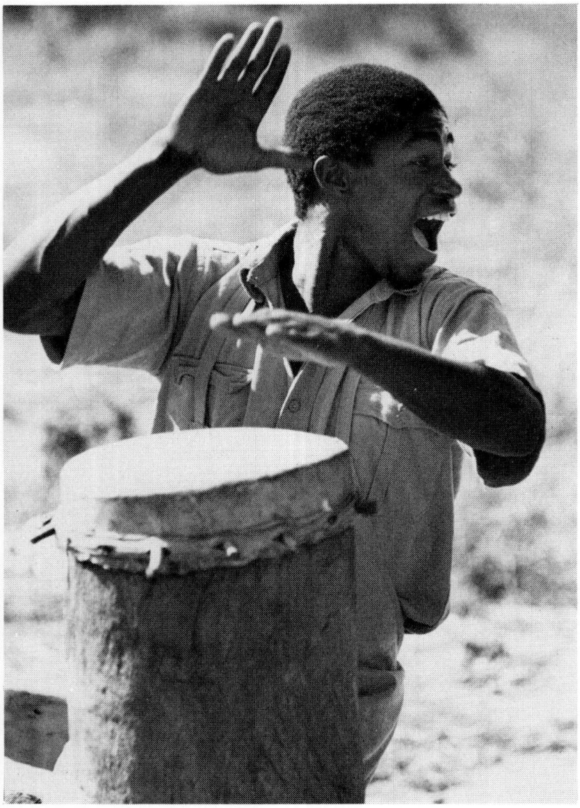

Karanga drummer, Rhodesia. A duty of this farmer was to sound mealtimes on a drum. During his performance for Robertson, he waxed enthusiastic and did a long drum solo accompanying a shouted chant. 135mm *f*/3.5 lens, Kodak Plus-X film, Rodinal.

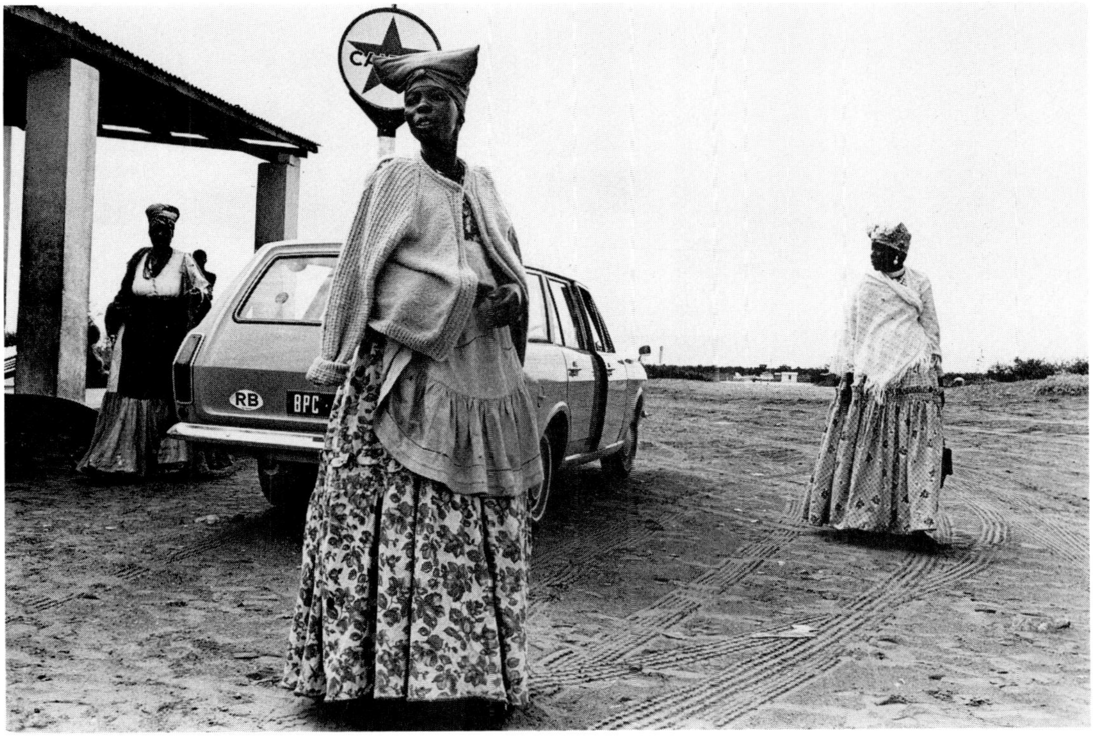

Herero women at Ghanzi still wear Mother Hubbard dresses introduced by Rhenish missionaries of 19th century. They avoid the camera which they regard as "Evil Eye." With prism finder removed, camera was used at waist level with a 35mm *f*/2 lens; it was zone-focused with screen image used for composition. In candid photography important not to stare at subject and to avoid having camera at eye. Kodak Plus-X film.

Struan Robertson

Portraits at street market, Botswana. To capture his subjects, Robertson used two cameras, one with 35mm lens and the other with 135mm. Latter used for selective recording of subjects as shown in accompanying pictures. Kodak Plus-X film, Rodinal 1:75.

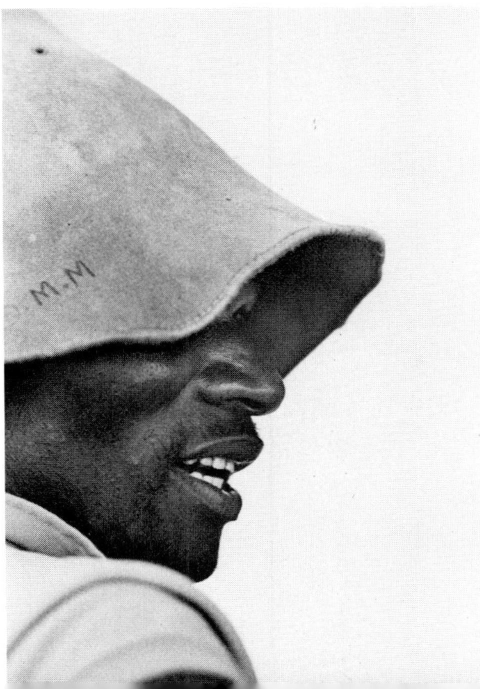

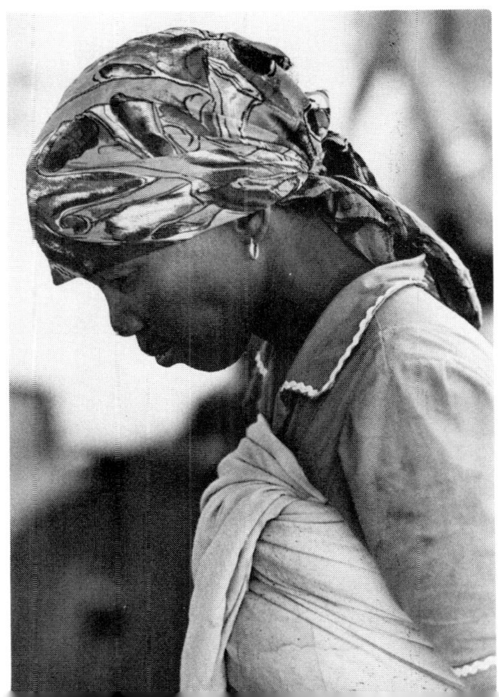

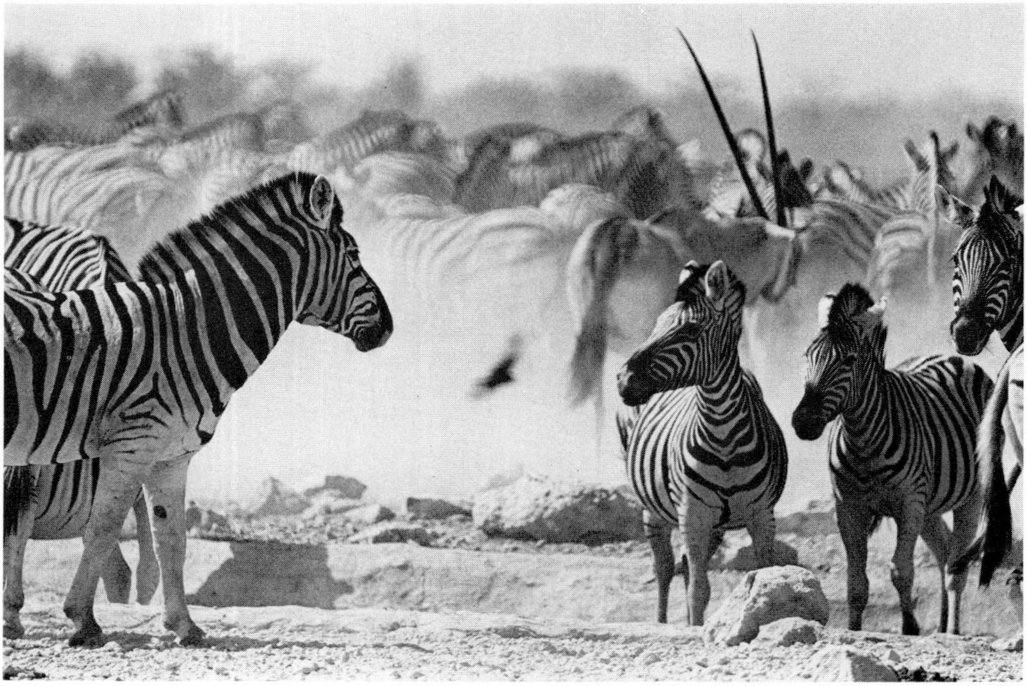

Zebra Herd at waterhole, Etosha pan, Namibia. Animals congregate in thousands at waterholes at edge of enormous pan in dry country, stirring up such clouds of alkali dust that sky has darkness of impending storm. One long-horned antelope (Gemsbok) wandered into herd. Note background out-of-focus pattern. 500mm *f*/8 lens, Kodak Plus-X, Rodinal.

Struan Robertson

Gemsbok (oryx gazella). The Gemsbok are continuously in motion—pushing, wheeling, bucking and lowering their heads to threaten others with their razor-sharp horns, making it very difficult to photograph them. They engage in endless status-fighting hierarchy defense at waterholes. Use of super-telephotos essential, with high shutter speeds to stop movement. 500mm *f*/8 lens, Kodak Plus-X film, Rodinal.

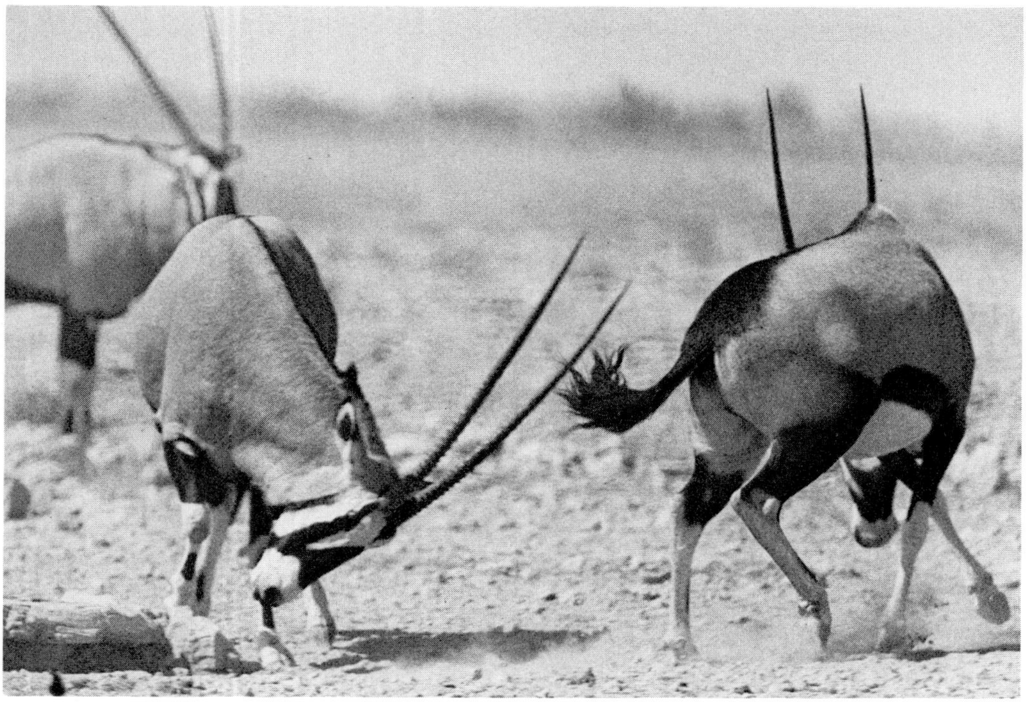

CHAPTER 2

Nikkor Lenses: General Range

The full range of Nikkor lenses for picture taking under a diversity of conditions extends from the extremely wide 15mm lens to the extremely long 2000mm lens. For convenience, these lenses have been grouped into discussion categories designated as wide-angle, standard (or normal), intermediate telephoto, and long-range tele lenses.

The technically knowledgeable photographer may point out that the term *telephoto* pertains solely to lenses that achieve shorter physical lengths than their optical focal lengths through the device of using negative rear elements to diverge the image projected toward the film. For convenience, however, the term telephoto is used to cover both lenses that qualify under the technical definition and lenses of long focus.

The categories used here are not absolutely clear-cut; they have some overlapping. Traditionally, lenses of about 50mm in focal length have been designated as standard for the 24 × 36mm image area. Wide-angle lenses have traditionally taken in all focal lengths from 35mm on down through the shortest. Quite a few photographers, however, have used the 35mm lens as a standard; this trend has been strengthened since the introduction of the 35mm *f*/1.4 Nikkor lens. There is no difficulty in starting the telephoto group with the 85mm lens, but the arbitrary break between 300mm and 400mm may introduce some argument as to where each belongs. The criterion used here is hand-held convenience. While many photographers are able to take hand-held pictures that show no blur with 300mm, 400mm, and even 500mm lenses, there is still a greater need for using a tripod or other firm support with these and longer lenses, particularly under adverse light conditions which require long exposure times.

Special-purpose lenses are covered in the next chapter. These include the fish-eyes, the zooms, the 45mm GN Auto Nikkor (discontinued), the various close-up lenses, the PC-Nikkors for perspective correction, and the El-Nikkor enlarging lenses.

This chapter discusses the working attributes of each category of lenses and their particular photographic applications. Comparatively little need be said about the standard lenses because they are, after all, designed to cover the norm—the average. They present few management problems. As one moves to the extremes on either end of the range of focal lengths, however, there is more and more to say about specialized uses and optical management problems.

In addition to the general narrative, this chapter includes individual data sheets for all of the lenses and numerous examples of pictorial results achieved within each focal length category.

WIDE-ANGLE LENSES

Wide-angle lenses in the Nikkor range begin with a shortest focal length of 13mm and progress in increments through 15mm, 18mm, 20mm, 24mm, 28mm, and 35mm. While these are seemingly small increments, they compare proportionately with advances from 85mm to 105mm to 135mm, or even from 300mm to 400mm. For example, there is the same ratio between the focal lengths of the 400mm and 300mm lenses as between the 20mm and 15mm lenses, but in the first case there is a difference of 100mm while in the second the difference is only 5mm. The jump in size of detail from 15mm to 35mm—a focal-length difference of 20mm—is enormously greater than the move from 85mm to 105mm. The professional or advanced amateur might select one or more of the lenses in the 20 to 35mm group. If the photographer uses the "normal," 50mm lens to any substantial degree, he might bypass the 35mm in favor of the 28mm. If the photographer needs exceptionally wide-angle coverage, he would favor either the 24mm, 20mm, or 18mm lens. If his interests include giving prominence to foreground or achieving unique perspective effects, he would also favor these wide-angle lenses. The 13mm, 15mm, and 16mm (the latter is a full-frame fisheye) lenses, with their exceptionally wide angles of view, are primarily special-purpose lenses.

The uses of wide-angle lenses range widely, both in conventional photography where the wide view is desired or in the creative use of perspective effects achieved by being able to focus as close as one foot (0.3 meter). Some of the unique effects achieved with wide-angle lenses are easily identifiable as the "wide-angle look"—especially the recognizable distortion—but these are functions of working distance rather than optical design. The characteristics of wide-angle lenses, some of their design features, their applications to photography, and the particular management problems they introduce are described in this part of the chapter.

Characteristics of Wide-Angle Lenses

The physical size of a wide-angle lens for an SLR may be greater than that of a standard lens of equivalent or wider aperture. Originally, the focal length of a lens was equivalent to the distance of travel of the image from the approximate center of the lens to the image plane. Hence, a 50mm lens would extend that same distance from the image plane, while a 25mm (or 24mm) lens would extend only half that distance from the image or focal plane. With the earlier nonreflex cameras, such as the Leica and Contax, the wide-angle or short focal-length lenses could be deeply recessed in the camera body so as to bring them closer to the film. With the development of single-lens reflex cameras, however, it became necessary to reformulate the lenses by extending them forward so that they would not interfere with the movement of the reflex mirror. Obviously, this required new optical approaches, which were achieved through the retrofocus or inverted telephoto design. Even so, the older Nikkor 21mm *f*/4 lens could be used only with the mirror in the locked-up position in conjunction with an external view finder. Today, this difficulty has been overcome in all Nikkor wide-angle lenses with the exception of Even the exceptionally wide-angle 13mm lens can be used with the mirror functioning normally for reflex focusing and viewing.

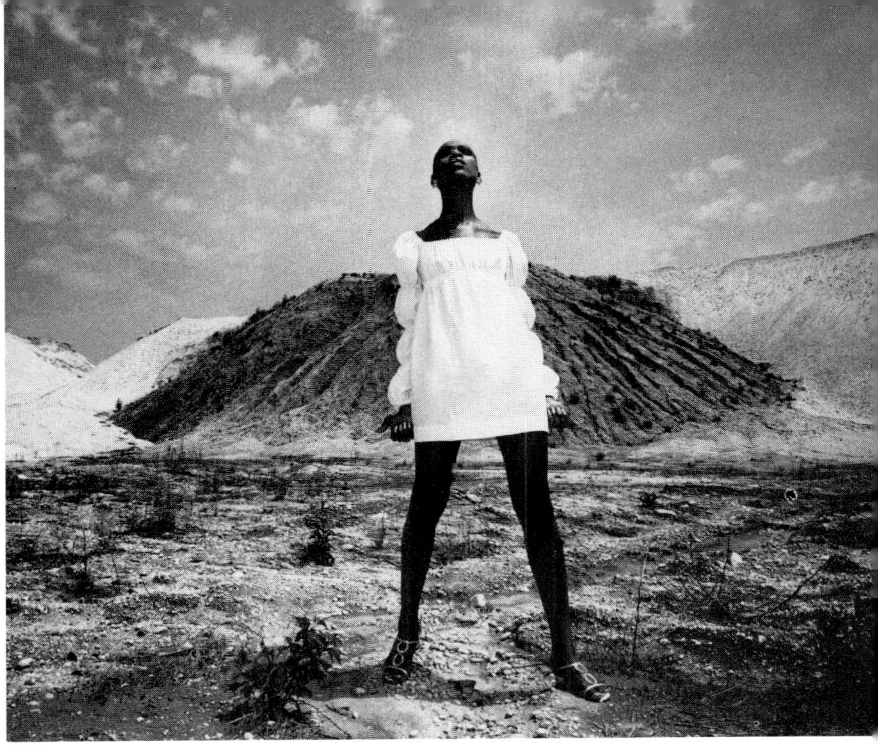

Douglas T. Mesney

Model Naomi Simms is given foreground prominence through moving in close with 20mm *f*/3.5 lens while background is diminished in relative size. Sl ghtly lowered camera position, closer to lower body, creates a geometric parallelism between foreground and background. Panatomic-X exposed at E.I. 64, 1/60 sec. at *f*/8, red filter.

The foreground figure is given prominence by being photographed with the 20mm lens at close range while the wide-angle capabilities bring in enough of the background to provide a story context. The story was about the Ir sh border for the *Daily Telegraph Magazine*. *f*/8, 1/250 sec. Ilford FP4.

Graham Finlayson

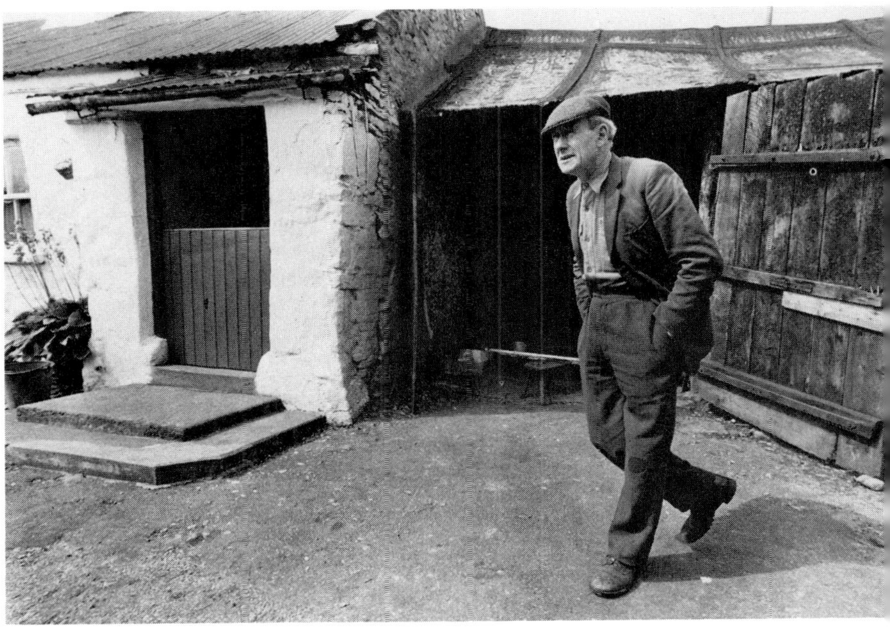

The impact of wide-angle lenses on photojournalism, advertising, and other areas of creative photography is due to a combination of factors—the increasing availability of wide-angle lenses with wider apertures, the ability of these lenses to be used very close to their subjects, and the improved optical performance resulting from advanced retrofocus design. Traditionally, especially for photographers on a limited lens budget, the 35mm lens was the most popular of the wide-angles due in no small part to the fact that they had the widest apertures among the wide-angle lenses. The availability of a 28mm *f*/2 has opened up a whole new field of adventure for that lens.

Wide-Angle Optics

Traditionally, wide-angle lenses were of fairly symmetrical design and relatively small apertures due to difficulties in correcting optical aberrations. One disadvantage of these lenses, which rendered them particularly unsuitable for color work, was an unevenness of illumination away from the center towards the edges and corners. Also, wide-angle lens apertures were relatively small, a disadvantage when working with color. The retrofocus design, originally developed by Angenieux of France, overcame these difficulties by providing even illumination and wider lens apertures, as well as generally improving optical performance.

Someone once said that a retrofocus or inverted telephoto lens can be likened to an ordinary lens that has a close-up attachment lens permanently attached to its front end. In a typical retrofocus design, a negative group of lens elements at the front gathers the image, which is then projected by positive elements in a convergent configuration to fill the image area at the desired back focus.

Another optical advance in the design of wide-angle lenses is the use of so-called floating elements. This means the automatic realignment of distances between certain internal lens elements to correct

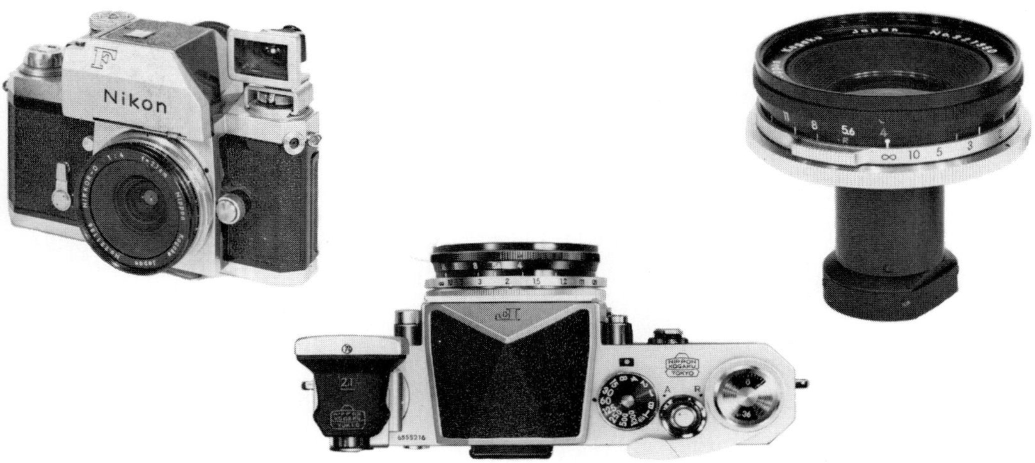

The 21mm *f*/4 Nikkor-O extreme wide-angle lens was most popular even though it had to be used with an externally mounted optical viewfinder. The very short back-focus required that the reflex mirror be locked up when this lens was mounted on the camera. The overhead view of lens on camera with standard pentaprism finder shows the most compact of configurations. It fit all Nikon camera bodies but only those from Serial No. 225001 could be mounted on Nikkormat camera bodies. Still to be found in use, this lens has a near-focusing distance of 0.9m (3 feet). It takes standard 52mm filter-thread attachments.

distortions or aberrations that occur when the lens is focused at close distances. This accommodates the fact that wide-angle lenses are frequently used at close range and that ordinary lenses with fixed positions for the internal components are normally corrected for infinity focus. The floating element design now provides corrections at ordinary shooting distances as well as at very close range.

Wide-Angle Applications

The two major areas of usage for wide-angle lenses are in achieving wide coverage—crowding more material into the picture area than is feasible with the normal lens—and achieving unique or arresting perspective effects that result from working at close range.

Under the wide coverage category comes architectural picture taking, especially horizontal format, scenes across narrow streets, interiors of all kinds, landscapes in which the broad sweep or large configurations predominate, crowd pictures, "establishing shots" as used in documentaries and photo essays, blind shooting when accurate focusing and viewing are not feasible, sports scenes in which close-in wide coverage is needed, and wide-field surveillance.

Wide-angle perspective effects, achieved by getting in close to main or foreground subjects, consist of:

1. Separating looming foreground (or frontal) objects from middle ground objects and the latter from diminished background objects.

2. Giving size dominance to frontal objects.

3. Stretching out the foreground even if it is devoid of individualized objects apart from ground or water.

A detailed description of the perceptual bases for these effects is beyond the scope of this book. Here, it is sufficient to state that it is the act of getting in close that yields these effects, rather than any optical attribute of wide-angle lenses. In fact, subjects photographed with both wide-angle and longer-focus lenses, from the same distance, will yield the same perspective effects.

Psychologically, the ability of a photographer to inject himself into a scene, bringing him very close to his living subjects, gives him a feeling of stark intimacy.

Another advantage of wide-angle lenses (and sometimes disadvantage) is they yield great depth of field. When the lenses are stopped down to $f/11$ or $f/16$ at their hyperfocal distances, images are defined sharply from the closest subjects out to infinity.

Several of the wide-angle lenses can be used in close-up photography when mounted in reverse position, using the BR-2 Reverse Adapter. The 24mm $f/2.8$ lens is particularly recommended for this purpose. In reverse mode, suitable wide-angle lenses give improved optical performance and greater magnification, as covered in the lens data sheets.

Wide-Angle Technique

Exact focusing in dim lights with wide-angle lenses may constitute a problem because of the great depth of field of wide-angle lenses. This is more of a problem at intermediate distances, for at very close focusing distances at full aperture, there is much less sharpness in depth. When working under adverse lighting conditions, the larger aperture lenses should be used—the 28mm $f/2$ compared to 28mm $f/3.5$, or the 35mm $f/1.4$ compared to 35mm $f/2$ or $f/2.8$. Magnifying eyepiece attachments are also useful in achieving optical "blow-ups" of the image through the viewfinder in order to zero in most critically on the zone of sharpest focus.

Exaggerated perspective, as already emphasized, is a function of usage rather than of optical attributes. The disturbing convergence of lines in some pictures is a familiar example. With long lenses, one ordinarily works at some distance from his subject, whereas with wide-angle lenses, the tendency to move in closer in order to show prominent details in larger scale, results in a rapid diminution in size of objects at greater distances from the camera. Parallel lines tend to converge toward some imaginary point in the background at a more rapid rate. When shooting from a height at a downward angle, full figure pictures are recorded in exaggerated perspective as though the models are carrot-shaped; the bodies taper off in size rapidly until the feet are shown to be very small. A correction of this convergence is to hold the camera so that the back is parallel to the subject, at eye level or waist level.

A more acceptable kind of exaggerated perspective can be seen when objects of similar size, especially people's heads, are placed close to the main subjects but at different distances from the camera. A dramatic fall-off in size of the objects beyond can be perceived. This can be used as a clue to the fact that a wide-angle lens was used to take a particular picture. If maintenance of relative size is important, objects should be arranged as nearly as possible at equal distances from the camera, either by actual placement or by choosing an appropriate shooting distance.

Ugliness or gross distortion, particularly of the human face, should be avoided. When using a wide-angle lens, if you get too close to a subject in order to fill the picture frame, a direct frontal view will depict protruding features as grossly distorted in size. Shooting downward and close to a face will exaggerate the size of the forehead. Shooting a head close up from a low angle will exaggerate the size of the chin. If there is no other choice but to use a wide-angle lens, a compromise position is to shoot a three-quarter view at eye level so as to avoid distortion of facial features.

In general scenic photography, distracting elements should be removed from the foreground, either by selection of a convenient position or by actual physical removal. Keep in mind that the eye may accommodate what ordinarily is a small and unobtrusive object, but when it is recorded by the lens, which makes no psychological accommodations, it might be reproduced as a distractingly large object.

The same area of coverage recorded with the wide-angle lens compared with a longer lens may yield entirely different effects. When you get close to large structures, the peripheral vision of the wide-angle lens will capture the insides of doorways at the side of the picture and the undersides of structural overhangs at the top of the picture. If the same area is photographed with a larger lens at a greater distance, it will not show any of these side details to any noticeable degree.

Extreme wide-angle lenses generally produce certain elliptical distortions at the edges of the image area, especially towards the corners and along the extreme ends of the wide dimensions of the image frame. This is another aspect of the problem of peripheral optical perception. Objects that are depicted as round in the center of the picture may be seen oval toward the extreme ends and corners of the picture. In a long row of people photographed with a wide-angle lens, those in the center would have both of their ears showing while those at the ends would have only one of their ears showing. The only way to correct this problem is to line the people up in a shallow semicircle with each person facing toward the lens.

Because of the possibility of wide variations in light reflections within the scene area, it is important that exposure determinations be based on the most significant areas of coverage. Clouds, buildings, trees, and other structures cast shadows that must be taken into account. While this is true of all picture taking, it constitutes an additional problem in wide-angle photography in that there is more opportunity for lighting variations to occur within a single perceived scene. One technique is to take an exposure reading with a longer focal length lens on the camera and then shoot the actual photograph with the wide-angle lens attached.

In flash photography, bounce and multiple flash techniques should be used, particularly when using lenses wider than 35mm. If a single flash is used in frontal lighting in conjunction with a wide lens, the light will not cover to the edges of the scene; rather a circular or rectangular light configuration—depending on the reflector shape—will be seen in the center of the picture.

Another reason for avoiding the use of direct flash with wide-angle lenses is that at very close distances there is a sharp rate of fall-off in the intensity of illumination. This is caused by the workings of the Inverse Square Law, which is discussed in the chapter on artificial lighting. If the closest objects to the camera are properly exposed, those objects a short distance behind will be markedly underexposed. On the other hand, if exposure is computed for middle ground objects, those in front will be "burned out" or grossly overexposed. This argues for the use of indirect flash illumination with wide-angle lenses.

THE NORMAL LENSES

The focal length of a normal or standard lens for a 35mm camera is considered to be 45mm to 58mm because a lens in this range produces the most natural perspective image in relation to the picture area.

Dating back to the original Leica camera, which pioneered the 35mm format, 50mm has been the most popular length of the normal lens. Theoretically a normal focal length for any given film format is supposed to correspond approximately to the diagonal of the image frame. In the case of the 24 × 36mm image frame, standard for 35mm photography, the diagonal is 43.2mm. The choice of a slightly longer focal length is a matter of comparability to normal eye perception and convenience in optical design.

Two lenses in the Nikkor range, designed for special purposes, may be considered as dual purpose lenses, because they can be used alternatively as normal lenses. One is the 55mm *f*/3.5 Micro-Nikkor. The other is the 45mm *f*/2.8 GN Auto Nikkor (discontinued). These lenses, intended for use in close-up photography and in distance-compensating flash photography, are described in the chapter on special lenses.

Uses of the Normal Lens

The reason it is much easier to describe performance of the shortest wide-angle lenses or the longer and longest telephoto lenses is that both categories constitute deviations from a norm or average. Unique properties are always so much more fascinating to describe and, indeed, call for more extensive description. The normal lens is by-passed by many working photographers who strive constantly for effect, either by giving prominence to the foreground or by collapsing space and bridging distance with long lenses.

Nevertheless, the normal lens is most popularly used, partly because it is ordinarily sold as original equipment with

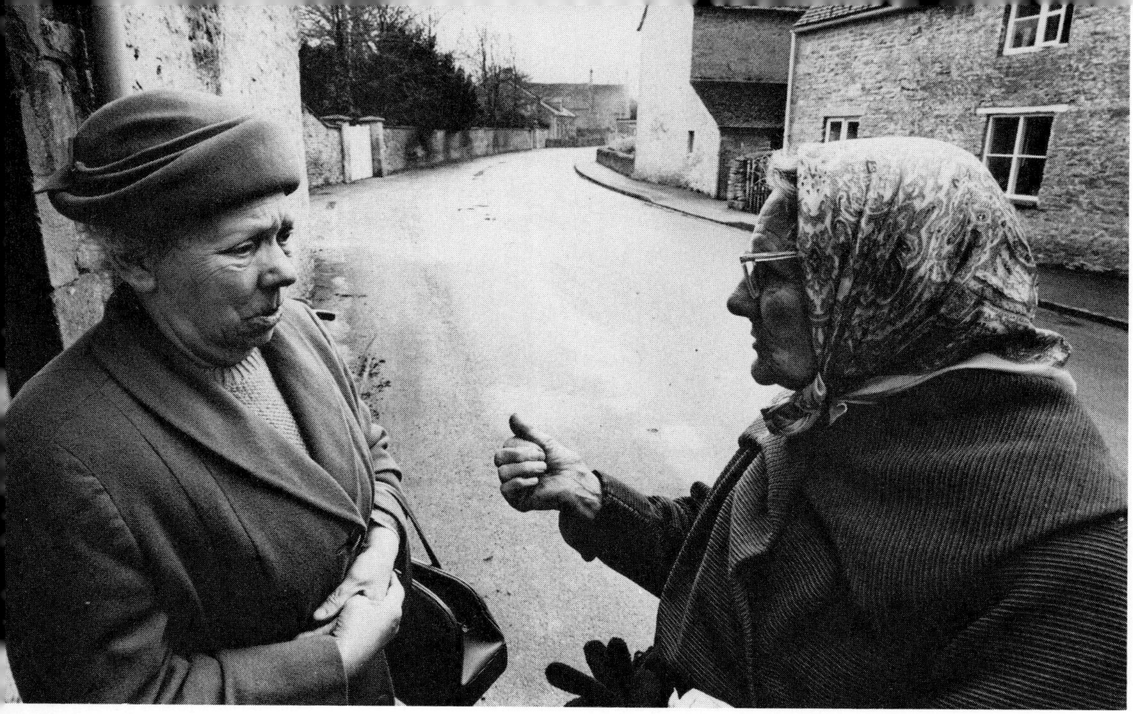

Graham Finlayson

In an Oxfordshire village two ladies are settling the affairs of the day or of the past. In picture above, wide-angle lens is used close to give them size while background is depicted in breadth to provide a setting with appropriate atmosphere. In picture below, normal 50mm lens with narrower angle of view cropped out the background and lost the setting; depth of field at this close-working distance is also at minimum as compared to upper picture. Both f/5.6, 1/60 sec., Ilford FP4.

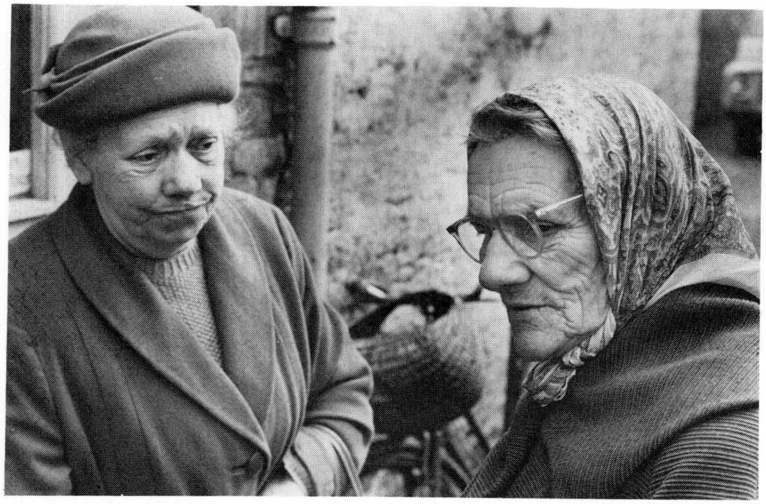

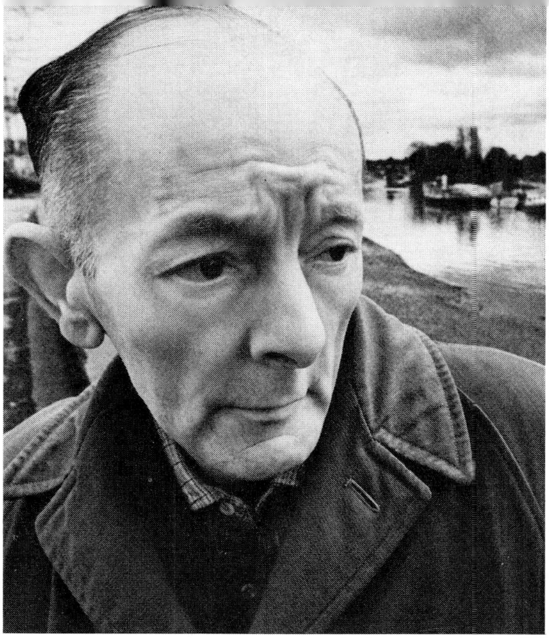

Chris Smith 24mm *f*/11, © *The Observer*

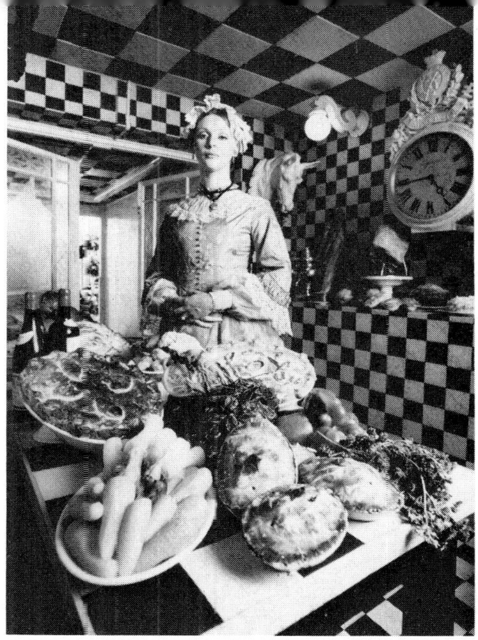

Graham Finlayson 28mm

Wide-angle lenses are used creatively here, through working close to the subjects, to bring out particular emphases. Smith sought to expand the mind of the self-searching ex-prisoner. Finlayson "pulled out" the culinary display. Reinstein put emphasis on handcrafts. Hoferichter pointed to simple diet of subject.

Anne B. Reinstein 20mm at *f*/4

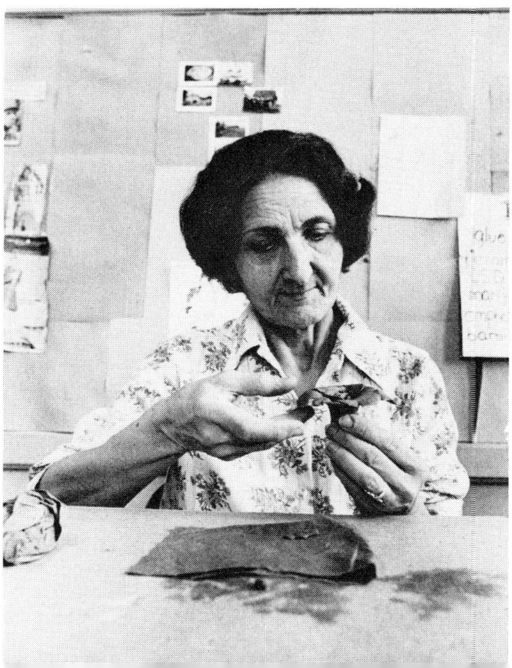

N. R. Hoferichter 24mm

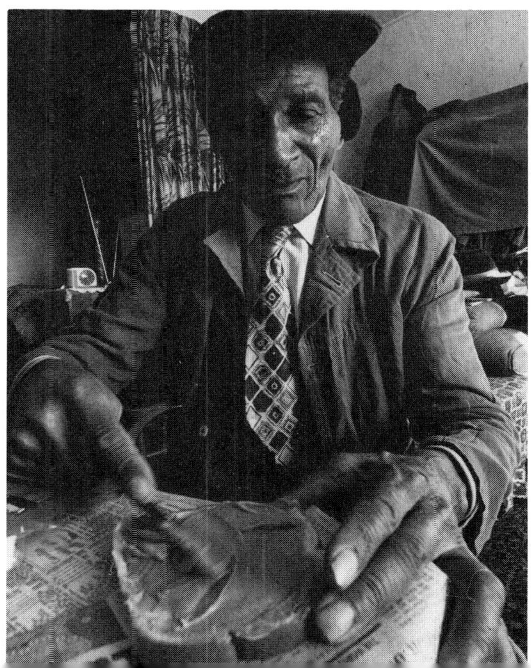

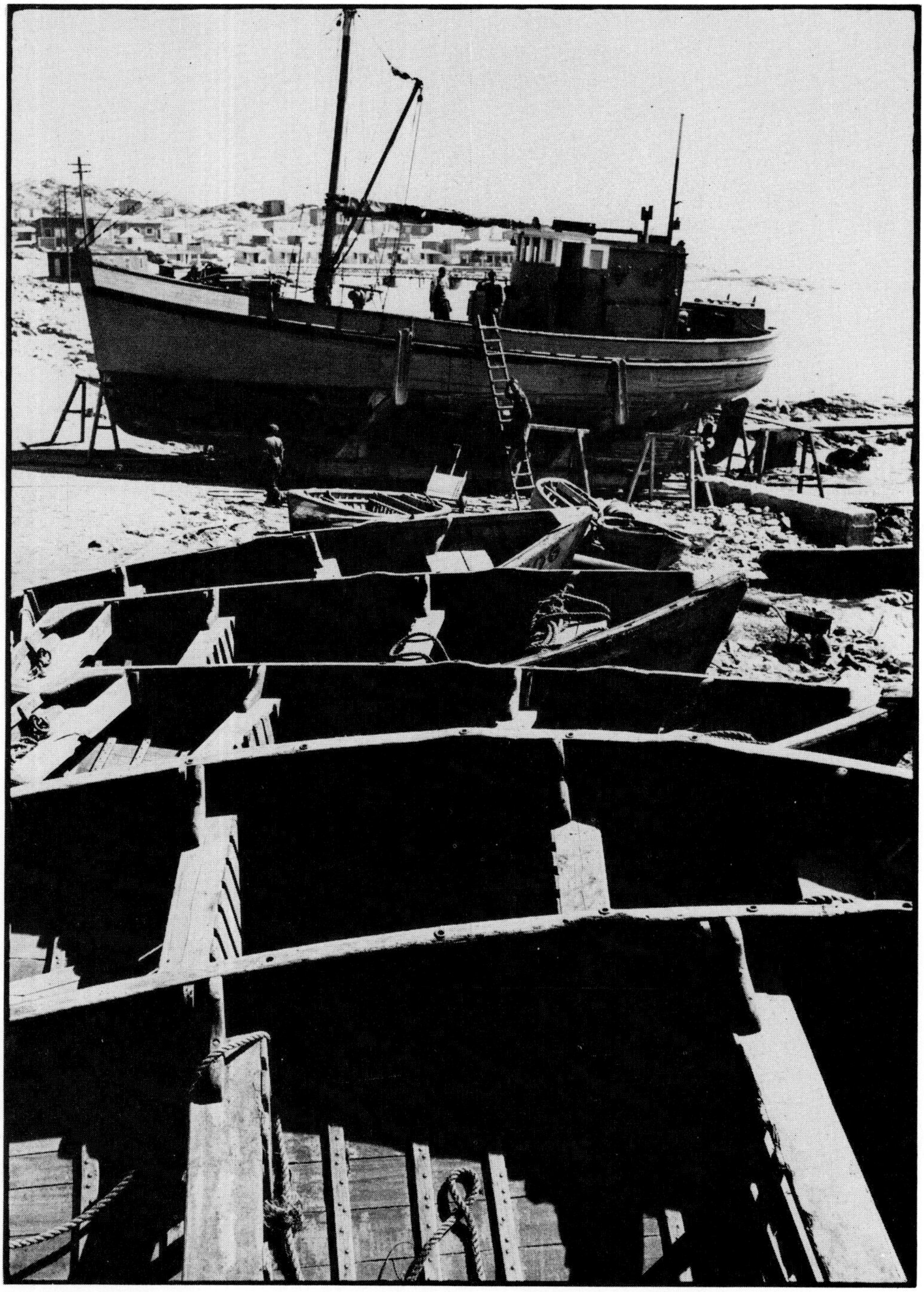

Struan Robertson

Portuguese fishing boat Luderitz Harbour, Namibia. Brilliant backlighting created harsh shadows and interesting patterns maximized by high angle using 35mm f/2.8 lens. This harbor, first discovered in 1486, is used by Portuguese fishing fleets from Madeira for repair and refitting after working the rich fishing grounds off the coast.

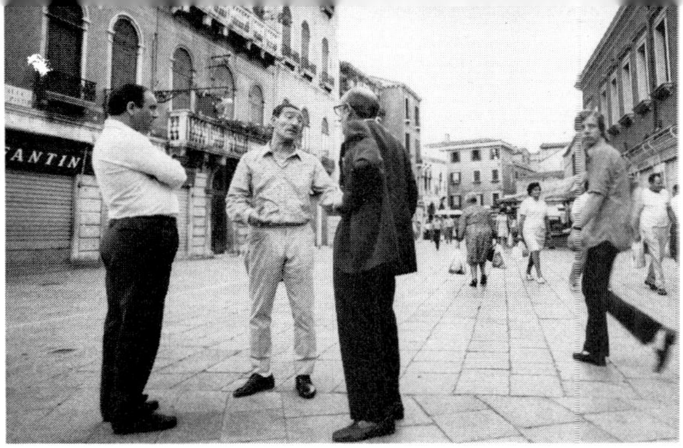
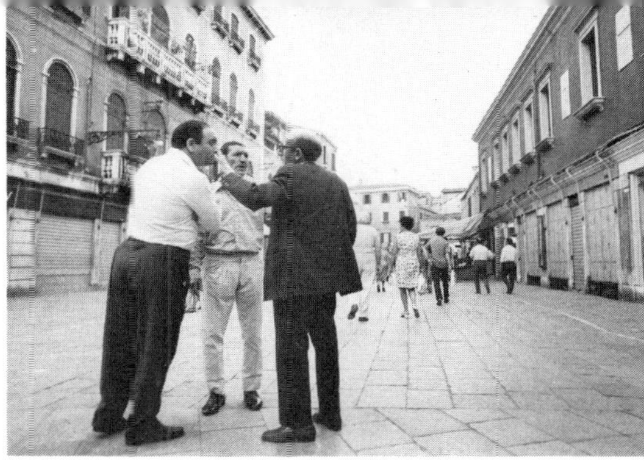

Joseph D. Cooper

Wide-angle lens also subordinates background as desired when working close to shift attention to foreground subjects. 24mm lens, GAF 2681 film.

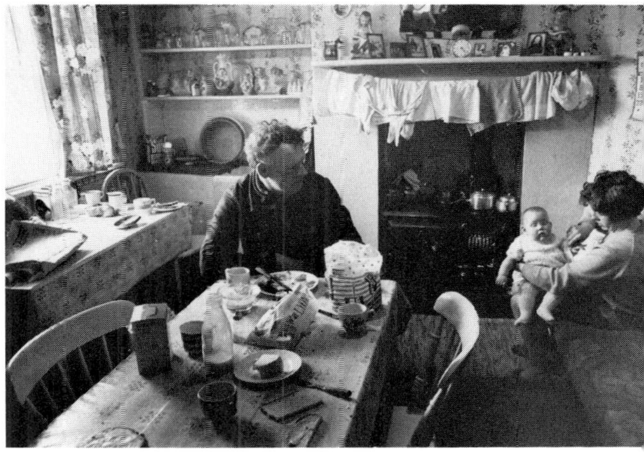

John Minihan

Wide-angle lenses are usually the choice for interior settings. Favorites are 28mm (in this case) and 35mm. Window lighting brings out starkness of abode. *f*/4, 1/60 sec.

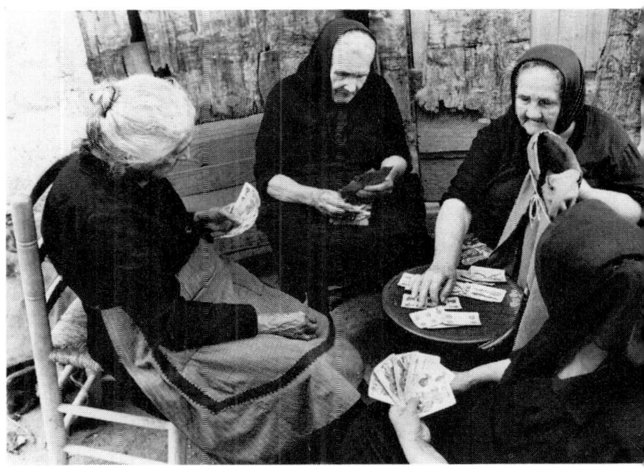

Francisco Hidalgo

The sharp-cutting 35mm PC-Nikkor is useable as a general-purpose lens. Shooting slightly downward, the lens embraces the group activity. *f*/5.6, 1/30 sec., Kodak Plus-X.

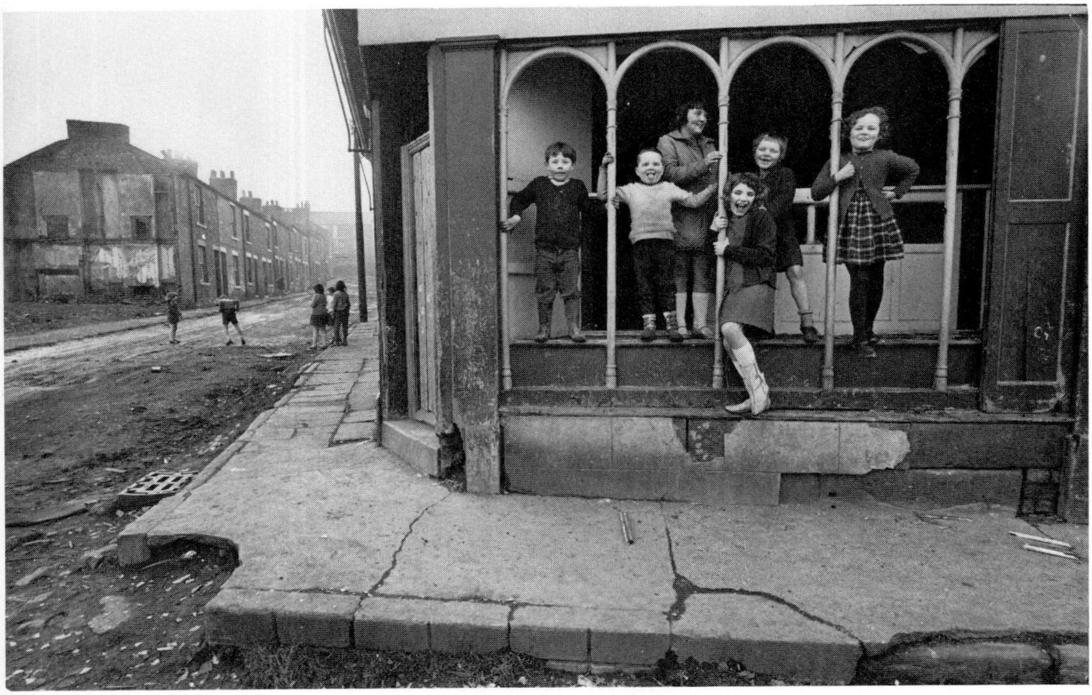

Graham Finlayson

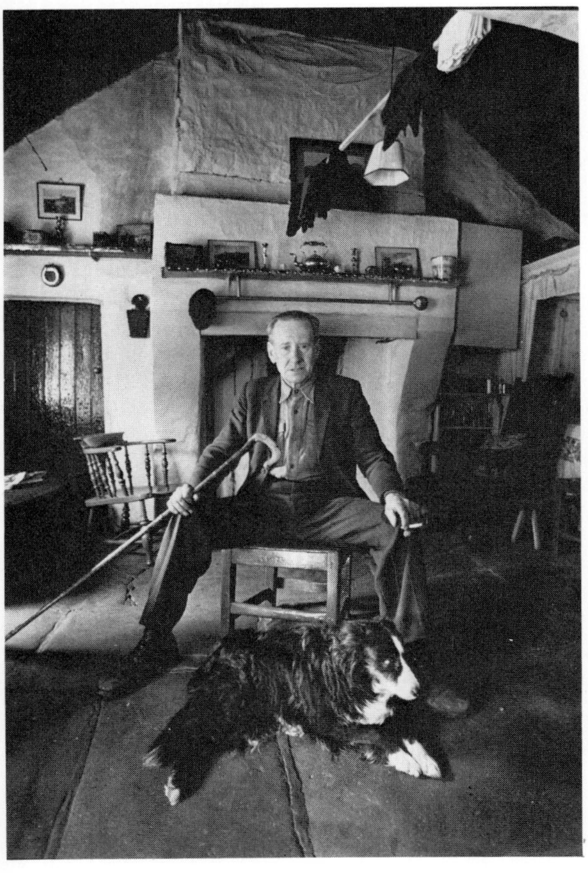

Two additional uses of 20mm *f*/3.5 lens to emphasize foreground within broad background setting. A particular property of extreme wide-angle lenses, however, is that pictorial information diverges or elongates toward extreme edges or corners. Note the elongation of the girl's head at extreme right of picture above. With many subjects, however, this effect is not noticeable particularly when objects of recognizable form are not in the corners, as at left. Both pictures for *Daily Telegraph Magazine*. Above, Northeast England Clearance Area *f*/5.6. Left, Irish border story, Blacksmith and his sheepdog trainer, *f*/3.5, 1/30 sec.

The 50mm lens under low-light levels or when working close is highly selective as regards depth of field. It alters natural, pleasing perspective although it is not best for foreground or background manipulation except to exclude the latter. Informal portrait angles must be carefully chosen to avoid apparent perspective distortion.

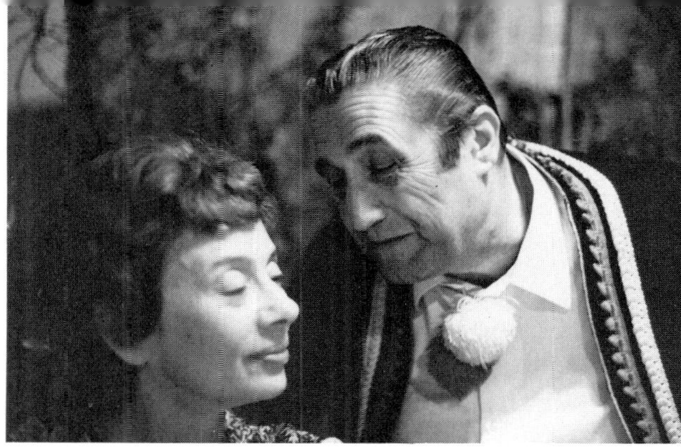

Joseph D. Cooper

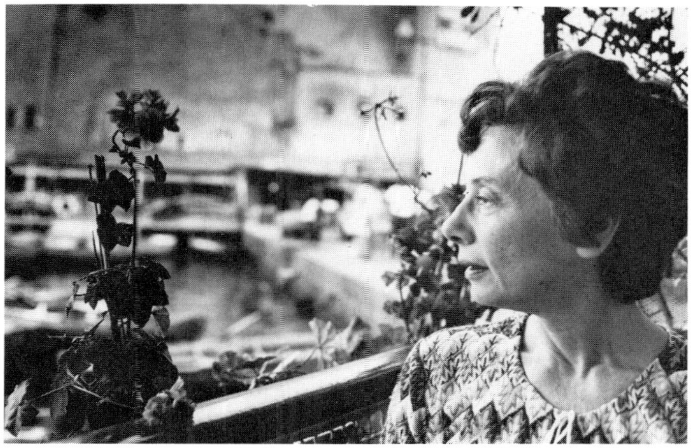

John Minihan

The photographer's mother at Somerset, England. The 50mm lens, used at *f*/2.8, allows the background to be blurred sufficiently so that, while retaining identifiable form, it does not compete with the main subject.

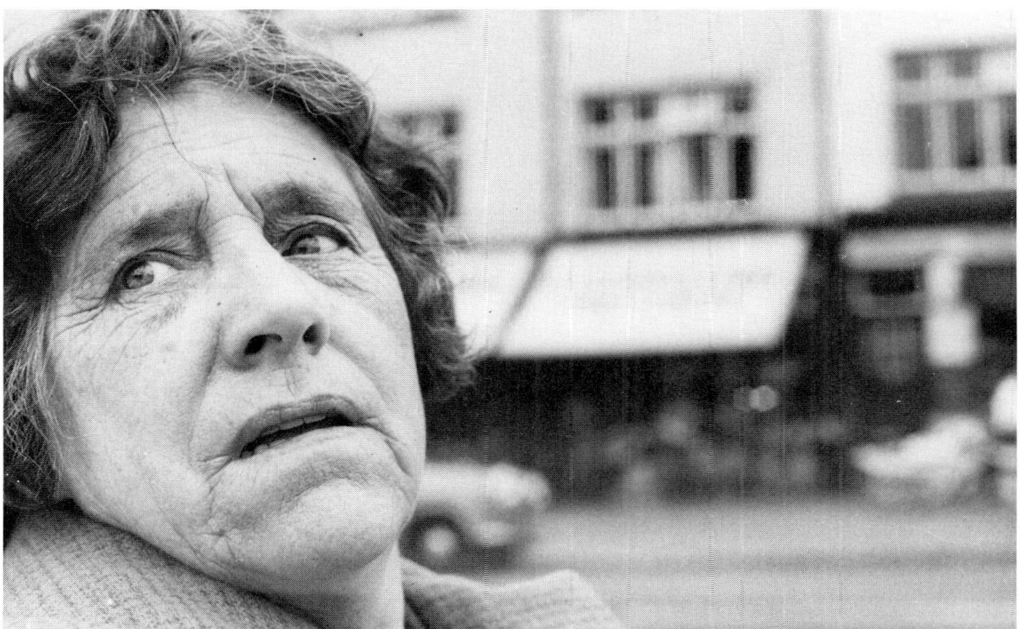

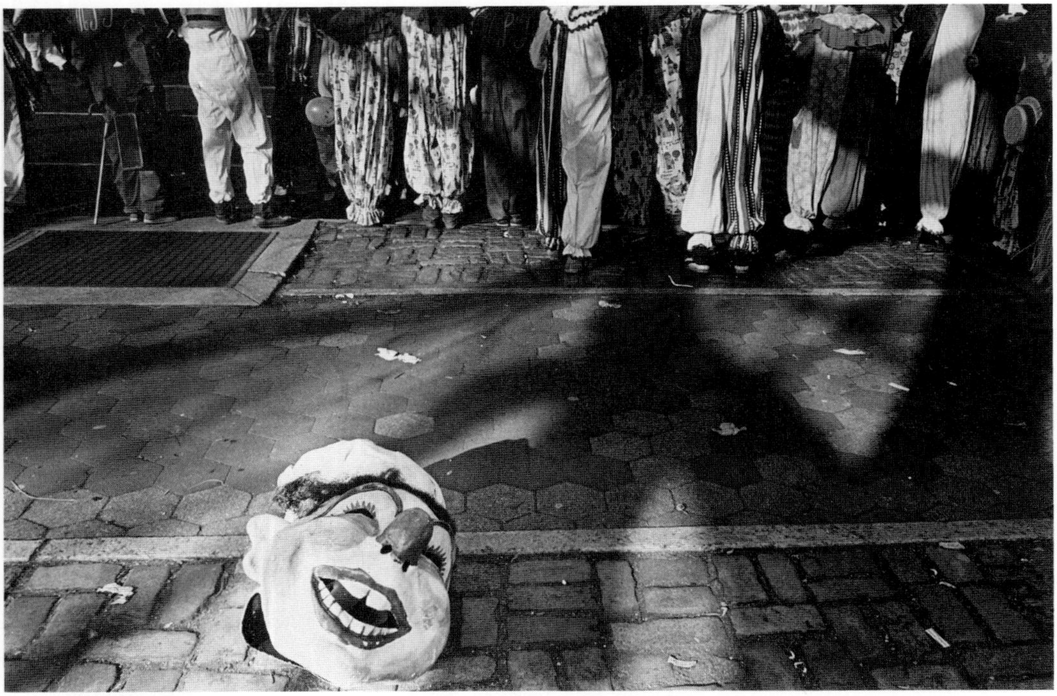

J. D. Levine

Wide-angle lenses emphasize foregrounds while retaining important background information. (Above) Thanksgiving Day Parade, New York. 35mm lens. (Below) Scene photographed during live news broadcast, WOR-TV, New York. 24mm lens.

Mark Iocolano

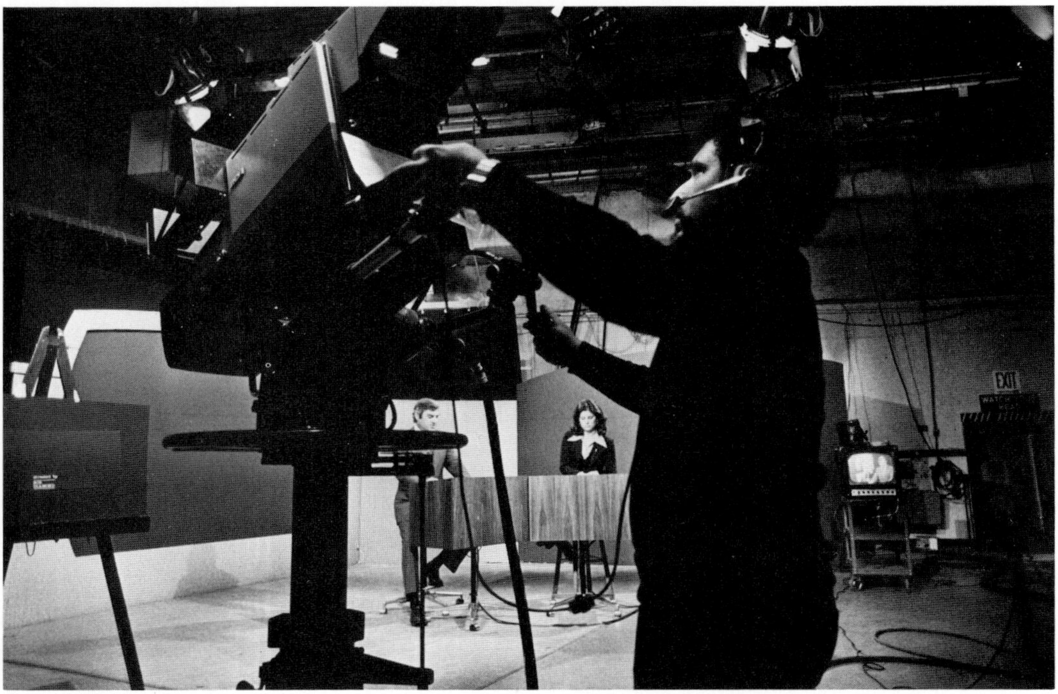

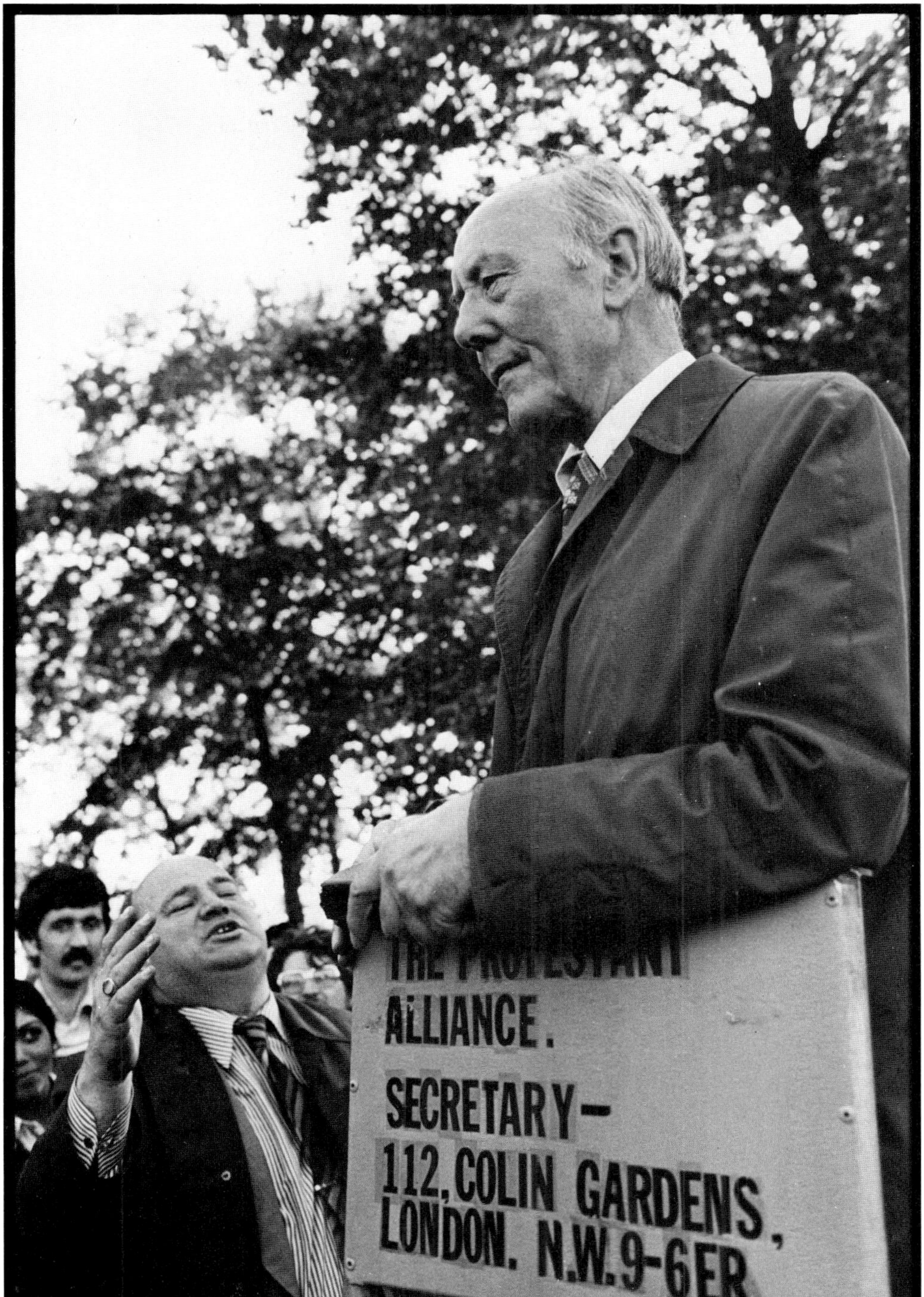

Mark Iocolano

Wide-angle lenses are often indispensable for working in crowds. Here, the 24mm *f*/2.8 brought the speaker well into the foreground, and also brought the heckler into view. Speaker's Corner, Hyde Park, London.

the camera body and partly because it is an all-purpose or workhorse lens.

The normal lens is easiest to correct from an optical standpoint. It has a minimum of optical aberrations. It is offered in a range of wide apertures—$f/2$, $f/1.4$, and $f/1.2$—which make it convenient to focus under adverse light conditions, particularly in conjunction with split-image and rangefinder screens.

Particularly at close working distances and at the wider apertures, the depth of field of these lenses, less than that of the wide-angles, enables one to frame and focus selectively, rendering critical areas most sharp and adjacent areas appropriately soft, depending upon the effects desired.

The Nikkor normal lenses focus as close as two feet (0.6 meters). Hence, with a somewhat narrower field, many of the effects of the so-called "wide-angle look" can be achieved by working close to main subjects. When this is done, the familiar predominance of foreground objects and rapid fall-off in size of receding detail will be observed.

From the standpoint of perspective, the normal lens is probably best in putting both background and foreground into proper size perspective. These size relationships will be achieved when the lens is focused on the middle ground, such as at the hyperfocal distance.

If there is only room for one lens when traveling or vacationing, for most people the normal lens is the best selection. It is most satisfactory for recording general scenes, groups, children, animals, floral displays, and so forth. However, when it is used in portraiture, a distance of at least three feet should be maintained to avoid feature distortion at close camera-to-subject distances. At three feet or closer, the subject should be positioned so that protruding features do not face directly toward the camera.

Business travelers and convention goers will also find the normal lens to be an ideal choice for taking pictures of documents and exhibits. Any of the Nikkor normal lenses will photograph a letterhead so that the frame is completely filled. Most slides and chart presentations can also be reproduced with the normal lens under existing light, although in some cases either a wide-angle or telephoto lens may be necessary.

Selection of a Normal Lens

For most picture-taking needs, 50 mm Nikkor lenses having maximum apertures of $f/2$, $f/1.8$, or $f/1.4$ will be adequate. The $f/2$ or $f/1.8$ offer more than enough light transmission at full aperture to accommodate practically all daylight conditions at safe shutter speeds. The $f/1.4$ lens offers a wider margin of safety in this regard and also extends the range of picture taking to adverse lighting conditions, including indoor photography under existing light. The $f/1.2$ lens can be regarded as a specialty lens for use when the photographer wishes to be prepared for a great variety of lighting conditions. Any of these lenses, stopped down for other picture taking to the same aperture, may be expected to yield equivalent fine results.

Comparing light transmission of the three lenses, there is approximately one-half stop difference between $f/1.2$ and $f/1.4$, and one full stop difference between $f/1.4$ and $f/2$.

An additional use for the 50mm $f/2$ or $f/1.8$ is in slide copying in conjunction with a bellows focusing attachment. The 50mm $f/1.4$ and $f/1.2$ and the 55mm $f/1.2$ lenses are not recommended for close-up work.

If cost is a factor, provided the greater light-gathering abilities of the other lenses is not an overriding consideration, the 50mm $f/2$ or $f/1.8$ lenses are desirable choices.

THE TELEPHOTO LENSES

The range of telephoto lenses covered here begins with 85mm and ends with 300mm. These lenses can all be conveniently hand-held, although some greater skill in this regard may be required with the 180mm, 200mm, and 300mm lenses, particularly under difficult light conditions when shutter speeds are likely to be somewhat slower.

The trend of optical design of telephoto lenses is toward compactness and wider apertures. A distinction must be made between a telephoto lens and a long focus lens. The latter is a lens whose physical length plus the back-focus to the focal plane is equivalent to the focal length. Curiously, as modern wide-angle lenses tend to become longer, modern telephoto lenses tend to become shorter. This optical achievement is accomplished through the use of negative lens elements at the rear of the lens; these have a diverging effect in that they expand the image gathered by the front elements.

In the classical sense, long lenses or telephoto lenses have two principal usages—portraiture, in order to eliminate close-up perspective problems and to give the photographer more room for his lighting; and long distance photography in order to magnify details. The contemporary mood is to achieve interesting perspective effects with long lenses—either to maintain the relative size of objects spaced out in depth, to collapse space between distant objects, or to emphasize pictorial attributes of distant haze and mists.

Portraits With Telephoto Lenses

When shooting a head or head-and-shoulders portrait with a standard lens, you need to get very close to the subject —from two to three feet, depending on how much more than the head alone you want to fill the image frame. At such close shooting distances, however, the leading features of the face will appear distorted, due to the simple rule that the closer objects are to the camera, the bigger they will be recorded on film. At very close shooting distances, relative size disproportion, as perceived and recorded by the lens and camera, can be be quite impressive; even when the head is tilted downward so that the forehead is the leading feature, it will appear to be disproportionately large. With the head in normal position, erect, facing toward the camera, the nose, lips, and chin will be pulled forward. These are reasons why the camera often does seem to distort truth; the subject is optically perceived and recorded from a closer distance than that from which he would ordinarily be viewed in real life. If portraits made at very close distances were also looked at from very close distances, these apparent perspective distortions would not be apparent or troublesome.

An ideal focal length for portraits is one that would correspond to an average distance at which people view each other. The average concept is important because we actually "see" in terms of perceptual averages. Either standing or seated, two people might be inches away or many feet apart. They do not study each other's features to make comparative analyses of how they look a foot away at one moment and how they appear when they are five feet apart, or seven or nine, seated on the other side of the room. When someone is very close to you, you automatically compensate for leading features; you do not see them as being overemphasized. Conversely, when an individual is at some distance from you, the rules of perspective viewing dictate that the features will be flattened or compressed. But in real life, you perceive the individual as he would appear to you at a closer, more comfortable viewing distance. Once you have gotten to know a person quite well, his features are programmed into your mind with the effect that no matter what your viewing distance might be, he always evokes an image of how you expect him to appear. The point of this is that psychologically you perceive an individual as a programmed average, strange though this may seem.

The lens and two-dimensional film are not capable of making these psychological adjustments in perception; they have no memory bank from which to draw stored perceptions. Hence, the representation of normalcy in portraiture done with the 35mm camera calls for the use of a lens in the range of 85–135mm used at subject distances ranging from about four feet up to five or six feet. The most popular of the three focal lengths, 85, 105 and 135mm, is the 105mm, although an excellent case can be made for the 85mm lens. However, if artificial light is to be used, the photographer needs more working room between himself and his subject. Hence, he is more likely to favor either the 105mm or 135mm lenses, with some leaning toward the latter. When using the 135mm lens, the photographer must be sensitive to the lens' tendency toward flattening facial features, which calls for some care in positioning the subject, possibly turning the head slightly to the side.

Some photographers like to use longer lenses, particularly in standard portraiture or when they are not able to be close to the subject, for example, when the subject is on a stage. Hence, you may see examples of the 180mm, 200mm, and 300mm lenses used in portraiture. The interesting thing here is that it is not the focal length that governs, but the shooting distance. With these longer lenses, the film frame might have to be filled very tightly, perhaps cropping off some of the head and certainly the space around it. Consider that with the 300mm lens, the average shooting distance for a head shot is about 15 feet. This certainly would flatten facial features. Although this may be unavoidable in spectator events where you cannot get close to the subject, the more interesting portrait study requires that you frame only the main features, cropping out the rest. The same problems occur, but in lesser degree, with the 180mm and 200mm lenses.

General Uses of Telephoto Lenses

In addition to use in portraiture, telephoto lenses in the intermediate range commonly are used in candid photography of children and adults, sports photography, wildlife photography, magnification of distant scenes, stage and theater photography, surveillance photography, and selective landscape picture taking. These and other such applications are quite conventional. More creative uses of the telephoto lens occur when advantage is taken of unique performance characteristics of the lens, as stated in the following list:

1. Increasing selectivity of field corresponding to longer focal length accompanied by greater magnification of image details and narrower angle of view for any given distance from the camera.
2. Increasingly shallow depth of field at any given distance from the camera corresponding to increases in focal length.
3. Maximizing of background effects together with the compression of objects (or information) in the background.
4. Rendition of distant objects in their normal size relationships with a minimum of size diminution due to perspective fall-off.
5. Attainment of greater depth of illumination evenness when working with artificial light sources.
6. Emphasis of aerial perspective effects.

The factor of field-selectivity relates particularly to the "tele" component of the lens category. Particularly in dealing with color transparency or slide film, it is advantageous to use a lens that selectively covers only that part of the total scene that is of pictorial interest. One might choose a telephoto lens with which to select a detail out of a more general scene or a landscape or an individual within a group. One should think of telephoto lenses as tools of selective composition. They can also be used for achieving dramatic close-up effects when extended beyond their normal close-focusing range through use of intermediate extension rings (focusing must then be done critically on the plane of primary interest concentrated largely within the central area of the image frame).

The shallow depth of field, most noticeable at the widest lens apertures, enables the photographer to determine where best to put the emphasis. Ordinarily this emphasis is on the image plane of primary interest, but as different scenes are amenable to different interpretations by the photographer, he can extend or retract the limited zone of softness by manipulating the focusing ring to achieve different effects in the viewing screen.

The background effects are applications of the laws of perspective. The distance between objects photographed at a great distance away closes up, such as between automobiles in a traffic jam or marching troops photographed from a distance. Each object appears to be right next to the object in front of it. This type of pictorial compressing is not a function of the lens but of distance; the lens really magnifies the stacking or pancaking effects, as these are sometimes called.

A related optical perspective effect of telephoto lenses is the maintenance of relative sizes of objects so that one person standing behind another will be seen almost in the same size relative to the person in front of him. Again, this effect will be recorded by any lens at the same distance from the subject, but telephoto lenses emphasize the effect.

The phenomenon of greater depth of artificial illumination relates to the operation of the inverse square law. Briefly, the greater the distance of the subject from the source of the illumination, the slower will be the rate of fall-off in the intensity of illumination. Hence, people standing at varying distances from the camera, when a flash is used near the camera, will be more evenly exposed if the photographer backs away from them and uses a telephoto lens to increase their pictorial size.

The creative use of aerial perspective lies in emphasizing phenomena associated with distance. These include haziness or clouding and a loss of contrast in distant objects. Sometimes it is important to minimize these effects—more easily done with black-and-white film than with color film—but the contemporary approach is to utilize or enhance these effects whenever they lend pictorial strength. In any event, where present, these effects cannot be excluded.

Selection of Telephoto Lenses

Stated generally, selection of telephoto lenses includes the following criteria:

1. Attainment of a particular pictorial effect as described above.
2. Adequacy of the lens aperture for existing light and action conditions.
3. Suitability for hand-held picture taking.
4. Near focusing limits.
5. Convenience of size and weight.
6. Cost.

These criteria are not mutually exclusive. For example, one photographer might prefer the 180mm *f*/2.8 lens because it is one aperture wider than the 200mm *f*/4 lens. On the other hand, another photographer may feel that for his picture-taking situations, the smaller lens aperture of the 200mm *f*/4 lens is adequately balanced out by the combination of the smaller size, lighter weight,

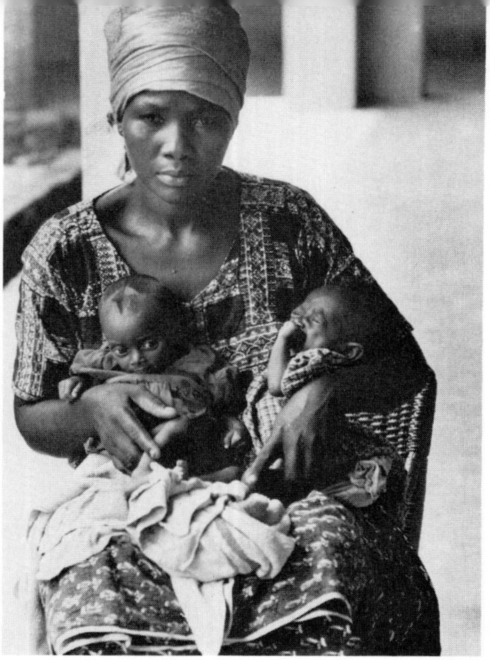

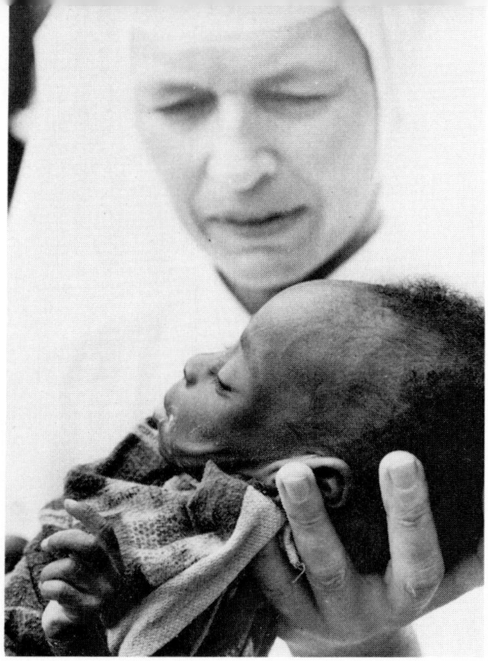

Ian Bradshaw

The most generally used portrait lenses are the 85mm *f*/1.8 and the 105mm *f*/2.8. For single portraits they enable one to work at a distance that offers optimum facial modelling without perspective distortion of leading features. They are not so long, however, as to preclude use with larger subject areas. At wider apertures they permit putting emphasis selectively through depth-of-field control. Pictures above made in Biafra with 85mm lens.

Francisco Hidalgo

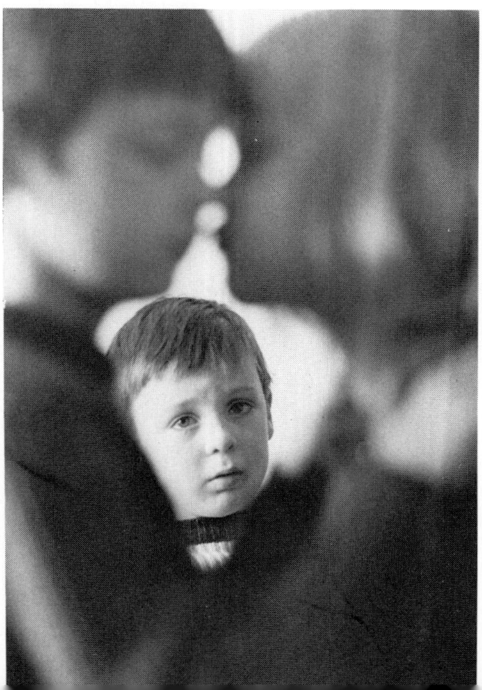

Picture to left made with 105mm lens; note creative use of out-of-focus area for framing and gentle modelling of frontal features of boy.

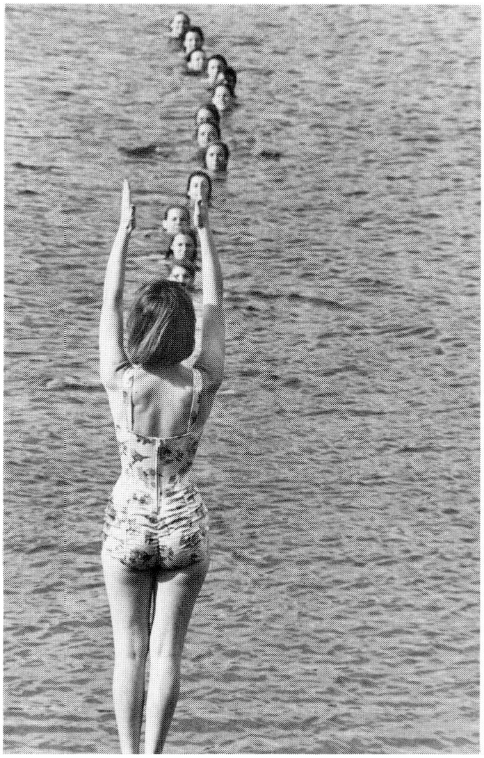

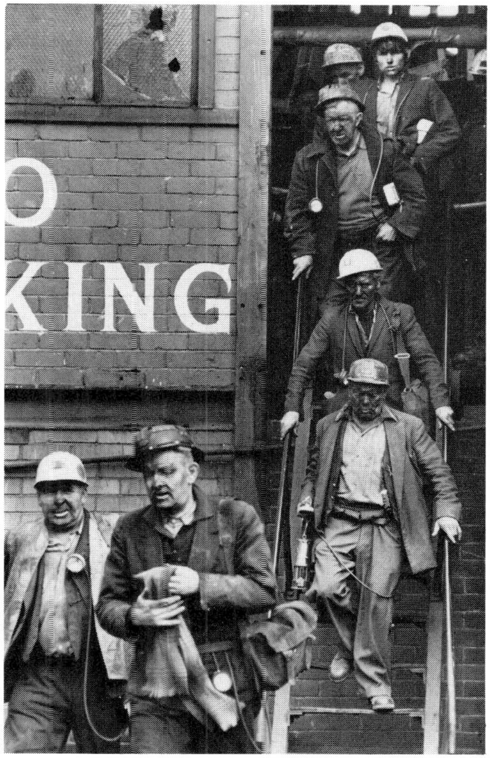

Al Satterwhite

John Minihan

The 200mm lens is ideal for maintaining relative size of objects in depth at a distance. Note almost identical size of swimmer heads in Satterwhite picture. The Minihan picture of miners in Wales was made with 135mm lens at f/5.6 yielding almost the same effect. Cooper's picture in Venice was made with 200mm end of 80–200 Zoom Nikkor.

Joseph D. Cooper

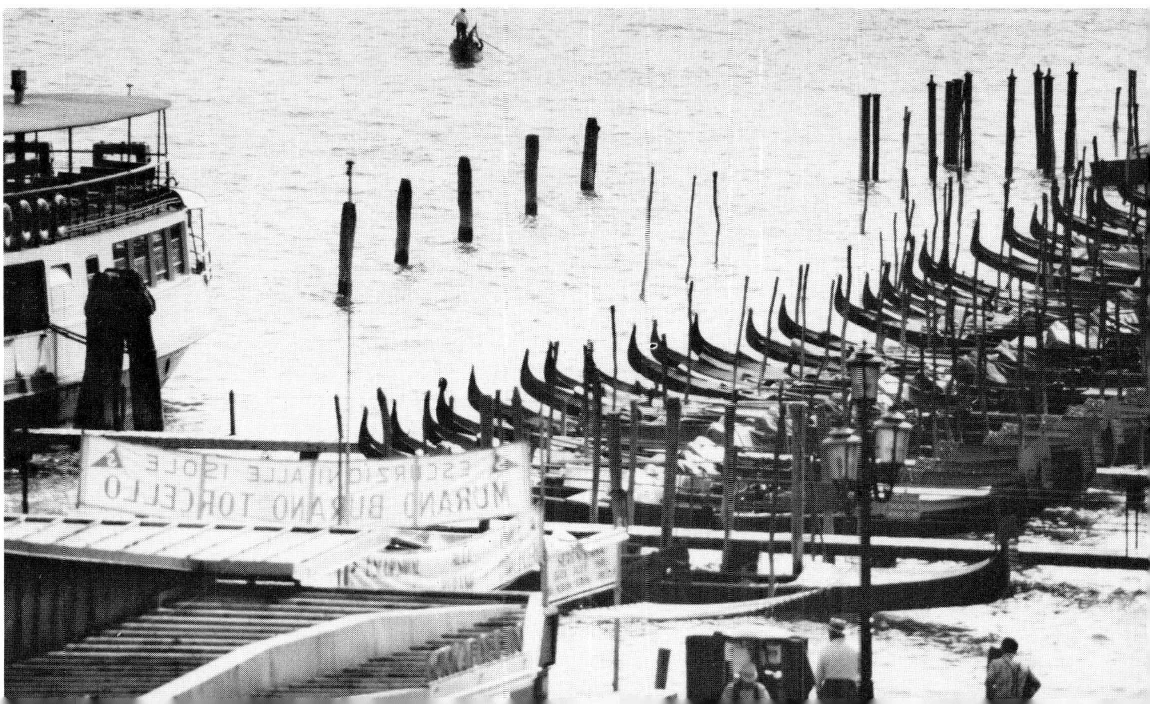

and lower cost. The portrait photographer working under dim existing light conditions might consider it important to have a one stop advantage over the 105mm *f*/2.5 lens by giving preference to the 85mm *f*/1.8. The same kinds of considerations pertain to other lenses that are closely related in focal length but have wider or smaller lens apertures.

Care in making a hand-held exposure is important with lenses of any focal length. Some photographers expose at not less than 1/125 sec. regardless of the lens on the camera. Inasmuch as the camera shake that one seeks to avoid by using faster shutter speeds is magnified by using telephoto lenses, faster shutter speeds are favored in using these lenses. With both the 135mm and the 180mm/200mm lenses, hand-held exposures can be made quite safely, but care must be taken when squeezing the shutter to avoid camera shake.

The near-focusing limit may be important in particular situations where you cannot back off sufficiently from the subject to get it adequately framed within the image area. The near-focusing limit is easily ascertainable by reference to the focusing rings of the lens, for selection purposes, or the lens data sheets included in this chapter.

From an operational standpoint, the 135mm lenses should be considered as being closer to the 180mm/200mm lenses than to the 105mm lens. The 135mm lens begins to introduce some flattening of features. It compels a greater separation from subject accompanied by a loss of intimacy. Also, with the 135mm lens, background compression and size equalization begin manifesting themselves. With the 200mm and 300mm lenses, these perspective effects are quite noticeable. These are popular lenses for spectator sports, particularly when you are limited to taking pictures from the stands. The 300mm lens opens up a whole new world of bird photography and big suns and moons on the horizon, and longer lenses will yield even more dramatic effects in animal photography, unobtrusive surveillance activity, and the rendition of the delicate mists of distant backgrounds.

Usage Problems With Telephoto Lenses

The more critical problems of handling telephoto lenses are discussed in the succeeding section on the Nikkor Super Telephoto Lenses. Here we will discuss briefly aspects of camera support, shutter speeds, and focusing pertinent to three groupings—the 85mm to 135mm lenses, the 180mm and 200mm lenses, and the 300mm lens. The first group constitutes no real problem in providing camera support. Tripods are really no more necessary than with lenses of shorter focal lengths. With the 135mm lens one should cradle both camera and lens to minimize any downward pull from the extended lens. The minimum shutter speed should be 1/125 sec.

The same precautions pertain to the 180mm and 200mm lenses, except that one should cradle the lens directly in front of the camera body in the left palm. A minimum safe exposure would be 1/250 sec. The 300mm lens is on the borderline between hand-held treatment and support by a tripod, monopod, or other solid supports.

When working in an area in which there are available solid supports, tripods should not be necessary. At the most, one might want to use a monopod or a chain pod. Where there is a car door, a window, a fence, or any other upright solid object, a beanbag filled with dried beans, peas, or lentils offers a conforming and shock-absorbing cradle-support. A beanbag should be standard equipment on field trips. A truly vibration-free tripod is heavy, bulky, and not particularly helpful when you desire maneuverability.

When using the split-image rangefinder prism with the 180mm to 300mm lenses, particularly with the latter, one half of the focusing disc may darken. If you are able to align your eye with the optical axis extended through the viewfinder, you may be able to see both halves of the circular focusing disc free of darkening. With the slightest shift off axis one or the other of the optical wedges will darken, thereby rendering this focusing aid inoperative. Therefore, a microprism focusing screen may be preferred for use with these lenses.

SUPER TELEPHOTO LENSES

The lenses covered here range from 300mm through 2000mm and are of three different types. One group includes the telephoto lenses that feature extra-dispersion (ED) glass and are highly corrected for chromatic and other optical aberrations. These lenses which mount directly to the camera with full auto-diaphragm operation and full-aperture metering, range in focal length from 300 to 1200mm. Many of these lenses feature internal focusing (IF), whereby the physical length of the lens does not change as it is focused.

A second category is a series of optical units of 400mm, 600mm, 800mm, and 1200mm focal lengths that must be used with an accessory focusing unit, that is placed between the camera and any one of these lenses for focusing and diaphragm control. A third category consists of mirror-reflex lenses of catadioptric design—a combination of mirrors and lenses resulting in compactness of the lens barrel for the focal length.

These are specialty lenses whose long focal lengths are of particular value in wildlife photography, surveillance photography, astronomical photography, and special effects photography of distant phenomena. While they magnify images, they also magnify environmental hazards and obstacles, which makes it necessary to use camera supports, avoid camera shake during exposure, and utilize appropriate filters.

The N-F adapter tube is necessary for attaching older 180mm, 250mm, 350 mm, or 500mm telephoto Nikkor lenses to the camera. This group of lenses was designed primarily for Nikon S series rangefinder models to be used in conjunction with the reflex housing.

Lenses Used with Focusing Units

The focusing unit is an intermediate tube that fits between the camera body and the following lenses: 400mm *f*/4.5 Auto Nikkor, 600mm *f*/5.6 Auto Nikkor, 600 mm *f*/5.6 Nikkor ED, 800mm *f*/8 Auto Nikkor, 800mm *f*/8 Nikkor ED, 1200 *f*/11 Auto Nikkor, and 1200mm *f*/11 Nikkor ED. The focusing unit does not contain optics. It has a built-in diaphragm that operates automatically for all lenses except the 1200mm. The Focusing Unit AU-1 contains a filter drawer which enables 52mm-diameter filters to be used with the long lenses. The smaller and lighter Standard Focusing Unit has no filter drawer. The aperture markings of *f*/4.5 to *f*/22 on the barrel are common for all the lenses except for the maximum aperture, which naturally must correspond to that of the lens attached.

Each of the applicable lenses comes with a removable distance scale that can be detached or attached to the focusing unit by means of screws.

An accessory cradle for the focusing unit contributes to smoother focusing by providing a firm support to the total assembly. It is available on order as an optional accessory

Each of the four lenses includes a built-in telescopic lens hood. While the

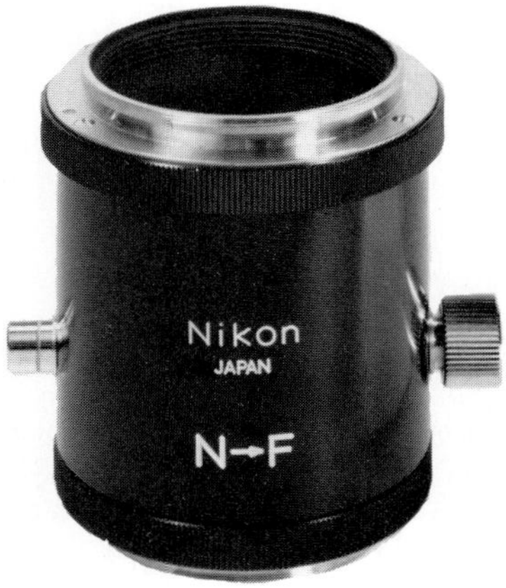

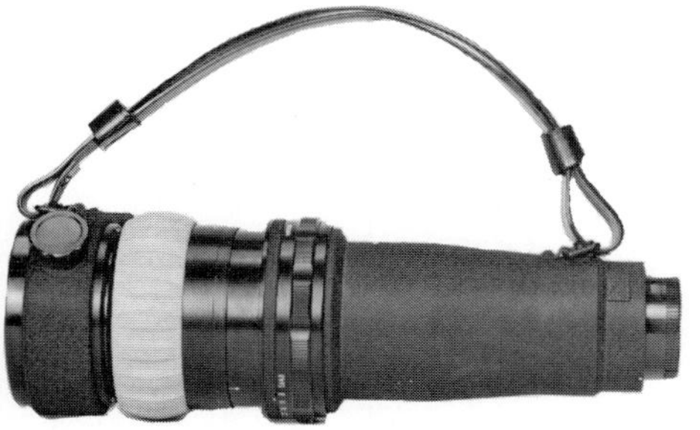

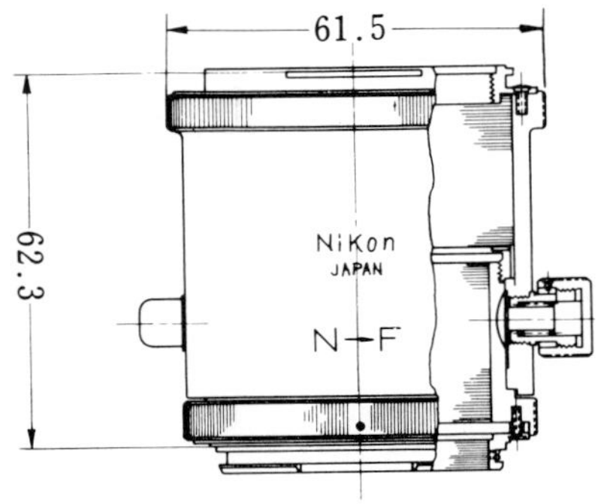

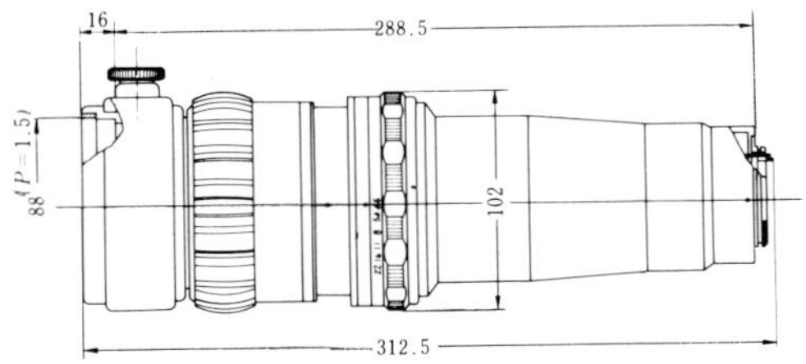

Focusing unit for supertelephoto lenses shown in above illustration. Unit has automatic diaphragm, lens-aperture markings, and focusing ring.

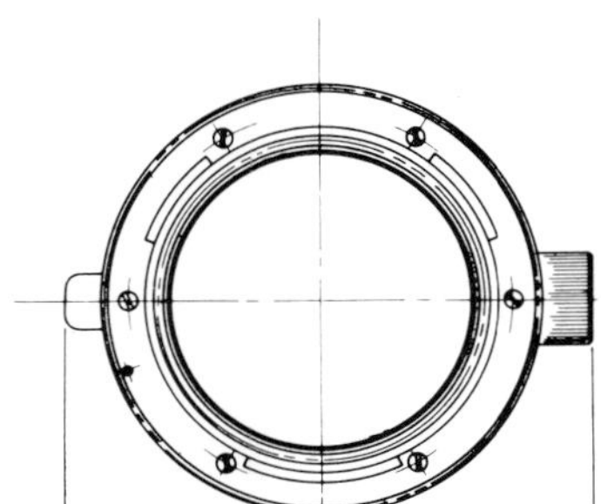

N-F Adapter tube permits use of certain older Nikon-S series lenses with Nikon and Nikkormat reflex cameras. These include 180mm, 250mm, 350mm, and 500mm lenses.

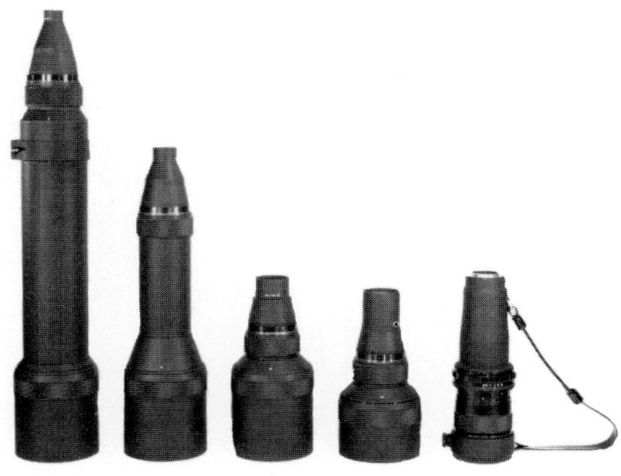

Lenses for use with focusing unit: 400mm, 600mm, 800mm, and 1200mm.

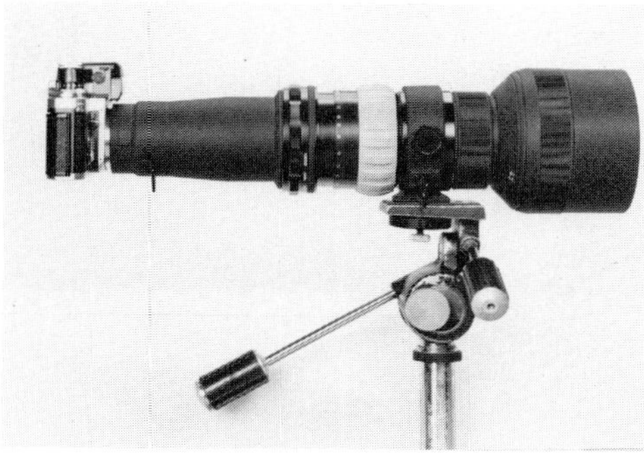

400mm *f*/4.5 lens mounted in focusing Unit and attached to Nikon F. Lenses in this group ordinarily will be used on tripod.

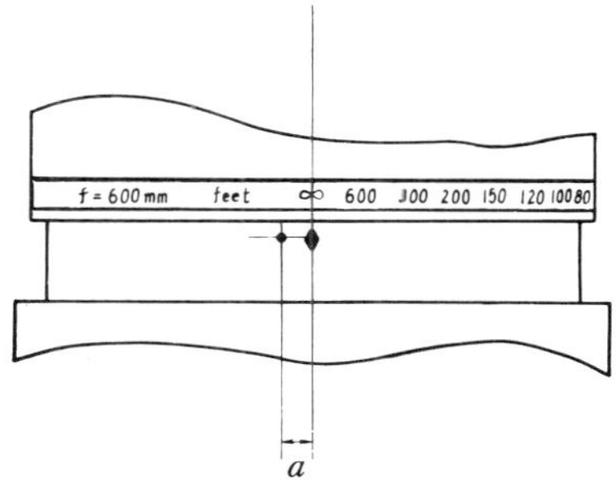

Lens	400mm	600mm	800mm	1200mm
Shift in focus (*a* mm)	3.6	6.1	4.9	8.9

For infrared photography, image is first focused sharply through viewfinder and then compensatory shift is made by turning focusing ring to the left by the number of millimeters shown in the table.

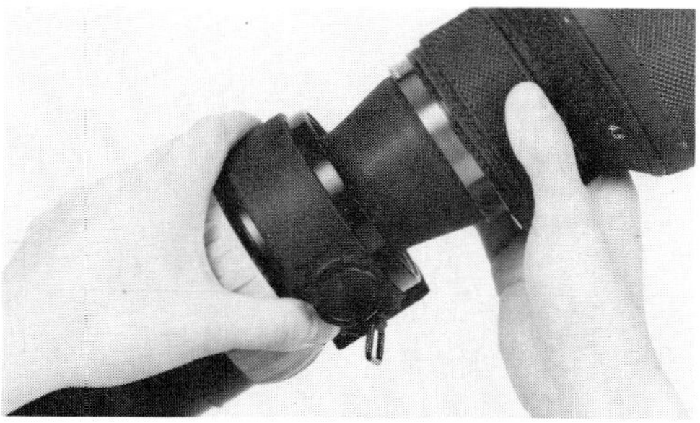

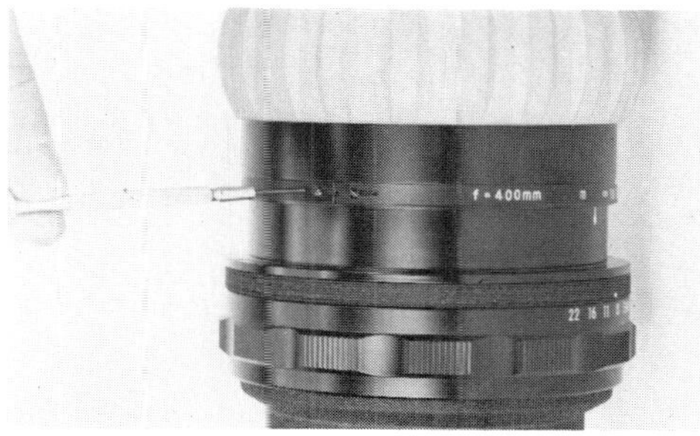

Since focusing unit is used with lenses of four different focal lengths, distance scale must be adjusted for particular lens in use. A removable distance scale is supplied with each of the lenses; it must be attached to the focusing unit, replacing any distance scale for a lens of different focal length. First, combine the lens with the focusing unit, attach the combination to the camera, and focus on extremely distant object until it appears sharp and crisp on focusing screen. With the lens thus focused at infinity, place distance scale around focusing unit and adjust it until infinity mark on scale lines up with white index line of focusing unit. Screw scale into place with two locking screws supplied with distance scale. Rectangular holes at either end of distance scale permitted to slide to compensate for thermal expansion of lens barrel.

aperture scales on the 400mm and 600mm lenses go down to *f*/22, corresponding with the smallest aperture on the focusing units, the 800mm and 1200mm lenses have manual diaphragms within the lens itself that permit dropping down to *f*/64 to insure greater depth of field. When using the manual diaphragm, the focusing unit should be set at *f*/4.5. Since the 800mm lens can be used with either manual or automatic diaphragm, whichever is used the other must be set at widest aperture.

The longest of these four lenses, the 1200mm, can be used only with subjects at some substantial distance from the camera. While the 400mm lens may be focused down to 5 meters, the 600mm lens demands a minimum separation of 11 meters from the subject, the 800mm lens may be focused only as close as 19 meters and the 1200mm lens at 43 meters.

500mm *f*/8 REFLEX-NIKKOR
PARTS NOMENCLATURE

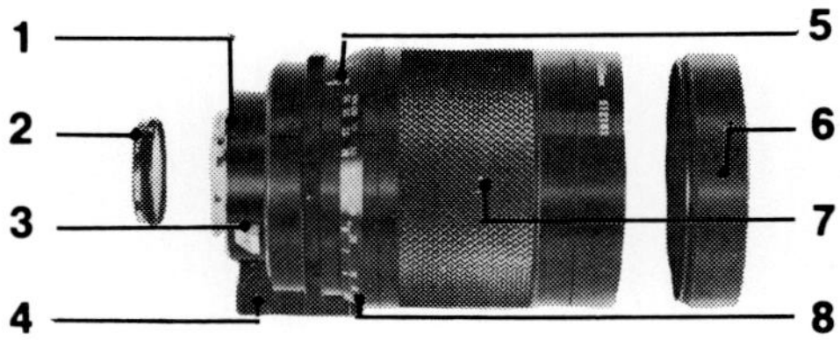

1. Attaching index to camera
2. Filter
3. Spring catch
4. Tripod socket
5. Distance scale index line
6. Hood
7. Focusing ring
8. Distance ring

Reflex-Nikkor Lenses

The Reflex-Nikkor Lenses—500mm, 1000mm, and 2000mm in focal length—are a combination of mirror and lens elements. The technical name for the optical design used in these lenses is catadioptric. Actually, this term is derived from a combination of two other terms—catoptric, which denotes a system for reflecting and altering light, and dioptric, which refers to a system that transmits and alters light. Hence, catadioptric is a combination of transmission and reflection that relates to lens and mirror. This definition is somewhat simplified since each of the Reflex-Nikkor lenses utilizes more than one lens and more than one mirror, as shown in the data sheets.

In the design of the telephoto lenses, discussed earlier, negative lens elements are used at the rear of the total lens assembly in order to diverge images, enlarging them, and thereby reduce the length and weight, for greater convenience and ease of handling. A similar end is accomplished in the design of the Reflex-Nikkor by a device that reflects incoming light twice on the mirror surfaces, thereby reducing physical length to less than half of the effective focal length, achieving great compactness and lightweight in comparison to long or telephoto lenses of equivalent focal lengths.

Catadioptric lenses are based on design principles used in large astronomical telescopes. They have a variety of special uses, depending on their focal length. The 500mm *f*/8 has been a favorite in sports and wildlife photography, particularly in photographing birds. This lens has been used extensively by photographers who want to maximize background effects and make pictorial use of aerial perspective. In some cases they have even utilized the characteristic "doughnut rings," which are the magnified out-of-focus circles of confusion associated particularly with light reflective points. Generally speaking, this group of lenses may be regarded as extreme close-up lenses for use in bringing in specific objects at high magnification when they cannot or should not be approached more closely for picture taking. Military and investigational surveillance are obvious specialized uses, but there are many situations involving industrial or scientific testing where personnel need to work at great distances from their subjects.

Another advantage to these lenses is that they minimize or eliminate chromatic aberrations because they rely on reflecting surfaces to form the primary images rather than refracting or transmitting lenses that introduce a variety of aberrations in the process of gathering and transmitting their optical images. This makes it possible to achieve unsurpassed sharpness of a focused image. It also obviates the need for the infrared mark on the focusing scale.

To compensate for minute displacement of focus caused by temperature changes, the focusing ring on each Reflex-Nikkor lens may be turned beyond the infinity marking. The lenses are used at full aperture since there are no diaphragm rings to stop down to achieve greater depth of field or engage in compensatory interplay between lens aperture and shutter speed. Exposure is controlled through shutter speed and the use of neutral density or other filters. (A rotating filter wheel is located in the rear of the 1000mm and 2000mm lenses.)

Out-of-focus subjects appear as blurred rings, as already mentioned, or as separated blurred lines, the latter constituting a linear adaptation of the same phenomena.

The 500mm lens is very compact and focuses as close as 12.4 feet (4 meters), thereby making it possible to achieve an unusually arresting effect. The 1000mm lens can be focused as close as 25 feet (8 meters) while the 2000mm lens, whose magnification is 40 times that of a normal 50mm lens, can be focused at a near distance of 60 feet (20 meters). The 2000mm lens, being of comparatively great size and weight—but still rather small relative to its focal length—has a special tripod mounting base that permits tilting upward or downward to a wide arc. It also incorporates a peepsight in the carrying handle to help the photographer succeed in bringing his photographic targets into an approximate field of view.

Operational Management of Super Telephotos

Whereas extreme wide-angle lenses present problems in perspective largely related to the foreground, extremely long lenses present problems of perspective pertaining to the background of distant subjects extending into infinity. The extreme compression associated with magnification of distant images, discussed earlier, serves as both a creative advantage, if handled in that way, and a problem to be overcome by selecting an appropriate lens or viewpoint, or both. When a very long lens is directed toward what is, in fact, a gentle rise in a road or hillside, that grade will appear as though it were an abrupt rise because of the compression effect. The viewer might regard that as a distortion. In this respect, the camera is truthfully recording

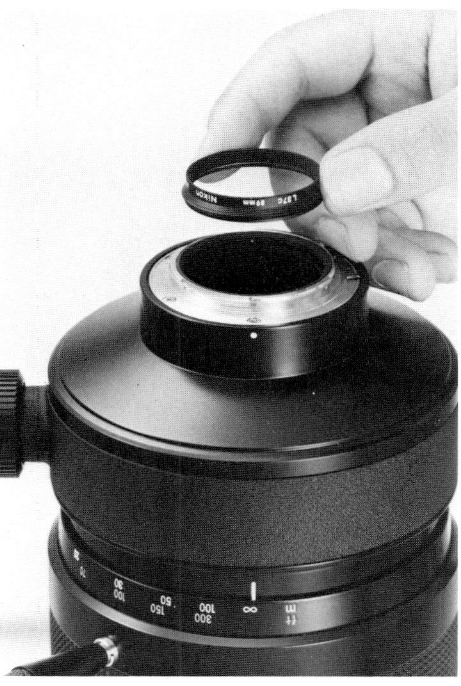

The 1000mm Reflex-Nikkor accepts 39mm screw-in filters that attach to the rear of the lens. Filters provided are L37C, A2, B2, 056, and ND4X.

what was to be perceived if the eye could actually reach out into the distance. To the extent that the camera depicts the unattainable and unfamiliar as reality, it appears to present distortion of the truth.

Aerial interference constitutes a second area of special concern. Pictures taken with long lenses have a characteristic veiling over of details, loss of contrast, and superimposing of a bluish or grayish cast over the subject matter. This is attributable to the cumulative recording of particulate matter in the air between the camera and the most distant object photographed, which could actually be infinity if it should include the horizon. The particulate matter consists of dust, moisture particles, and air pollution. These screen and alter the light coming toward the camera. Additionally, the camera lens gathers the cumulative ultraviolet radiation existing in the distance, invisible to the eye, but not to the film. Hence, if landscape pictures taken with any lens appear to be excessively bluish, this is attributable both to the bouncing around of a great deal of ultraviolet radiation, intermingling with moisture in the air—each droplet serving as a tiny lens to refract and diffuse this radiation—and to the reflection of blue skylight onto the subject.

With color films, only two remedies are available: using a skylight or UV filter to screen out excess ultraviolet radiation and choosing a shooting time immediately after a heavy rainfall which clears and cools the atmosphere.

Associated effect is the distortion of images due to heated air circulating upward and downward from and toward the ground creating an aerial turbulence. This is called the *schlieren effect.* While you might want to avoid this effect in the manner described, there may be instances when you will want to capture it, because it conveys the reality of shimmering heat waves on a hot day.

Lens hoods, built into the longest lenses, are essential in minimizing the bombardment of the subsurface of the

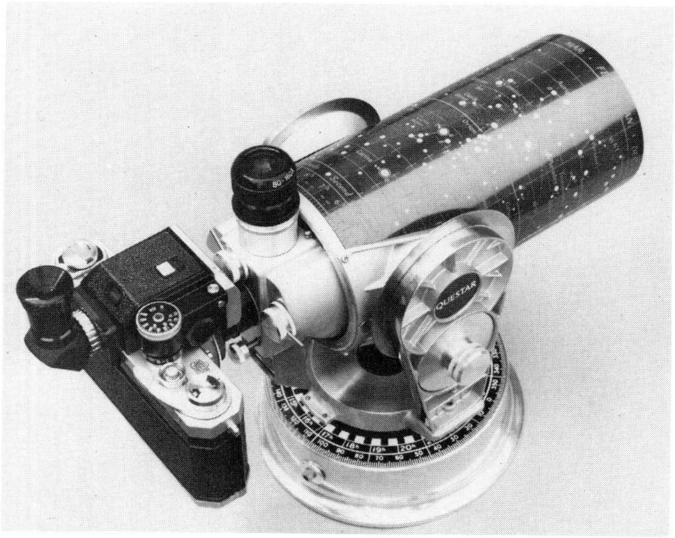

Questar Telescope mounted on Nikon camera (or vice versa). The Questar compresses a focal length of 56 inches into a closed tube of 8 inches with a relative aperture of *f*/16 and a clear aperture of 89mm (3.5 inches). This reflex lens is of Maksutov Cassegrain Catadioptric design. It boasts of no coma, astigmatism, or spherical aberrations. The photographic model has a field of view of 1 degree 30 minutes. As shown, the Questar is on an equatorial mount powered by a synchronous-drive motor. Other basic field models are available for both the 3.5-inch lens and a 7-inch lens.

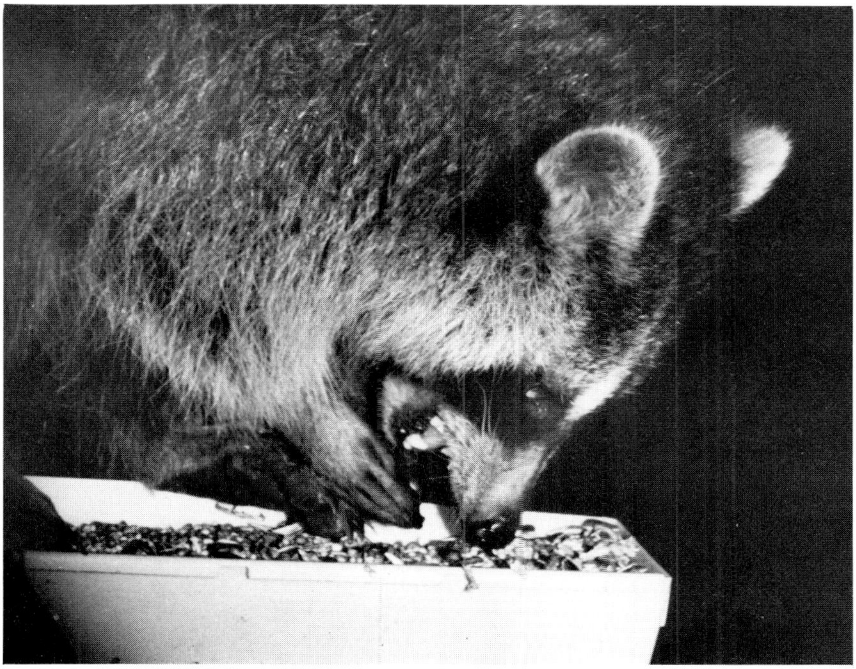

Edwin Hirsch

Questar and Nikon with Q-modification Raccoon photographed at distance of 60 feet. Single flash set off 13 feet from subject. Kodak Tri-X.

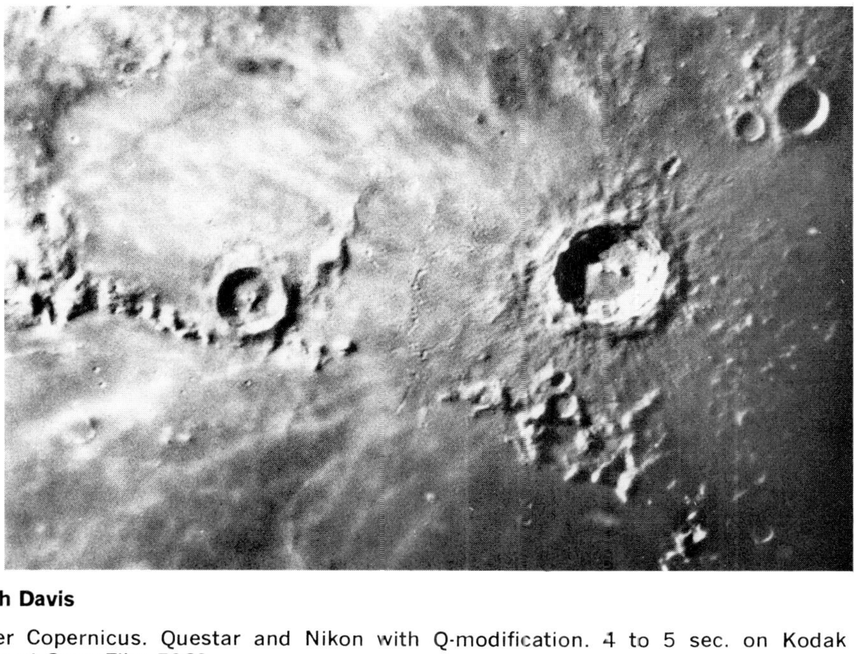

Ralph Davis

Crater Copernicus. Questar and Nikon with Q-modification. 4 to 5 sec. on Kodak High Contrast Copy Film 5069.

lens with ambient light that serves no other purpose than to degrade image quality.

With black-and-white films, the additional remedy of contrast correction is also available. The use of a yellow, orange, or red filter will, in the first instance, serve in lieu of a UV filter to screen out excessive ultraviolet radiation. Secondly, each of these filters, in successive order of greater effect, will sharpen contrast and darken the sky provided it is blue. While haze is not actually eliminated, as distinct from ultraviolet radiation, the filters make it less apparent by creating pictorial contrast.

Focusing before reaching infinity must be done critically and exactly, for with the longest lens one is often working with a zone of sharpness (or depth of field) measured in inches or millimeters. Consider that at a distance of 13 feet or 4 meters, the 500mm *f*/8 Reflex-Nikkor will record a depth of field of one inch or 0.02 meters. This is about the amount of sharpness to be expected at the closest focusing ranges of the 1000mm and 2000mm reflex lenses as well as with all the other super telephotos in the range of 400mm through 1200mm. The focusing strategy is to "tune in" on the most critical plane to which the viewer's attention is to be drawn. The viewer then will impute to the overall scene a psychoperceptual sense of greater sharpness in depth than actually was depicted on film and in the print. Split-image- and microprism-type focusing screens are not useful with the super telephotos. With Nikkormat cameras, whose focusing screens are not interchangeable, focusing should be done with the groundglass collar surrounding the central split-image or microprism focusing circle. With Nikon cameras, a groundglass screen without the central focusing aide should be substituted.

From a theoretical standpoint, it might be useful to know that most telephoto lenses are optically designed to yield optimal performance at a distance of about 26 times the focal length of the lens. With a 400mm lens this would be about 34 feet (10.4 meters), while with a 500mm lens this would be about 42 feet (13 meters). As a practical matter, the photographer is most likely to compose and shoot the picture from the most feasible distance to achieve the desired effect whether or not the shooting distance corresponds to the optical distance. Focusing the 400mm *f*/4.5 or the 400mm *f*/5.6 at the nearest ranges will not yield as good a result optically as focusing at greater distances reaching into infinity. The loss of image quality tends to be most noticeable at the edges of the image area.

A common problem encountered in using the super telephotos is camera shake during exposure even at the fastest shutter speeds. All of the long lenses covered in this group have tripod sockets on the underside of the lens barrels in order to move the center of gravity forward. One trouble with this arrangement is that the free-standing camera may move with the force of wind and will also respond to the mirror and shutter release actions that precede the actual opening of the shutter. The slightest vibration during exposure is magnified geometrically in relation to the focal length of the lens. One elaborate solution is to mount the lens and camera on two separate tripods. Andreas Feininger has at various times published specifications for the construction of a five-legged tripod to support both camera and lens that can be used to solve this problem. Simpler solutions include cradling both lens and camera in beanbags or other shock absorption materials, physically cradling the camera in both hands during exposure triggered off by either the self-timer or a cable release, and timing the moment of exposure to occur between gusts of wind or protecting oneself from high, steady winds.

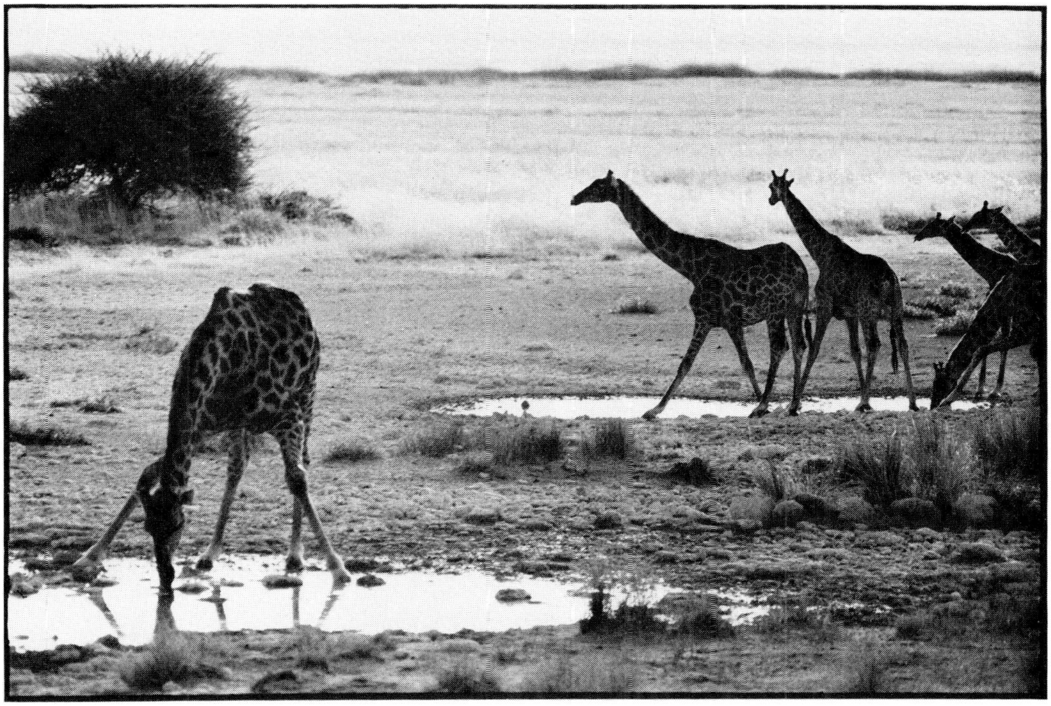

Struan Robertson

Giraffe drinking at waterhole, Etosha. At sunset with long light effects, the 300mm *f*/4.5 lens was selected because it had just enough reach and enough speed. Because slow film, Kodak Panatomic X, was in camera, slow shutter speeds had to be squeezed off gently with camera supported by gunstock grip and car window ledge. Everytime the camera clicked the animals would raise their heads.

Francisco Hidalgo

The 300mm lens may be considered among the hand-holdable group, but it calls for skill to avoid movement. This lens is used for special effects and for bringing in distant objects. As can be seen, it cuts sharply. *f*/5.6, 1/30 sec. Kodak Plus-X.

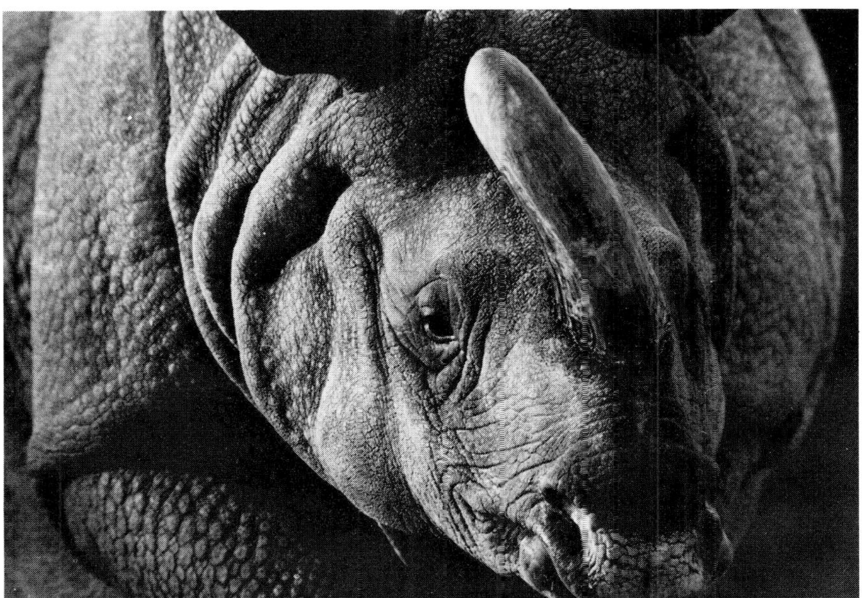

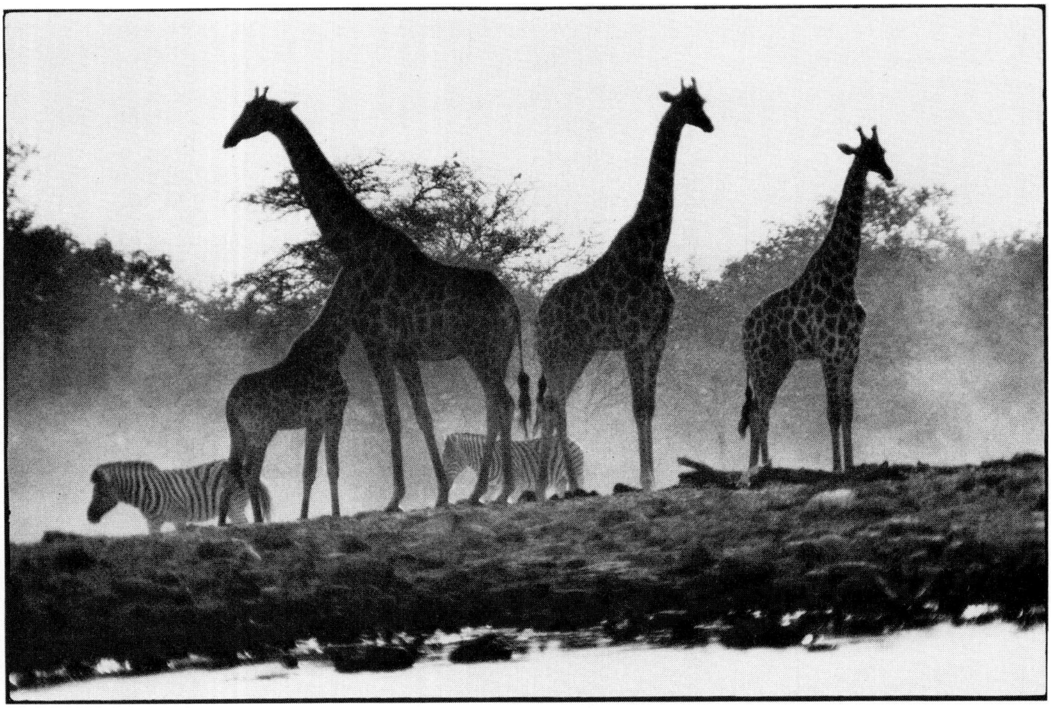

Struan Robertson

Giraffe and zebra at a waterhole, Etosha. Early morning, dust created by zebra in background coming down to waterhole. Sun behind animals caused great deal of flair in 500mm *f*/8 Reflex-Nikkor (which has difficulty coping with backlight). Ilford FP4 developed in Rodinal. To get contrast, printed on Agfa No. 6.

Douglas T. Mesney

Typical example of "pancaking" of objects photographed at distance with 500mm *f*/8 Reflex-Nikkor. Bridgehampton Can-Am Race. 1/250 sec. Dark sky achieved with red filter. Broken cross-line highlights achieved with household screen material in front of lens. Kodak Tri-X.

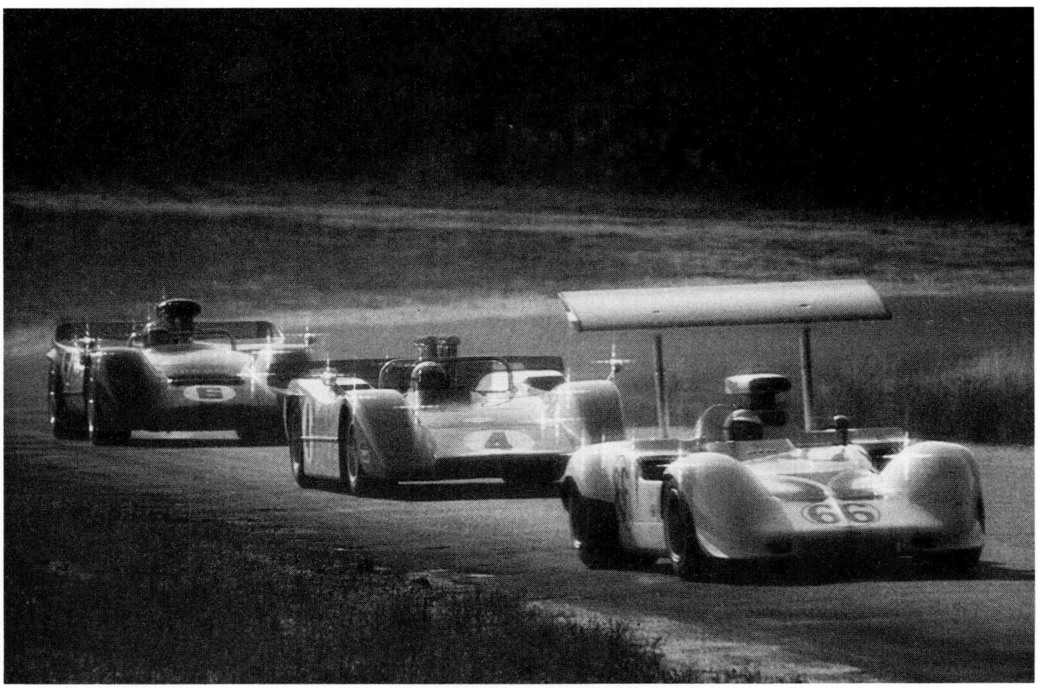

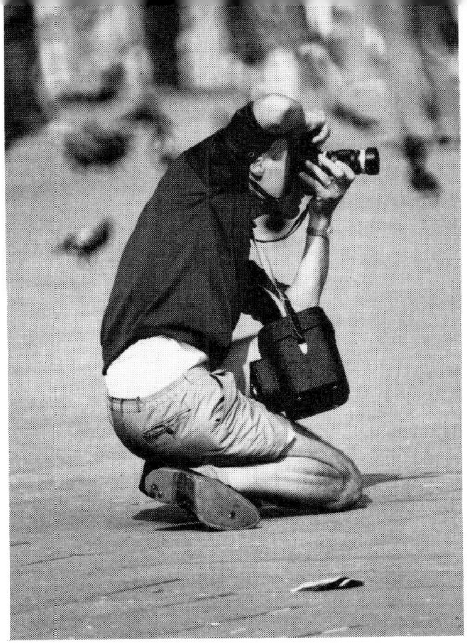
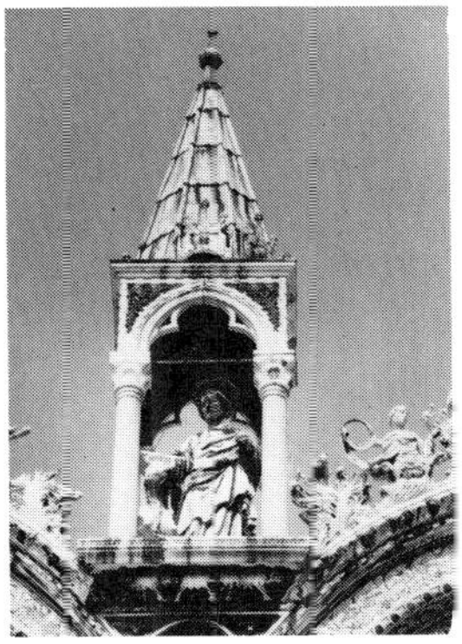
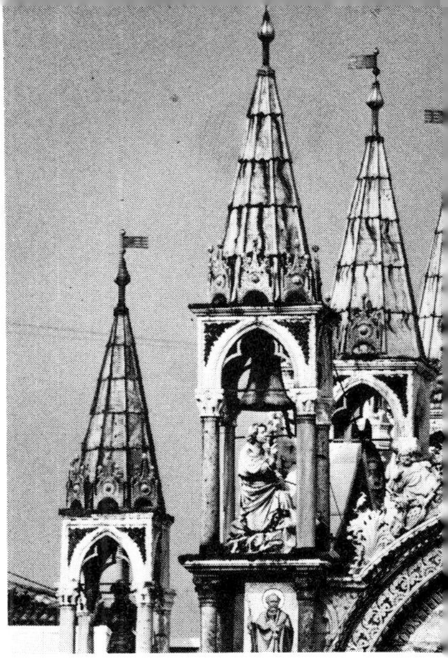

Joseph D. Cooper

The long 500mm lens permits taking objects at ground level or higher without much change in shooting angle and without development of lines of convergence. The inset photo shows effect of shooting upward at tower of Saint Mark's Cathedral, Venice with 200mm lens; adjacent photo was made with 500mm Reflex-Nikkor. Sharply delineated photographer at ground level made with same lens; note background rendition.

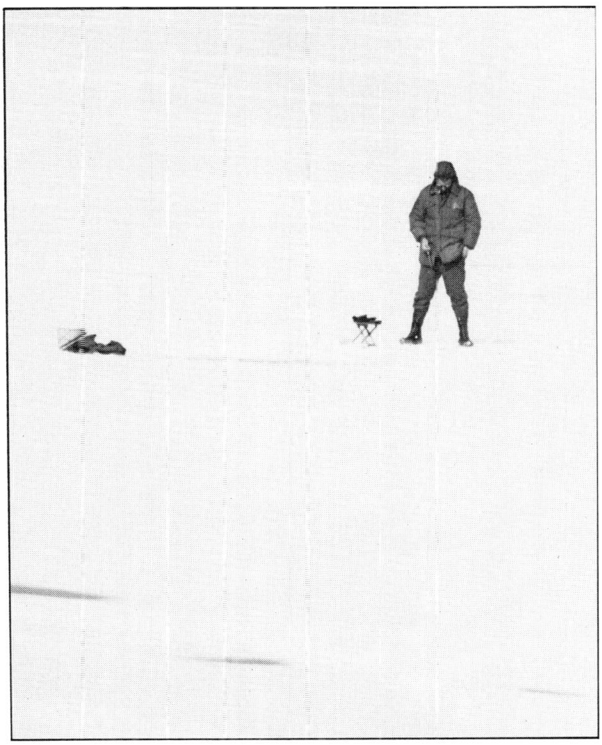

R. K. Bickerton

Ice Fishing. Abundant ambient light under these conditions creates some flair within 500mm *f*/8 Reflex-Nikkor lens to interfere with sharpness of rendition. Newer coated version of this lens would minimize flare problem. 1/500 sec. Kodak Plus-X.

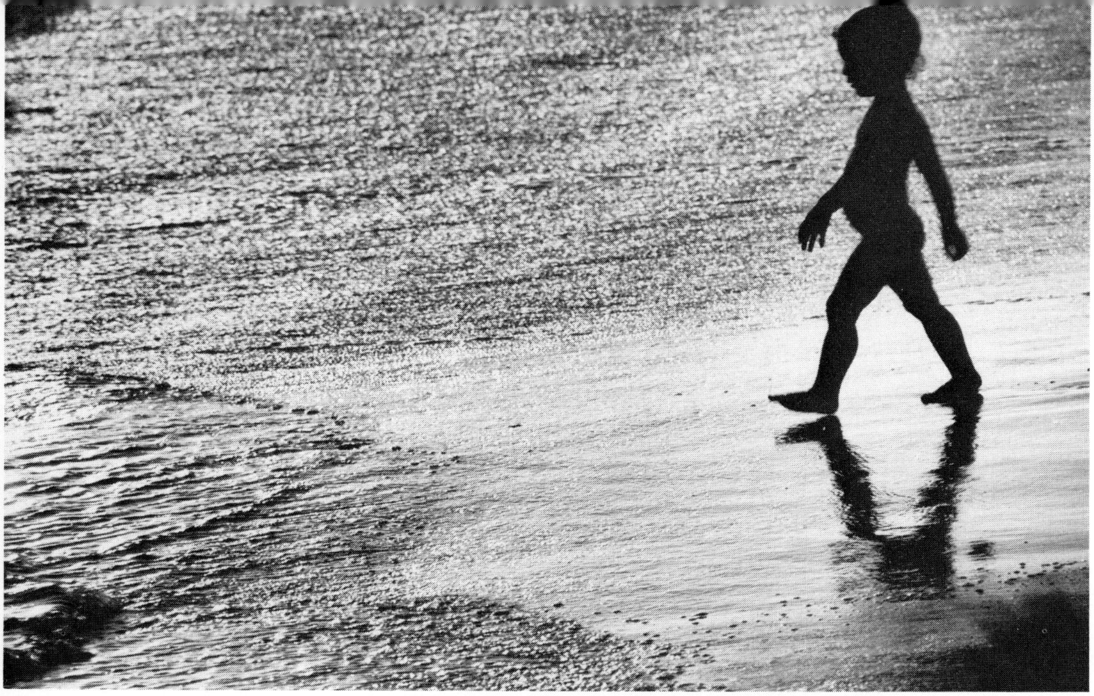

The silhouetted daughter of the photographer was made with the 1200mm long focus lens in focusing unit, isolated from other background objects. The smaller picture made with normal lens shows setting and comparison of long lens with results achieved with normal.

Tom Carroll

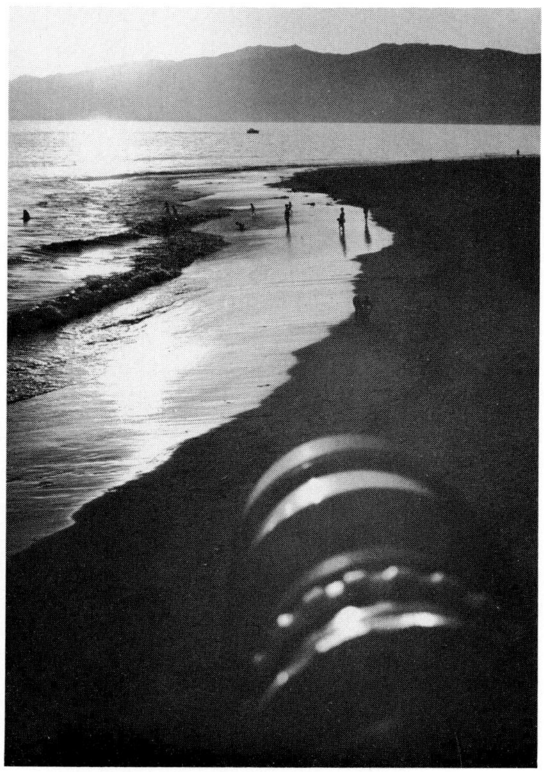

Directory of Nikkor Lenses General Range

GUIDE TO THE LENS DATA SHEETS

The lens data sheets have been designed as technical monographs presenting reference information pertaining to the optical and mechanical attributes of each lens, selection factors, working characteristics, relevant close-up information, focusing screen selection and use, and availability of accessories. Hence, the reader has one central point of reference for each lens.

The lenses are presented in groups assigned to this and the succeeding chapter. In this chapter are presented all lenses in what may be called the general range from extreme wide-angle through super-telephoto, including the mirror-reflex lenses. Shortest focal lengths (wide-angle) are presented first, with succeeding lenses having longer focal lengths on through normal, telephoto, and super-telephoto. Where two or more lenses are available in the same focal length, the widest aperture is presented first.

Chapter 3 covers special-purpose lenses, including Fisheye-Nikkors, Zoom-Nikkors, close-up Nikkors, the GN Nikkor, the enlarging lenses—El Nikkors—that may also be used in certain close-up work, and the PC (Perspective Control) Nikkors.

Factors in selection of a lens include:

Magnification or angle of view needed for subject categories from anticipated working distances.

Maximum aperture needed either for convenience in focusing (the brilliance factor) or for use in picture taking under adverse lighting conditions.

Near-focusing characteristics, if relevant to intended uses, such as when wide-angle lenses are used to achieve striking foreground dominance against clearly defined backgrounds or when close focusing with a telephoto lens may have advantages as against other alternatives.

Special purposes served uniquely by particular lenses.

Desirable optical characteristics of particular lenses as described or as determined through individual experience.

Tabular data are presented in metric form although dimensional attributes are given both in metric and feet-inches.

Discontinued lenses and their key attributes are listed in tables at the end of the lens data sheet presentations in each of the two specific lens chapters.

NIKKOR LENSES THAT CAN BE MODIFIED TO AI AND ADR

Lens	Serial Numbers
13mm f/5.6	175021—and higher
15mm f/5.6	321001—and higher
18mm f/4	173111—and higher
20mm f/3.5	421241—and higher
20mm f/4	103001—and higher
24mm f/2.8	242821—257010 257011—and higher
28mm f/2	280001—335000 335001—and higher
28mm f/2.8	382011—and higher
28mm f/3.5	195531—301010 625611—and higher
35mm f/1.4	350001—385000 385001—and higher
35mm f/2	690101—and higher
35mm f/2.8	255311—920110
50mm f/1.4	532011—635510 635511—2797020 2797021—3750400 3750401—and higher
50mm f/2	742111—785010 785011—and higher
55mm f/1.2	184711—970110
85mm f/1.8	219901—and higher
105mm f/2.5	234011—and higher
135mm f/2	175011—and higher

Lens	Serial Numbers
135mm f/2.8	189311—430000 430001—730000 730001—and higher
135mm f/3.5	111111—720100 831211—and higher
180mm f/2.8	312011—and higher
200mm f/4	304411—420000 420001—670002 670003—and higher
300mm f/4.5	326511—480000 480001—and higher
300mm f/4.5 ED	173101—and higher
400mm f/5.6	256031—and higher
400mm f/5.6 ED	260001—and higher
6mm f/2.8	628001—and higher
8mm f/2.8	230011—and higher
16mm f/3.5	272281—and higher
45mm f/2.8 GN	710101—and higher
† 55mm f/3.5 Micro	238011—and higher
† 105mm f/4 Micro	174011—and higher
28-45mm Zoom f/4.5	174011—and higher
43-86mm Zoom f/3.5	438611—and higher
50-300mm Zoom f/4.5	740101—and higher
80-200mm Zoom f/4.5	101911—and higher
85-250mm Zoom f/4	184711—and higher

†New AI extension rings (PK-13 for 55mm Micro-Nikkor, PN-11 for 105mm Micro-Nikkor), available as accessories, must be used for full-aperture meter operation in the 1:2—1:1 range. Original rings may be used with stop-down metering. *Modification of previous PK and PN-series extension rings is not available.*

Lens/Focusing Screen Selection
The characteristics of a screen when used with a specific lens should always be considered carefully before making the final selection. The following chart provides convenient reference when selecting the best model screen for the application at hand.

Focusing Screen Selector Guide

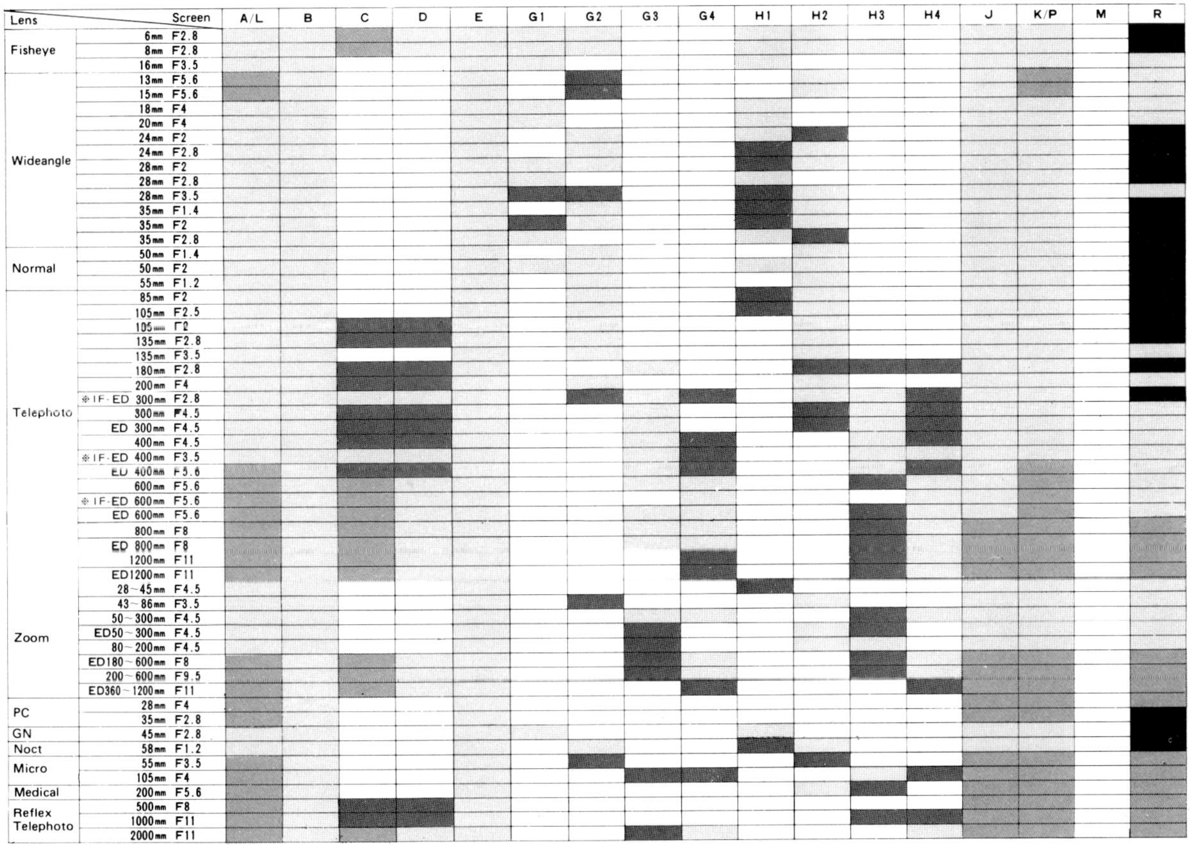

*Internal focusing type

Excellent

Acceptable
The image is brilliant from edge to edge, but the center area (rangefinder, microprism or cross-hair) is dim. Focusing should be performed on the surrounding matte area.

Acceptable
Slight vignetting (or moire phenomenon, in the case of the microprism) affects the screen image. The image on the film, however, shows no trace of this.

Acceptable
Focusing by split image prism or microprism may be inaccurate for bright lenses of f/1.2 ~ f/2.8 because of shallow angle of prism. Focusing should be performed on the surrounding matte area.

Not Usable

Exposure compensation chart/metering method. F2A Photomic

Lens	Screen	A/L	B	C	D	E	G1	G2	G3	G4	H1	H2	H3	H4	J	K/P	M	R
Fisheye	6mm F2.8	0	0	−½	−½	0	0	0			0	0			0	0		0
	8mm F2.8	0	0	−½	−½	0	0	0			0	0	0		0	0		0
	16mm F3.5	0	0			0	−½				0				0	0		0
Wideangle	13mm F5.6	0	0			0		−1				−½			0	0		0
	15mm F5.6	0	0			0		−1·½				−½			0	0		0
	18mm F4	0	0			0	−1				−1				0	0		0
	20mm F4	0	0			0	−1				−½				0	0		0
	24mm F2	0	0			0		0			+½	0			0	0		0
	24mm F2.8	0	0			0		0			+½	0			0	0		0
	28mm F2	0	0			0	+½	+½			+½	+½			0	0		0
	28mm F2.8	0	0			0	−½				0				0	0		0
	28mm F3.5	0	0			0	−1	−½			0	0			0	0		0
	35mm F1.4	0	0			0		+½			+½	+½			0	0		0
	35mm F2	0	0			0	+½	0			+½	0			0	0		0
	35mm F2.8	0	0			0	0				0	0			0	0		0
Normal	50mm F1.4	0	0			0		+½				+½			0	0		0
	50mm F2	0	0			0	+½	+½			+½	+½			0	0		0
	55mm F1.2	0	0			0		0				0			0	0		0
Telephoto	85mm F2	0	0			0		+½			+½	+½			0	0		0
	105mm F2.5	0	0			0		0			+½	+½			0	0		0
	135mm F2	0	0	0	0	0		+½				+½			0	0		0
	135mm F2.8	0	0	0	0	0		0				+½			0	0		0
	135mm F3.5	0	0			0		−½				+½			0	0		0
	180mm F2.8	0	0	0	0	0			0			0	0	0	0	0		0
	200mm F4	0	0	0	0	0		−1½				−1			0	0		0
	※IF-ED 300mm F2.8	0	0	0	0	0		0	0	0		+½	0	0	0	0		0
	300mm F4.5	0	0	0	0	0			−1·½			−1½	−1	−1½	0	0		0
	ED 300mm F4.5	0	0	0	0	0			−1·½			−1½	−1	−1½	0	0		0
	400mm F4.5	0	0	0	0	0									0	0		0
	※IF-ED 400mm F3.5	0	0	0	0	0			−1	−½			0	−½	0	0		0
	ED 400mm F5.6	0	0	0	0	0									0	0		0
	600mm F5.6	0	0	0	0	0									0	0		0
	※IF-ED 600mm F5.6	0	0	0	0	0									0	0		0
	ED 600mm F5.6	0	0	0	0	0									0	0		0
	800mm F8	0	0	0	0	0									0	0		0
	ED 800mm F8	0	0	0	0	0									0	0		0
	1200mm F11	0	0	0	0	0									0	0		0
	ED1200mm F11	0	0	0	0	0									0	0		0
Zoom	28~45mm F4.5	0	0			0					−1½				0	0		0
	43~86mm F3.5	0	0			0		−½				−½			0	0		0
	50~300mm F4.5	0	0			0			−2				−1·½		0	0		0
	ED50~300mm F4.5	0	0			0			−1			−1·½	−½		0	0		0
	80~200mm F4.5	0	0			0			−1			−1·½	−½		0	0		0
	ED180~600mm F8	0	0	0	0	0									0	0		0
	200~600mm F9.5	0	0	0	0	0									0	0		0
	ED360~1200mm F11	0	0	0	0	0									0	0		0
PC	28mm F4	0	0			0									0	0		0
	35mm F2.8	0	0			0									0	0		0
GN	45mm F2.8	0	0			0	0				0				0	0		0
Noct	58mm F1.2	0	0			0		0			0	0			0	0		0
Micro	55mm F3.5	0	0			0									0	0		0
	105mm F4	0	0			0									0	0		0
Medical	200mm F5.6	0	0			0									0	0		0
Reflex Telephoto	500mm F8	0	0	0	0	0									0	0		0
	1000mm F11	0	0	0	0	0									0	0		0
	2000mm F11	0	0	0	0	0									0	0		0

※Internal focusing type

- ▢ (light grey) Exposure measurement via full-aperture method
- ■ (dark grey) Exposure measurement via stop-down method
- ■ (black) Exposure measurement not possible; lens/screen combination permits only focusing operation.
- □ Not Usable

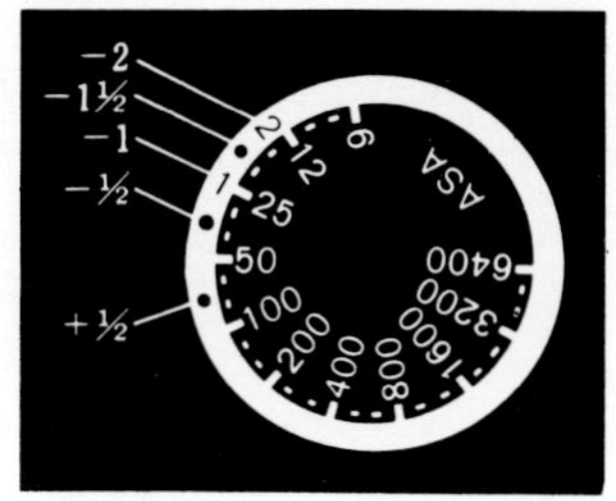

Exposure compensation chart/metering method. F2AS Photomic

Lens	Screen	A/L	B	C	D	E	G1	G2	G3	G4	H1	H2	H3	H4	J	K/P	M	R
Fisheye	6mm F2.8	0	0	−½	−½	0	−½	0			0	0			0	0		0
	8mm F2.8	0	0	−½	−½	0	−½	0			0	0	0		0	0		0
	16mm F3.5	0	0			0	−½				0				0	0		0
Wideangle	13mm F5.6	0	0			0		−1				−½			0	0		0
	15mm F5.6	0	0			0		−1				−½			0	0		0
	18mm F4	0	0			0	−1½				−1				0	0		0
	20mm F4	0	0			0	−1				−½				0	0		0
	24mm F2	0	0			0		0			+½	0			0	0		0
	24mm F2.8	0	0			0		0			+½	0			0	0		0
	28mm F2	0	0			0	+½	+½			+½	+½			0	0		0
	28mm F2.8	0	0			0	0				+½				0	0		0
	28mm F3.5	0	0			0	−1	−½			0	0			0	0		0
	35mm F1.4	0	0			0		+½			+½	+½			0	0		0
	35mm F2	0	0			0	+½	+½			+½	+½			0	0		0
	35mm F2.8	0	0			0	0				+½	0			0	0		0
Normal	50mm F1.4	0	0			0		+½				+½			0	0		0
	50mm F2	0	0			0	+½	+½			+½	+½			0	0		0
	55mm F1.2	0	0			0		0				0			0	0		0
Telephoto	85mm F2	0	0			0		+½			+½	+½			0	0		0
	105mm F2.5	0	0			0		0			+½	+½			0	0		0
	135mm F2	0	0	0	0	0		+½				+½			0	0		0
	135mm F2.8	0	0	0	0	0		0				+½			0	0		0
	135mm F3.5	0	0			0		−1				0			0	0		0
	180mm F2.8	0	0	0	0	0			0			0	0	0	0	0		0
	200mm F4	0	0	0	0	0		−1½				−½			0	0		0
	※IF-ED 300mm F2.8	0	0	0	0	0		0	0	0		+½	0	0	0	0		0
	300mm F4.5	0	0	0	0	0			−1½			−2	−1	−1	0	0		0
	300mm F4.5	0	0	0	0	0			1			−1½	−½	−½	0	0		0
	400mm F4.5	0	0	0	0	0									0	0		0
	※IF-ED 400mm F3.5	0	0	0	0	0			−1	−½			0	−½	0	0		0
	ED 400mm F5.6	0	0	0	0	0									0	0		0
	600mm F5.6	0	0	0	0	0									0	0		0
	※IF-ED 600mm F5.6	0	0	0	0	0									0	0		0
	ED 600mm F5.6	0	0	0	0	0									0	0		0
	800mm F8	0	0	0	0	0									0	0		0
	ED 800mm F8	0	0	0	0	0									0	0		0
	1200mm F11	0	0	0	0	0									0	0		0
	ED1200mm F11	0	0	0	0	0									0	0		0
Zoom	28~45mm F4.5	0	0			0					−½				0	0		0
	43~86mm F3.5	0	0			0		−1				−½			0	0		0
	50~300mm F4.5	0	0			0			−2				−1		0	0		0
	ED50~300mm F4.5	0	0			0			−1			−1½	−½		0	0		0
	80~200mm F4.5	0	0			0			−1			−1½	−½		0	0		0
	ED180~600mm F8	0	0	0	0	0									0	0		0
	200~600mm F9.5	0	0	0	0	0									0	0		0
	ED360~1200mm F11	0	0	0	0	0									0	0		0
PC	28mm F4	0	0			0									0	0		0
	35mm F2.8	0	0			0									0	0		0
GN	45mm F2.8	0	0			0	0				0				0	0		0
Noct	58mm F1.2	0	0			0		0			0	0			0	0		0
Micro	55mm F3.5	0	0			0									0	0		0
	105mm F4	0	0			0									0	0		0
Medical	200mm F5.6	0	0			0									0	0		0
Reflex Telephoto	500mm F8	0	0	0	0	0									0	0		0
	1000mm F11	0	0	0	0	0									0	0		0
	2000mm F11	0	0	0	0	0									0	0		0

※Internal focusing type

- Exposure measurement via full-aperture method
- Exposure measurement via stop-down method
- Exposure measurement not possible; lens/screen combination permits only focusing operation.
- Not Usable

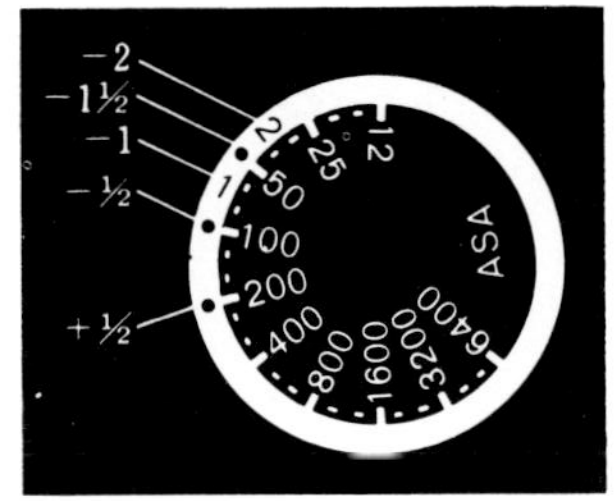

13mm *f*/5.6 NIKKOR

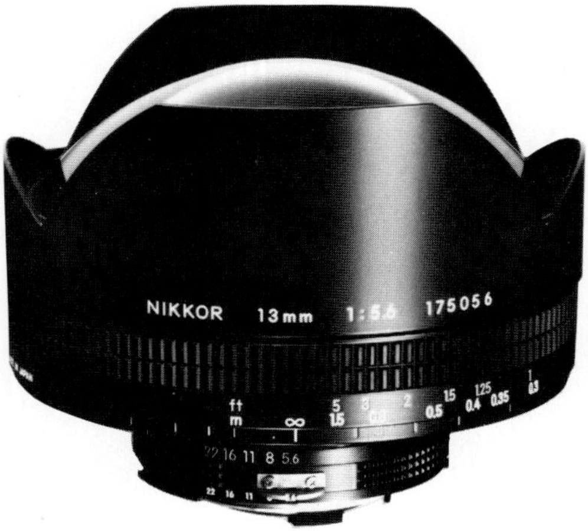

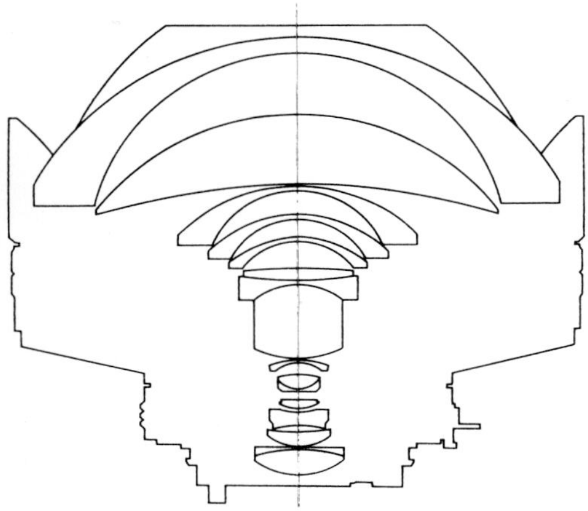

DESCRIPTION

The 13mm *f*/5.6 Nikkor is a super-wide-angle lens which accurately reproduces straight lines without the pronounced curvature effects common to fisheye lenses. The optics are corrected for evenness of illumination across the entire frame. The Nikon close-focus correction system permits optimum performance at the 0.3m (1 ft) closest focusing distance. The retrofocus configuration of the lens enables all normal reflex-mirror and through-the-lens metering functions. Four bayonet-mount filters are included with the lens (one must always be in place). These filters attach to the special filter mount provided at the rear of the lens.

SPECIFICATIONS

Smallest aperture: 22
Nearest focus distance: 0.3m (1 ft)
Image ratio at nearest distance: 1:22
Angles of view:
Diagonal: 118°
Horizontal: 100°20′
Vertical: 69°40′
Ratio of image size at infinity to image of 50mm lens: 0.26:1
Filters: Provided with a set of four bayonet-mount filters for attachment to the rear of the lens: Y48, O56, R60, and plain glass (N)
Lens hood: Built-in
Front lens cap: Slip on; provided
Lens case: CL-14
Overall size: 115mm ø × 101mm
Weight: 1.2kg (2.6 lb)

DEPTH OF FIELD TABLE

(m)

focus distance	depth of field				
	f/5.6	8	11	16	22
0.3	0.28361–0.32212	0.27781–0.33416	0.27137–0.35226	0.26224–0.39356	0.25330–0.47794
0.35	0.32021–0.39489	0.31031–0.42195	0.29966–0.46672	0.28516–0.59244	0.27161–1.03531
0.4	0.35373–0.47806	0.3392–0.53077	0.32403–0.62928	0.30407–1.01602	0.28612–∞
0.5	0.41292–0.68601	0.38832–0.85123	0.36385–1.30786	0.33344–∞	0.30767–∞
0.8	0.54559–2.14295	0.49034–23.87595	0.44069–∞	0.38527–∞	0.34297–∞
1.5	0.71951–∞	0.60937–∞	0.52149–∞	0.43383–∞	0.37327–∞
∞	1.11259–∞	0.83041–∞	0.65084–∞	0.50119–∞	0.41141–∞

15mm f/5.6 NIKKOR

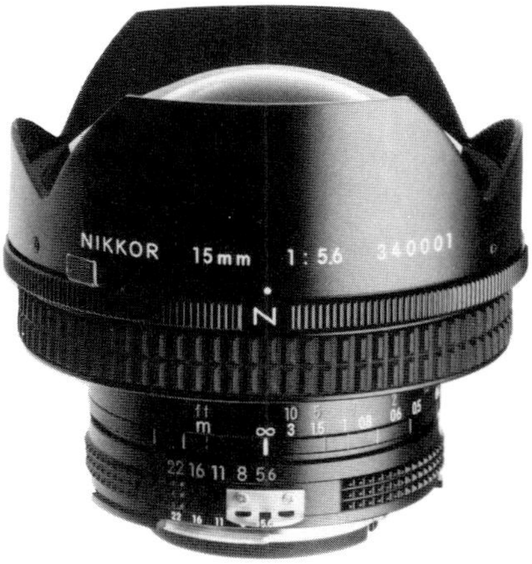

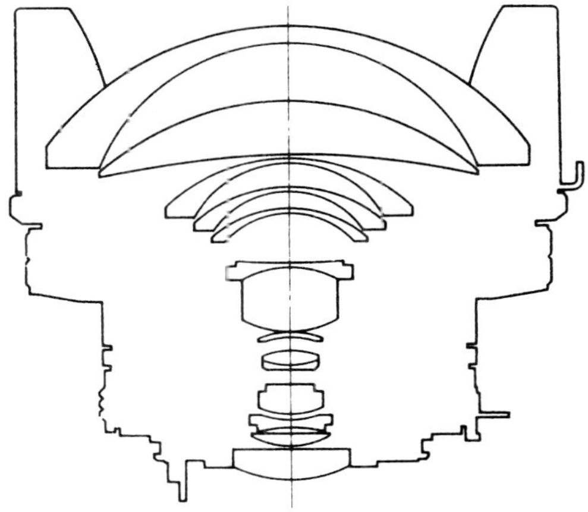

DESCRIPTION

The 15mm Nikkor encompasses 3.3× subject matter in linear dimension as compared to standard 50mm lens. Useful primarily in architectural, panoramic, and other wide-field applications, as well as in extreme close-quarter situations. Special applications in underwater photography. Tremendous focusing latitude due to great depth of field; almost no need to focus if diaphragm is closed down slightly. Retrofocus design permits through-the-lens viewing and metering. Rear elements shift as lens is focused at close distances to provide excellent resolution. Four built-in filters.

SPECIFICATIONS

Smallest aperture: 22
Nearest focus distance: 0.3m (1 ft)
Subject field at nearest distance: 3.29 × 4.93cm
Image ratio at nearest distance: 1:13.7
Focusing distances:
One head vertical: 0.22m (0.8 ft) subject to perspective distortion
Two heads horizontal: 0.27m (0.9 ft) subject to perspective distortion
One to three adults standing: 0.9m (3 ft) subject to perspective distortion
Angles of view:
Diagonal: 110°
Horizontal: 100°
Vertical: 77°
Ratio of image size at infinity to image of 50mm lens: 0.33:1
Filters: Built-in; Y48, O56, R60, and plain glass (N)
Lens hood: Built-in
Front lens cap: 64mm slip-on
Lens case: CL-26
Overall size: 92mm ϕ × 88mm
Weight: 645g (1.4 lb)

DEPTH OF FIELD TABLE

Meters

m \ f/	5.6	8	11	16	22	Magnification
0.3	0.268—0.346	0.257—0.373	0.244—0.420	0.229—0.522	0.212—0.858	1/13.7
0.35	0.303—0.423	0.288—0.469	0.270—0.558	0.250—0.790	0.228—0.858	1/17.0
0.4	0.336—0.509	0.316—0.583	0.293—0.743	0.268—1.29	0.241—∞	1/20.3
0.5	0.396—0.711	0.366—0.887	0.333—1.40	0.298—14.1	0.262—∞	1/26.8
0.6	0.449—0.969	0.409—1.36	0.366—3.43	0.321—∞	0.279—∞	1/33.4
0.8	0.539—1.78	0.478—4.21	0.417—∞	0.357—∞	0.302—∞	1/46.5
1.0	0.613—3.57	0.532—∞	0.455—∞	0.382—∞	0.318—∞	1/59.5
1.5	0.750—∞	0.626—∞	0.517—∞	0.421—∞	0.341—∞	1/92.2
3.0	0.962—∞	0.761—∞	0.598—∞	0.468—∞	0.368—∞	1/190
∞	1.34—∞	0.967—∞	0.710—∞	0.528—∞	0.399—∞	1/∞

18mm *f*/4 NIKKOR

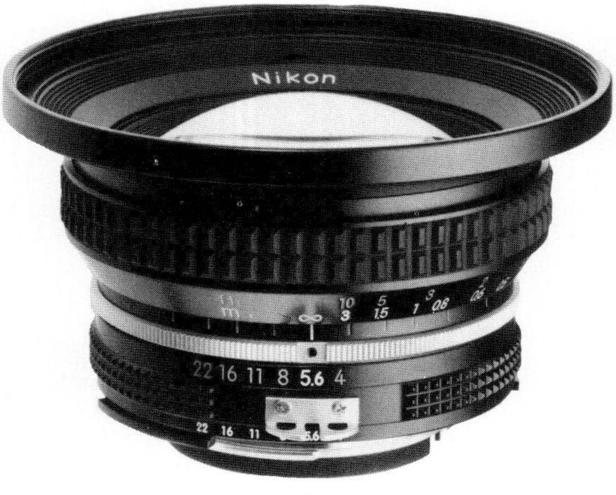

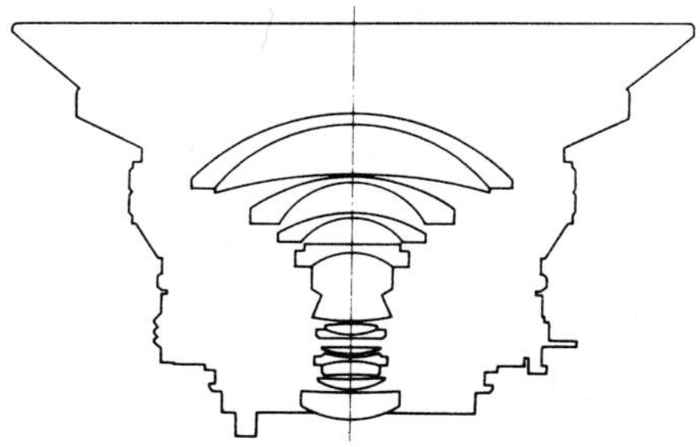

DESCRIPTION

This wide-angle lens, which covers a picture angle of 100 degrees, features a retrofocus design enabling the photographer to compose, focus, and perform metering operations through the camera's viewfinder. With its *f*/4 speed, the lens retains image field flatness and provides sufficient edge-to-edge illumination for uniformly sharp and bright images over the entire picture field. The ultra-wide picture angle tends to exaggerate the image perspective for striking effects, making the lens especially useful for commercial, advertising, architectural, and panoramic photography.

SPECIFICATIONS

Smallest aperture: 22
Nearest focus distance: 0.3m (1 ft)
Image ratio at nearest distance: 1:15.7
Focusing distances:
  One head vertical: 0.3m (1 ft) subject to perspective distortion
  Two heads horizontal: 0.37m (1.2 ft) subject to perspective distortion
  One to three adults standing: 1.2m (4 ft) subject to perspective distortion
Angles of view:
  Diagonal: 100°
  Horizontal: 85°
  Vertical: 59°
Ratio of image size at infinity to image of 50mm lens: 0.36:1
Attachment size (inside screw diameter): 86mm (P = 1.00)
Lens hood: HN-15
Front lens cap: 86mm screw-in
Lens case: CL-28, flexible pouch 54
Overall size: 89mm ø × 58.5mm
Weight: 325g (11.5 oz)

DEPTH OF FIELD TABLE

(m)

focus distance	depth of field						repro-duction ratio
	f/4	5.6	8	11	16	22	
0.3	0.280–0.324	0.273–0.335	0.263–0.354	0.253–0.381	0.237–0.442	0.222–0.555	1/12.3
0.35	0.321–0.386	0.311–0.404	0.298–0.434	0.283–0.480	0.262–0.590	0.242–0.838	1/15.0
0.4	0.361–0.451	0.348–0.477	0.330–0.522	0.311–0.595	0.285–0.789	0.260–1.37	1/17.7
0.5	0.436–0.591	0.416–0.639	0.389–0.730	0.361–0.897	0.324–1.50	0.290–12.0	1/23.2
0.6	0.507–0.744	0.478–0.827	0.442–0.997	0.404–1.36	0.356–3.81	0.315– ∞	1/28.6
0.8	0.635–1.10	0.588–1.31	0.531–1.83	0.475–3.85	0.407– ∞	0.351– ∞	1/39.5
1	0.748–1.55	0.682–2.01	0.604–3.71	0.531– ∞	0.445– ∞	0.377– ∞	1/50.4
1.5	0.982–3.39	0.867–7.11	0.740– ∞	0.629– ∞	0.508– ∞	0.418– ∞	1/77.6
3	1.43– ∞	1.19– ∞	0.954– ∞	0.771– ∞	0.592– ∞	0.469– ∞	1/159
∞	2.61– ∞	1.89– ∞	1.34– ∞	0.996– ∞	0.707– ∞	0.534– ∞	1/∞

20mm *f*/3.5 NIKKOR

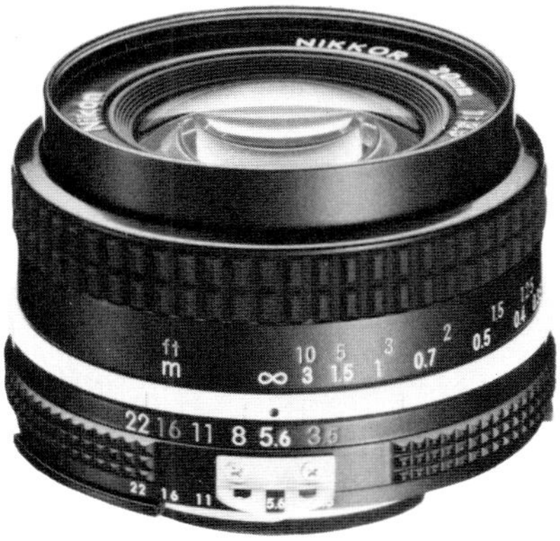

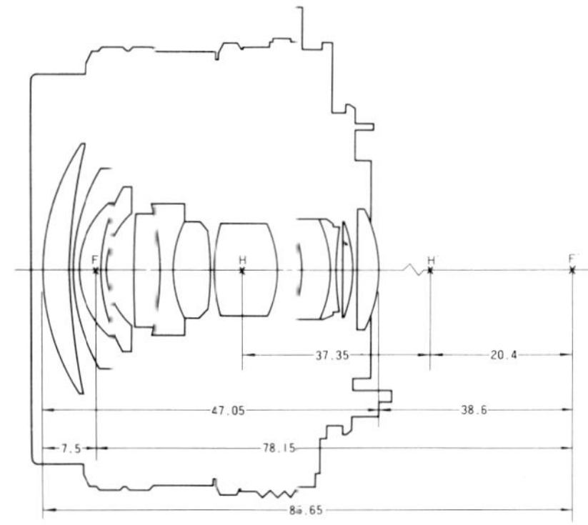

DESCRIPTION

The 20mm *f*/3.5 Nikkor inherits the compactness and light weight of the 20mm *f*/4 lens, which it replaces. It provides a slightly brighter viewfinder image over its predecessor, due to its increase in speed. The helicoidal turning angle of 100° from its nearest focusing distance to infinity ensures easier and quicker focusing. The 20mm *f*/3.5 is designed to produce improved results in the reproduction of corner images and distant subjects. The combination of wide depth of field and extreme wide field coverage make this lens useful in panoramic photography, architectural photography, and constricted interior areas. When the lens is stopped down to achieve maximum depth of field, striking background/foreground effects are possible.

SPECIFICATIONS

Smallest aperture: 22
Nearest focus distance: 0.3m (1 ft)
Subject field at nearest distance: 26.4 × 39.6cm
Image ratio at nearest distance: 1:11
Focusing distances:
One head vertical: 0.3m (1 ft)
Two heads horizontal: 0.37m (1.2 ft)
One to three adults standing: 1.2m (4 ft)
Angles of view:
Diagonal: 94°
Horizontal: 83°30′
Vertical: 61°30′
Ratio of image size at infinity to image of 50mm lens: 0.4:1
Attachment size (inside screw diameter): 52mm (P = 0.75)
Lens hood: 52mm slip-on HK-6
Front lens cap. 52mm snap-on
Lens case: CL-31, flexible pouch 54, plastic case CP-1
Overall size: 65.5mm ϕ × 50.5mm
Weight: 235g (8.4 oz)

DEPTH OF FIELD TABLE

Meters

m \ f/	3.5	4	5.6	8	11	16	22	Magnification
0.3	0.288−0.314	0.286−0.316	0.281−0.323	0.274−0.335	0.265−0.352	0.253−0.382	0.239−0.438	1/11
0.35	0.331−0.371	0.329−0.375	0.321−0.386	0.311−0.405	0.298−0.434	0.282−0.487	0.263−0.596	1/13
0.4	0.374−0.431	0.371−0.436	0.360−0.453	0.347−0.480	0.329−0.527	0.308−0.615	0.284−0.821	1/15
0.45	0.416−0.492	0.411−0.499	0.398−0.523	0.380−0.562	0.358−0.632	0.333−0.773	0.303−1.17	1/18
0.5	0.456−0.555	0.451−0.564	0.434−0.597	0.412−0.651	0.386−0.752	0.355−0.974	0.320−1.76	1/20
0.6	0.535−0.687	0.527−0.702	0.502−0.758	0.471−0.855	0.435−1.05	0.394−1.60	0.349−7.67	1/25
0.7	0.609−0.829	0.598−0.852	0.565−0.939	0.525−1.10	0.478−1.48	0.427−2.99	0.373−∞	1/30
0.8	0.680−0.980	0.666−1.01	0.624−1.14	0.574−1.41	0.517−2.12	0.456−8.55	0.394−∞	1/35
1	0.812−1.32	0.792−1.38	0.731−1.65	0.660−2.30	0.583−5.43	0.504−∞	0.426−∞	1/45
1.5	1.10 −2.43	1.06 −2.68	0.945−4.03	0.825−15.2	0.702−∞	0.585−∞	0.478−∞	1/69
2	1.33 −4.22	1.27 −5.04	1.11 −14.5	0.942−∞	0.782−∞	0.636−∞	0.509−∞	1/94
5	2.15 −∞	1.99 −∞	1.61 −∞	1.27 −∞	0.983−∞	0.754−∞	0.576−∞	1/241
∞	3.66 −∞	3.21 −∞	2.29 −∞	1.65 −∞	1.19 −∞	0.866−∞	0.637−∞	1/∞

20mm f/4 NIKKOR

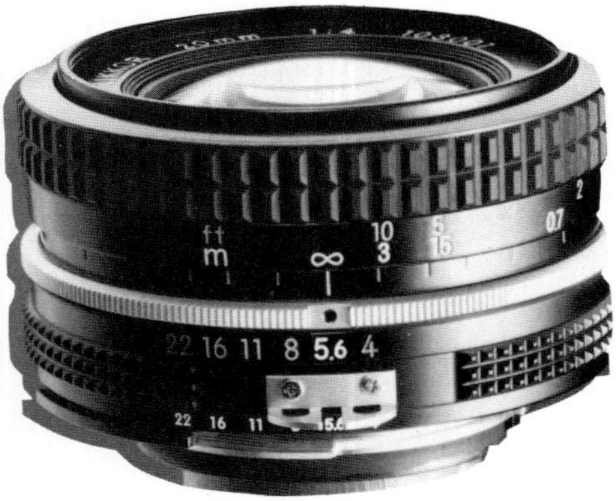

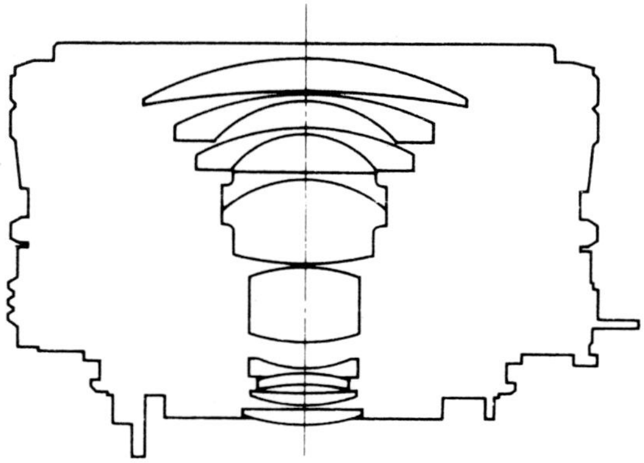

DESCRIPTION

Combination of extreme wide-field coverage and extreme depth of field (particularly when diaphragm is closed down slightly at near-focusing distances) make this a popular lens for architectural photography, panoramic situations, and constricted interior areas. Widely used in underwater photography. Striking foreground/background effects achieved at close working distances with lens stopped down. Flash and other artificial lighting must be evenly distributed over entire picture area. Retrofocus design permits viewing through reflex mechanism with mirror in normal position.

SPECIFICATIONS

Smallest aperture: 22
Nearest focus distance: 0.3m (1 ft)
Subject field at nearest distance: 26.4 × 39.6cm
Image ratio at nearest distance: 1:11
Focusing distances:
One head vertical: 0.3m (1 ft) subject to perspective distortion
Two heads horizontal: 0.37m (1.2 ft) subject to perspective distortion
One to three adults standing: 1.2m (4 ft) subject to perspective distortion
Angles of view:
Diagonal: 94°
Horizontal: 83°30′
Vertical: 61°30′
Ratio of image size at infinity to image of 50mm lens: 0.4:1
Attachment size (inside screw diameter): 52mm (P = 0.75)
Lens hood: HN-14
Front lens cap: 52mm screw-in
Lens case: CL-31, flexible pouch 54, plastic case CP-1
Overall size: 63.5mm ϕ × 47.5mm
Weight: 210g (7.4 oz)

DEPTH OF FIELD TABLE

Meters

m \ f/	4	5.6	8	11	16	22	Magnification
0.3	0.286−0.316	0.281−0.323	0.274−0.335	0.265−0.352	0.253−0.382	0.239−0.438	1/11
0.35	0.329−0.375	0.321−0.386	0.311−0.405	0.298−0.434	0.282−0.487	0.263−0.596	1/13
0.4	0.371−0.436	0.360−0.453	0.347−0.480	0.329−0.527	0.308−0.615	0.284−0.821	1/15
0.45	0.411−0.499	0.398−0.523	0.380−0.562	0.358−0.632	0.333−0.773	0.303−1.17	1/18
0.5	0.451−0.564	0.434−0.597	0.412−0.651	0.386−0.752	0.355−0.974	0.320−1.76	1/20
0.6	0.527−0.702	0.502−0.758	0.471−0.855	0.435−1.05	0.394−1.60	0.349−7.67	1/25
0.7	0.598−0.852	0.565−0.939	0.525−1.10	0.478−1.48	0.427−2.99	0.373−∞	1/30
0.8	0.666−1.01	0.624−1.14	0.574−1.41	0.517−2.12	0.456−8.55	0.394−∞	1/35
1	0.792−1.38	0.731−1.65	0.660−2.30	0.583−5.43	0.504−∞	0.426−∞	1/45
1.5	1.06 −2.68	0.945−4.03	0.825−15.2	0.702−∞	0.585−∞	0.478−∞	1/69
2	1.27 −5.04	1.11 −14.5	0.942−∞	0.782−∞	0.636−∞	0.509−∞	1/94
5	1.99 −∞	1.61 −∞	1.27 −∞	0.983−∞	0.754−∞	0.576−∞	1/241
∞	3.21 −∞	2.29 −∞	1.65 −∞.	1.19 −∞	0.866−∞	0.637−∞	1/∞

24mm *f*/2 NIKKOR

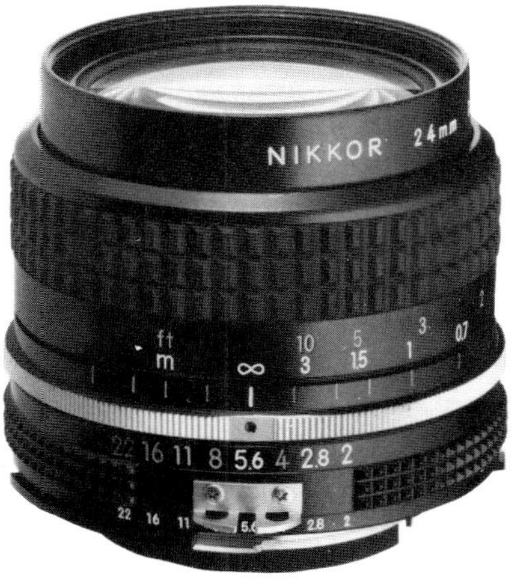

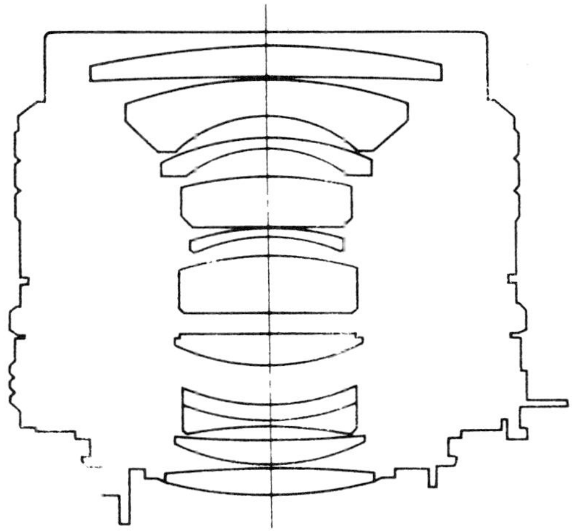

DESCRIPTION

The 24mm *f*/2 Nikkor is a wide-angle lens of retrofocus design featuring a bright maximum aperture that makes for easier focusing even under dark lighting conditions. This lens is fully corrected for aberrations and is designed for uniform brightness over the entire field. Top performance at close-working distances is ensured by the adoption of floating rear elements. Applications include architectural exteriors and interiors, landscapes, and travel. Great depth of field makes lens especially useful for candid "grab" shots.

SPECIFICATIONS

Smallest aperture: 22
Nearest focus distance: 0.3m (1 ft)
Subject field at nearest distance: 21.8 × 32.8cm
Image ratio at nearest distance: 1:9.1
Focusing distances:
  One head vertical: 0.35m (1.12 ft) subject to perspective distortion
  Two heads horizontal: 0.45m (1.5 ft) subject to perspective distortion
  One to three adults standing: 1.5m (5 ft)
Angles of view:
  Diagonal: 84°
  Horizontal: 74°
  Vertical: 53°
Ratio of image size at infinity to image of 50mm lens: 0.48:1
Attachment size (inside screw diameter): 52mm (P = 0.75)
Lens hood: HK-2
Front lens cap: 52mm snap-on
Lens case: CL-31, flexible pouch 54, plastic case CP-1
Overall size: 63.5mm ø × 63.5mm
Weight: 300g (10.6 oz)

DEPTH OF FIELD TABLE

(m)

focus distance	depth of field								reproduction ratio
	f/2	f/2.8	f/4	f/5.6	f/8	f/11	f/16	f/22	
0.3	0.295–0.306	0.293–0.308	0.240–0.312	0.286–0 317	0.280–0.325	0.273–0.336	0.263–0.356	0.253–0.386	1/8.64
0.35	0.342–0.359	0.339–0.362	0.334–0.368	0.329–0 376	0.320–0.388	0.311–0.406	0.297–0.440	0.282–0.491	1/10.7
0.4	0.389–0.412	0.384–0.417	0.378–0.425	0.370–0 437	0.359–0.455	0.347–0.481	0.328–0.534	0.309–0.619	1/12.8
0.5	0.481–0.521	0.474–0.530	0.463–0.544	0.451–0 565	0.433–0.600	0.413–0.651	0.384–0.763	0.356–0.974	1/16.9
0.7	0.659–0.747	0.645–0.768	0.624–0.801	0.598–0 852	0.565–0.943	0.528–1.092	0.478–1.502	0.431–2.866	1/25.0
1	0.914–1.11	0.884–1.16	0.842–1.24	0.794–1 38	0.731–1.65	0.667–2.23	0.585–5.58	0.512–∞	1/37.3
1.5	1.31–1.77	1.24–1.91	1.16–2.16	1.06–2.64	0.949–4.00	0.839–11.7	0.707–∞	0.599–∞	1/57.7
3	2.28–4.41	2.09–5.45	1.85–8.48	1.61–33 9	1.35–∞	1.13–∞	0.893–∞	0.721–∞	1/119
∞	9.09–∞	6.52–∞	4.59–∞	3.30–∞	2.34–∞	1.72–∞	1.21–∞	0.90–∞	1/∞

24mm f/2.8 NIKKOR

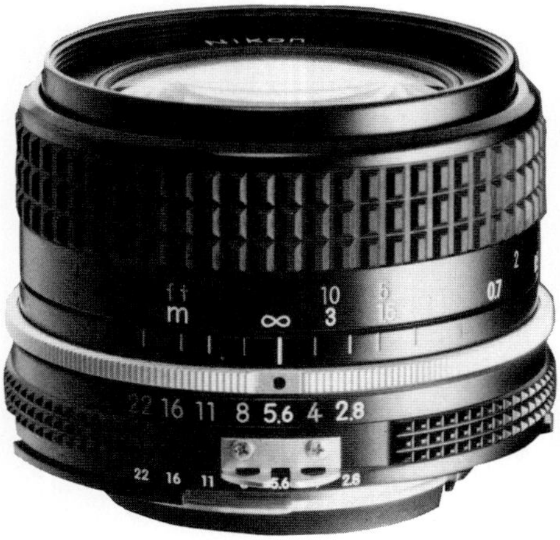

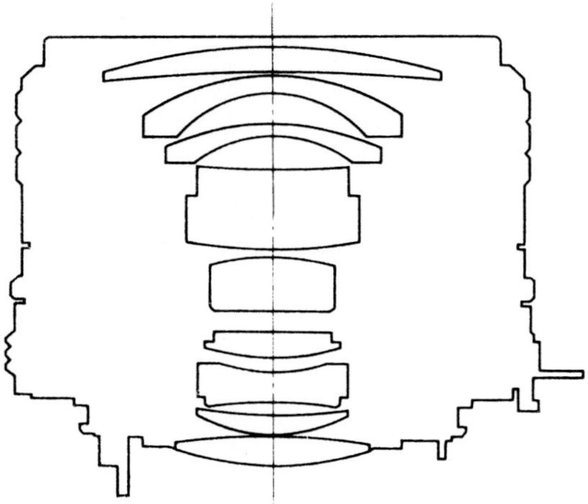

DESCRIPTION

Popular wide-angle lens utilizing standard 52mm lens front attachments. "Floating element" design, coupled to focusing ring, provides automatic correction of image quality at close distances. Unusually compact with relatively high-speed aperture of *f*/2.8 for this focal length. Applications include architectural exteriors and interiors, landscapes, travel, and candid, manually focused "grab" shots. Macro performance in reverse mode best at *f*/8 with image quality loss at smaller apertures.

SPECIFICATIONS

Smallest aperture: 22
Nearest focus distance: 0.3m (1 ft)
Subject field at nearest distance: 21.8 × 32.8cm
Image ratio at nearest distance: 1:9
Focusing distances:
  One head vertical: 0.35m (1.12 ft) subject to perspective distortion
  Two heads horizontal: 0.45m (1.5 ft) subject to perspective distortion
  One to three adults standing: 1.5m (5 ft)
Angles of view:
  Diagonal: 84°
  Horizontal: 74°
  Vertical: 53°
Ratio of image size at infinity to image of 50mm lens: 0.48:1
Attachment size (inside screw diameter): 52mm (P = 0.75)
Lens hood: HN-1
Front lens cap: 52mm snap-on
Lens case: CL-31, flexible pouch 54, plastic case CP-1
Overall size: 63.5mm ϕ × 58mm
Weight: 270g (9.5 oz)

DEPTH OF FIELD TABLE

(m)

focus distance	depth of field							reproduction ratio
	f/2.8	f/4	f/5.6	f/8	f/11	f/16	f/22	
0.3	0.292–0.308	0.289–0.312	0.285–0.318	0.279–0.326	0.272–0.337	0.262–0.359	0.251–0.390	1/8.8
0.35	0.338–0.363	0.334–0.369	0.328–0.377	0.319–0.390	0.310–0.408	0.295–0.443	0.280–0.498	1/11
0.4	0.384–0.418	0.378–0.426	0.369–0.438	0.358–0.457	0.345–0.484	0.326–0.539	0.307–0.629	1/13
0.5	0.473–0.531	0.463–0.546	0.449–0.567	0.431–0.603	0.411–0.655	0.382–0.772	0.353–0.996	1/17
0.7	0.644–0.769	0.622–0.804	0.597–0.855	0.562–0.949	0.525–1.10	0.475–1.53	0.428–3.03	1/25
1	0.882–1.16	0.840–1.25	0.791–1.38	0.738–1.67	0.663–2.27	0.580–5.95	0.507–∞	1/38
1.5	1.24–1.91	1.15–2.18	1.06–2.67	0.94–4.09	0.83–12.8	0.70–∞	0.59–∞	1/58
3	2.08–5.50	1.84–8.64	1.60–37.7	1.34–∞	1.12–∞	0.88–∞	0.713–∞	1/120
∞	6.46–∞	4.55–∞	3.27–∞	2.31–∞	1.71–∞	1.20–∞	0.894–∞	1/∞

28mm *f*/2 NIKKOR

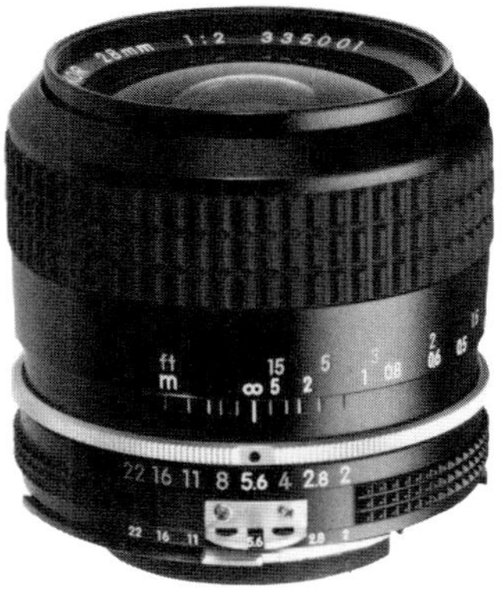

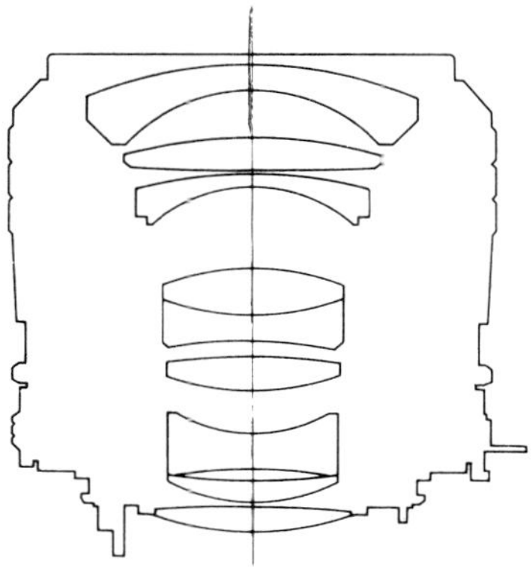

DESCRIPTION

Exceptionally wide *f*/2 aperture makes this lens unusually attractive for existing-light photography. Wide aperture extremely useful in focusing under dim-light conditions. "Floating element" coupled to focusing ring maintains image quality at close-focusing distances. Recommended for news and magazine photographers. Applications in industrial, architectural, commercial, travel, and landscape photography. Close focusing at 0.3m (1 ft) offers flexible depth-of-field control depending on selected aperture. For macro work in reverse mode on bellows, image quality best at apertures *f*/8 to *f*/11; in normal mode, image quality improves the further lens is stopped down. Unsuitable for copying.

SPECIFICATIONS

Smallest aperture: 22
Nearest focus distance: 0.3m (1 ft)
Subject field at nearest distance: 17 × 25.6cm
Image ratio at nearest distance: 1:7
Focusing distances:
- One head vertical: 0.5m (1.75 ft) subject to perspective distortion
- Two heads horizontal: 0.6m (2.1 ft) subject to perspective distortion
- One to three adults standing: 1.7m (5.5 ft)

Angles of view:
- Diagonal: 74°
- Horizontal: 64°
- Vertical: 45°30′

Ratio of image size at infinity to image of 50mm lens: 0.56:1
Attachment size (inside screw diameter): 52mm (P = 0.75)
Lens hood: HN-1
Front lens cap: 52mm snap-on
Lens case: CL-31, flexible pouch 54, plastic case CP-1
Overall size: 64.5mm ϕ × 70.5mm
Weight: 355g (12.5 oz)

DEPTH OF FIELD TABLE

Meters

m \ f/	2	2.8	4	5.6	8	11	16	22	Magnification
0.3	0.296—0.304	0.295—0.306	0.293—0.308	0.290—0.312	0.286—0.317	0.280—0.325	0.273—0.337	0.264—0.356	1/7.1
0.35	0.344—0.356	0.342—0.359	0.339—0.362	0.334—0.368	0.329—0.376	0.321—0.383	0.310—0.408	0.297—0.440	1/8.9
0.4	0.392—0.409	0.389—0.412	0.384—0.418	0.378—0.426	0.370—0.437	0.360—0.456	0.345—0.485	0.328—0.536	1/11
0.5	0.486—0.515	0.481—0.521	0.473—0.531	0.463—0.545	0.450—0.567	0.432—0.602	0.410—0.661	0.384—0.772	1/14
0.6	0.579—0.623	0.571—0.633	0.559—0.648	0.544—0.671	0.525—0.707	0.500—0.766	0.469—0.872	0.433—1.09	1/18
0.8	0.760—0.845	0.745—0.866	0.724—0.896	0.697—0.944	0.663—1.02	0.621—1.16	0.571—1.45	0.514—2.29	1/25
1	0.936—1.07	0.912—1.11	0.880—1.16	0.839—1.25	0.788—1.40	0.727—1.69	0.656—2.42	0.580—6.71	1/32
2	1.74 —2.36	1.65 —2.55	1.54 —2.88	1.41— 3.54	1.26 —5.27	1.10 —17.8	0.935—∞	0.777—∞	1/67
5	3.59 —8.30	3.22 —11.5	2.81 —25.2	2.39 —∞	1.97 —∞	1.59 —∞	1.26 —∞	0.976—∞	1/172
∞	12.4 —∞	8.77 —∞	6.23 —∞	4.43 —∞	3.16 —∞	2.26 —∞	1.63 —∞	1.18 —∞	1/∞

28mm *f*/2.8 NIKKOR

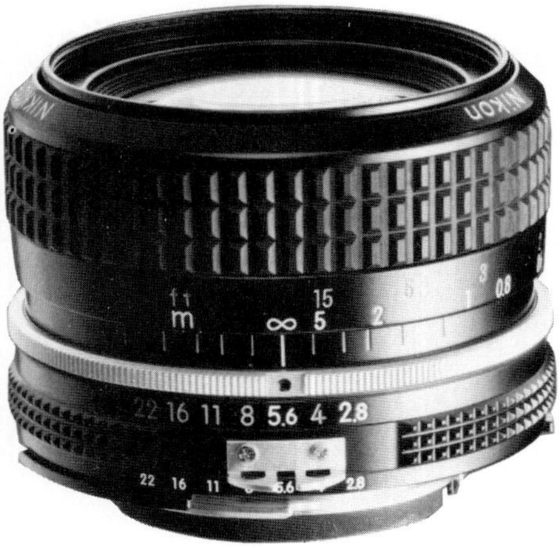

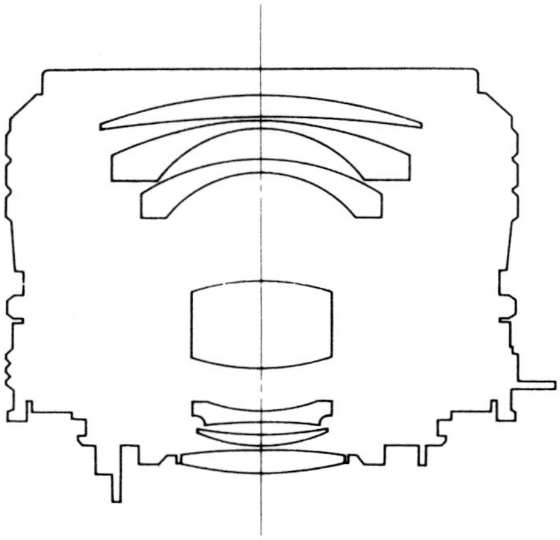

DESCRIPTION

The 28mm *f*/2.8 is a relatively fast, lightweight, and compact wide-angle lens. A favorite of photojournalists and candid "street" photographers, the 28mm also has applications in industrial, architectural, commercial, travel, and landscape photography. The application of Nikon Integrated Coating on air-glass surfaces minimizes ghost and flare for improved contrast and color rendition.

SPECIFICATIONS

Smallest aperture: 22
Nearest focus distance: 0.3m (1 ft)
Subject field at nearest distance: 17 × 25.6cm
Image ratio at nearest distance: 1:7
Focusing distances:
- One head vertical: 0.5m (1.75 ft) subject to perspective distortion
- Two heads horizontal: 0.6m (2.1 ft) subject to perspective distortion
- One to three adults standing: 1.7m (5.5 ft)

Angles of view:
- Diagonal: 74°
- Horizontal: 64°
- Vertical: 45°30′

Ratio of image size at infinity to image of 50mm lens: 0.56:1
Attachment size (inside screw diameter): 52mm (P = 0.75)
Lens hood: HN-2
Front lens cap: 52mm snap-on
Lens case: CL-31, flexible pouch 54, plastic case CP-1
Overall size: 63.5mm ø × 56.5mm
Weight: 245g (8.7 oz)

DEPTH OF FIELD TABLE

(m)

focus distance	depth of field							repro-duction ratio
	f/2.8	4	5.6	8	11	16	22	
0.3	0.294–0.306	0.292–0.309	0.289–0.313	0.284–0.318	0.279–0.326	0.271–0.340	0.262–0.360	1/7.5
0.35	0.341–0.359	0.338–0.363	0.333–0.369	0.327–0.378	0.319–0.390	0.307–0.413	0.295–0.445	1/9.3
0.4	0.388–0.413	0.383–0.419	0.377–0.427	0.368–0.440	0.358–0.458	0.342–0.491	0.326–0.541	1/11
0.5	0.480–0.522	0.472–0.533	0.462–0.547	0.447–0.571	0.431–0.604	0.406–0.670	0.381–0.776	1/15
0.6	0.570–0.634	0.558–0.650	0.543–0.673	0.522–0.712	0.498–0.767	0.464–0.885	0.430–1.09	1/18
0.8	0.744–0.867	0.722–0.899	0.696–0.947	0.660–1.03	0.620–1.16	0.565–1.48	0.513–2.25	1/25
1	0.911–1.11	0.877–1.17	0.837–1.25	0.784–1.41	0.727–1.68	0.650–2.48	0.579–6.12	1/32
2	1.65–2.55	1.54–2.89	1.41–3.53	1.26–5.33	1.11–15.1	0.927–∞	0.781–∞	1/67
5	3.23–11.4	2.80–25.5	2.39–∞	1.96–∞	1.61–∞	1.25–∞	0.987–∞	1/172
∞	8.85–∞	6.22–∞	4.46–∞	3.15–∞	2.31–∞	1.62–∞	1.20–∞	1/∞

28mm *f*/3.5 NIKKOR

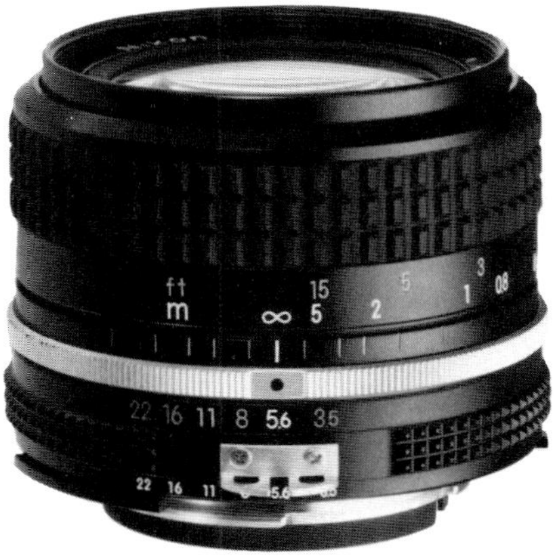

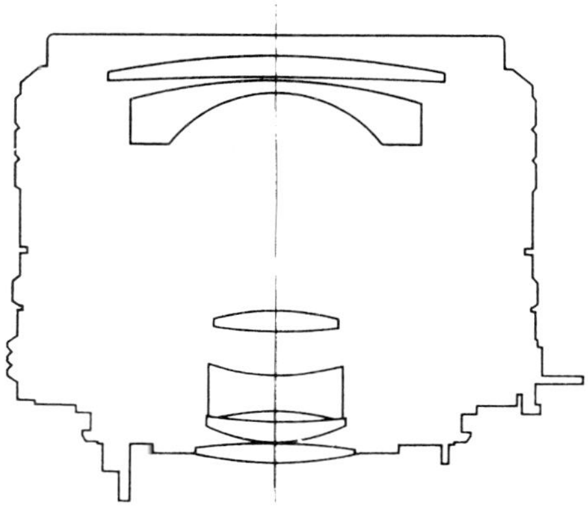

DESCRIPTION

Long-standing favorite, general-purpose, wide-angle lens adequate for most lighting situations other than dim light. Retrofocus design, unusually compact. Vivid contrast and brilliance even at full aperture with minimum coma and distortion. Corrected for spherical aberrations, eliminating displacement of focus as diaphragm is stopped down. Optimal aperture *f*/5.6, but if maximum corner correction desired stop down to *f*/11 or *f*/16. On bellows for macro work in reverse mode image quality best at *f*/8; in normal mode, stopping down improves image quality. Unsuitable for copying.

SPECIFICATIONS

Smallest aperture: 22
Nearest focus distance: 0.3m (1 ft)
Subject field at nearest distance: 17 × 25.6cm
Image ratio at nearest distance: 1:7
Focusing distances:
One head vertical: 0.5m (1.75 ft) subject to perspective distortion
Two heads horizontal: 0.6m (2.1 ft) subject to perspective distortion
One to three adults standing: 1.7m (5.5 ft)
Angles of view:
Diagonal: 74°
Horizontal: 64°
Vertical: 45°30′
Ratio of image size at infinity to image of 50mm lens: 0.56:1
Attachment size (inside screw diameter): 52mm (P = 0.75)
Lens hood: HN-2
Front lens cap: 52mm snap-on
Lens case: CL-31, flexible pouch 54, plastic case CP-1
Overall size: 63.5mm ⌀ × 58.5mm
Weight: 235g (8.3 oz)

DEPTH OF FIELD TABLE

(m)

focus distance	depth of field							reproduction ratio
	f/3.5	f/4	f/5.6	f/8	f/11	f/16	f/22	
0.3	0.293–0.308	0.292–0.309	0.289–0.312	0.284–0.318	0.279–0.326	0.271–0.340	0.262–0.359	1/7.4
0.35	0.339–0.361	0.338–0.363	0.334–0.369	0.327–0.378	0.319–0.390	0.308–0.412	0.295–0.444	1/9.2
0.4	0.385–0.416	0.383–0.419	0.377–0.427	0.368–0.440	0.358–0.457	0.343–0.490	0.326–0.539	1/11
0.5	0.475–0.528	0.472–0.532	0.462–0.547	0.448–0.570	0.431–0.603	0.407–0.669	0.382–0.774	1/15
0.6	0.563–0.643	0.558–0.650	0.543–0.673	0.522–0.711	0.499–0.766	0.465–0.883	0.431–1.09	1/18
0.8	0.731–0.885	0.723–0.899	0.696–0.946	0.660–1.03	0.621–1.16	0.566–1.47	0.514–2.23	1/25
1	0.891–1.14	0.878–1.17	0.838–1.25	0.784–1.41	0.728–1.672	0.651–2.47	0.580–6.05	1/32
2	1.58–2.74	1.54–2.89	1.41–3.53	1.26–5.32	1.11–15.0	0.29–∞	0.782–∞	1/67
5	2.97–16.8	2.81–25.4	2.39–∞	1.97–∞	1.61–∞	1.25–∞	0.988–∞	1/172
∞	7.10–∞	6.22–∞	4.47–∞	3.15–∞	2.31–∞	1.62–∞	1.20–∞	1/∞

35mm *f*/1.4 NIKKOR

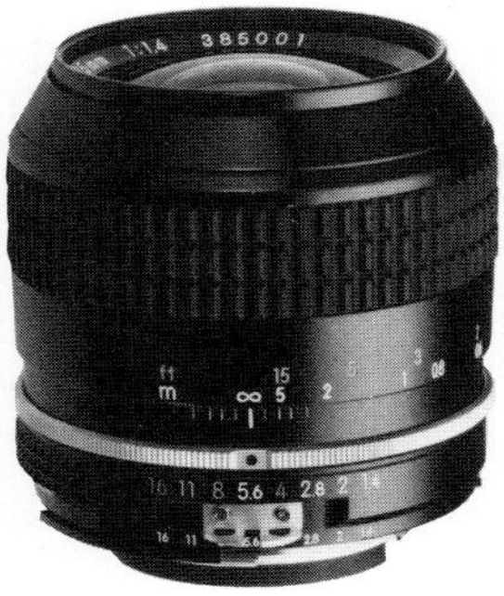

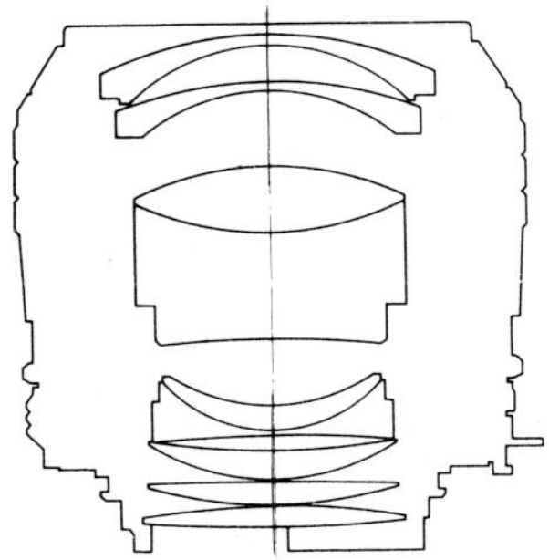

DESCRIPTION

Combination of high speed of *f*/1.4—fastest Nikkor wide-angle lens—and close-focusing "floating element" correction down to 0.3m (1 ft) makes this one of the most versatile of optical tools. 35mm focal length used by many as alternative to standard 50mm. Wide aperture extremely useful in focusing under dim-light conditions. Excellent for documentary photography and people reportage where normalcy of perspective rendition is important, but wider coverage is desired with slightly enhanced depth of field: also, greater foreground dominance with only slight subordination of background. For macro work in reverse mode on bellows, image quality best at *f*/11; in normal mode, image quality improves with stopping down. Not recommended for copying.

SPECIFICATIONS

Smallest aperture: 16
Nearest focus distance: 0.3m (1 ft)
Subject field at nearest distance: 13.2 × 19.8cm
Image ratio at nearest distance: 1:5.5
Focusing distances:
 One head vertical: 0.5m (1.7 ft) subject to perspective distortion
 Two heads horizontal: 0.6m (2.1 ft) subject to perspective distortion
 One to three adults standing: 2.1m (7 ft)
Angles of view:
 Diagonal: 62°
 Horizontal: 53°
 Vertical: 37°
Ratio of image size at infinity to image of 50mm lens: 0.7:1
Attachment size (inside screw diameter): 52mm (P = 0.75)
Lens hood: HN-3
Front lens cap: 52mm snap-on
Lens case: CL-32, flexible pouch 54, plastic case CP-1
Overall size: 67.5mm ø × 74mm
Weight: 400g (14.1 oz)

DEPTH OF FIELD TABLE

Meters

m \ f/	1.4	2	2.8	4	5.6	8	11	16	22	Magnification
0.3	0.298−0.302	0.298−0.302	0.297−0.303	0.294−0.305	0.294−0.307	0.291−0.310	0.288−0.314	0.283−0.321	0.277−0.330	1/5.5
0.35	0.347−0.353	0.346−0.354	0.345−0.355	0.343−0.357	0.340−0.361	0.336−0.365	0.332−0.372	0.324−0.383	0.316−0.397	1/6.9
0.4	0.396−0.404	0.395−0.405	0.393−0.407	0.390−0.411	0.386−0.415	0.381−0.422	0.374−0.431	0.364−0.448	0.352−0.470	1/8.3
0.45	0.445−0.455	0.443−0.457	0.441−0.460	0.437−0.464	0.432−0.471	0.424−0.480	0.416−0.493	0.402−0.516	0.387−0.547	1/9.7
0.5	0.494−0.506	0.491−0.509	0.488−0.513	0.483−0.519	0.476−0.527	0.467−0.539	0.456−0.556	0.439−0.587	0.421−0.631	1/11
0.6	0.591−0.610	0.587−0.614	0.583−0.620	0.574−0.629	0.564−0.642	0.550−0.662	0.534−0.690	0.509−0.742	0.483−0.818	1/14
0.7	0.687−0.714	0.681−0.720	0.674−0.729	0.663−0.742	0.650−0.761	0.630−0.791	0.608−0.832	0.575−0.913	0.541−1.04	1/17
0.8	0.782−0.819	0.774−0.828	0.765−0.839	0.751−0.858	0.733−0.883	0.708−0.925	0.679−0.985	0.637−1.11	0.594−1.30	1/19
1	0.971−1.03	0.959−1.05	0.943−1.07	0.921−1.10	0.893−1.14	0.854−1.22	0.811−1.33	0.749−1.57	0.688−2.02	1/25
1.5	1.48 −1.58	1.40 −1.61	1.37 −1.66	1.32 −1.74	1.26 −1.87	1.18 −2.09	1.09 −2.46	0.979−3.53	0.871−7.60	1/39
2	1.88 −2.14	1.83 −2.21	1.77 −2.31	1.68 −2.47	1.59 −2.74	1.46 −3.26	1.33 −4.31	1.16 −9.47	1.01 −∞	1/53
5	4.26 −6.06	4.01 −6.67	3.71 −7.70	3.35 −10.1	2.96 −17.0	2.53 −∞	2.14 −∞	1.71 −∞	1.39 −∞	1/136
∞	27.9 −∞	19.6−∞	14.0 −∞	9.83 −∞	7.05 −∞	4.96 −∞	3.63 −∞	2.53 −∞	1.87 −∞	1/∞

35mm *f*/2 NIKKOR

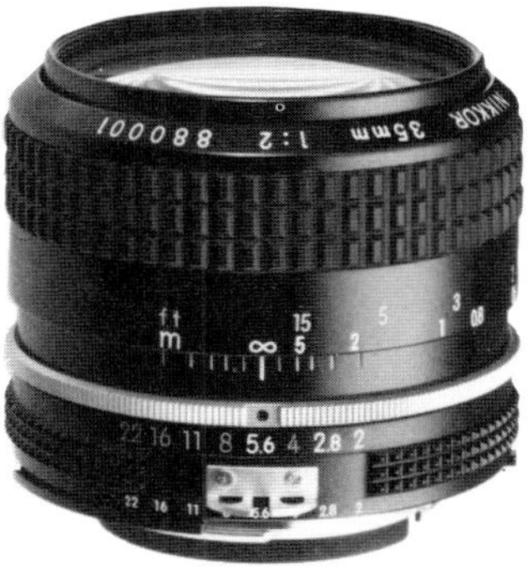

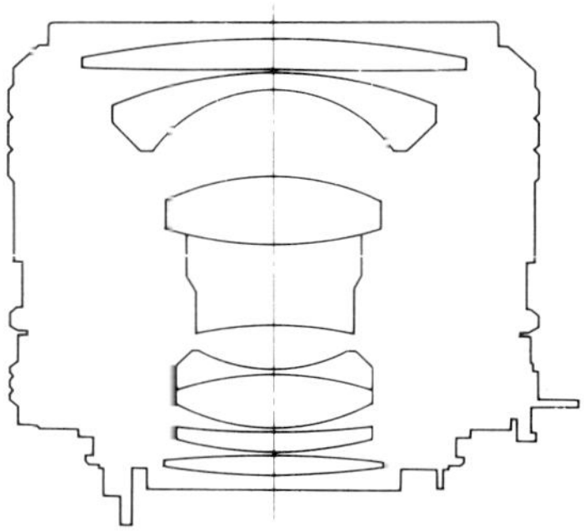

DESCRIPTION

Relatively high-speed *f*/2 aperture provides ability to work under wide range of lighting conditions other than very poor. Advantages of wide-aperture focusing, near-focusing distance of 0.3m (1 ft), and compact retrofocus design make this a preferred selection. Optical design eliminates coma and other aberrations to give crisply sharp picture of high contrast at full lens aperture with optimum performance in range of *f*/4 to *f*/5.6. As general-purpose lens it covers more scene with selectivity governed by working distance. For macro work in reverse mode on bellows, image quality best at *f*/8; in normal mode, image quality improves with stopping down.

SPECIFICATIONS

Smallest aperture: 22
Nearest focus distance: 0.3m (1 ft)
Subject field at nearest distance: 13.7 × 20.5cm
Image ratio at nearest distance: 1:5.7
Focusing distances:
- One head vertical: 0.5m (1.7 ft) subject to perspective distortion
- Two heads horizontal: 0.6m (2.1 ft) subject to perspective distortion
- One to three adults standing: 2.1m (7 ft)

Angles of view:
- Diagonal: 62°
- Horizontal: 53°
- Vertical: 37°

Ratio of image size at infinity to image of 50mm lens: 0.7:1
Attachment size (inside screw diameter): 52mm (P = 0.75)
Lens hood: HN-3
Front lens cap: 52mm snap-on
Lens case: CL-31, flexible pouch 54, plastic case CP-1
Overall size: 63.5mm ø × 63.5mm
Weight: 280g (9.9 oz)

DEPTH OF FIELD TABLE

Meters

m \ f/	2	2.8	4	5.6	8	11	16	22	Magnification
0.3	0.298–0.302	0.297–0.303	0.294–0.305	0.294–0.307	0.291–0.310	0.238–0.314	0.283–0.321	0.277–0.330	1/5.5
0.35	0.346–0.354	0.345–0.355	0.343–0.357	0.340–0.361	0.336–0.365	0.332–0.372	0.324–0.383	0.316–0.397	1/6.9
0.4	0.395–0.405	0.393–0.407	0.390–0.411	0.386–0.4[illegible]5	0.381–0.422	0.374–0.431	0.364–0.448	0.352–0.470	1/8.3
0.45	0.443–0.457	0.441–0.460	0.437–0.464	0.432–0.471	0.424–0.480	0.416–0.493	0.402–0.516	0.387–0.547	1/9.7
0.5	0.491–0.509	0.488–0.513	0.483–0.519	0.476–0.527	0.467–0.539	0.456–0.556	0.439–0.587	0.421–0.631	1/11
0.6	0.587–0.614	0.583–0.620	0.574–0.629	0.564–0.642	0.550–0.662	0.534–0.690	0.509–0.742	0.483–0.818	1/14
0.7	0.681–0.720	0.674–0.729	0.663–0.742	0.650–0.761	0.630–0.791	0.608–0.832	0.575–0.913	0.541–1.04	1/17
0.8	0.774–0.828	0.765–0.839	0.751–0.858	0.733–0.883	0.708–0.925	0.679–0.985	0.637–1.11	0.594–1.30	1/19
1	0.959–1.05	0.943–1.07	0.921–1.10	0.893–1.1[illegible]	0.854–1.22	0.8[illegible]1–1.33	0.749–1.57	0.688–2.02	1/25
1.5	1.40 –1.61	1.37 –1.66	1.32 –1.74	1.26 –1.8[illegible]	1.18 –2.09	1.09 –2.46	0.979–3.53	0.871–7.60	1/39
2	1.83 –2.21	1.77 –2.31	1.68 –2.47	1.59 –2.7[illegible]	1.46 –3.26	1.33 –4.31	1.16 –9.47	1.01 –∞	1/53
5	4.01 –6.67	3.71 –7.70	3.35 –10.1	2.96 –17.0	2.53 –∞	2.14 –∞	1.71 –∞	1.39 –∞	1/136
∞	19.6–∞	14.0 –∞	9.83 –∞	7.05 –∞	4.96 –∞	3.63 –∞	2.53 –∞	1.87 –∞	1/∞

35mm *f*/2.8 NIKKOR

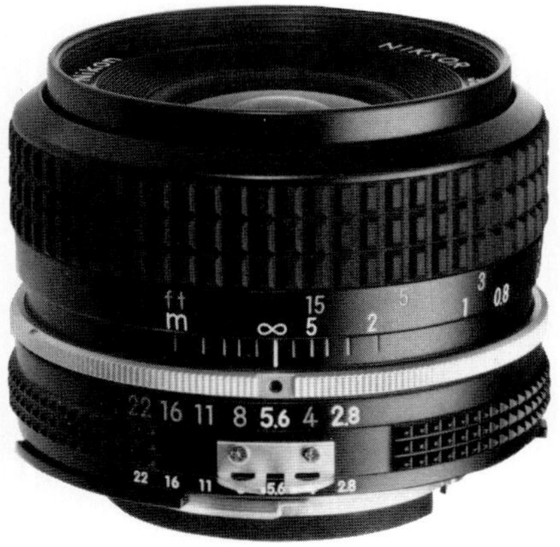

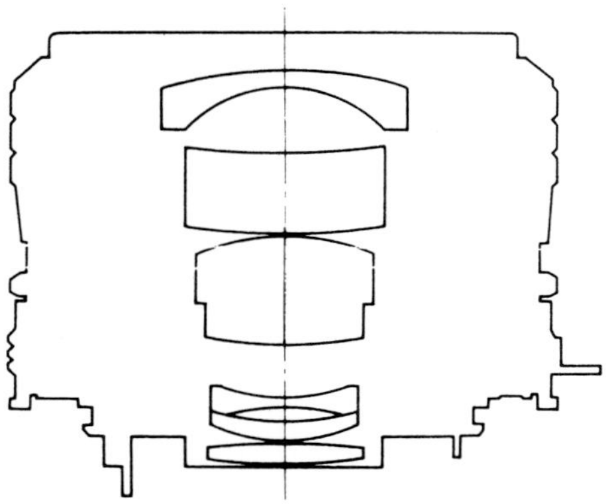

DESCRIPTION

Among 35mm lens options, if existing-light (low-level) photography is not a governing requirement this highly compact retrofocus-type lens, which offers close focusing down to 0.3m (1 ft), is an excellent choice. As general-purpose lens it covers more scene with selectivity governed by working distance. For macro work in reverse mode on bellows, image quality best at *f*/8; in normal mode, image quality improves with stopping down.

SPECIFICATIONS

Smallest aperture: 22
Nearest focus distance: 0.3m (1 ft)
Subject field at nearest distance: 13.9 × 20.9cm
Image ratio at nearest distance: 1:5.8
Focusing distances:
  One head vertical: 0.5m (1.7 ft) subject to perspective distortion
  Two heads horizontal: 0.6m (2.1 ft) subject to perspective distortion
  One to three adults standing: 2.1m (7 ft)
Angles of view:
  Diagonal: 62°
  Horizontal: 53°
  Vertical: 37°
Ratio of image size at infinity to image of 50mm lens: 0.7:1
Attachment size (inside screw diameter): 52mm (P = 0.75)
Lens hood: HN-3
Front lens cap: 52mm snap-on
Lens case: CL-31, flexible pouch 54, plastic case CP-1
Overall size: 63.5mm ϕ × 56.5mm
Weight: 240g (8.5 oz)

DEPTH OF FIELD TABLE

Meters

m \ f/	2.8	4	5.6	8	11	16	22	Magnification
0.3	0.297–0.303	0.294–0.305	0.294–0.307	0.291–0.310	0.288–0.314	0.283–0.321	0.277–0.330	1/5.5
0.35	0.345–0.355	0.343–0.357	0.340–0.361	0.336–0.365	0.332–0.372	0.324–0.383	0.316–0.397	1/6.9
0.4	0.393–0.407	0.390–0.411	0.386–0.415	0.381–0.422	0.374–0.431	0.364–0.448	0.352–0.470	1/8.3
0.45	0.441–0.460	0.437–0.464	0.432–0.471	0.424–0.480	0.416–0.493	0.402–0.516	0.387–0.547	1/9.7
0.5	0.488–0.513	0.483–0.519	0.476–0.527	0.467–0.539	0.456–0.556	0.439–0.587	0.421–0.631	1/11
0.6	0.583–0.620	0.574–0.629	0.564–0.642	0.550–0.662	0.534–0.690	0.509–0.742	0.483–0.818	1/14
0.7	0.674–0.729	0.663–0.742	0.650–0.761	0.630–0.791	0.608–0.832	0.575–0.913	0.541–1.04	1/17
0.8	0.765–0.839	0.751–0.858	0.733–0.883	0.708–0.925	0.679–0.985	0.637–1.11	0.594–1.30	1/19
1	0.943–1.07	0.921–1.10	0.893–1.14	0.854–1.22	0.811–1.33	0.749–1.57	0.688–2.02	1/25
1.5	1.37 –1.66	1.32 –1.74	1.26 –1.87	1.18 –2.09	1.09 –2.46	0.979–3.53	0.871–7.60	1/39
2	1.77 –2.31	1.68 –2.47	1.59 –2.74	1.46 –3.26	1.33 –4.31	1.16 –9.47	1.01 –∞	1/53
5	3.71 –7.70	3.35 –10.1	2.96 –17.0	2.53 –∞	2.14 –∞	1.71 –∞	1.39 –∞	1/136
∞	14.0 –∞	9.83 –∞	7.05 –∞	4.96 –∞	3.63 –∞	2.53 –∞	1.87 –∞	1/∞

50mm *f*/1.2 NIKKOR

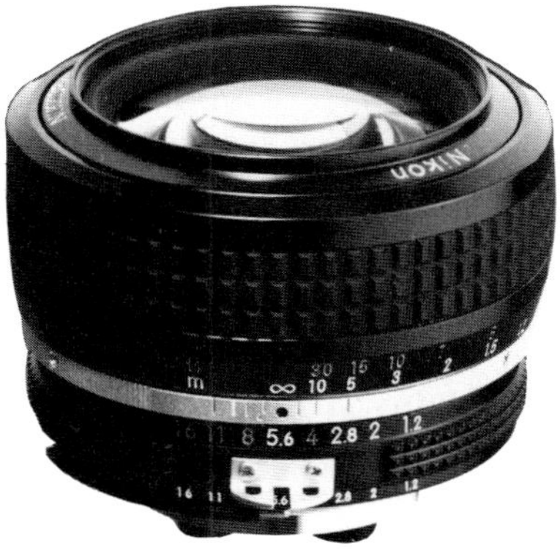

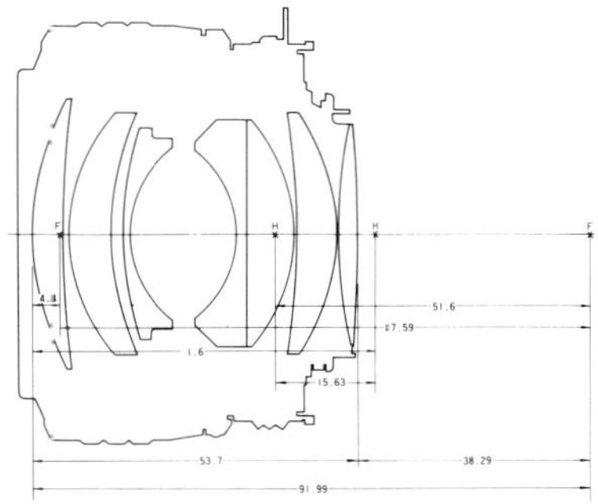

DESCRIPTION

The advantages of the 50mm *f*/1.2 Nikkor are twofold. The first is that the lens can be used in low-light-level shooting, either indoors or outdoors under very dull conditions, particularly when working with very slow color film. The second advantage is ease of focusing. The resultant bright image appears on the viewing screen. The lens has very little depth of field at its maximum aperture, which can help the creative photographer achieve interesting selective focusing effects.

SPECIFICATIONS

Smallest aperture: 16
Nearest focus distance: 0.5m (1.7 ft)
Subject field at nearest distance: 23.1 × 34.6cm
Image ratio at nearest distance: 1:10
Focusing distances:
One head vertical: 0.7m (2.25 ft) subject to perspective distortion
Two heads horizontal: 0.9m (3 ft) subject to perspective distortion
One to three adults standing: 3m (10 ft)
Angles of view:
Diagonal: 46°
Horizontal: 39°
Vertical: 26°
Attachment size (inside screw diameter): 52mm (P = 0.75)
Lens hood: HR-2
Front lens cap: 52mm snap-on
Lens case: CL-34A, flexible pouch 54, plastic case CP-1
Overall size: 70.5mm ø × 59mm
Weight: 340g (14.4 oz)

DEPTH OF FIELD TABLE

(m)

focus distance	depth of field									repro-duction ratio
	f/1.2	f/1.4	f/2	f/2.8	f/4	f/5.6	f/8	f/11	f/16	
0.5	0.497–0.503	0.497–0.503	0.495–0.505	0.494–0.507	0.491–0.510	0.487–0.513	0.482–0.5 9	0.476–0.527	0.466–0.541	1/7.9
0.55	0.547–0.554	0.546–0.554	0.544–0.556	0.542–0.558	0.539–0.562	0.534–0.567	0.528–0.574	0.520–0.584	0.508–0.602	1/8.8
0.6	0.596–0.604	0.595–0.605	0.593–0.607	0.590–0.610	0.585–0.615	0.581–0.621	0.573–0.630	0.564–0.642	0.549–0.664	1/9.8
0.7	0.694–0.706	0.693–0.707	0.690–0.710	0.686–0.714	0.681–0.721	0.673–0.729	0.662–0.743	0.649–0.761	0.629–0.793	1/12
0.8	0.792–0.808	0.791–0.810	0.787–0.814	0.782–0.819	0.771–0.828	0.764–0.840	0.750–0.858	0.733–0.883	0.706–0.927	1/14
0.9	0.890–0.911	0.888–0.912	0.883–0.918	0.876–0.925	0.867–0.936	0.854–0.952	0.836–0.976	0.814–1.01	0.781–1.07	1/16
1	0.987–1.01	0.985–1.02	0.979–1.02	0.970–1.03	0.953–1.05	0.943–1.07	0.920–1.10	0.894–1.14	0.853–1.22	1/18
1.2	1.18–1.22	1.18–1.22	1.17–1.23	1.16–1.25	1.14–1.27	1.12–1.30	1.08–1.35	1.05–1.41	0.990–1.54	1/22
1.5	1.47–1.53	1.46–1.54	1.45–1.55	1.43–1.58	1.40–1.61	1.37–1.66	1.32–1.74	1.26–1.86	.18–2.08	1/27
2	1.95–2.06	1.94–2.07	1.91–2.10	1.88–2.14	1.83–2.21	1.77–2.30	1.69–2.47	1.59–2.71	46–3.24	1/37
3	2.88–3.14	2.86–3.16	2.80–3.23	2.73–3.34	2.62–3.51	2.50–3.76	2.33–4.23	2.16–5.01	92–7.25	1/56
5	4.66–5.40	4.67–5.47	4.46–5.70	4.27–6.03	4.02–6.62	3.73–7.62	3.37–9.85	3.01–15.6	2.55–836	1/95
10	8.71–11.7	8.53–12.1	8.02–13.3	7.43–15.3	6.70–19.9	5.92–33.0	5.05–4530	4.27–∞	3.40–∞	1/192
∞	66.7–∞	57.1–∞	40.0–∞	28.6–∞	20.1–∞	14.4–∞	10.1–∞	7.35–∞	5.08–∞	1/∞

50mm *f*/1.4 NIKKOR

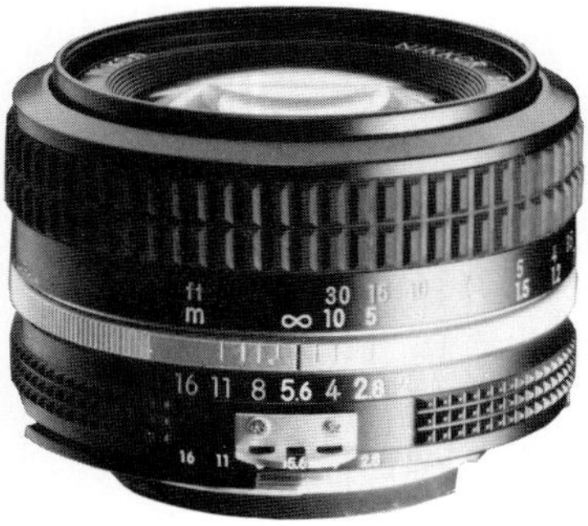

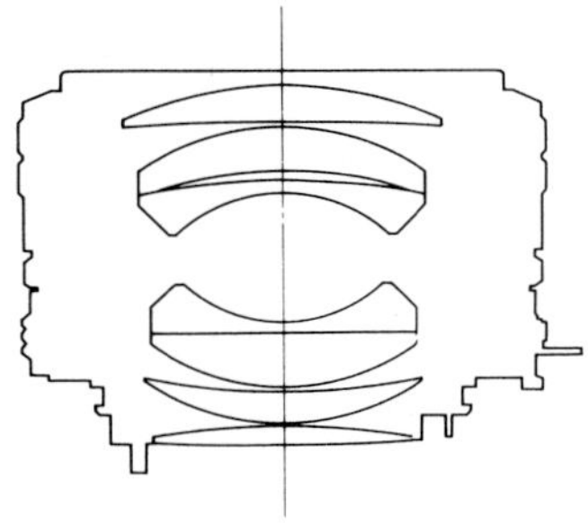

DESCRIPTION

Standard or nomal lens approximates angle of view of human eye to produce natural perspectives. Middle-ground objects rendered with greater dominance while retaining adequate background scale. When working close, background limited in coverage and sharpness. Easy-focusing lens due to exceptionally bright viewfinder image and shallow depth of field. Displacement of focus resulting from stopping down is virtually eliminated. At full aperture, but vignetting, but critical focusing needed due to shallow depth of field. Excellent performance at full aperture with flare potential eliminated through integrated multi-layer coating on air surfaces of individual elements. When used for macro work in reverse mode on bellows, corner image quality deteriorates at low image ratios; in normal mode, image quality improves with stopping down of lens. Not suitable for copying.

SPECIFICATIONS

Smallest aperture: 16
Nearest focus distance: 0.45m (1.5 ft)
Subject field at nearest distance: 20.8 × 31.2cm
Image ratio at nearest distance: 1:8.7
Focusing distances:
  One head vertical: 0.7m (2.25 ft) subject to perspective distortion
  Two heads horizontal: 0.9m (3 ft) subject to perspective distortion
  One to three adults standing: 3m (10 ft)
Angles of view:
  Diagonal: 46°
  Horizontal: 39°
  Vertical: 26°
Attachment size (inside screw diameter): 52mm (P = 0.75)
Lens hood: HS-5, HR-1
Front lens cap: 52mm snap-on
Lens case: CL-34A, flexible pouch 54, plastic case CP-1
Overall size: 64mm ϕ × 51.5mm
Weight: 255g (9oz)

DEPTH OF FIELD TABLE

Meters

m \ f/	1.4	2	2.8	4	5.6	8	11	16	Magnification
0.6	0.595−0.605	0.593−0.607	0.591−0.610	0.587−0.614	0.582−0.620	0.574−0.628	0.564−0.641	0.551−0.660	1/9.8
0.7	0.693−0.707	0.691−0.710	0.687−0.714	0.681−0.720	0.674−0.728	0.664−0.741	0.650−0.760	0.631−0.788	1/12
0.8	0.791−0.809	0.787−0.813	0.782−0.819	0.775−0.827	0.765−0.839	0.751−0.856	0.733−0.882	0.709−0.921	1/14
0.9	0.888−0.912	0.883−0.917	0.877−0.925	0.868−0.935	0.855−0.951	0.837−0.974	0.814−1.01	0.784−1.06	1/16
1	0.985−1.02	0.979−1.02	0.971−1.03	0.959−1.04	0.943−1.06	0.922−1.09	0.893−1.14	0.856−1.21	1/18
1.2	1.18 −1.22	1.17 −1.23	1.16 −1.25	1.14 −1.27	1.12 −1.30	1.09 −1.34	1.05 −1.41	0.994−1.52	1/22
1.5	1.47 −1.54	1.45 −1.55	1.43 −1.58	1.41 −1.61	1.37 −1.66	1.32 −1.74	1.26 −1.86	1.18 −2.06	1/27
1.7	1.66 −1.75	1.64 −1.77	1.61 −1.80	1.58 −1.84	1.53 −1.91	1.47 −2.01	1.40 −2.18	1.30 −2.48	1/31
2	1.94 −2.07	1.91 −2.10	1.88 −2.14	1.83 −2.20	1.77 −2.30	1.69 −2.46	1.59 −2.72	1.46 −3.20	1/37
3	2.86 −3.16	2.80 −3.23	2.73 −3.34	2.63 −3.50	2.50 −3.76	2.34 −4.21	2.14 −5.06	1.92 −7.10	1/56
5	4.61 −5.46	4.46 −5.69	4.27 −6.04	4.03 −6.61	3.73 −7.63	3.37 −9.77	2.98 −16.2	2.55 −∞	1/95
10	8.53 −12.1	8.03 −13.3	7.42 −15.4	6.71 −19.8	5.90 −33.3	5.05 −∞	4.20 −∞	3.39 −∞	1/192
∞	57.2 −∞	40.1 −∞	28.4 −∞	20.1 −∞	14.2 −∞	10.1 −∞	7.16 −∞	5.09 −∞	1/∞

50mm *f*/1.8 NIKKOR

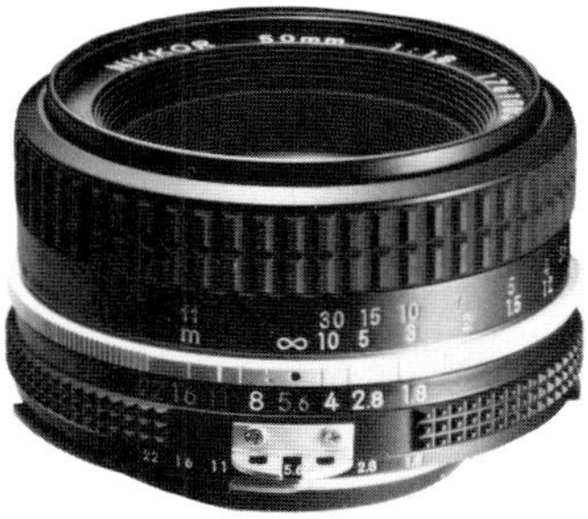

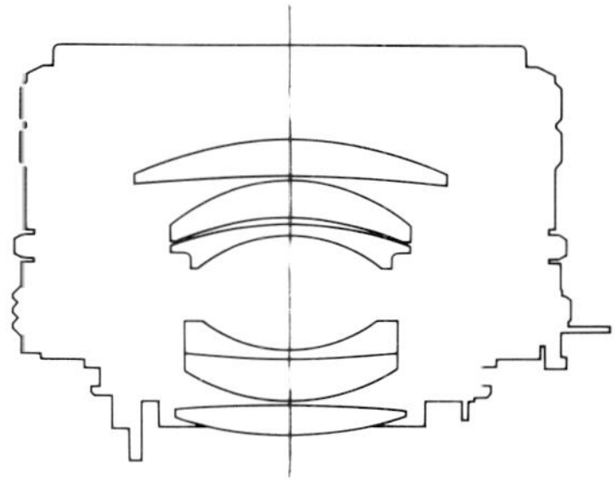

DESCRIPTION

The Nikkor 50mm *f*/1.8 is ideally suited for general photography, including travel and scenics, group shots, and full-length portarits. The lens is well-suited for close-up work such as document copying, still lifes, and flower photography, especially when used in the reverse mode with various Nikon extension and close-up accessories. The Nikon Teleconverter TC-200 doubles the effective focal length of the lens, while permitting the lens to be focused to its minimum focusing distance of 0.45m (1.5 ft). When the Teleconverter TC-200 is used, the aperture ring of the lens should not be set to an aperture greater than *f*/2.

SPECIFICATIONS

Smallest aperture: 22
Nearest focus distance: 0.45m (1.5 ft)
Subject field at nearest distance: 20.8 × 31.2cm
Image ratio at nearest distance: 1:8.7
Focusing distances:
  One head vertical: 0.7m (2.25 ft) subject to perspective distortion
  Two heads horizontal: 0.9m (3 ft) subject to perspective distortion
  One to three adults standing: 3m (10 ft)
Angles of view:
  Diagonal: 46°
  Horizontal: 39°
  Vertical: 26°
Attachment size (inside screw diameter): 52mm (P = 0.75)
Lens hood: HS-11
Front lens cap: 52mm snap-on
Lens case: CL-34A, flexible pouch 54, plastic case CP-1
Overall size: 63.5mm ϕ × 48mm
Weight: 220g (7.8 oz)

DEPTH OF FIELD TABLE

(m)

focus distance	depth of field								repro-duction ratio
	f/1.8	f/2	f/2.8	f/4	f/5.6	f/8	f/11	f/16	
0.45	0.447–0.453	0.447–0.453	0.445–0.455	0.443–0.457	0.441–0.460	0.437–0.464	0.432–0.470	0.425–0.480	1/6.7
0.5	0.496–0.504	0.496–0.505	0.494–0.506	0.491–0.509	0.488–0.513	0.483–0.519	0.477–0.526	0.467–0.539	1/7.7
0.55	0.545–0.555	0.544–0.556	0.542–0.558	0.539–0.561	0.535–0.566	0.529–0.574	0.521–0.583	0.509–0.600	1/8.7
0.6	0.594–0.606	0.593–0.607	0.591–0.610	0.587–0.614	0.582–0.620	0.574–0.629	0.565–0.641	0.550–0.662	1/9.7
0.7	0.691–0.709	0.690–0.710	0.687–0.714	0.681–0.720	0.674–0.729	0.663–0.742	0.651–0.759	0.631–0.790	1/11.6
0.8	0.788–0.812	0.787–0.814	0.782–0.819	0.775–0.827	0.765–0.839	0.751–0.857	0.734–0.880	0.709–0.924	1/13.6
0.9	0.885–0.916	0.883–0.917	0.877–0.925	0.867–0.936	0.855–0.951	0.837–0.975	0.816–1.006	0.783–1.065	1/15.5
1	0.981–1.020	0.979–1.022	0.770–1.031	0.959–1.045	0.944–1.064	0.922–1.095	0.896–1.136	0.856–1.212	1/17.4
1.2	1.172–1.229	1.169–1.233	1.157–1.246	1.140–1.267	1.118–1.297	1.086–1.344	1.049–1.408	0.994–1.530	1/21.3
1.5	1.456–1.547	1.451–1.553	1.432–1.575	1.405–1.610	1.370–1.659	1.322–1.739	1.266–1.851	1.184–2.075	1/27.2
2	1.920–2.088	1.911–2.098	1.878–2.140	1.830–2.206	1.771–2.302	1.689–2.403	1.597–2.700	1.465–3.222	1/36.9
3	2.819–3.207	2.800–3.232	2.728–3.335	2.626–3.564	2.502–3.758	2.337–4.219	2.161–4.990	1.921–7.205	1/56.2
5	4.508–5.616	4.459–5.694	4.275–6.030	4.025–6.618	3.736–7.609	3.374–9.828	3.012–15.525	2.558–637.240	1/95.0
10	8.186–12.864	8.024–13.287	7.438–15.307	6.706–19.842	5.930–32.870	5.056–3195.7	4.274–∞	3.405–∞	1/191.9
∞	44.477–∞	40.039–∞	28.627–∞	20.068–∞	14.362–∞	10.082–∞	7.359–∞	5.089–∞	1/∞

50mm *f*/2 NIKKOR

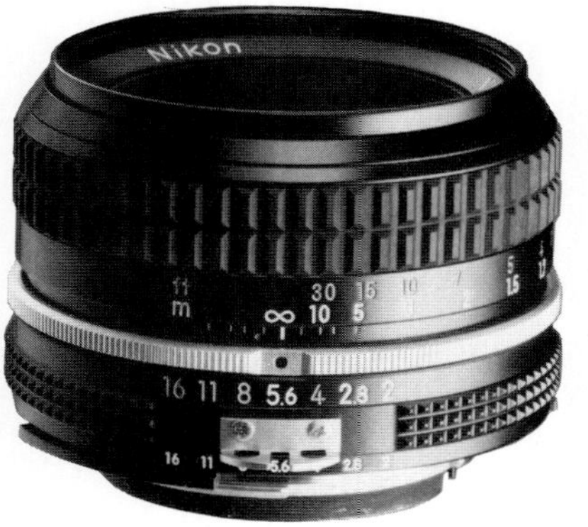

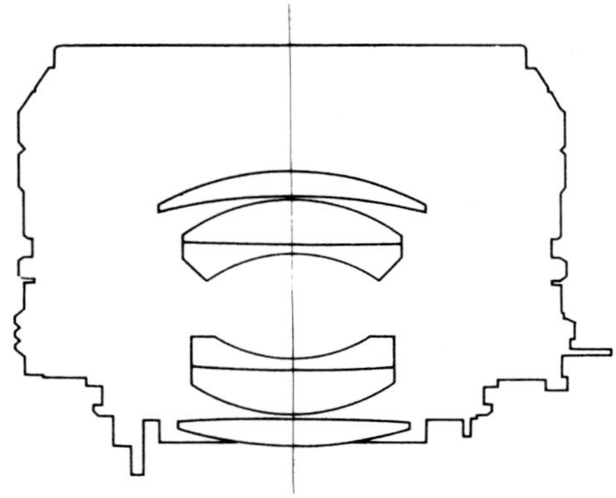

DESCRIPTION

Standard or normal lens approximates angle of view of human eye to produce natural perspectives. Middle-ground objects rendered with greater dominance while retaining adequate background scale. When working close, background limited in coverage and sharpness. Highly useful in close-up work. Compact and lightweight. Very high resolution and outstanding color rendition at full aperture although performance is improved through stopping down optimally at *f*/4 or *f*/5.6. For macro work, in reverse mode, at high image ratios, corner quality deteriorates somewhat at smaller apertures than *f*/8; in normal mode, image quality improves with stopping down, thereby permitting use in copying.

SPECIFICATIONS

Smallest aperture: 16
Nearest focus distance: 0.45m (1.5 ft)
Subject field at nearest distance: 20.8 × 31.2cm
Image ratio at nearest distance: 1:8.7
Focusing distances:
  One head vertical: 0.7m (2.25 ft) subject to perspective distortion
  Two heads horizontal: 0.9m (3 ft) subject to perspective distortion
  One to three adults standing: 3m (10 ft)
Angles of view:
  Diagonal: 46°
  Horizontal: 39°
  Vertical: 26°
Attachment size (inside screw diameter): 52mm (P = 0.75)
Lens hood: HS-6, HR-1
Front lens cap: 52mm snap-on
Lens case: CL-34A, flexible pouch 54, plastic case CP-1
Overall size: 63.5mm ø × 53mm
Weight: 220g (7.8 oz)

DEPTH OF FIELD TABLE

Meters

m \ f/	2	2.8	4	5.6	8	11	16	Magnification
0.6	0.593−0.607	0.591−0.610	0.587−0.614	0.581−0.620	0.574−0.629	0.564−0.641	0.551−0.660	1/9.7
0.7	0.690−0.710	0.637−0.714	0.681−0.720	0.674−0.729	0.664−0.741	0.650−0.760	0.631−0.788	1/12
0.8	0.787−0.813	0.782−0.819	0.775−0.827	0.765−0.839	0.751−0.856	0.733−0.882	0.708−0.921	1/14
0.9	0.883−0.917	0.877−0.925	0.867−0.935	0.855−0.951	0.837−0.974	0.814−1.01	0.783−1.06	1/16
1	0.979−1.02	0.971−1.03	0.959−1.04	0.943−1.06	0.922−1.09	0.893−1.14	0.856−1.21	1/18
1.2	1.17 −1.23	1.16 −1.25	1.14 −1.27	1.12 −1.30	1.09 −1.34	1.05 −1.41	0.993−1.52	1/21
1.5	1.45 −1.55	1.43 −1.58	1.41 −1.61	1.37 −1.66	1.32 −1.74	1.26 −1.86	1.18 −2.06	1/27
1.7	1.64 −1.77	1.61 −1.80	1.58 −1.84	1.53 −1.91	1.47 −2.01	1.40 −2.18	1.30 −2.48	1/31
2	1.91 −2.10	1.88 −2.14	1.83 −2.20	1.77 −2.30	1.69 −2.46	1.59 −2.72	1.46 −3.20	1/37
3	2.80 −3.23	2.73 −3.34	2.63 −3.50	2.50 −3.76	2.34 −4.21	2.14 −5.05	1.92 −7.09	1/56
5	4.46 −5.69	4.27 −6.04	4.03 −6.61	3.73 −7.63	3.37 −9.77	2.97 −16.2	2.55 −∞	1/95
10	8.02 −13.3	7.42 −15.4	6.70 −19.8	5.90 −33.3	5.05 −∞	4.20 −∞	3.39 −∞	1/192
∞	40.1 −∞	28.4 −∞	20.1 −∞	14.2 −∞	10.1 −∞	7.17 −∞	5.09 −∞	1/∞

55mm *f*/1.2 NIKKOR

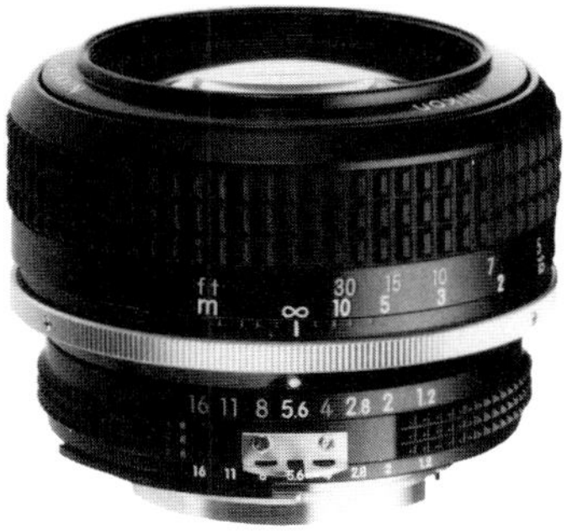

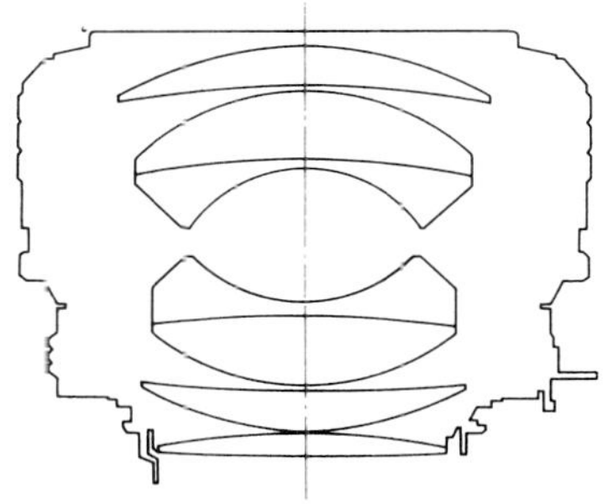

DESCRIPTION

General-purpose lens with *f*/1.2 aperture—brightest among Nikkor lenses for existing light use—provides advantage of one-half *f*/stop for bright-screen focusing and shallowest depth of field at full aperture, the latter being an advantage in viewing and focusing. Stopping lens down below maximum aperture yields performance comparable to other standard lenses with optimum performance at about *f*/5.6. At full aperture, curvilinear and spherical aberrations are corrected to highest degree. In macro work on bellows in reverse mode, corner image quality deteriorates at low angle image ratios; in normal mode, suitable for small objects close up but unsuitable for copying. Where corner image quality is needed in normal mode, lens should be stopped down as far as possible.

SPECIFICATIONS

Smallest aperture: 16
Nearest focus distance: 0.5m (1.7 ft)
Subject field at nearest distance: 21.9 × 32.8cm
Image ratio at nearest distance: 1:9
Focusing distances:
  One head vertical: 0.7m (2.5 ft) subject to perspective distortion
  Two heads horizontal: 1m (3.3 ft) subject to perspective distortion
  One to three adults standing: 3.1m (11 ft)
Angles of view:
  Diagonal: 43°
  Horizontal: 36°10′
  Vertical: 24°40′
Ratio of image size at infinity to image of 50mm lens: 1.1:1
Attachment size (inside screw diameter): 52mm (P = 0.75)
Lens hood: HS-7, HR-2
Front lens cap: 52mm snap-on
Lens case: CL-34A, flexible pouch 54, plastic case CP-1
Overall size: 72mm ø × 61mm
Weight: 410g (14.5 oz)

DEPTH OF FIELD TABLE

Meters

m \ f/	1.2	1.4	2	2.8	4	5.6	8	11	16	Magnification
0.6	0.596−0.604	0.596−0.604	0.594−0.606	0.592−0.608	0.589−0.612	0.584−0.617	0.578−0.624	0.569−0.635	0.557−0.651	1/9.0
0.7	0.695−0.705	0.694−0.706	0.692−0.708	0.688−0.712	0.684−0.717	0.677−0.724	0.668−0.735	0.656−0.751	0.640−0.774	1/11
0.8	0.793−0.807	0.792−0.808	0.789−0.811	0.784−0.816	0.778−0.823	0.770−0.833	0.758−0.848	0.742−0.869	0.720−0.902	1/13
0.9	0.891−0.909	0.890−0.910	0.886−0.915	0.980−0.921	0.872−0.930	0.861−0.943	0.846−0.963	0.825−0.991	0.798−1.04	1/16
1	0.989−1.01	0.987−1.01	0.982−1.02	0.975−1.03	0.965−1.04	0.951−1.05	0.932−1.08	0.907−1.12	0.873−1.17	1/16
1.2	1.18 −1.22	1.18 −1.22	1.17 −1.23	1.16 −1.24	1.15 −1.26	1.13 −1.28	1.10 −1.32	1.06 −1.38	1.02 −1.47	1/20
1.5	1.47 −1.53	1.47 −1.53′	1.46 −1.55	1.44 −1.56	1.42 −1.59	1.39 −1.64	1.34 −1.70	1.29 −1.80	1.22 −1.96	1/25
1.7	1.67 −1.74	1.66 −1.74	1.64 −1.76	1.62 −1.78	1.59 −1.82	1.55 −1.88	1.50 −1.96	1.43 −2.10	1.34 −2.33	1/29
2	1.95 −2.05	1.96 −2.06	1.92 −2.08	1.89 −2.12	1.85 −2.17	1.80 −2.26	1.73 −2.38	1.63 −2.59	1.52 −2.95	1/34
3	2.89 −3.12	2.87 −3.14	2.83 −3.20	2.76 −3.29	2.67 −3.42	2.56 −3.64	2.41 −3.99	2.23 −4.62	2.02 −5.97	1/52
5	4.70 −5.34	4.66 −5.40	4.53 −5.59	4.36 −5.87	4.14 −6.33	3.86 −7.12	3.53 −8.54	3.15 −12.4	3.73 −32.7	1/88
10	8.85 −11.5	8.69 −11.8	8.25 −12.7	7.69 −14.3	7.02 −17.5	6.25 −25.3	5.41 −69.5	4.55 −∞	3.72 −∞	1/179
∞	75.9 −∞	65.5 −∞	46.3 −∞	32.8 −∞	23.2 −∞	16.4 −∞	11.7 −∞	8.27 −∞	5.87 −∞	1/∞

85mm *f*/2 NIKKOR

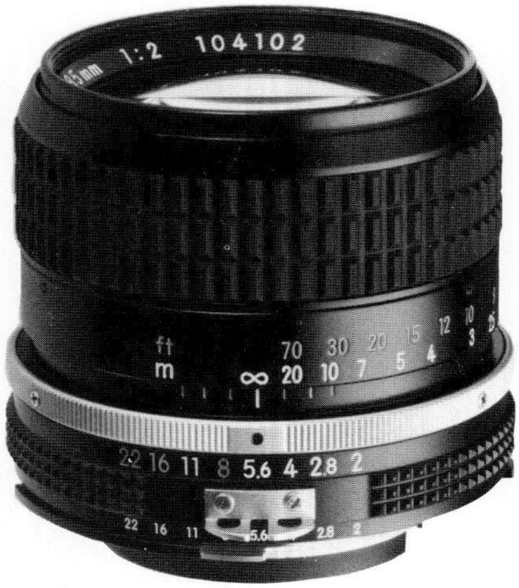

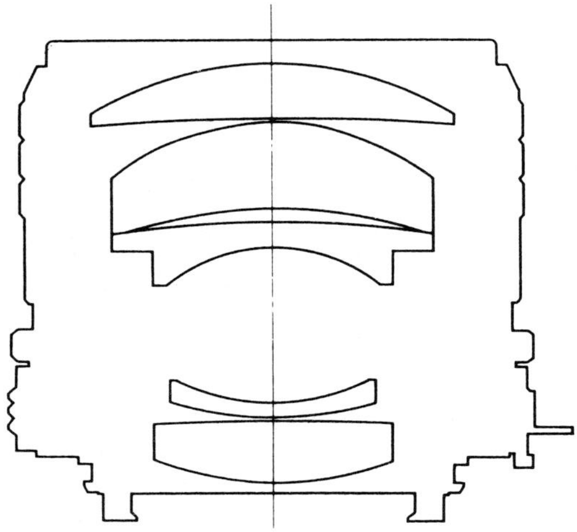

DESCRIPTION

The 85mm *f*/2 Nikkor is ideal for portraiture; especially so under poor light conditions where the *f*/2 aperture isolates image planes for ease in focusing. The moderately long focal length provides natural perspective when making head-and-shoulders portraits. It is ideal for photojournalism when working at relatively short distances. Its relatively wide coverage for a telephoto makes it easy to track moving subjects as in child studies, some sports, and various group situations. Nikon Integrated Coating on air-to-glass surfaces reduces flare and ghost, further increasing contrast and improving color rendition.

SPECIFICATIONS

Smallest aperture: 22
Nearest focus distance: 0.85m (3 ft)
Subject field at nearest distance: 23.9 × 35.9cm
Image ratio at nearest distance: 1:10
Focusing distances:
  One head vertical: 1.2m (4 ft)
  Two heads horizontal: 1.5m (5 ft)
  One to three adults standing: 5.3m (17 ft)
Angles of view:
  Diagonal: 28°30′
  Horizontal: 23°50′
  Vertical: 16°
Ratio of image size at infinity to image of 50mm lens: 1.7:1
Attachment size (inside screw diameter): 52mm (P = 0.75)
Lens hood: HS-10
Front lens cap: 52mm snap-on
Lens case: CL-31, flexible pouch 54, plastic case CP-1
Overall size: 63.5mm ϕ × 61mm
Weight: 310g (11 oz)

DEPTH OF FIELD TABLE

(m)

Focused distance	Depth of field								Repro.ratio
	f/2	f/2.8	f/4	f/5.6	f/8	f/11	f/16	f/22	
0.85	0.845–0.855	0.843–0.857	0.840–0.860	0.837–0.864	0.831–0.870	0.824–0.878	0.813–0.891	0.800–0.908	1/8.1
1	0.993–1.007	0.990–1.010	0.986–1.015	0.981–1.020	0.972–1.030	0.963–1.041	0.947–1.061	0.928–1.087	1/9.9
1.2	1.189–1.211	1.185–1.215	1.179–1.222	1.171–1.231	1.159–1.245	1.144–1.263	1.120–1.294	1.094–1.334	1/12.2
1.5	1.483–1.518	1.476–1.525	1.466–1.536	1.452–1.551	1.433–1.574	1.410–1.605	1.372–1.658	1.331–1.727	1/15,8
1.7	1.677–1.723	1.668–1.733	1.655–1.748	1.638–1.768	1.613–1.798	1.582–1.839	1.535–1.910	1.482–2.005	1/18.1
2	1.968–2.033	1.955–2.047	1.937–2.068	1.913–2.097	1.878–2.141	1.836–2.200	1.771–2.306	1.699–2.448	1/21.7
2.5	2.449–2.554	2.429–2.576	2.400–2.610	2.362–2.657	2.307–2.731	2.243–2.829	2.144–3.012	2.037–3.266	1/27,6
3	2.925–3.079	2.896–3.112	2.854–3.162	2.800–3.233	2.723–3.345	2.632–3.496	2.495–3.784	2.348–4.203	1/33.5
4	3.866–4.145	3.814–4.206	3.740–4.301	3.646–4.434	3.513–4.652	3.361–4.957	3.136–5,570	2.904–6.550	1/45.2
5	4.789–5.231	4.710–5.329	4.596–5.485	4.453–5.707	4.254–6.077	4.031–6.616	3.707–7.771	3.384–9.851	1/57
7	6.589–7.468	6.438–7.673	6.224–8.004	5.961–8.493	5.606–9.352	5.219–10.713	4.684–14.168	4.174–23.229	1/80.5
10	9.174–10.993	8.881–11.449	8.475–12.209	7.990–13.397	7.359–15.696	6.701–20.000	5.836–37.025	5.058–∞	1/115.8
20	16.917–24.472	15.937–26.881	14.664–31.545	13.255–41.064	11.589–75.200	10.021–∞	8.185–∞	6.720–∞	1/233.9
∞	108.540–∞	77.572–∞	54.347–∞	38.863–∞	27.250–∞	19.860–∞	13.702–∞	10.007–∞	1/∞

105mm f/2.5 NIKKOR

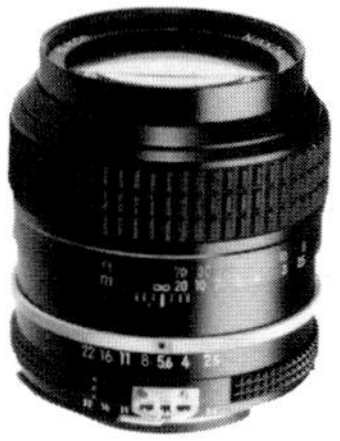

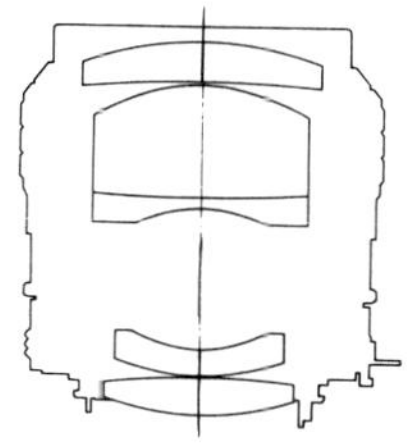

DESCRIPTION

Compared with standard lenses, 105mm has a focal length of about twice as long and a picture angle about half as wide. Picture coverage is about one-fourth the area of normal or standard lens. For the same coverage of a head-and-shoulders portrait, the photographer can work at twice the distance enabling him to take pictures in greater natural portrait perspective corresponding to distances at which people perceive each other across the table or in small social groups and to set up lighting equipment. High speed of *f*/2.5 facilitates focusing under indoor lighting conditions. Excellent for indoor sports coverage or stage photography. Near focus of 1m (3.3 ft) permits very tight framing. Diaphragm design overcomes hexagonal form of out-of-focus bright spots. Very compact. Optimum performance about *f*/5.6. For close-up work, best used in normal mode with image quality improved by stopping down.

SPECIFICATIONS

Smallest aperture: 22
Nearest focus distance: 1m (3.3 ft)
Subject field at nearest distance: 22.8 × 34.4cm
Image ratio at nearest distance: 1:9.5
Focusing distances:
One head vertical: 1.5m (5.5 ft)
Two heads horizontal: 1.9m (6.3 ft)
One to three adults standing: 6.4m (2.1 ft)
Angles of view:
Diagonal: 23°20′
Horizontal: 19°30′
Vertical: 13°
Ratio of image size at infinity to image of 50mm lens: 2.1:1
Attachment size (inside screw diameter): 52mm (P = 0.75)
Lens hood: HS-8
Front lens cap: 52mm snap-on
Lens case: CL-32, flexible pouch 55, plastic case CP-2
Overall size: 66mm ϕ × 78mm
Weight: 435g (15.5 oz)

DEPTH OF FIELD TABLE

Meters

m \ f/	2.5	2.8	4	5.6	8	11	16	22	Magnification
1	0.994−1.01	0.994−1.01	0.991−1.01	0.988−1.01	0.983−1.02	0.976−1.03	0.966−1.04	0.953−1.05	1/7.7
1.1	1.09 −1.11	1.09 −1.11	1.09 −1.11	1.08 −1.12	1.08 −1.12	1.07 −1.13	1.06 −1.15	1.04 −1.17	1/8.7
1.2	1.19 −1.21	1.19 −1.21	1.19 −1.21	1.18 −1.22	1.17 −1.23	1.16 −1.24	1.14 −1.26	1.13 −1.28	1/9.6
1.3	1.29 −1.31	1.29 −1.31	1.28 −1.32	1.28 −1.32	1.27 −1.33	1.26 −1.35	1.24 −1.37	1.21 −1.40	1/11
1.4	1.39 −1.41	1.39 −1.41	1.38 −1.42	1.37 −1.43	1.36 −1.44	1.35 −1.46	1.33 −1.48	1.30 −1.52	1/12
1.5	1.49 −1.51	1.48 −1.52	1.48 −1.52	1.47 −1.53	1.46 −1.55	1.44 −1.57	1.42 −1.60	1.38 −1.64	1/13
1.7	1.68 −1.72	1.68 −1.72	1.67 −1.73	1.66 −1.74	1.64 −1.76	1.62 −1.79	1.59 −1.83	1.55 −1.89	1/14
2	1.97 −2.03	1.97 −2.03	1.96 −2.04	1.94 −2.06	1.92 −2.09	1.89 −2.13	1.85 −2.19	1.79 −2.27	1/17
2.5	2.46 −2.54	2.45 −2.55	2.43 −2.57	2.41 −2.60	2.37 −2.64	2.32 −2.71	2.26 −2.81	2.17 −2.96	1/22
3	2.94 −3.06	2.93 −3.07	2.90 −3.10	2.87 −3.15	2.81 −3.21	2.74 −3.31	2.65 −3.46	2.53 −3.70	1/27
4	3.89 −4.12	3.88 −4.13	3.83 −4.19	3.76 −4.27	3.67 −4.40	3.55 −4.59	3.39 −4.89	3.19 −5.40	1/36
5	4.83 −5.19	4.81 −5.21	4.73 −5.31	4.63 −5.44	4.49 −5.65	4.31 −5.98	4.07 −6.51	3.79 −7.45	1/46
7	6.66 −7.38	6.62 −7.43	6.47 −7.62	6.28 −7.92	6.02 −8.37	5.69 −9.12	5.29 −10.4	4.81 −13.1	1/65
10	9.31 −10.8	9.23 −10.9	8.95 −11.3	8.58 −12.0	8.10 −13.1	7.51 −15.0	6.81 −19.1	6.03 −30.7	1/94
20	17.4 −23.5	17.1 −24.1	16.2 −26.3	15.0 −30.2	13.6 −38.4	12.0 −62.4	10.3 −548	8.57 −∞	1/189
∞	132 −∞	117 −∞	82.9 −∞	58.6 −∞	41.5 −∞	29.4 −∞	20.9 −∞	14.8 −∞	1/∞

135mm *f*/2 NIKKOR

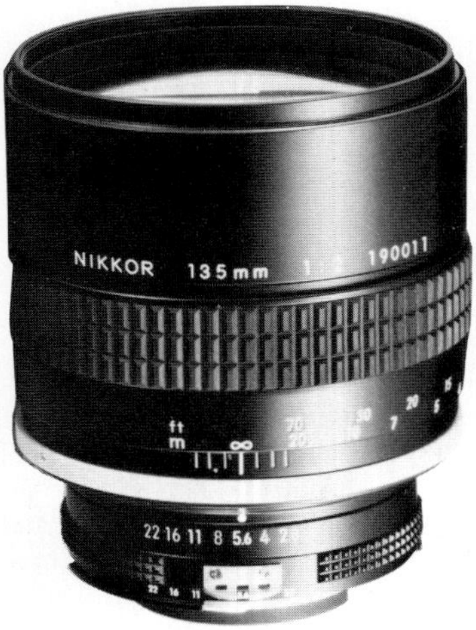

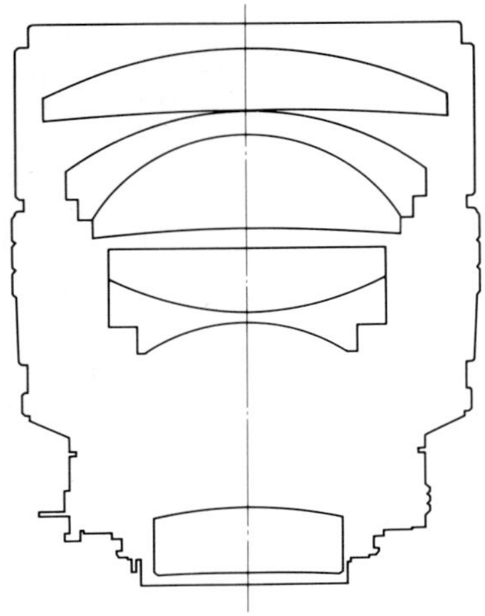

DESCRIPTION

The Nikkor 135mm *f*/2 is one of the fastest of the Nikkor medium-telephoto lenses. The speed of this lens makes it especially useful for photographing dimly lit or fast-action events, especially indoors. The compact lens size ensures comfortable hand-held shooting. Nikon Integrated Coating has been applied to air-to-glass surfaces to minimize ghost and flare and to improve contrast and color rendition.

SPECIFICATIONS

Smallest aperture: 22
Nearest focus distance: 1.3m (4.5 ft)
Focusing distances:
One head vertical: 2m (6.5 ft)
Two heads horizontal: 2.4m (8 ft)
One to three adults standing: 8.2m (27 ft)
Angles of view:
Diagonal: 18°
Horizontal: 15°
Vertical: 10°
Ratio of image size at infinity to image of 50mm lens: 2.7:1
Attachment size (inside screw diameter): 72mm (P = 0.75)
Lens hood: Built-in
Front lens cap: 72mm screw-in
Lens case: CL-15, flexible pouch 55, plastic case CP-2
Overall size: 81mm ø × 103mm
Weight: 860g (1.9 lb)

DEPTH OF FIELD TABLE

(m)

focus distance	depth of field								reproduction ratio
	f/2	2.8	4	5.6	8	11	16	22	
1.3	1.30–1.30	1.29–1.31	1.29–1.31	1.29–1.31	1.28–1.32	1.28–1.32	1.27–1.33	1.26–1.35	1/7.46
1.5	1.49–1.51	1.49–1.51	1.49–1.51	1.48–1.52	1.48–1.52	1.47–1.53	1.45–1.55	1.44–1.57	1/8.96
1.7	1.69–1.71	1.69–1.71	1.68–1.72	1.68–1.72	1.67–1.73	1.66–1.75	1.64–1.77	1.62–1.79	1/10.5
2	1.99–2.01	1.98–2.02	1.98–2.02	1.97–2.03	1.95–2.05	1.94–2.07	1.91–2.10	1.88–2.14	1/12.7
2.5	2.48–2.52	2.47–2.53	2.46–2.54	2.45–2.55	2.43–2.58	2.40–2.61	2.36–2.66	2.31–2.73	1/16.4
3	2.97–3.03	2.96–3.04	2.94–3.06	2.92–3.08	2.89–3.12	2.85–3.17	2.79–3.25	2.72–3.35	1/20.1
4	3.95–4.05	3.93–4.07	3.90–4.11	3.86–4.15	3.80–4.22	3.73–4.31	3.62–4.47	3.50–4.68	1/27.6
5	4.92–5.09	4.89–5.12	4.84–5.17	4.78–5.25	4.69–5.36	4.58–5.51	4.41–5.78	4.23–6.15	1/35.0
7	6.84–7.17	6.77–7.24	6.68–7.36	6.56–7.51	6.39–7.75	6.19–8.08	5.88–8.69	5.55–9.56	1/49.8
10	9.66–10.4	9.53–10.5	9.35–10.8	9.11–11.1	8.77–11.6	8.39–12.4	7.82–13.9	7.24–16.4	1/72.0
20	18.7–21.5	18.2–22.2	17.5–23.4	16.7–25.0	15.6–28.1	14.4–33.1	12.8–47.4	11.2–98.4	1/146
∞	274–∞	196–∞	137–∞	97.9–∞	68.6–∞	50.0–∞	34.5–∞	25.1–∞	1/∞

135mm f/2.8 NIKKOR

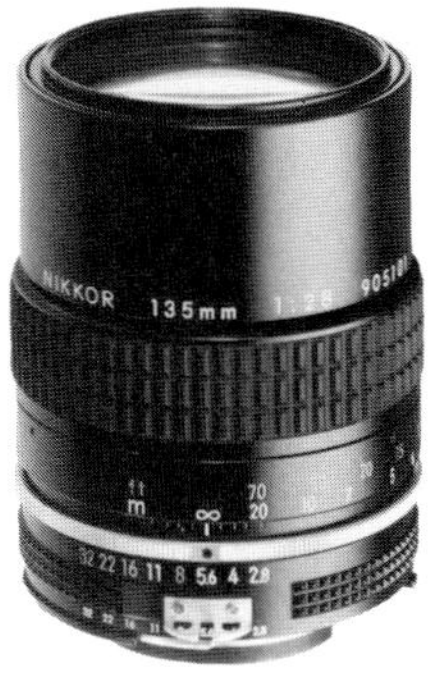

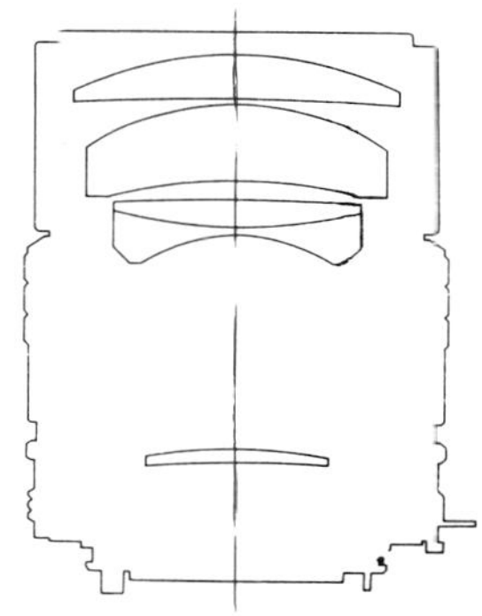

DESCRIPTION

Large *f*/2.8 aperture of this 135mm telephoto lens extends picture-taking capabilities of one of the most popular of lens focal lengths. The 135mm lens is the ideal all-purpose telephoto for indoor sports, many outdoor sporting events, zoo pictures, set-up portraiture, travel photography, candid shooting, and selective landscape photography. Optical performance excellent at full aperture with optimum quality at *f*/4. Built-in lens hood. For close-up work, best used in normal mode with lens stopped down maximally for best image quality.

SPECIFICATIONS

Smallest aperture: 32
Nearest focus distance: 1.3m (4.5 ft)
Focusing distances:
One head vertical: 2m (6.5 ft)
Two heads horizontal: 2.4m (8 ft)
One to three adults standing: 8.2m (27 ft)
Angles of view:
Diagonal: 18°
Horizontal: 15°
Vertical: 10°
Ratio of image size at infinity to image of 50mm lens: 2.7:1
Attachment size (inside screw diameter): 52mm (P = 0.75)
Lens hood: Built-in
Front lens cap: 52mm snap-on
Lens case. CL-33A, flexible pouch 55, plastic case CP-2
Overall size: 64.5mm ϕ × 91.5mm
Weight: 430g (15.2 oz)

DEPTH OF FIELD TABLE

(m)

focus distance	depth of field								reproduction ratio
	2.8	4	5.6	8	11	16	22	32	
1.3	1.29–1.31	1.29–1.31	1.29–1.31	1.28–1.32	1.28–1.32	1.27–1.34	1.26–1.35	1.24–1.37	1/7.49
1.5	1.49–1.51	1.49–1.51	1.48–1.52	1.48–1.52	1.47–1.53	1.45–1.55	1.44–1.57	1.41–1.60	1/8.99
1.7	1.69–1.71	1.68–1.72	1.68–1.72	1.67–1.73	1.66–1.75	1.64–1.77	1.62–1.79	1.58–1.84	1/10.5
2	1.98–2.02	1.98–2.02	1.97–2.03	1.95–2.05	1.94–2.07	1.91–2.10	1.88–2.14	1.83–2.21	1/12.7
2.5	2.47–2.53	2.46–2.54	2.45–2.55	2.43–2.58	2.40–2.61	2.36–2.66	2.31–2.73	2.23–2.86	1/16.4
3	2.96–3.04	2.94–3.06	2.92–3.08	2.89–3.12	2.85–3.17	2.79–3.25	2.72–3.35	2.61–3.55	1/20.2
4	3.93–4.08	3.90–4.11	3.86–4.15	3.80–4.22	3.73–4.31	3.62–4.47	3.50–4.68	3.31–5.09	1/27.6
5	4.89–5.12	4.84–5.17	4.78–5.25	4.69–5.36	4.58–5.51	4.41–5.78	4.23–6.15	3.95–6.88	1/35.0
7	6.77–7.24	6.68–7.36	6.56–7.51	6.39–7.75	6.18–8.08	5.88–8.69	5.55–9.56	5.07–11.5	1/49.8
10	9.53–10.5	9.35–10.8	9.11–11.1	8.77–11.6	8.39–12.4	7.82–13.9	7.24–16.4	6.44–23.3	1/72.0
20	18.2–22.2	17.5–23.4	16.7–25.0	15.6–28.1	14.4–33.1	12.7–47.4	11.2–98.5	9.40–∞	1/146
∞	196–∞	137–∞	97.9–∞	68.6–∞	50.0–∞	34.4–∞	25.1–∞	17.4–∞	1/∞

135mm *f*/3.5 NIKKOR

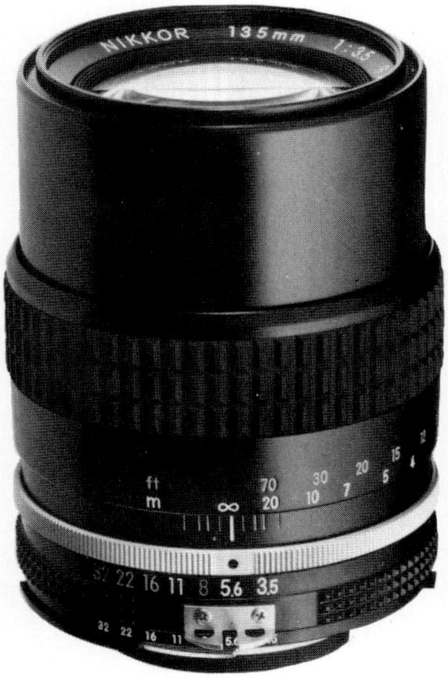

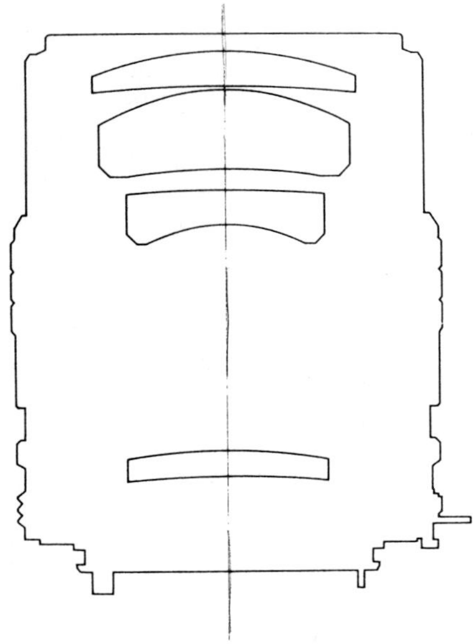

DESCRIPTION

Compact and lightweight, this 135mm lens is one of the most popular Nikkor telephotos. It is the obvious choice if the additional aperture power of the 135mm *f*/2.8 or *f*/2 is not needed. It has the same applications in sports, candid shooting, visits to the zoo, travel, landscapes, and close-up photography as the other 135mm lenses. Lens barrel is comparatively short for its focal length—only 89.5mm.

SPECIFICATIONS

Smallest aperture: 32
Nearest focus distance: 1.3m (4.5 ft)
Focusing distances:
  One head vertical: 2m (6.5 ft)
  Two heads horizontal: 2.4m (8 ft)
  One to three adults standing: 8.2m (27 ft)
Angles of view:
  Diagonal: 18°
  Horizontal: 15°
  Vertical: 10°

Ratio of image size at infinity to image of 50mm lens: 2.7:1
Attachment size (inside screw diameter): 52mm (P = 0.75)
Lens hood: Built-in
Front lens cap: 52mm snap-on
Lens case: CL-33A, flexible pouch 55, plastic case CP-2
Overall size: 65mm ϕ × 89.5mm
Weight: 400g (14.1 oz)

DEPTH OF FIELD TABLE

(m)

focus distance	depth of field								repro-duction ratio
	f/3.5	f/4	f/5.6	f/8	f/11	f/16	f/22	f/32	
1.3	1.29–1.31	1.29–1.31	1.29–1.31	1.28–1.32	1.28–1.32	1.27–1.33	1.26–1.35	1.24–1.37	1/7.47
1.5	1.49–1.51	1.49–1.51	1.48–1.52	1.48–1.52	1.47–1.53	1.45–1.55	1.44–1.57	1.41–1.6	1/8.98
1.7	1.69–1.71	1.68–1.72	1.68–1.72	1.67–1.73	1.66–1.75	1.64–1.77	1.62–1.79	1.58–1.84	1/10.5
2	1.98–2.02	1.98–2.02	1.97–2.03	1.95–2.05	1.94–2.07	1.91–2.10	1.88–2.14	1.83–2.21	1/12.7
2.5	2.47–2.53	2.46–2.54	2.45–2.55	2.43–2.58	2.40–2.61	2.36–2.66	2.31–2.73	2.23–2.85	1/16.4
3	2.95–3.05	2.94–3.06	2.92–3.08	2.89–3.12	2.85–3.17	2.79–3.25	2.72–3.35	2.61–3.55	1/20.1
4	3.91–4.09	3.90–4.11	3.86–4.15	3.80–4.22	3.73–4.31	3.62–4.47	3.50–4.68	3.31–5.09	1/27.6
5	4.86–5.15	4.84–5.17	4.78–5.25	4.69–5.36	4.58–5.51	4.41–5.78	4.23–6.15	3.95–6.88	1/35.0
7	6.72–7.31	6.68–7.36	6.56–7.51	6.39–7.75	6.18–8.08	5.88–8.69	5.55–9.56	5.07–11.5	1/49.8
10	9.42–10.7	9.35–10.8	9.11–11.1	8.77–11.6	8.39–12.4	7.82–13.9	7.24–16.4	6.44–23.3	1/72.0
20	17.8–22.9	17.5–23.4	16.7–25.0	15.6–28.1	14.4–33.1	12.7–47.4	11.2–98.5	9.40–∞	1/146
∞	157–∞	137–∞	97.9–∞	68.6–∞	50.0–∞	34.4–∞	25.1–∞	17.4–∞	1/∞

180mm f/2.8 NIKKOR

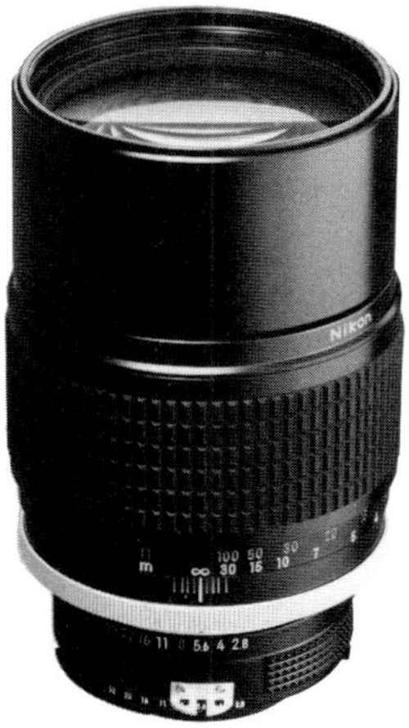

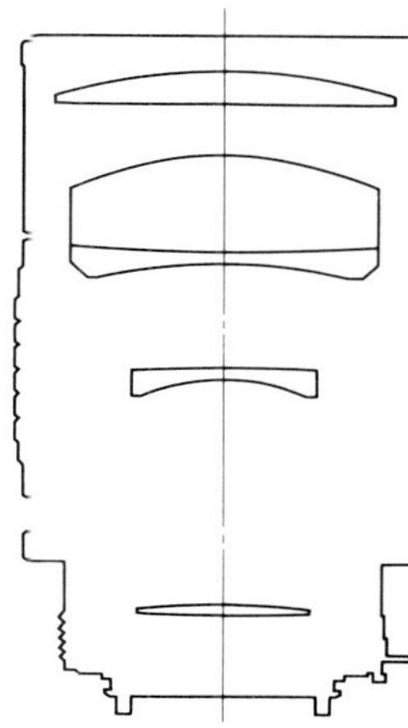

DESCRIPTION

High-speed lens aperture of $f/2.8$—one full stop greater than the well-established 200mm $f/4$ lens which is very close in focal length—has made the 180mm lens extremely popular with photojournalists and other working photographers who often need to obtain sharp images with high contrast under difficult light conditions. Brilliant finder image makes focusing much easier under such conditions. Useful also in spectator events of all kinds. Although not an ideal portrait lens, it is excellent for photo reportage of indoor events at a distance. Can be used for closeups in normal mode but should be stopped down for best image quality.

SPECIFICATIONS

Smallest aperture: 32
Nearest focus distance: 1.8m (6 ft)
Subject field at nearest distance: 19.0 × 28.4cm
Image ratio at nearest distance: 1:7.9
Focusing distances:
  One head vertical: 2.6m (9.6 ft)
  Two heads horizontal: 3.2m (10.8 ft)
  One to three adults standing: 10.9m (36 ft)
Angeles of view:
  Diagonal: 13°40′
  Horizontal: 11°30′
  Vertical: 7°40′
Ratio of image size at infinity to image of 50mm lens: 3.6 1
Attachment size (inside screw diameter): 72mm (P = 0.75)
Lens hood: Built-in
Front lens cap: 72m screw-in
Lens case: CL-35A, flexible pouch 56, plastic case CO-2
Overall size: 82mm ø × 141mm
Weight: 880g (1.9 lb)

DEPTH OF FIELD TABLE

Meters

m \ f/	2.8	4	5.6	8	11	16	22	32	Magnification
1.8	1.79—1.81	1.79—1.81	1.79—1.81	1.78—1.82	1.77—1.83	1.76—1.84	1.75—1.86	1.73—1.88	1/8.0
2	1.99—2.01	1.99—2.01	1.98—2.02	1.98—2.03	1.97—2.04	1.95—2.05	1.93—2.07	1.91—2.11	1/9.2
2.5	2.49—2.51	2.48—2.52	2.47—2.53	2.46—2.54	2.44—2.56	2.42—2.59	2.39—2.62	2.35—2.68	1/12
3	2.98—3.02	2.97—3.03	2.96—3.04	2.94—3.06	2.92—3.09	2.88—3.13	2.84—3.19	2.77—3.27	1/15
4	3.96—4.04	3.94—4.06	3.92—4.08	3.89—4.12	3.84—4.17	3.78—4.25	3.70—4.36	3.59—4.53	1/20
5	4.94—5.07	4.91—5.09	4.87—5.14	4.82—5.19	4.75—5.28	4.66—5.40	4.53—5.59	4.36—5.88	1/26
7	6.87—7.13	6.82—7.19	6.74—7.28	6.64—7.40	6.51—7.58	6.33—7.85	6.08—8.26	5.77—8.94	1/37
10	9.73—10.3	9.62—10.4	9.48—10.6	9.28—10.9	9.01—11.3	8.65—11.9	8.20—12.9	7.63—14.6	1/54
15	14.4—15.7	14.2—16.0	13.8—16.4	13.4—17.0	12.8—18.1	12.1—19.7	11.2—22.7	10.2—29.0	1/82
30	27.7—32.8	26.8—34.2	25.6—36.2	24.1—39.7	22.4—45.8	20.2—58.7	17.8—97.5	15.3—1700	1/165
∞	347—∞	243—∞	172—∞	122—∞	86.3—∞	61.1—∞	43.3—∞	30.7—∞	1/∞

200mm f/4 NIKKOR

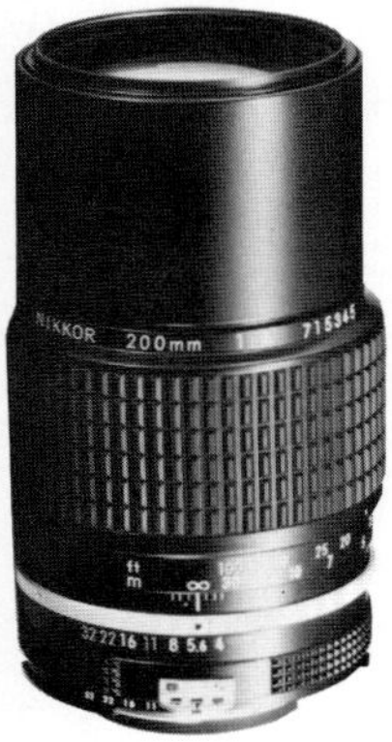

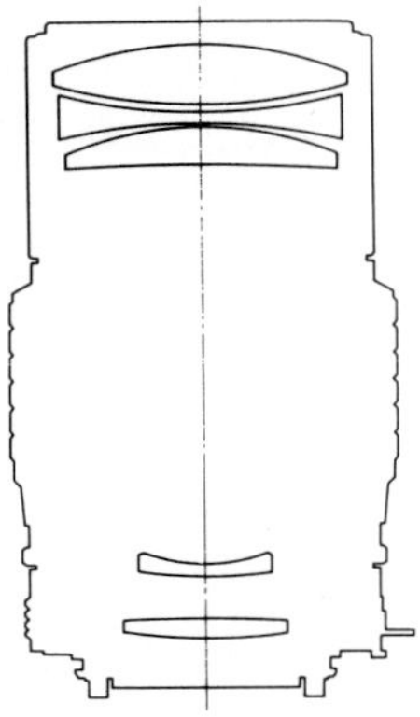

DESCRIPTION

Since debut of Nikon F in 1959, the 200mm *f*/4 lens has been considered "standard" gear when pronounced telephoto capabilities are needed. It provides four times image magnification over the 50mm normal lens. Because it is compact and light, it can be used for rapid hand-held shooting of action-packed subject matter—news events, sports, animals, travel photography, selective landscape scenes, and candid shooting, among others. At a distance from several objects behind each other, telephoto perspective maintains relative sizes of these objects without maximizing compression effect. Excellent at full aperture with optimum performance at *f*/5.6. Close-up pictures may be taken in normal mode with best results when lens is stopped down to a maximum.

SPECIFICATIONS

Smallest aperture: 32
Nearest focus distance: 2m (7 ft)
Subject field at nearest distance: 28.8 × 43.2cm
Image ratio at nearest distance: 1:12
Focusing distances:
  One head vertical: 2.9m (9.5 ft)
  Two heads horizontal: 3.7m (12 ft)
  One to three adults standing: 12.2m (40 ft)
Angles of view:
  Diagonal: 12°20′
  Horizontal: 10°20′
  Vertical: 6°50′
Ratio of image size at infinity to image of 50mm lens: 4:1
Attachment size (inside screw diameter): 52mm (P = 0.75)
Lens hood: Built-in
Front lens cap: 52mm snap-on
Lens case: CL-13, flexible pouch 56, plastic case CP-2
Overall size: 68mm ϕ × 126mm
Weight: 530g (1.2 lb)

DEPTH OF FIELD TABLE

(m)

focus distance	depth of field							repro-duction ratio
	4	5.6	8	11	16	22	32	
2	1.99–2.01	1.99–2.01	1.98–2.02	1.98–2.02	1.97–2.03	1.96–2.05	1.94–2.07	1/7.44
2.5	2.49–2.51	2.48–2.52	2.47–2.53	2.46–2.54	2.44–2.56	2.42–2.58	2.39–2.02	1/9.97
3	2.98–3.02	2.97–3.03	2.96–3.05	2.94–3.06	2.91–3.09	2.88–3.13	2.83–3.19	1/12.5
4	3.96–4.04	3.94–4.06	3.92–4.09	3.88–4.12	3.83–4.18	3.78–4.26	3.68–4.38	1/17.5
5	4.93–5.07	4.90–5.10	4.86–5.15	4.81–5.20	4.73–5.30	4.64–5.43	4.50–5.65	1/22.5
7	6.86–7.15	6.80–7.21	6.72–7.31	6.62–7.43	6.46–7.64	6.29–7.91	6.01–8.42	1/32.6
10	9.70–10.3	9.59–10.5	9.42–10.7	9.22–10.9	8.91–11.4	8.56–12.1	8.04–13.3	1/47.6
15	14.3–15.8	14.1–16.1	13.7–16.6	13.3–17.3	12.6–18.6	11.9–20.4	10.9–24.4	1/72.7
30	27.3–33.3	26.4–34.8	25.1–37.3	23.7–41.1	21.6–49.5	19.6–65.5	16.9–144	1/148
∞	300–∞	214–∞	150–∞	109–∞	75.3–∞	54.9–∞	37.9–∞	1/∞

300mm *f*/2.8 NIKKOR IF-ED

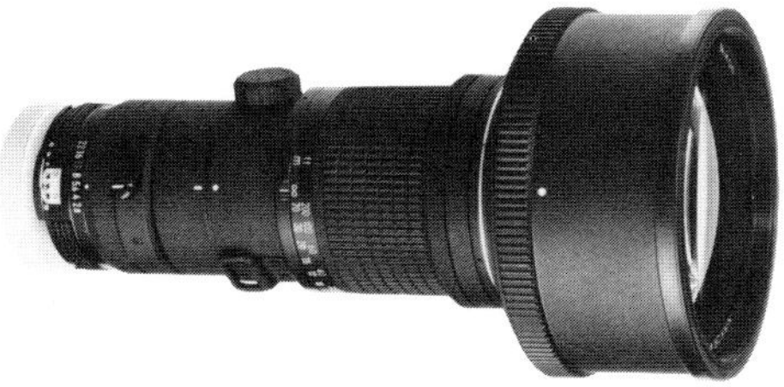

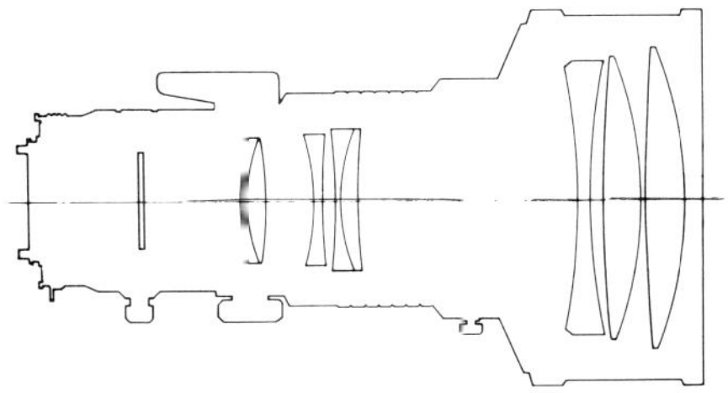

DESCRIPTION

The Nikkor ED 300mm *f*/2.8 is a fast, hand-holdable telephoto lens. Its *f*/2.8 maximum aperture enables photographers, particularly those working with slow-speed, fine-grain color film, to overcome technical limitations which have hindered their ability to shoot action scenes under conditions of low illumination. The lens' internal focusing (IF) mechanism enables the weight and bulk of the focusing helicoid to be drastically reduced, permitting relatively easy hand-held focusing. Other features include a preset focusing mechanism which enables the lens to be preset to a focusing distance to be relocated quickly and easily. The focusing ring also includes a provision for turning past the infinity index to compensate for thermal expansion when the lens is used under extreme climatic conditions. The lens is fitted with a plug-in filter slide that accepts standard Nikon 39mm filters, one of which must be mounted in the lens at all times. For specialized shooting applications, a gelatine filter holder is supplied, and standard gelatine filters can easily be trimmed to fit.

SPECIFICATIONS

Smallest aperture: 22
Nearest focus distance: 4m (13 ft)
Subject field at nearest distance: 26.4 × 39.6cm
Image ratio at nearest distance: 1:11
Focusing distances:
- One head vertical: 4.4m (14.5 ft)
- Two heads horizontal: 5.5m (18 ft)
- One to three adults standing: 18.3m (60 ft)

Angles of view:
- Diagonal: 8°10′
- Horizontal: 6°50′
- Vertical: 4°30′

Ratio of image size at infinity to image of 50mm lens: 6:1
Attachment size (inside screw diameter): 122mm (P = 1.00)
Lens hood: Built-in
Front lens cap: Leather slip-on lens cap supplied
Lens case: CL-63
Overall size: 138mm ⌀ × 249mm
Weight: 2.5kg (5.5 lb)

DEPTH OF FIELD TABLE

(m)

Focused distance	Depth of field							Repro. ratio
	f/2.8	f/4	f/5.6	f/8	f/11	f/16	f/22	
4	3.99–4.01	3.98–4.02	3.97–4.03	3.96–4.04	3.95–4.05	3.93–4.07	3.9–4.1	1/11.71
5	4.98–5.02	4.97–5.03	4.96–5.04	4.94–5.06	4.92–5.08	4.88–5.[illegible]2	4.84–5.17	1/15.04
6	5.97–6.03	5.96–6.05	5.94–6.06	5.91–6.09	5.88–6.13	5.83–6.[illegible]9	5.76–6.26	1/18.37
7	6.96–7.04	6.94–7.06	6.91–7.09	6.88–7.13	6.83–7.18	6.76–7.26	6.67–7.37	1/21.71
8	7.94–8.06	7.92–8.08	7.88–8.12	7.84–8.17	7.78–8.24	7.68–8.35	7.57–8.49	1/25.04
10	9.91–10.09	9.87–10.14	9.82–10.19	9.74–10.28	9.65–10.33	9.49–10.57	9.32–10.8	1/31.71
12	11.86–12.14	11.81–12.2	11.73–12.28	11.62–12.41	11.43–12.57	11.27–12.84	11.0[illegible]–13.19	1/38.37
15	14.78–15.22	14.69–15.32	14.58–15.45	14.40–15.65	14.19–15.91	13.85–16.37	13.47–16.95	1/48.37
20	19.61–20.4	19.45–20.58	19.24–20.82	18.93–21.2	18.56–21.69	17.98–22.55	17.33–23.69	1/65.04
30	29.12–30.93	28.76–31.35	28.3–31.92	27.63–32.83	26.83–34.04	25.61–36.26	24.28–39.35	1/98.37
70	65.33–75.4	63.51–77.98	61.24–81.71	58.13–83.04	54.66–97.43	49.73–118.74	44.88–160.98	1/231.71
∞	964.87–∞	675.59–∞	482.73–∞	338.09–∞	246.04–∞	169.34–∞	123.31–∞	1/∞

NIKKOR 300mm *f*/4.5 IF-ED

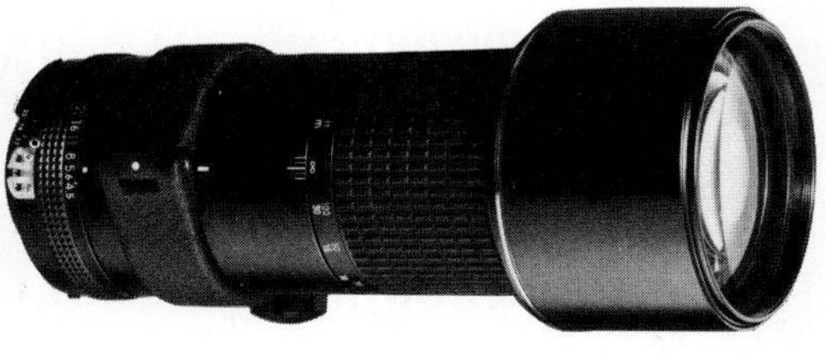
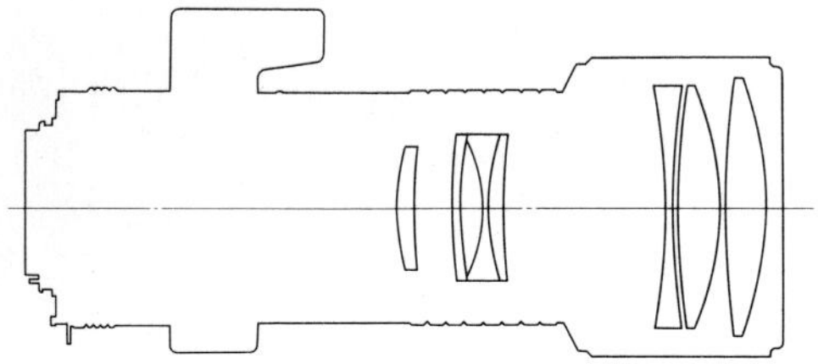

DESCRIPTION

The Nikkor 300mm *f*/4.5 IF-ED telephoto lens incorporates Nikon's Internal Focusing (IF) system. The result is a lightweight, relatively compact lens due to the elimination of bulky and heavy focusing mechanisms. The physical length of the lens does not change as it is focused. The weight and configuration of the lens enables stable and easy hand-held shooting. The 300mm *f*/4.5 IF-ED comprises elements made of Nikon Extra Low Dispersion (ED) glass for optimum correction of chromatic and other aberrations, even at full aperture. Nikon Integrated Coating is applied to air-to-glass surfaces to provide excellent contrast and color rendition. Excellent for sports photography. Closest focusing distance is 2.5m, exceptionally close for a lens of this focal length. Rotating tripod collar provided.

SPECIFICATIONS

Smallest aperture: 22
Nearest focus distance: 2.5m (10 ft)
Subject field at nearest distance: 16.8 × 25.2cm
Image ratio at nearest distance: 1:7
Focusing distances:
One head vertical: 4.4m (14.5 ft)
Two heads horizontal: 5.5m (18 ft)
One to three adults standing: 18.3m (60 ft)

Angeles of view:
Diagonal: 8°10′
Horizontal: 6°50′
Vertical: 4°30′
Ratio of image size at infinity to image of 50mm lens: 6:1
Attachment size (inside screw diameter): 72mm (P = 0.75)
Overall size: 80mm ø × 200mm
Weight: 990g (2.2 lb)

DEPTH OF FIELD TABLE

Meters

m \ f/	4.5	5.6	8	11	16	22	Magnification
4	3.98–4.02	3.97–4.03	3.96–4.04	3.95–4.05	3.92–4.08	3.89–4.11	1/11
5	4.96–5.04	4.96–5.04	4.94–5.06	4.91–5.09	4.88–5.13	4.83–5.18	1/14
6	5.95–6.05	5.93–6.07	5.91–6.09	5.87–6.13	5.82–6.19	5.75–6.28	1/17
7	6.93–7.07	6.91–7.09	6.87–7.13	6.82–7.19	6.75–7.27	6.65–7.39	1/21
8	7.90–8.10	7.88–8.12	7.83–8.18	7.76–8.25	7.67–8.36	7.54–8.52	1/24
9	8.88–9.13	8.85–9.16	8.78–9.23	8.70–9.32	8.58–9.46	8.42–9.67	1/27
10	9.85–10.2	9.81–10.2	9.73–10.3	9.63–10.4	9.48–10.6	9.28–10.8	1/31
12	11.8–12.2	11.7–12.3	11.6–12.4	11.5–12.6	11.2–12.9	11.0–13.3	1/37
15	14.7–15.4	14.6–15.5	14.4–15.7	14.2–16.0	13.8–16.4	13.4–17.0	1/47
20	19.4–20.7	19.2–20.8	18.9–21.2	18.5–21.8	17.9–22.6	17.2–23.8	1/64
30	28.6–31.5	28.3–32.0	27.6–32.8	26.7–34.2	25.6–36.3	24.1–39.7	1/97
60	54.6–66.6	53.4–68.5	51.0–72.8	48.1–79.8	44.4–92.4	40.1–119	1/197
∞	601 –∞	479 –∞	339 –∞	240 –∞	170 –∞	120 –∞	1/∞

300mm f/4.5 NIKKOR ED

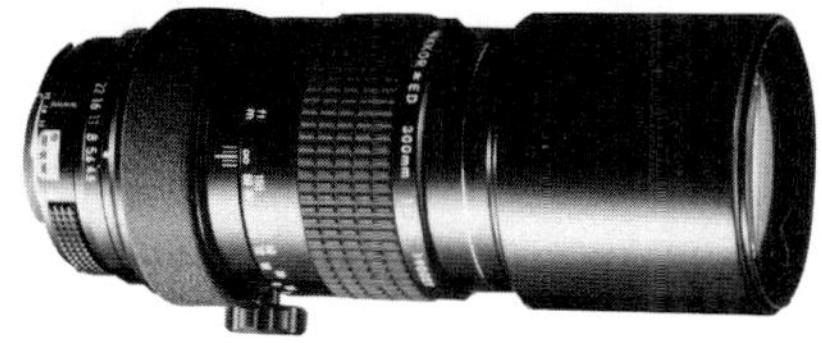

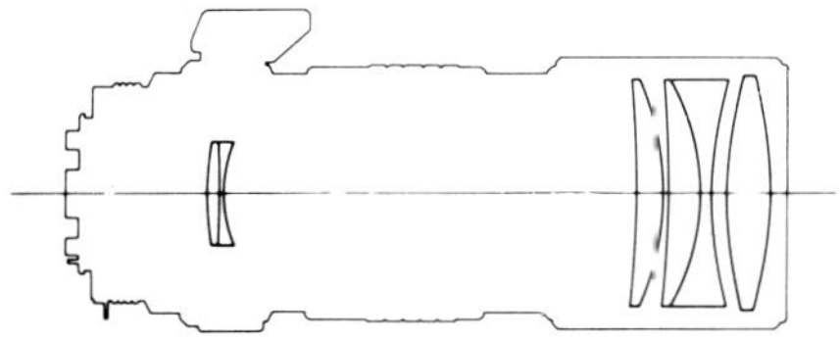

DESCRIPTION

The 300mm Nikkor *f*/4.5 ED is a compact, lightweight telephoto lens with a construction of 6 elements in 4 groups. It differs from the standard 300mm *f*/4.5 primarily in the use of ED (Extra Low Dispersion) glass. The unique dispersion characteristics of this glass eliminate approximately 90 percent of the secondary spectrum across the 400 to 1000 nanometer wavelength range, providing an exceptional degree of chromatic aberration correction. The use of ED glass also contributes to the elimination of other aberrations. Corrective refocusing for infrared photography is not necessary with this lens. The 300mm *f*/4.5 ED has the same applications in sports, wildlife, and close-up photography as the standard 300mm *f*/4.5. A rotating tripod collar is provided.

SPECIFICATIONS

Smallest aperture: 22
Nearest focus distance: 4m (13 ft)
Subject field at nearest distance: 26.4 × 39.6cm
Image ratio at nearest distance: 1:11
Focusing distances:
  One head vertical: 4.4m (14.5 ft)
  Two heads horizontal: 5.5m (18 ft)
  One to three adults standing: 18.3m (60 ft)
Angles of view:
  Diagonal: 8°10′
  Horizontal: 6°50′
  Vertical: 4°30′
Ratio of image size at infinity to image of 50mm lens: 6:1
Attachment size (inside screw diameter): 72mm (P = 0.75)
Lens hood: Built-in
Front lens cap: 72mm screw-in
Lens case: CL-20A
Overall size: 78.5mm ø × 201mm
Weight: 1.1kg (2.4 lb)

DEPTH OF FIELD TABLE

Meters

m \ f/	4.5	5.6	8	11	16	22	Magnification
4	3.98–4.02	3.97–4.03	3.96–4.04	3.95–4.05	3.92–4.08	3.89–4.11	1/11
5	4.96–5.04	4.96–5.04	4.94–5.06	4.91–5.09	4.88–5.13	4.83–5.18	1/14
6	5.95–6.05	5.93–6.07	5.91–6.09	5.87–6.13	5.82–6.19	5.75–6.28	1/17
7	6.93–7.07	6.91–7.09	6.87–7.13	6.82–7.19	6.75–7.27	6.65–7.39	1/21
8	7.90–8.10	7.88–8.12	7.83–8.18	7.76–8.25	7.67–8.36	7.54–8.52	1/24
9	8.88–9.13	8.85–9.16	8.78–9.23	8.70–9.32	8.58–9.46	8.42–9.67	1/27
10	9.85–10.2	9.81–10.2	9.73–10.3	9.63–10.4	9.48–10.6	9.28–10.8	1/31
12	11.8–12.2	11.7–12.3	11.6–12.4	11.5–12.6	11.2–12.9	11.0–13.3	1/37
15	14.7–15.4	14.6–15.5	14.4–15.7	14.2–16.0	13.8–16.4	13.4–17.0	1/47
20	19.4–20.7	19.2–20.8	18.9–21.2	18.5–21.8	17.9–22.6	17.2–23.8	1/64
30	28.6–31.5	28.3–32.0	27.6–32.8	26.7–34.2	25.6–36.3	24.1–39.7	1/97
60	54.6–66.6	53.4–68.5	51.0–72.8	48.1–79.8	44.4–92.4	40.1–119	1/197
∞	601 –∞	479 –∞	339 –∞	240 –∞	170 –∞	120 –∞	1/∞

300mm *f*/4.5 NIKKOR

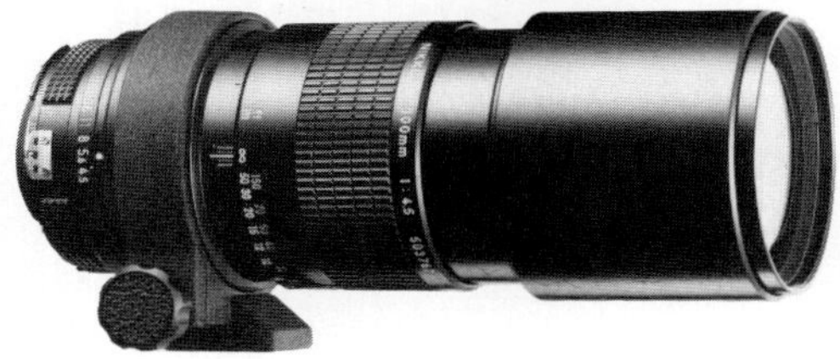

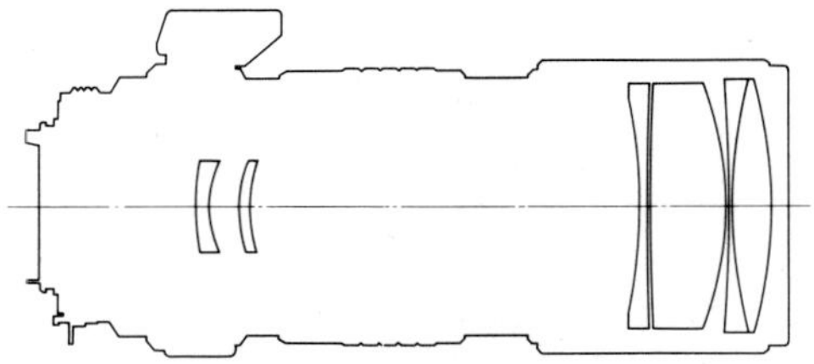

DESCRIPTION

The 300mm telephoto lens is considered to be longest for relatively safe hand-held shooting. Its pictorial scope is the background in action—sports and scenic photography—for it overshoots both foreground and middle ground. Telephoto design affords a relatively short barrel. Excellent at full aperture, but performance is optional at *f*/5.6 to *f*/8. When used at nearest focusing limits, lens isolates image planes because of very shallow depth of field. Closeups in normal mode yield interesting effects with maximum separation between lens and object, but focusing must be critical.

SPECIFICATIONS

Smallest aperture: 22
Nearest focus distance: 4m (13 ft)
Subject field at nearest distance: 26.4 × 39.6cm
Image ratio at nearest distance: 1:11
Focusing distances:
  One head vertical: 4.4m (14.5 ft)
  Two heads horizontal: 5.5m (18 ft)
  One to three adults standing: 18.3m (60 ft)
Angles of view:
  Diagonal: 8°10′
  Horizontal: 6°50′
  Vertical: 4°30′
Ratio of image size at infinity to image of 50mm lens: 6:1
Attachment size (inside screw diameter): 72mm (P = 0.75)
Lens hood: Built-in
Front lens cap: 72mm screw-in
Lens case: CL-20A
Overall size: 78.5mm ø × 203mm
Weight: 1.1kg (2.4 lb)

DEPTH OF FIELD TABLE

Meters

m \ f/	4.5	5.6	8	11	16	22	Magnification
4	3.98–4.02	3.97–4.03	3.96–4.04	3.95–4.05	3.92–4.08	3.89–4.11	1/11
5	4.96–5.04	4.96–5.04	4.94–5.06	4.91–5.09	4.88–5.13	4.83–5.18	1/14
6	5.95–6.05	5.93–6.07	5.91–6.09	5.87–6.13	5.82–6.19	5.75–6.28	1/17
7	6.93–7.07	6.91–7.09	6.87–7.13	6.82–7.19	6.75–7.27	6.65–7.39	1/21
8	7.90–8.10	7.88–8.12	7.83–8.18	7.76–8.25	7.67–8.36	7.54–8.52	1/24
9	8.88–9.13	8.85–9.16	8.78–9.23	8.70–9.32	8.58–9.46	8.42–9.67	1/27
10	9.85–10.2	9.81–10.2	9.73–10.3	9.63–10.4	9.48–10.6	9.28–10.8	1/31
12	11.8–12.2	11.7–12.3	11.6–12.4	11.5–12.6	11.2–12.9	11.0–13.3	1/37
15	14.7–15.4	14.6–15.5	14.4–15.7	14.2–16.0	13.8–16.4	13.4–17.0	1/47
20	19.4–20.7	19.2–20.8	18.9–21.2	18.5–21.8	17.9–22.6	17.2–23.8	1/64
30	28.6–31.5	28.3–32.0	27.6–32.8	26.7–34.2	25.6–36.3	24.1–39.7	1/97
60	54.6–66.6	53.4–68.5	51.0–72.8	48.1–79.8	44.4–92.4	40.1–119	1/197
∞	601 –∞	479 –∞	339 –∞	240 –∞	170 –∞	120 –∞	1/∞

400mm *f*/3.5 NIKKOR IF-ED

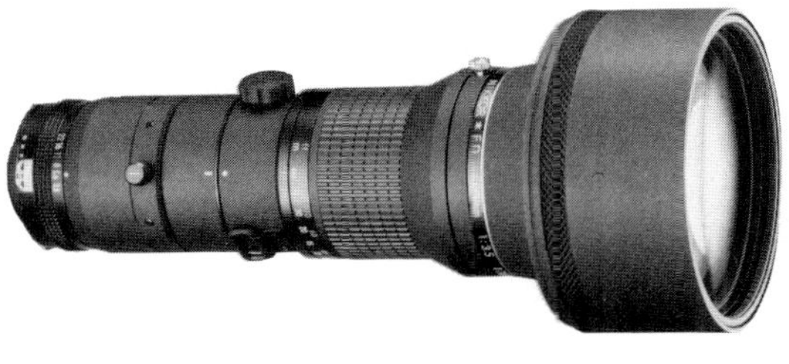

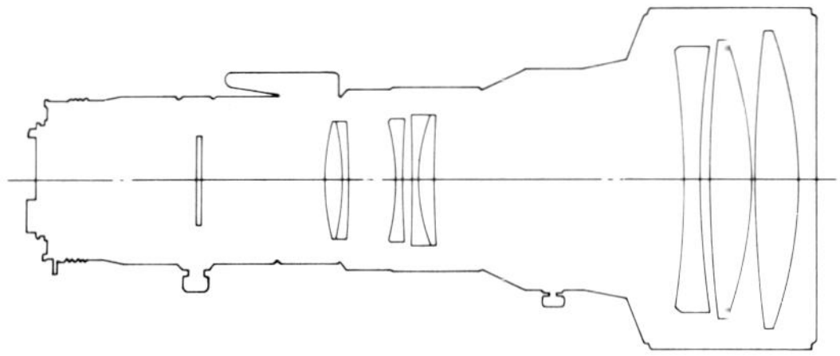

DESCRIPTION

The Nikkor 400mm *f*/3.5 ED IF lens employs Nikon Extra Low Dispersion glass for improved performance, which is characterized by high chromatic aberration correction, even when operated at the exceptionally fast *f*/3.5 aperture setting. The use of the Nikon Internal Focusing (IF) system provides for elimination of the normally bulky helicoid assembly associated with a lens of this focal length; thus, the lens is more compact, lightweight, and easier to balance (it does not change length during focusing) while shooting. Other features include a slip-in filter holder capable of accepting either standard 39mm glass filters or gelatine filters, a focus preset ring for refocusing operation by touch, and the capability of turning the focusing ring past the infinity mark for correcting the effects of thermal expansion under extreme climatic conditions. Built-in rotatable tripod collar provided.

SPECIFICATIONS

Smallest aperture: 22
Nearest focus distance: 4.5m (15 ft)
Focusing distances:
  One head vertical: 5.8m (19 ft)
  Two heads horizontal: 7.4m (24 ft)
  One to three adults standing: 24.4m (80 ft)
Angeles of view:
  Diagonal: 6°10′
  Horizontal: 5°10′
  Vertical: 3°30′
Ratio of image size at infinity to image of 50mm lens: 8:1
Attachment size (inside screw diameter): 122mm (P = 1.00)
Lens hood: Built-in
Front lens cap: 122mm screw-in
Lens case: CL-61
Overall size: 134mm ø × 304mm
Weight: 2.8kg (6.2 lb)

DEPTH OF FIELD TABLE

(m)

Focused distance	Depth of field							Repro. ratio
	f/3.5	f/4	f/5.6	f/8	f/11	f/16	f/22	
4.5	4.49–4.51	4.49–4.51	4.48–4.52	4.47–4.53	4.46–4.54	4.45–4.55	4.43–4.57	1/9.82
5	4.99–5.01	4.98–5.02	4.98–5.02	4.97–5.03	4.96–5.04	4.93–5.07	4.91–5.09	1/11.07
6	5.98–6.02	5.98–6.02	5.97–6.03	5.95–6.05	5.93–6.07	5.9–6.1	5.86–6.14	1/13.57
7	6.97–7.03	6.97–7.03	6.95–7.05	6.93–7.07	6.91–7.09	6.86–7.14	6.81–7.19	1/16.07
8	7.96–8.04	7.95–8.05	7.94–8.06	7.91–8.09	7.87–8.13	7.82–8.18	7.75–8.25	1/18.57
10	9.94–10.06	9.93–10.07	9.90–10.1	9.85–10.15	9.8–10.2	9.7–10.3	9.59–10.41	1/23.57
12	11.9–12.1	11.89–12.11	11.85–12.15	11.78–12.22	11.7–12.3	11.56–12.44	11.4–12.6	1/28.57
15	14.85–15.15	14.83–15.17	14.76–15.24	14.65–15.35	14.52–15.48	14.31–15.69	14.05–15.69	1/36.07
20	19.72–20.28	19.69–20.31	19.56–20.44	19.37–20.63	19.13–20.87	18.74–21.26	18.27–21.73	1/48.57
30	29.37–30.63	29.28–30.72	28.99–31.01	28.56–31.44	28.02–31.98	27.11–32.89	26.03–33.97	1/73.57
70	66.49–73.51	65.98–74.02	64.38–75.62	61.97–78.03	58.95–81.05	53.93–86.07	47.91–92.09	1/173.57
∞	1372–∞	1200.57–∞	857.71–∞	600.57–∞	436.94–∞	300.57–∞	218.75–∞	1/∞

400mm *f*/4.5 NIKKOR-Q AUTO

Requires Focusing Unit for which Optional Cradle is available

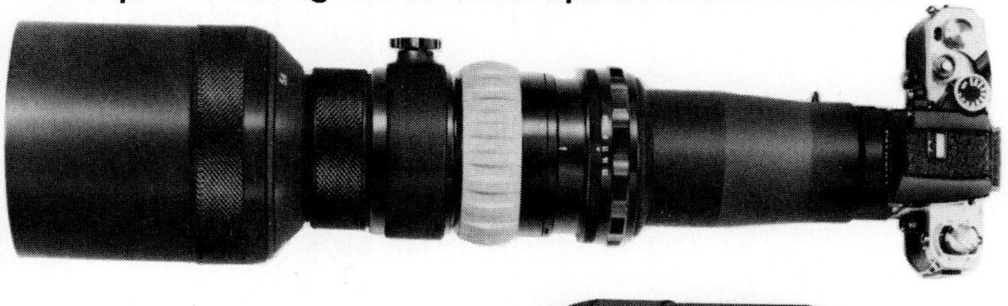

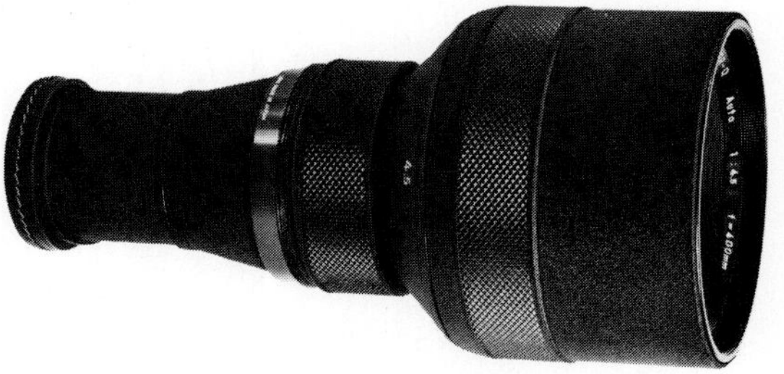

DESCRIPTION

This 400mm telephoto lens must be used with the accessory focusing unit for automatic diaphragm control and focusing. Intended mainly for use with tripod, this lens can occasionally be used hand-held, but handy solid supports should be utilized when available. Ideal for coverage of popular action sports, game stalking, and recording of distant events generally. High-speed films preferred in order to utilize fast shutter speeds under a wide range of lighting conditions.

SPECIFICATIONS

Smallest aperture: 22
Nearest focus distance: 5m (16 ft)
Subject field at nearest distance: 26.4 x 39.6cm
Image ratio at nearest distance: 1:11
Focusing distances:
- One head vertical: 5.8m (19.0 ft)
- Two heads horizontal: 7.4m (24 ft)
- One to three adults standing: 24.4m (80 ft)

Angles of view:
- Diagonal: 6°10′
- Horizontal: 5°10′
- Vertical: 3°30′

Ratio of image size at infinity to image of 50mm lens: 8:1
Attachment size (inside screw diameter): 122mm (P = 1.00)
Lens hood: Built-in telescopic type
Front lens cap: 133mm slip-on leather cap
Rear lens cap: Slip-on leather cap (U.S. 599)
Lens case: Wooden case (U.S. 462)
Overall size: 135mm ϕ x 471.5mm
Weight: 3.1 kg (6.8 lb)

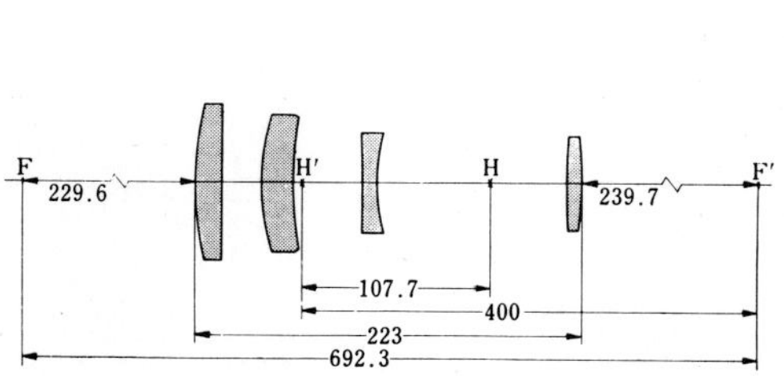

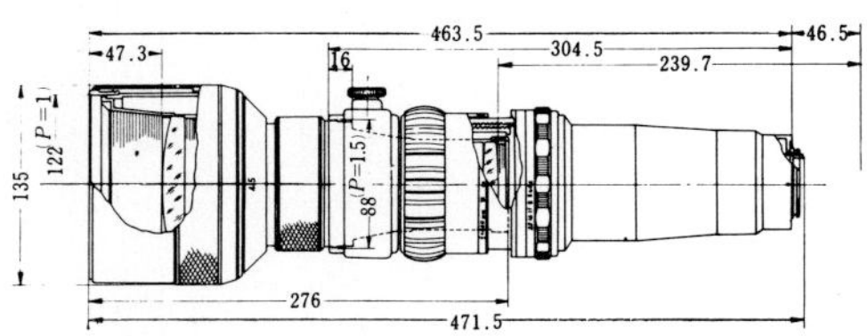

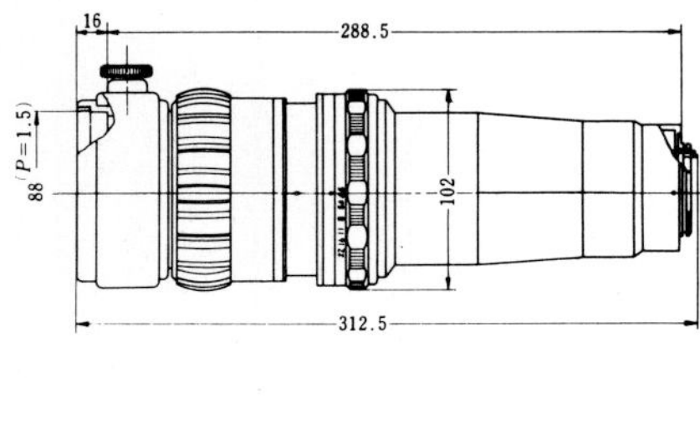

400mm *f*/5.6 NIKKOR IF-ED

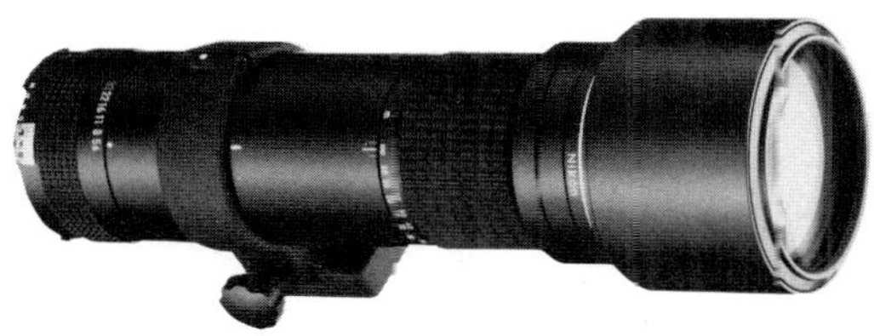

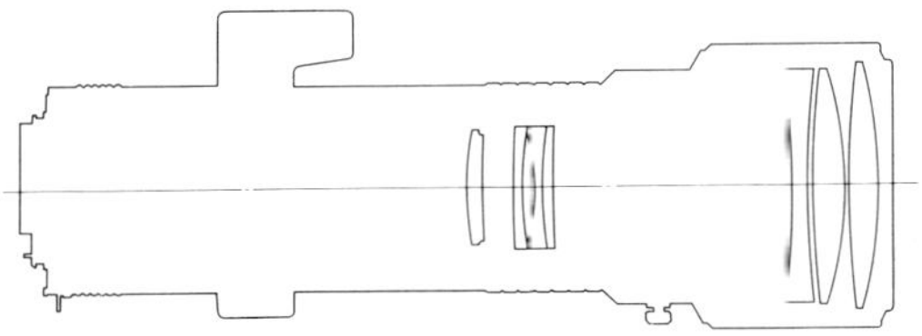

DESCRIPTION

The adoption of Nikon's Internal Focusing (IF) system in its design makes this Nikkor telephoto extremely compact and lightweight for its focal length. The lens barrel is well-shaped, enabling stable and easy hand-held shooting. The lens is comprised of elements made of Nikon Extra Low Dispersion (ED) glass, which provides optimum correction of chromatic aberration. The close focusing distance of 4m (15 ft) is exceptional for a lens of this focal length. A preset focusing ring enables the photographer to quickly return "by feel" to a preset position on the focusing ring, an especially valuable feature when photographing sports or other fast-moving action. Rotating tripod collar is provided.

SPECIFICATIONS

Smallest aperture: 32
Nearest focus distance: 4m (16 ft)
Subject field at nearest distance: 26.4 × 32.4cm
Image ratio at nearest distance: 1:9
Focusing distances:
One head vertical: 5.8m (19 ft)
Two heads horizontal: 7.4m (24 ft)
One to three adults standing: 24.4m (80 ft)

Angles of view:
Diagonal: 6°10′
Horizontal: 5°10′
Vertical: 3°30′
Ratio of image size at infinity to image of 50mm lens: 8:1
Attachment size (inside screw diameter): 72mm (P = 0.75)
Overall size: 85mm ϕ × 262mm
Weight: 1.17kg (2.6 lb)

DEPTH OF FIELD TABLE

Meters

m \ f/	5.6	8	11	16	22	32	Magnification
5	4.98–5.02	4.97–5.03	4.96–5.04	4.95–5.05	4.93–5.07	4.90–5.11	1/9.49
5.5	5.48–5.52	5.47–5.53	5.45–5.55	5.43–5.57	5.41–5.59	5.37–5.64	1/10.7
6	5.97–6.03	5.96–6.04	5.94–6.06	5.92–6.08	5.89–6.12	5.84–6.17	1/12.0
6.5	6.46–6.54	6.45–6.55	6.43–6.57	6.40–6.60	6.36–6.64	6.31–6.71	1/13.3
7	6.96–7.04	6.94–7.06	6.92–7.08	6.88–7.12	6.84–7.17	6.77–7.25	1/14.5
8	7.94–8.06	7.92–8.08	7.89–8.11	7.84–8.17	7.78–8.23	7.69–8.34	1/17.0
9	8.93–9.08	8.89–9.11	8.86–9.15	8.79–9.22	8.72–9.31	8.59–9.45	1/19.5
10	9.91–10.1	9.87–10.1	9.82–10.2	9.74–10.3	9.64–10.4	9.49–10.6	1/22.0
12	11.9–12.1	11.8–12.2	11.7–12.3	11.6–12.4	11.5–12.6	11.2–12.9	1/27.1
15	14.8–15.2	14.7–15.3	14.6–15.5	14.4–15.7	14.2–16.0	13.8–16.4	1/34.6
20	19.6–20.4	19.4–20.6	19.2–20.9	18.9–21.3	18.5–21.8	17.9–22.8	1/44.1
30	29.0–31.0	28.7–31.5	28.2–32.1	27.4–33.1	26.6–34.5	25.3–37.0	1/72.1
50	47.3–53.0	46.3–54.4	45.0–56.2	43.1–59.6	41.[illegible]–64.2	37.9–73.9	1/122
100	89.7–113	86.0–120	81.7–129	75.4–149	69.[illegible]–182	60.7–293	1/247
∞	858–∞	601–∞	438–∞	301–∞	219–∞	151–∞	1/∞

400mm *f*/5.6 NIKKOR ED

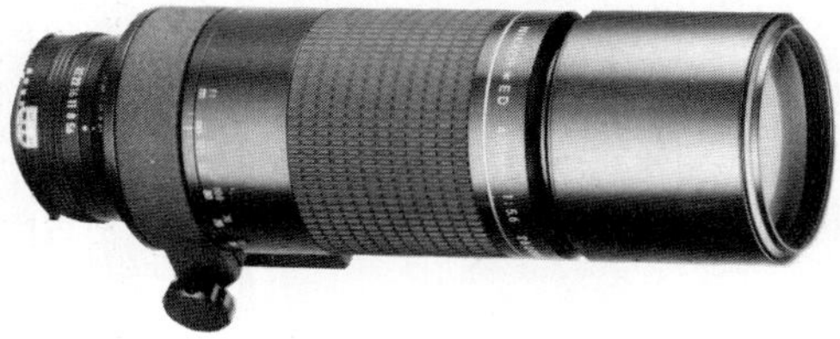

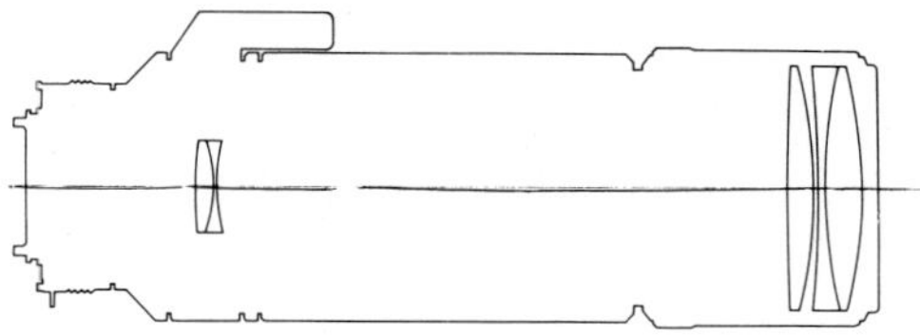

DESCRIPTION

The special feature of the Nikkor 400mm *f*/5.6 ED lens is the use of Nikon's Extra Low Dispersion (ED) glass for controlling chromatic aberration, even at full aperture. For infrared photography, corrective refocusing is necessary. Nikon Integrated Coating improves image contrast and color resolution. Compact design permits hand-holding the lens at fast shutter speeds for covering sports, wildlife, and fast-breaking action. Built-in rotating tripod mounting collar is provided.

SPECIFICATIONS

Smallest aperture: 32
Nearest focus distance: 5m (16 ft)
Subject field at nearest distance: 26.4 × 39.6cm
Image ratio at nearest distance: 1:11
Focusing distances:
One head vertical: 5.8m (19 ft)
Two heads horizontal: 7.4m (24 ft)
One to three adults standing: 24.4m (80 ft)
Angles of view:
Diagonal: 6°10′
Horizontal: 5°10′
Vertical: 3°30′
Ratio of image size at infinity to image of 50mm lens: 8:1
Attachment size (inside screw diameter): 72mm (P = 0.75)
Lens hood: Built-in
Front lens cap: 72mm screw-in
Lens case: CL-27A
Overall size: 83mm ϕ × 263mm
Weight: 1.4kg (3.1 lb)

DEPTH OF FIELD TABLE

Meters

m \ f/	5.6	8	11	16	22	32	Magnification
5	4.98–5.02	4.97–5.03	4.96–5.04	4.95–5.05	4.93–5.07	4.90–5.11	1/9.49
5.5	5.48–5.52	5.47–5.53	5.45–5.55	5.43–5.57	5.41–5.59	5.37–5.64	1/10.7
6	5.97–6.03	5.96–6.04	5.94–6.06	5.92–6.08	5.89–6.12	5.84–6.17	1/12.0
6.5	6.46–6.54	6.45–6.55	6.43–6.57	6.40–6.60	6.36–6.64	6.31–6.71	1/13.3
7	6.96–7.04	6.94–7.06	6.92–7.08	6.88–7.12	6.84–7.17	6.77–7.25	1/14.5
8	7.94–8.06	7.92–8.08	7.89–8.11	7.84–8.17	7.78–8.23	7.69–8.34	1/17.0
9	8.93–9.08	8.89–9.11	8.86–9.15	8.79–9.22	8.72–9.31	8.59–9.45	1/19.5
10	9.91–10.1	9.87–10.1	9.82–10.2	9.74–10.3	9.64–10.4	9.49–10.6	1/22.0
12	11.9–12.1	11.8–12.2	11.7–12.3	11.6–12.4	11.5–12.6	11.2–12.9	1/27.1
15	14.8–15.2	14.7–15.3	14.6–15.5	14.4–15.7	14.2–16.0	13.8–16.4	1/34.6
20	19.6–20.4	19.4–20.6	19.2–20.9	18.9–21.3	18.5–21.8	17.9–22.8	1/44.1
30	29.0–31.0	28.7–31.5	28.2–32.1	27.4–33.1	26.6–34.5	25.3–37.0	1/72.1
50	47.3–53.0	46.3–54.4	45.0–56.2	43.1–59.6	41.0–64.2	37.9–73.9	1/122
100	89.7–113	86.0–120	81.7–129	75.4–149	69.1–182	60.7–293	1/247
∞	858–∞	601–∞	438–∞	301–∞	219–∞	151–∞	1/∞

500mm f/8 REFLEX-NIKKOR

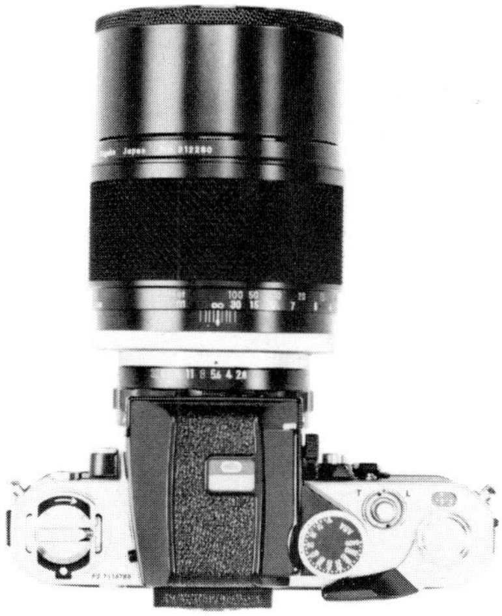

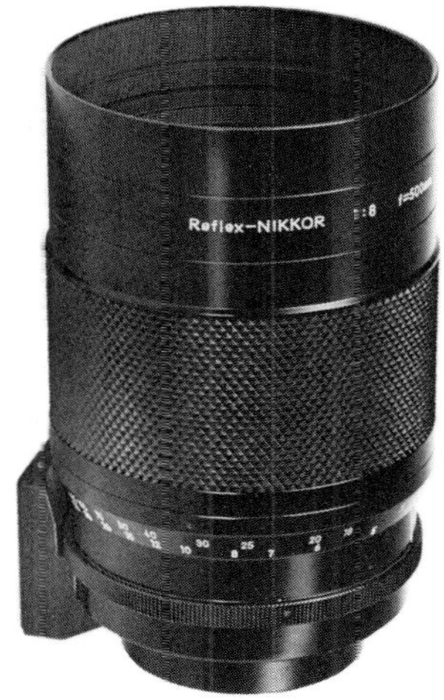

DESCRIPTION

Remarkably compact and lightweight 500mm Reflex-Nikkor may be hand-held for shooting by skilled photographer. It measures less than one-third its focal length and may therefore be carried easily for sports, wildlife, or general photojournalism. One of its great advantages over refractor-type lenses is its close-focusing capability—4m (13 ft.). Inexpensive filters are mounted at rear. Exposure control (which does not affect depth of field) is achieved with neutral density filters. On tripod, a vertical or horizontal format can be selected by pushing on knurled-spring catch at rear of lens.

SPECIFICATIONS

Smallest aperture: Single fixed aperture
Nearest focus distance: 4m (13 ft)
Subject field at nearest distance: 172.8 x 259.2
Image ratio at nearest distance: 1:7.2
Focusing distances:
One head vertical: 7.3m (23.8 ft)
Two heads horizontal: 9.2m (30 ft)
One to three adults standing: 30.5m (100 ft)
Angles of view:
Diagonal: 5°
Horizontal: 4°10′
Vertical: 2°50′

Ratio of image size at infinity to image of 50mm lens: 10:1
Attachment size (inside screw diameter):
Rear filter size 39mm (P = 1.00); built-in filters L-39, Y48, O56, R60, ND
Front attachment size: 88mm (P = 0.75)
Lens hood: Screw-in type 87mm
Front lens cap: 91mm slip-on leather cap (U.S. 625)
Lens case: CL-23
Overall size: 93mm ϕ x 141.5mm
Weight: 1 kg (2.2 lb)

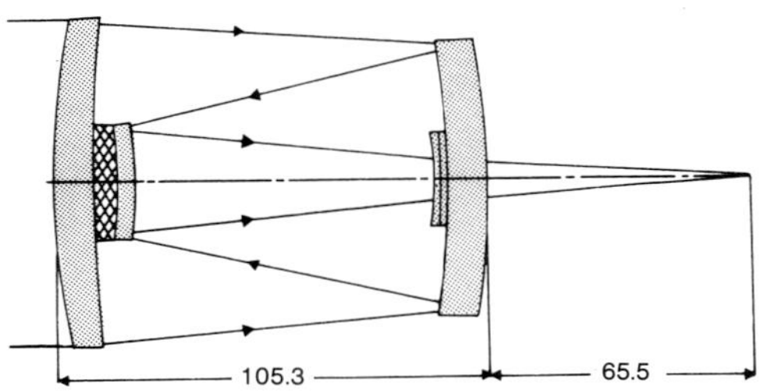

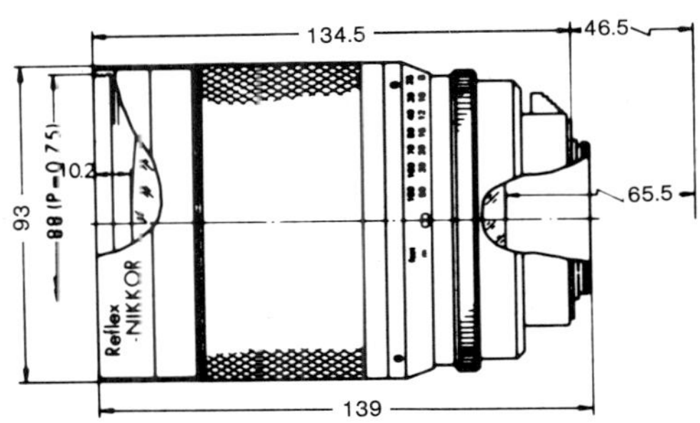

600mm *f*/5.6 NIKKOR IF-ED

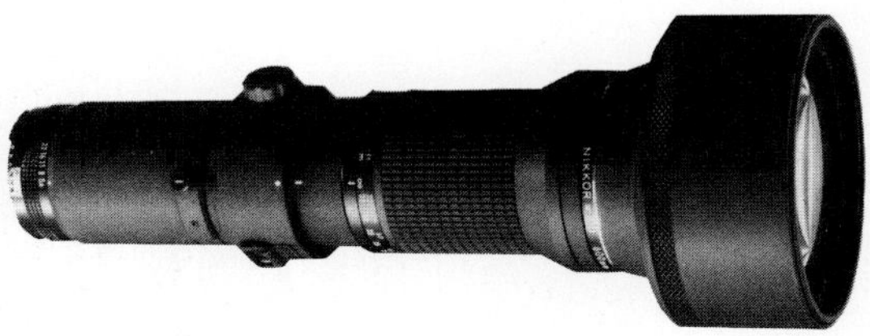

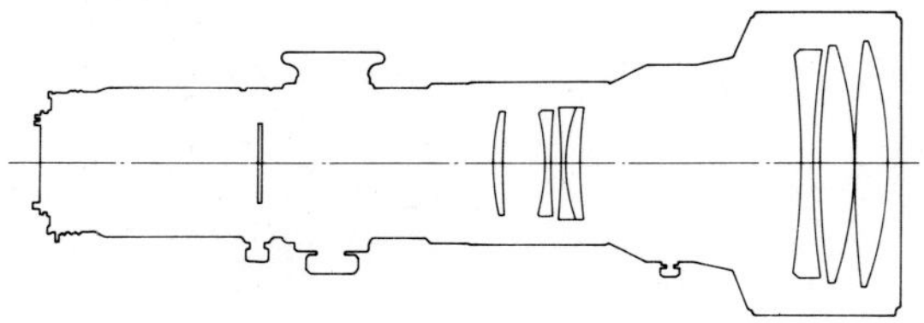

DESCRIPTION

The Nikkor 600mm *f*/5.6 is a super-telephoto lens of relatively compact size, featuring selected elements made of Nikon Extra Low Dispersion (ED) glass for control of chromatic aberration. The result is sharp, high-contrast images, even when the lens is operated at maximum aperture. This lens also features the Nikon Internal Focusing system, eliminating the need for a large and heavy focusing helicoid, normally found in lenses of this focal length. In addition to greater compactness and weight reduction, the IF system is easier to hand-hold, due to the fact that the lens does not change physical length during focusing. Other features include slip-in filter holders for inserting 39mm filters within the lens barrel, a preset focus feature for rapid refocusing by touch, and focusing adjustment past the infinity mark, which compensates for temperature-induced focus shift.

SPECIFICATIONS

Smallest aperture: 22
Nearest focus distance: 5.5m (20 ft)
Focusing distances:
One head vertical: 11.6m (38 ft)
Two heads horizontal: 14.8m (48 ft)
One to three adults standing: 48.8m (160 ft)
Angles of view:
Diagonal: 4°10′
Horizontal: 3°30′
Vertical: 2°20′
Ratio of image size at infinity to image of 50mm lens: 12:1
Attachment size (inside screw diameter): 122mm (P = 1.00)
Lens hood: Built-in
Front lens cap: 133mm slip-on leather cap provided
Lens case: CL-62
Overall size: 134mm ϕ × 382mm
Weight: 2.7kg (5.9 lb)

DEPTH OF FIELD TABLE

(m)

Focused distance	Depth of field *f*/4	*f*/5.6	*f*/8	*f*/11	*f*/16	*f*/22	*f*/32	Reproduction ratio
0.71	0.709–0.711	0.709–0.711	0.709–0.711	0.708–0.712	0.707–0.713	0.706–0.714	0.705–0.715	1/1.99
0.80	0.799–0.801	0.799–0.801	0.798–0.802	0.797–0.803	0.796–0.804	0.795–0.805	0.792–0.808	1/2.44
0.90	0.899–0.901	0.898–0.902	0.897–0.903	0.896–0.904	0.895–0.905	0.893–0.908	0.889–0.911	1/2.94
1.0	0.998–1.00	0.997–1.00	0.996–1.00	0.995–1.01	0.993–1.01	0.990–1.01	0.986–1.01	1/3.4
1.2	1.20–1.20	1.20–1.20	1.19–1.21	1.19–1.21	1.19–1.21	1.18–1.22	1.18–1.22	1/4.4
1.5	1.49–1.51	1.49–1.51	1.49–1.51	1.49–1.51	1.48–1.52	1.47–1.53	1.46–1.54	1/5.9
2.0	1.99–2.01	1.99–2.01	1.98–2.02	1.97–2.03	1.96–2.04	1.95–2.06	1.92–2.08	1/8.4
3.0	2.98–3.03	2.97–3.04	2.95–3.05	2.93–3.07	2.90–3.10	2.87–3.14	2.81–3.22	1/13.4
4.0	3.95–4.05	3.94–4.07	3.91–4.10	3.88–4.13	3.82–4.20	3.76–4.28	3.66–4.42	1/18.4
6.0	5.89–6.11	5.85–6.16	5.79–6.23	5.71–6.32	5.59–6.48	5.45–6.68	5.24–7.04	1/28.4
12.0	11.6–12.5	11.4–12.7	11.1–13.0	10.9–13.4	10.4–14.2	9.9–15.2	9.2–17.4	1/58.4
∞	300–∞	215–∞	150–∞	109–∞	75–∞	55–∞	38–∞	1/∞

600mm f/5.6 NIKKOR ED

Requires Focusing Unit for which Optional Cradle is available

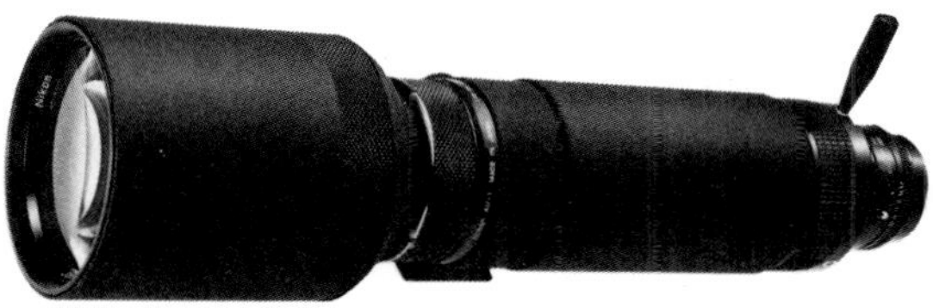

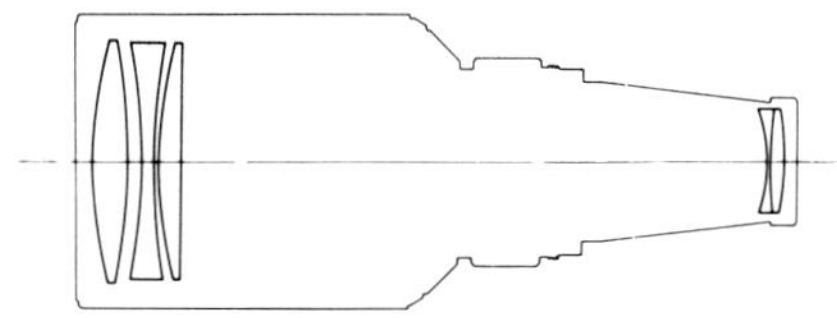

DESCRIPTION

The special feature of this long-focus lens is the use of Extra Low Dispersion (ED) glass, resulting in excellent correction of chromatic aberration, even at maximum aperture. The lens is intended for use with the focusing unit that includes the automatic diaphragm control and focusing mechanism. A tripod or other support is essential. Useful primarily in sports, wildlife, and surveillance photography.

SPECIFICATIONS

Smallest aperture: 22
Nearest focus distance: 11m (36 ft)
Subject field at nearest distance: 38.4 × 57.6cm
Image ratio at nearest distance: 1:16
Focusing distances:
  One head vertical: 11.6m (38 ft)
  Two heads horizontal: 14.8m (48 ft)
  One to three adults standing: 48.8m (160 ft)
Angles of view:
  Diagonal: 4°10′
  Horizontal: 3°30′
  Vertical: 2°20′
Ratio of image size at infinity to image of 50mm lens: 12:1
Attachment size (inside screw diameter): 122mm (P = 1.00)
Lens hood: Built-in
Front lens cap: 133mm slip-on leather cap provided
Lens case: CE-5
Overall size: 135mm φ × 517mm (including focusing unit)
Weight: 4.8 kg (10.6 lb)

DEPTH OF FIELD TABLE

Meters

m \ f/	5.6	8	11	16	22	Magnification
11	11.0–11.1	10.9–11.1	10.9–11.1	10.9–11.2	10.8–11.2	1/16
12	11.9–12.1	11.9–12.1	11.9–12.1	11.8–12.2	11.8–12.3	1/18
13	12.9–13.1	12.9–13.1	12.9–13.2	12.8–13.2	12.7–13.3	1/20
15	14.9–15.1	14.9–15.2	14.8–15.2	14.7–15.3	14.6–15.4	1/23
18	17.9–18.2	17.8–18.2	17.7–18.3	17.6–18.4	17.4–18.6	1/28
20	19.8–20.2	19.7–20.3	19.6–20.4	19.5–20.6	19.3–20.8	1/31
25	24.7–25.3	24.6–25.4	24.4–25.6	24.2–25.9	23.9–26.2	1/40
30	29.6–30.4	29.4–30.6	29.2–30.9	28.8–31.3	28.4–31.8	1/48
40	39.2–40.8	38.9–41.2	38.5–41.6	37.9–42.4	37.1–43.4	1/65
50	48.8–51.3	48.3–51.9	47.7–52.6	46.7–53.9	45.5–55.5	1/81
70	67.6–72.6	66.6–73.7	65.5–75.2	63.6–77.9	61.5–81.3	1/115
100	95.2–105	93.2–108	90.9–111	87.3–117	83.3–125	1/165
200	181 –223	174 –235	166 –251	155 –283	142 –336	1/331
∞	1930–∞	1350–∞	981 –∞	675 –∞	490 –∞	1/∞

600mm f/5.6 NIKKOR-P AUTO

Requires Focusing Unit for which Optional Cradle is available

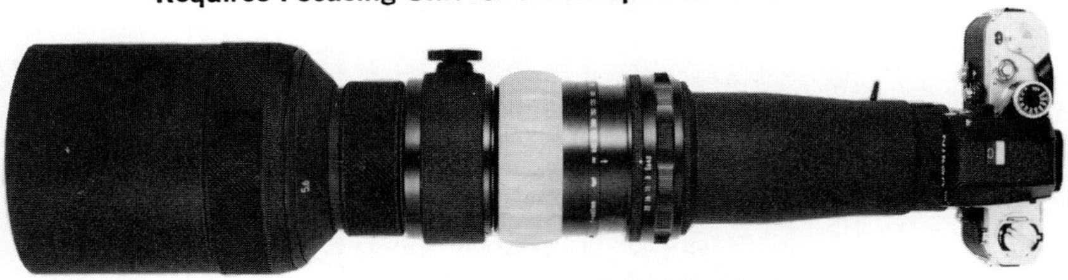

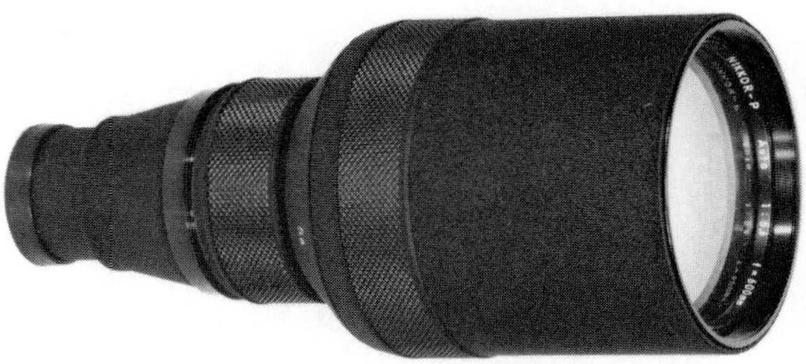

DESCRIPTION

Magnification of image with 600mm lens is twelve times that of normal 50mm lens. Intended for use with the focusing unit which includes the automatic diaphragm control and focusing mechanism. A tripod or other solid support is essential. Used primarily in sports and wildlife photography and in surveillance work at appropriate distances.

SPECIFICATIONS

Smallest aperture: 22
Nearest focus distance: 11m (35 ft)
Subject field at nearest distance: 38.4 x 57.6cm
Image ratio at nearest distance: 1:16
Focusing distances:
 One head vertical: 11.6m (38.0 ft)
 Two heads horizontal: 14.8m (48 ft)
 One to three adults standing: 48.8m (160 ft)
Angles of view:
 Diagonal: 4°10′
 Horizontal: 3°30′
 Vertical: 2°20′
Ratio of image size at infinity to image of 50mm lens: 12:1
Attachment size (inside screw diameter): 122mm (P = 1.0); slip-on outer diameter: 133mm
Lens.hood: Built-in telescopic type
Front lens cap: 133mm slip-on leather cap
Rear lens cap: Slip-on leather cap (U.S. 599)
Lens case: Wooden case (U.S. 462)
Overall size: 135mm ϕ x 516.5mm
Weight: 3.6 kg (7.9 lb)

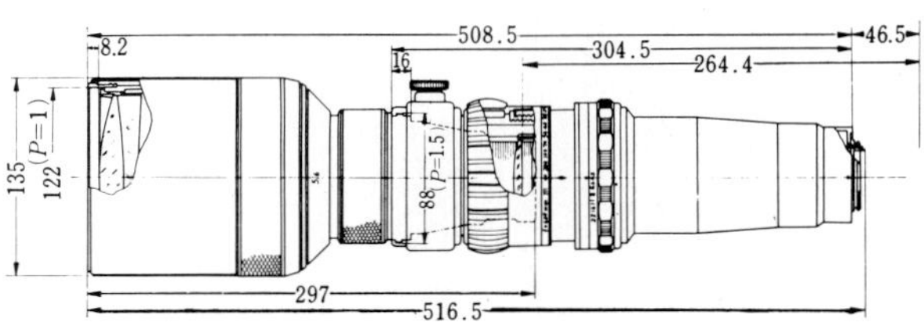

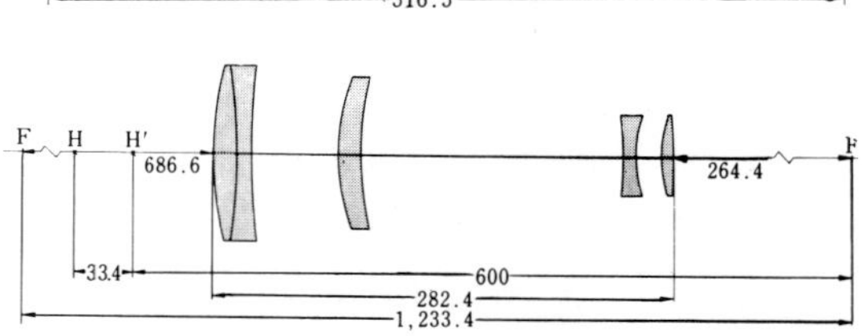

800mm *f*/8 NIKKOR IF-ED

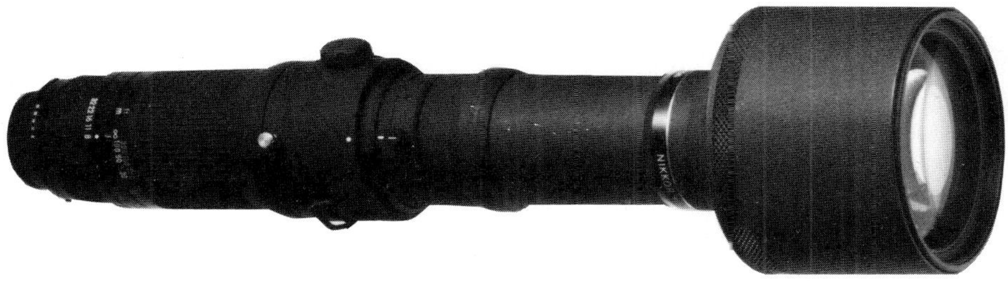

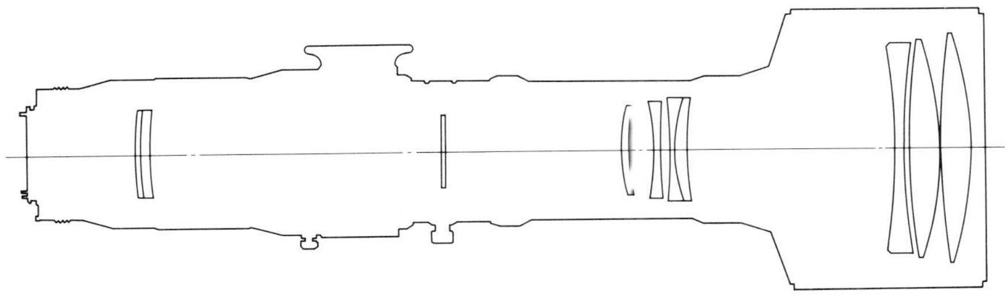

DESCRIPTION

This telephoto lens is one of the first of its kind; a super-telephoto lens with a built-in focusing unit, offering meter coupling for full-aperture metering. The 800mm *f*/8 IF-ED uses Nikon Extra Low Dispersion (ED) glass for optimum correction of chromatic aberration, even at full aperture. The Internal Focusing (IF) mechanism results in exceptional compactness and lightness for a lens of this focal length. The physical length of the lens does not change as focus is changed. A preset focusing ring permits the photographer to quickly return to a previously set position on the focusing ring. The lens also has a filter holder which accepts standard 39mm filters. Rotating tripod collar is provided.

SPECIFICATIONS

Smallest aperture: 32
Nearest focus distance: 10m (35 ft)
Subject field at nearest distance: 27.6 × 41.4cm
Image ratio at nearest distance: 1:11
Focusing distances:
  One head vertical: 14.5m (47.5 ft)
  Two heads horizontal: 18.5m (60 ft)
  One to three adults standing: 61m (200 ft)

Angles of view:
  Diagonal: 3°
  Horizontal: 2°30′
  Vertical: 1°40′
Ratio of image size at infinity to image of 50mm lens: 16:1
Attachment size (inside screw diameter): 122mm (P = 1.00); 39mm filter drawer
Overall size: 134mm ϕ × 458mm
Weight: 3.3kg (7.3 lb)

DEPTH OF FIELD TABLE

(m)

Focused distance	Depth of field					Reproduction ratio
	f/8	f/11	f/16	f/22	f/32	
10	9.96—10.0	9.95—10.1	9.93—10.1	9.90—10.1	9.86—10.1	1/11.6
12	11.9—12.1	11.9—12.1	11.9—12.1	11.9—12.2	11.8—12.2	1/14.1
15	14.9—15.1	14.9—15.1	14.8—15.2	14.8—15.2	14.7—15.4	1/17.8
20	19.8—20.2	19.8—20.2	19.7—20.3	19.6—20.4	19.4—20.6	1/24.1
30	29.6—30.4	29.5—30.5	29.3—30.7	29.0—31.0	28.6—31.5	1/36.6
50	49.0—51.0	48.6—51.4	48.0—52.1	47.4—53.0	46.3—54.4	1/61.6
100	96.0—104	94.6—106	92.4—109	89.9—113	85.9—120	1/124.0
∞	2402—∞	1747—∞	1202—∞	875—∞	602—∞	1/∞

800mm f/8 NIKKOR ED

Requires Focusing Unit for which Optional Cradle is available

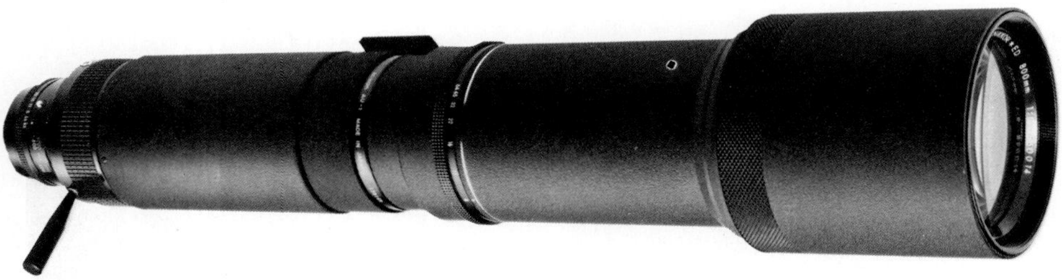

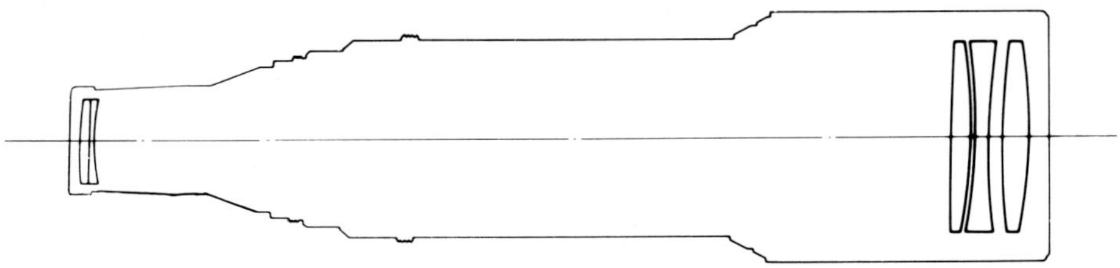

DESCRIPTION

The special feature of this super-telephoto, long-focus lens is the use of Extra Low Dispersion (ED) glass, resulting in excellent correction of chromatic aberration, even at maximum aperture. It must be used with the focusing unit which also provides automatic diaphragm control in the range of *f*/8 to *f*/22. The lens has its own manual diaphragm control, from *f*/8 to *f*/64, for greater depth of field. When one of these diaphragm controls is used, the other must be set at full opening. Intended for sports, nature, and surveillance photography.

SPECIFICATIONS

Smallest aperture: 22 (automatic); 64 (manual)
Nearest focus distance: 20m (70 ft)
Focusing distances:
One head vertical: 14.5m (47.5 ft)
Two heads horizontal: 18.5m (60 ft)
One to three adults standing: 61m (200 ft)
Angles of view:
Diagonal: 3°
Horizontal 2°30′
Vertical: 1°40′
Ratio of image size at infinity to image of 50mm lens: 16:1
Attachment size (inside screw diameter): 122mm (P = 1.00)
Lens hood: Built-in
Front lens cap: 133mm slip-on leather cap provided
Lens case: CE-6
Overall size: 133mm ϕ × 693mm (including focusing unit)
Weight: 5.3kg (11.7 lb)

DEPTH OF FIELD TABLE

Meters

m \ f/	8	11	16	22	Magnification
18	17.9−18.1	17.8−18.2	17.8−18.2	17.7−18.3	1/20
20	19.9−20.2	19.8−20.2	19.7−20.3	19.6−20.4	1/23
25	24.8−25.2	24.7−25.3	24.6−25.5	24.4−25.7	1/29
30	29.7−30.4	29.5−30.5	29.3−30.7	29.1−31.0	1/35
40	39.4−40.6	39.2−40.9	38.8−41.3	38.4−41.8	1/48
50	49.0−51.0	48.7−51.4	48.1−52.1	47.4−52.9	1/60
70	68.1−72.0	67.4−72.8	66.3−74.2	65.0−75.9	1/85
100	96.1−104	94.9−106	92.5−109	90.0−113	1/123
200	185 −219	180 −226	172 −239	163 −259	1/248
∞	2400−∞	1750−∞	1200−∞	872 −∞	1/∞

800mm *f*/8 NIKKOR

Requires Focusing Unit for which Optional Cradle is available

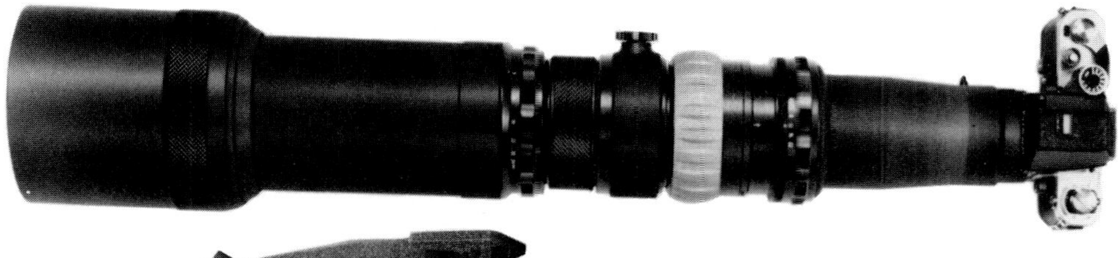

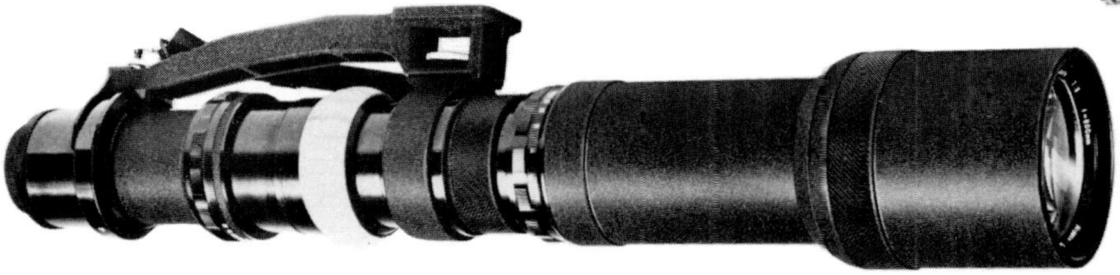

DESCRIPTION

Apochromatic design of 800mm lens in super-telephoto group minimizes chromatic aberration and insures superb image quality. Optics must be used with the focusing unit which provides automatic diaphragm control in the range of *f*/8-*f*/22 and focusing control. This lens additionally has its own manual diaphragm control from *f*/8 down to *f*/64 for greater depth of field. When one of these diaphragm controls is used, the other must be set at full opening. High-speed films are indicated for utilization of fastest shutter speeds in order to minimize vibrations. Intended for use in sports, nature and surveillance photography.

SPECIFICATIONS

Smallest aperture: 22
Nearest focus distance: 19m (61 ft)
Subject field at nearest distance: 48.0 x 72.0cm
Image ratio at nearest distance: 1:20
Focusing distances:
  One head vertical: 14.5m (47.5 ft)
  Two heads horizontal: 18.5m (60 ft)
  One to three adults standing: 61.0m (200 ft)
Angles of view:
  Diagonal: 3°
  Horizontal: 2°30′
  Vertical: 1°40′
Ratio of image size at infinity to image of 50mm lens: 16:1
Attachment size (inside screw diameter): 122mm (P = 1.00)
Lens hood: Built-in telescopic type
Front lens cap: 133mm slip-on leather cap
Rear lens cap: Slip-on leather cap (U.S. 599)
Lens case: Wooden case (U.S. 463)
Overall size: 135mm ϕ x 711.5mm
Weight: 3.5 kg (7.7 lb)

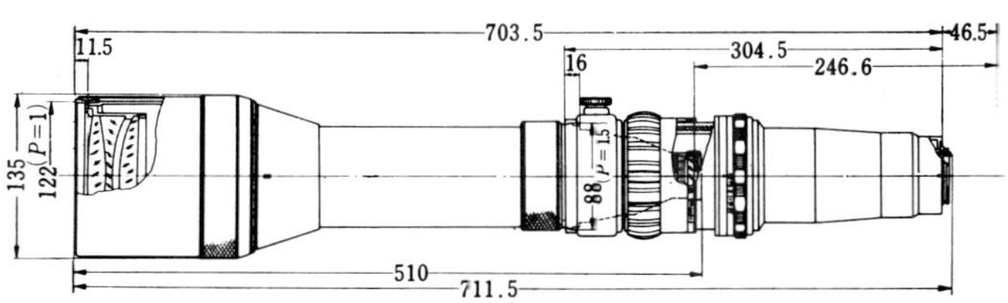

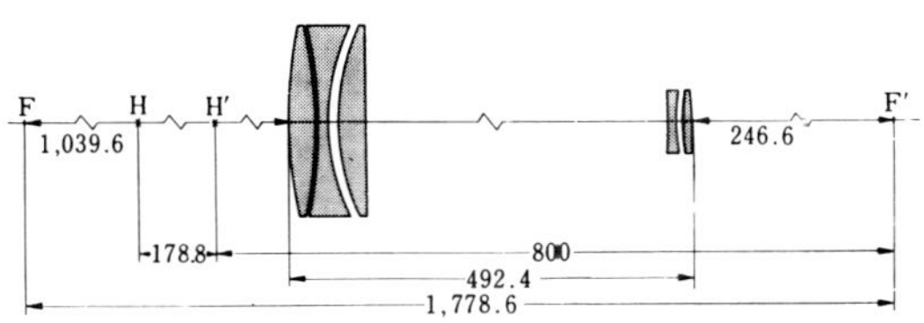

1000mm *f*/11 REFLEX-NIKKOR

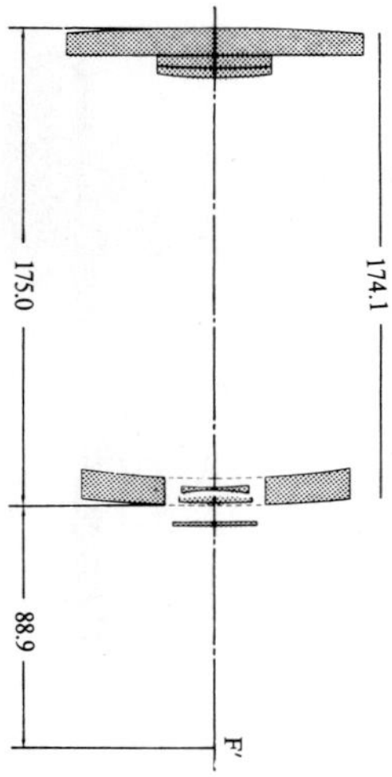

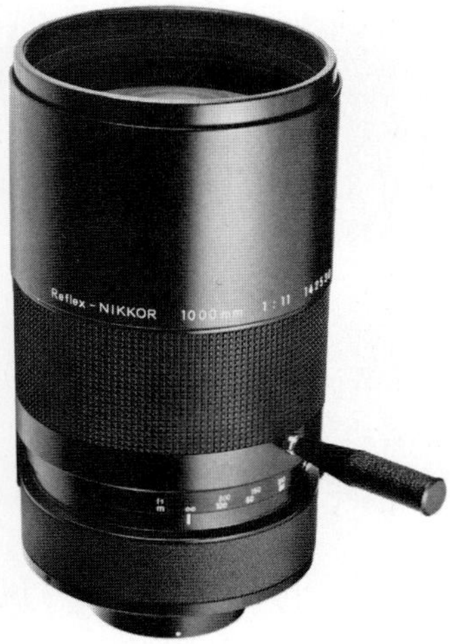

DESCRIPTION

Overall length of this lens is only 241mm, or less than one-fourth the 1000mm focal length. All aberrations, particularly chromatic aberration, have been well corrected. Nikon Integrated Coating (NIC) minimizes flare and ghost image, resulting in high-contrast images and good color rendition. A screw fitting at the rear of the lens accepts standard 39mm-diameter filters, five of which are supplied with the lens. The tripod mounting is a rotating collar with a locking screw; it is click-stopped at each 90° interval.

SPECIFICATIONS

Smallest aperture: Single fixed aperture
Nearest focus distance: 8m (25 ft)
Subject field at nearest distance: 17.7 x 26.6cm
Focusing distances:
One head vertical: 11.6m (48 ft)
Two heads horizontal: 18.3m (60 ft)
One to three adults standing: 61m (200 ft)
Angles of view:
Diagonal: 2°30′
Horizontal: 2°
Vertical: 1°20′

Ratio of image size at infinity to image of 50mm lens: 20:1
Attachment size (inside screw diameter): 108mm (P = 0.75)
Filters: 39mm-diameter screw-in via rear threaded mount; L37C, A2, B2, 056, and ND4X provided.
Lens hood: Built-in
Front lens cap: 115mm slip-on leather or 108mm screw-in metal
Lens case: CL-29
Overall size: 119mm ϕ x 241mm
Weight: 1.9kg. (4.2 lb)

DEPTH OF FIELD TABLE

Meters

m \ f/	11	Magnification
8	7.98—8.02	1/7.4
10	9.97—10.0	1/9.4
12	11.96—12.04	1/11
15	14.9—15.1	1/14
20	19.9—20.1	1/19
30	29.7—30.3	1/29
50	49.3—50.7	1/49
100	97.1—103	1/99
∞	3000—∞	1/∞

1200mm *f*/11 NIKKOR IF-ED

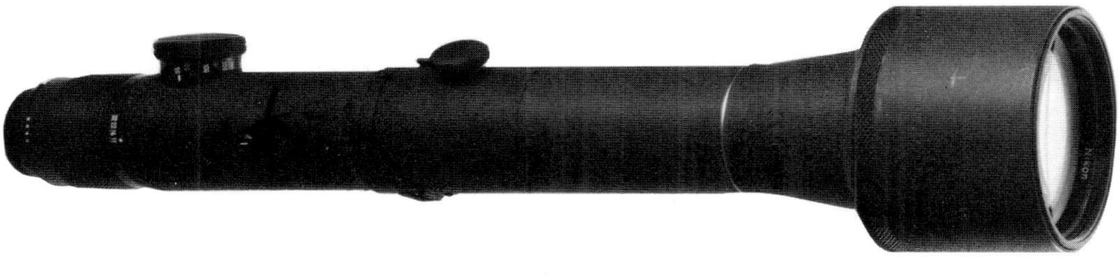

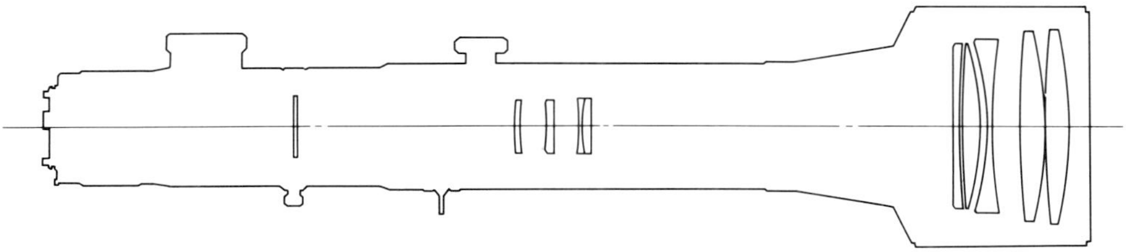

DESCRIPTION

The 1200mm *f*/11 Nikkor IF-ED is remarkably lightweight and compact for a lens of this focal length. It is the first Nikkor of this focal length to offer full-aperture metering. Nikon Extra Low Dispersion (ED) glass is employed to provide optimum correction of chromatic aberration. Much of the lens' lightness and compactness is due to the Nikon Internal Focusing (IF) system, which eliminates the need for heavy and bulky focusing mechanisms. In addition, the physical length of the lens does not change as focus is changed. Closest focusing is 14m (45 ft). A preset focusing ring is provided, which enables the photographer to return quickly to a previously set position on the focusing dial. A filter holder accepts optional 39mm filters. Generally, the lens should be used on a tripod. Rotating tripod mounting collar is provided.

SPECIFICATIONS

Smallest aperture: 32
Nearest focus distance: 14m (45 ft)
Subject field at nearest distance: 25.6 × 38.4cm
Image ratio at nearest distance: 1:11
Focusing distances:
One head vertical: 23.2m (76 ft)
Two heads horizontal: 29.6m (96 ft)
One to three adults standing: 97.6m (320 ft)

Angles of view:
Diagonal: 2°
Horizontal: 1°40′
Vertical: 1°10′
Ratio of image size at infinity to image of 50mm lens: 24:1
Attachment size (inside screw diameter): 122mm (P = 1.00); accepts 39mm filters
Overall size: 134mm φ × 577mm
Weight: 3.8kg (8.4 lb)

DEPTH OF FIELD TABLE

(m)

Focused distance					Reproduction ratio
	f/11	f/16	f/22	f/32	
14	14.0–14.0	13.9–14.1	13.9–14.1	13.9–14.1	1/10.9
15	14.9–15.1	14.9–15.1	14.9–15.1	14.9–15.2	1/11.7
17	16.9–17.1	16.9–17.1	16.9–17.1	16.8–17.2	1/13.4
20	19.9–20.1	19.9–20.1	19.8–20.2	19.7–20.3	1/15.9
30	29.8–30.2	29.7–30.3	29.6–30.4	29.4–30.6	1/24.2
50	49.4–50.6	49.1–50.9	48.8–51.3	48.3–51.9	1/40.9
100	97.6–103	96.5–104	95.2–105	93.2–108	1/83.0
∞	3931–∞	2704–∞	1968–∞	1354–∞	1/∞

1200mm *f*/11 NIKKOR ED

Requires Focusing Unit for which Optional Cradle is available

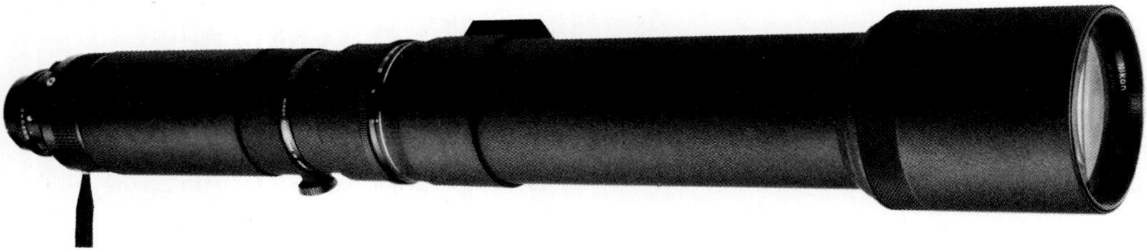

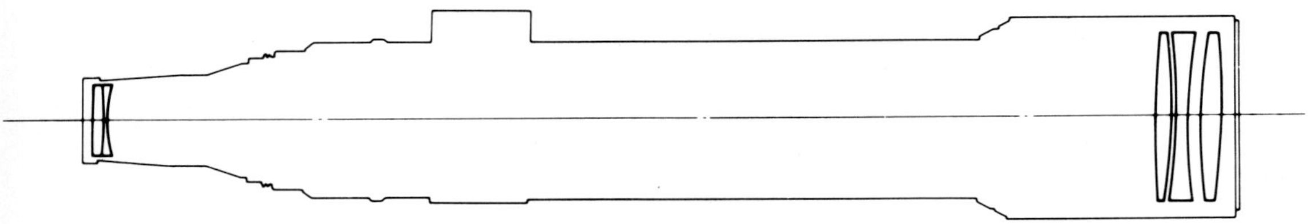

DESCRIPTION

The special feature of the 1200mm *f*/11 Nikkor ED is the use of Nikon Extra Low Dispersion (ED) glass, resulting in optimum correction of chromatic aberration, even at maximum aperture. This is the longest of the Nikon refractor-type lenses. It must be used with focusing unit. To avoid vignetting, automatic diaphragm of the focusing unit should be set to *f*/4.5, and manual diaphragm of the lens should be used. At great distances, the photographer will encounter problems of atmospheric interference, extreme compression effects, and camera-lens vibration, which degrade image sharpness.

SPECIFICATIONS

Smallest aperture: 64
Nearest focus distance: 50m (150 ft)
Focusing distances:
One head vertical: 23.2m (76 ft)
Two heads horizontal: 29.6m (96 ft)
One to three adults standing: 97.6m (320 ft)
Angles of view:
Diagonal: 2°
Horizontal: 1°40′
Vertical: 1°10′
Ratio of image size at infinity to image of 50mm lens: 24:1
Attachment size (inside screw diameter): 122mm (P = 1.00)
Lens hood: Built-in
Front lens cap: 133mm slip-on leather cap provided
Lens case: CE-7
Overall size: 133mm φ × 898mm
Weight: 6.1kg (13.4 lb)

DEPTH OF FIELD TABLE

Meters

m \ f/	11	16	22	32	45	65	Magnification
40	39.7–40.4	39.5–40.5	39.3–40.7	39.0–41.0	38.6–41.5	38.1–42.2	1/30
50	49.4–50.6	49.2–50.8	48.9–51.2	48.4–51.7	47.8–52.4	46.9–53.6	1/39
60	59.2–60.8	58.8–61.2	58.4–61.7	57.7–62.5	56.8–63.6	55.5–65.4	1/47
70	68.9–71.2	68.4–71.7	67.8–72.4	66.8–73.5	65.6–75.0	63.9–77.5	1/55
100	97.7–102	96.6–104	95.4–105	93.5–108	91.1–111	87.6–117	1/80
150	145 –156	142 –158	140 –162	136 –168	130 –177	123 –182	1/122
200	191 –210	187 –216	182 –222	175 –234	166 –251	155 –283	1/164
500	444 –572	423 –612	399 –669	366 –790	330 –1030	287 –1980	1/414
∞	3930–∞	2700–∞	1960–∞	1350–∞	960 –∞	664 –∞	1/∞

1200mm *f*/11 NIKKOR

Requires Focusing Unit for which Optional Cradle is available

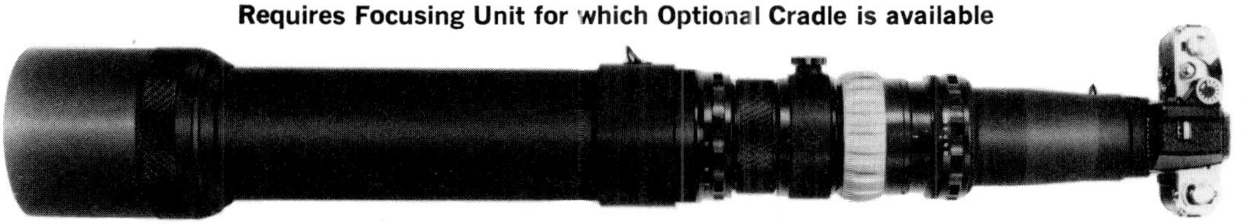

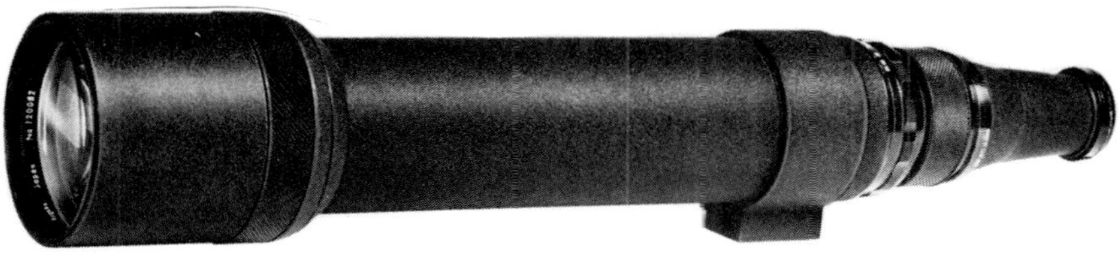

DESCRIPTION

The 1200mm lens is longest refractor-type Nikkor lens with diaphragm control. It must be used with focusing unit. To avoid vignetting, automatic diaphragm of focusing unit should be set at *f*/4.5 and manual diaphragm of lens should be used. Intended for use in stalking wildlife, in covering action sports from fixed positions in the stands, and in surveillance photography. Apochromatic lens design virtually eliminates chromatic aberration. Magnification is 24 times that of normal 50mm lens; an object recorded as 1mm in size with the 50mm lens will, at same distance, be recorded as 24mm. At great distances, the photographer will encounter problems of atmospheric interference, extreme compression effects, and camera-and-lens vibration which degrade image sharpness.

SPECIFICATIONS

Smallest aperture: 64
Aperture diaphragm: Manual, does not couple to exposure meter
Nearest focus distance: 43m (139 ft)
Subject field at nearest distance: 72.0 x 108.0cm
Image ratio at nearest distance: 1:30
Focusing distances:
- One head vertical: 23.2m (76.0 ft)
- Two heads horizontal: 29.6m (96 ft)
- One to three adults standing: 97.6m (320 ft)

Angles of view:
- Diagonal: 2°
- Horizontal: 1°40′
- Vertical: 1°10′

Ratio of image size at infinity to image of 50mm lens: 24:1
Attachment size (inside screw diameter): 122mm (P = 1.00)
Lens hood: Built-in telescopic type
Front lens cap: 133mm slip-on leather cap
Rear lens cap: Slip-on leather cap (U.S. 599)
Lens case: Wooden case (U.S. 464)
Overall size: 135mm ϕ x 922mm
Weight: 4.3 kg (9.5 lbs)

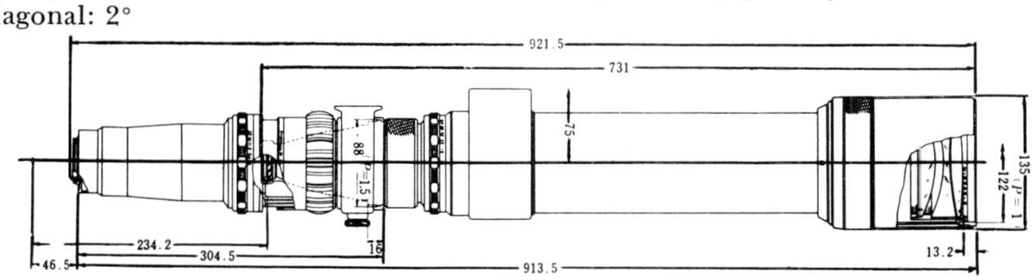

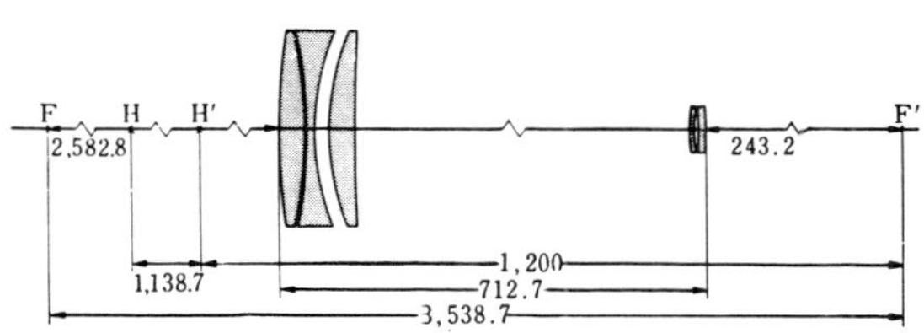

2000mm *f*/11 REFLEX-NIKKOR

Yoke mounting for turning and tilting separately available

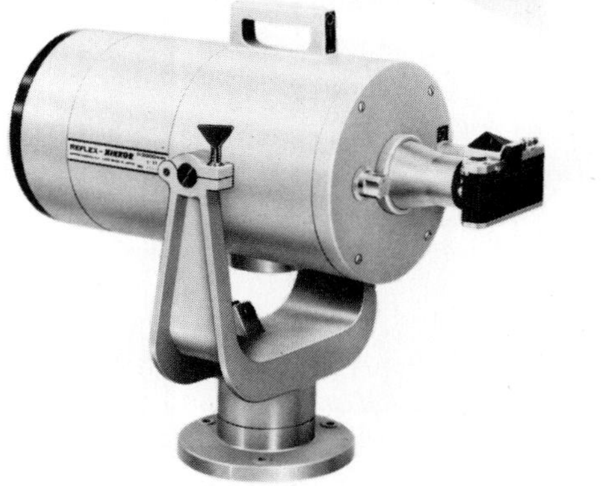

DESCRIPTION

This longest of Nikkor lenses magnifies 40 times that of 50mm normal lens. Catadioptric design minimizes and virtually eliminates optical aberrations of all kinds. A unique feature is ability to focus relatively close—20m (65 ft.). Four built-in filters in a turret mount move into optical path at turn of a knob. Carrying handle incorporates a peep sight to help photographer to prespot his subject, since angle of view of lens is only 1°10′. Lens mount rotates with click stops to permit vertical or horizontal format selection. In addition to terrestrial photographic applications, this lens is quite suitable for star and lunar photography. For terrestrial uses, high-speed films ordinarily should be used in order to obtain use of fastest possible shutter speeds.

SPECIFICATIONS

Smallest aperture: Single fixed aperture
Nearest focus distance: 18m (60 ft)
Subject field at nearest distance: 20.4 x 30.6cm
Image ratio at nearest distance: 1:8.5
Focusing distances:
One head vertical: 29.2m (95.2 ft)
Two heads horizontal: 36.8m (120 ft)
One to three adults standing: 122m (400 ft)
Angles of view:
Diagonal: 1°10′
Horizontal: 1°
Vertical: 40′
Ratio of image size at infinity to image of 50mm lens: 40:1
Filters: Built-in, L39, Y48, O56, R60
Lens hood: Integral
Front lens cap: Slip-on cap supplied
Lens case: Wooden case or metal case supplied
Overall size: 573mm high x 330mm wide
Weight: 7.5 kg (16.5 lb) lens only, less yoke mounting

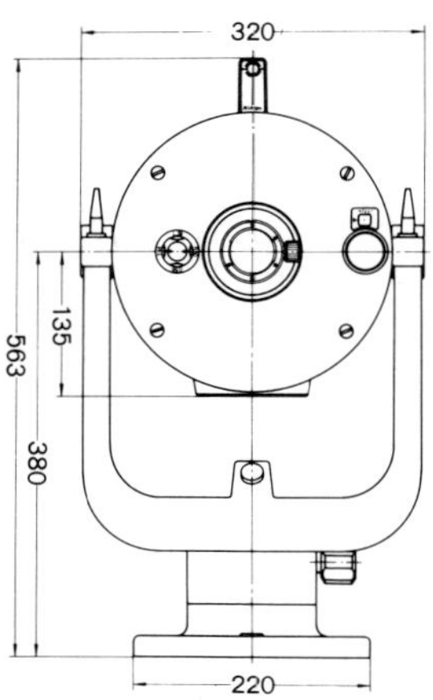

End view

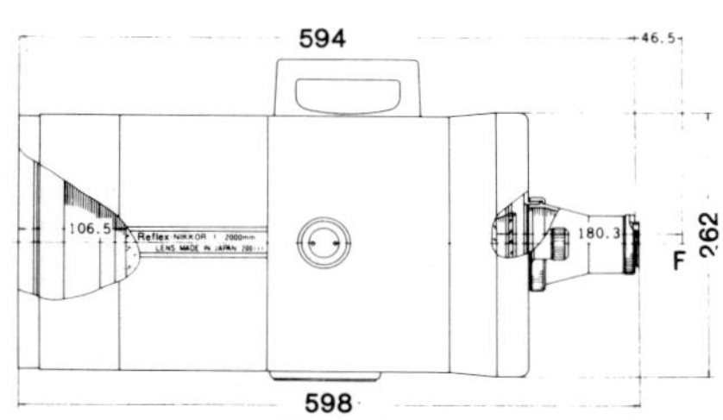

Side view

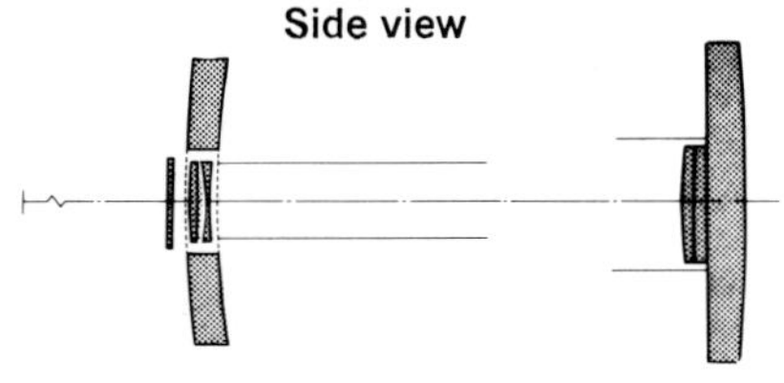

CHAPTER 3

Nikkor Lens Guide: Special Lenses

The lenses covered in this chapter fall into several unique categories, including the Fisheye Nikkor lenses, the Zoom-Nikkors, the PC (Perspective Control) Nikkors, the 45mm *f*/2.8 GN Auto-Nikkor (discontinued), close-up lenses, and the El-Nikkor (enlarging) lenses.

The Fisheye lenses are "special" in that they are not of the ordinary prime-field-rendering design. Otherwise, they are intended for general photographic use. As to the other lenses, in addition to their special uses, most can also be used in general photography as described below. The El-Nikkor enlarging lenses will be found to have special applications in photocopying.

THE FISHEYE NIKKOR LENSES

Two types of Fisheye Nikkor lenses are available: one records its field of view as a circular image; the other type—more properly termed a "semi-fisheye"—fills the entire image area on film. Most of the Fisheye Nikkor lenses are of the former type. To the general public, a fisheye picture may mean an enormous outstretched open hand thrusting toward the camera, attached to a tiny body. To an industrial photographer, the exceptionally wide field of coverage affords the ability to take pictures of otherwise inaccessible interiors. A city planner might use one of the Fisheye Nikkors to study sky illuminance. Advertising photographers who seek to create attention-getting pictures utilize the propensity of these lenses to see things "in the round" in order to convert what otherwise might be a commonplace scene into an arresting one. Underwater photographers use fisheye lenses to cover a wide field at close range, thereby overcoming the problem of cumulative interference by particulate matter at increasingly greater working distances.

The different types of Fisheye Nikkors are described below and in the lens data sheets. Additionally, operational information is included with respect to spherical composition, viewpoint management, camera handling, and exposure problems.

The Range of Fisheye Nikkor Lenses

Although, from an optical standpoint, there are two types of fisheye lenses—those that produce full hemispheric or greater images rendered as circles on the film and one lens that covers somewhat less than a hemisphere rendered on film as a full frame image—these will be described in three separate categories, taking account of operational attributes, as follows:

1. Fixed-focus lenses that cover fields of view of 180 or 220 degrees, whose images cannot be observed through the camera viewfinder.
2. Lenses that cover fields of view of 180 or 220 degrees and focus continually through the camera's viewfinder system from about one foot (0.3 meters) or less to infinity.
3. One lens that focuses fully and fills the total film area corner to corner with a diagonal field of view of 170 degrees.

All of the Fisheye Nikkor lenses are prime lenses, complete in themselves, attachable directly to any of the Nikon or Nikkormat reflex camera bodies. Adapters are available through independent sources for attaching these lenses to Nikonos cameras together with waterproof ports for underwater photography.

Fixed-Focus Fisheye Lenses. Three lenses of fixed-focus design are described. These include the 6mm, 7.5mm, and 10mm Fisheye Nikkor lenses, all of *f*/5.6 aperture. (The 7.5mm lens is not currently in production.) These lenses are used with the camera mirror locked in the up position. An auxiliary viewfinder must be used; a single common viewfinder, covering a field of 160 degrees, is used with all three of these lenses. The viewfinder is mounted on the camera accessory shoe. These lenses do not couple to any of the internal exposure metering and control systems; they require the use of separate exposure meters for measurement of light conditions. A set of built-in, turret-mounted filters is fixed to the rear of each of the lenses.

Depth of field is controllable only by changing the aperture setting. For all practical purposes, this is important only when working in near proximity to an object as depth of field at all settings is enormous with these extremely short focal-length lenses. At the smallest aperture of *f*/22, depth of field will range from about 8 inches (20 cm) to infinity, with variations governed by the lens used.

Some important differences are to be found among these three lenses. The 6mm Fisheye Nikkor has the widest angle of coverage with a field of 220 degrees, which is 40 degrees more than the other two. Whereas the latter have limits of perception at right angles to the optical axis, the 6mm lens "sees" behind the camera for an additional range of coverage of 20 degrees at either side; hence, it is especially useful for taking pictures of areas of the greatest constriction of view.

Any of these camera-mounted lenses can be introduced into areas where dimensional and environmental factors would not permit entry of a photographer. This includes pipeline sections, tanks, cavernous areas, and toxic areas, among others. Under these conditions, absence of a focusing ring is no disadvantage. Under such blind shooting conditions, incidentally, an auxiliary viewfinder is not needed. The 220-degree field of coverage of the 6mm lens offers greater flexibility in recording fields of view in which control personnel must operate, such as the cockpit of an airplane, the control panels of an operations center, the visibility range of a land vehicle, or the visibility range of an airport control tower.

The 10mm OP Fisheye-Nikkor lens is different from all others in the Nikkor series in both main purpose and optical

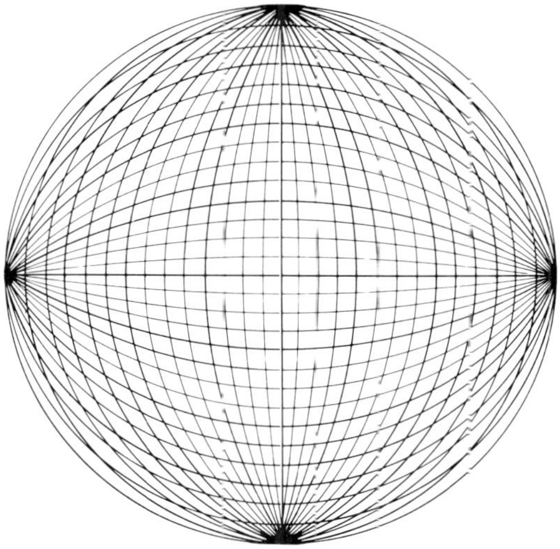

Conceptual diagram of spherical pattern of rendering subject matter. Only those lines that represent true radii (going to the center of the circular area) are rendered and perceived as straight lines. All other lines are rendered as curves with degree of curvature governed by position above or below (or to the sides) of the diameter. In reality since an infinite number of lines or diameters can intersect the center of the circular area the spherical effect is manifested in an infinite number of directions radiating from the center. These phenomena are most readily identifiable in familiar geometric forms such as buildings and more or less straight horizons. Distortion is not as readily perceivable in the central area with objects of irregular shape. The practical effects of the optical phenomena are demonstrated in the photo below taken with the 8mm *f*/2.8 lens. Model Ruthie Langstaff diminishes into the periphery of the circular image. Vertical and horizontal lines of woodwork show spherical attributes. Courtesy Nikon School.

John D. Slack

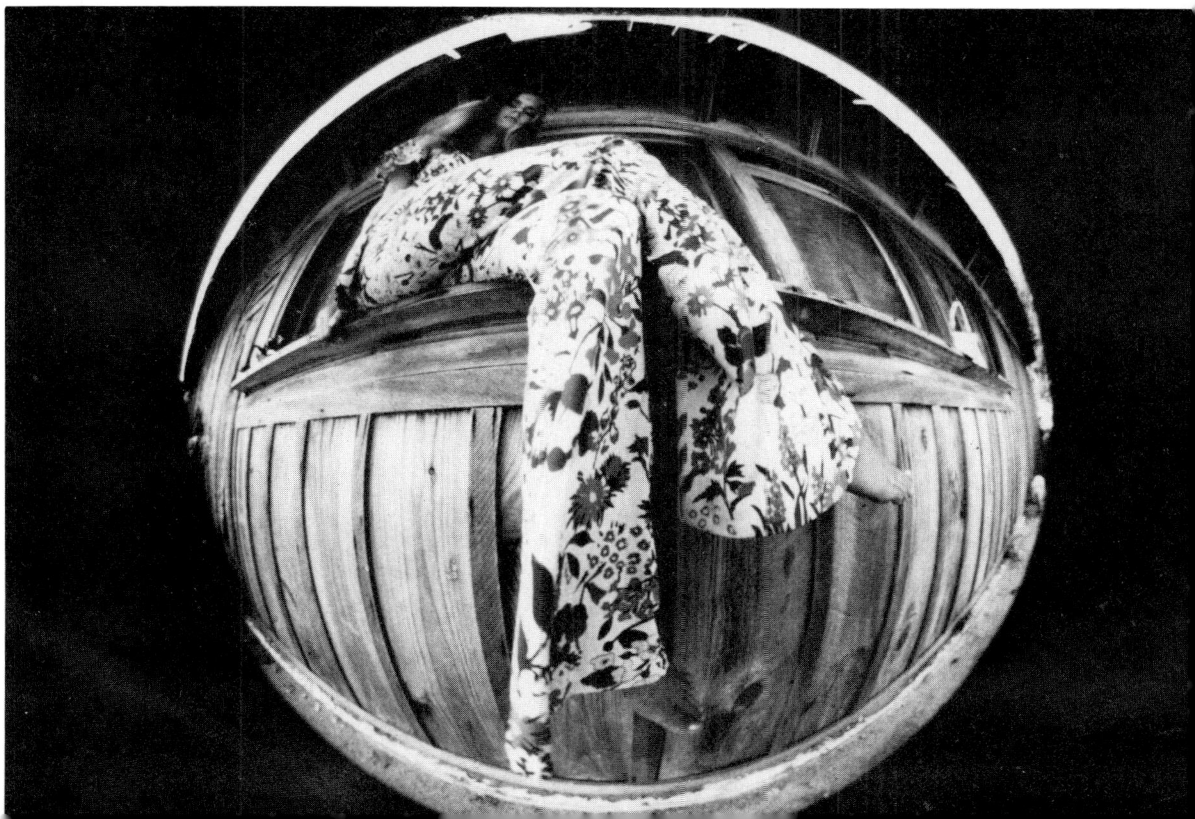

Angles of View (Areas of Coverage) of Fisheye Lenses Compared to Normal 50mm Lens

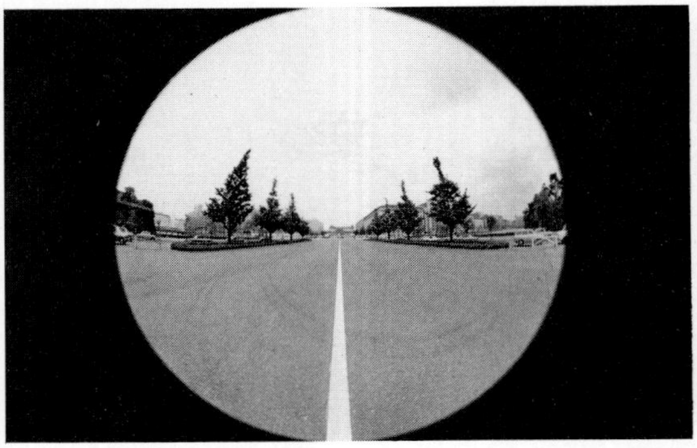

6mm fisheye lens

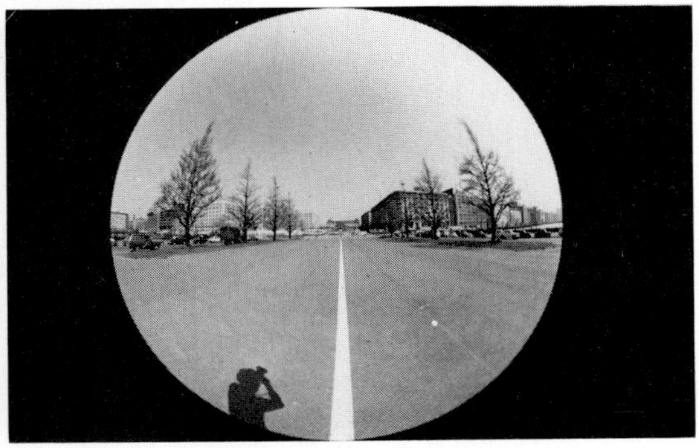

8mm fisheye lens

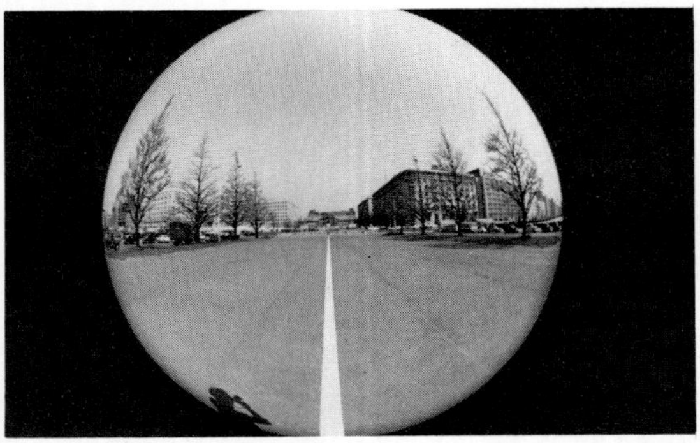

10mm fisheye lens

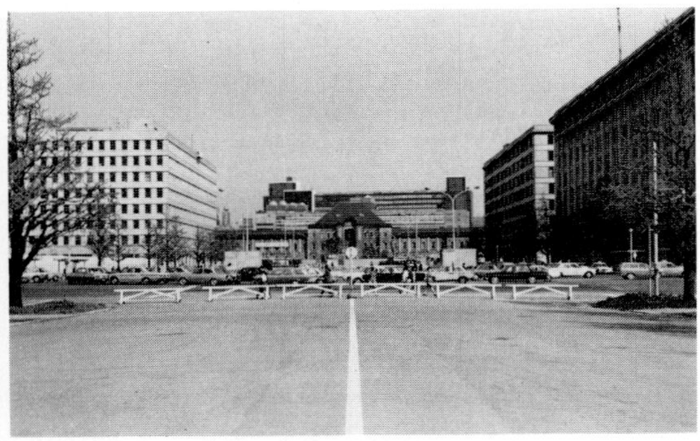

50mm normal lens

design. The 10mm lens has an orthographic projection design; objects of the same luminance photographed through this lens are recorded with the same density regardless of their position within the entire picture field ranging from center to periphery. This is not possible when using any of the other Fisheye Nikkors, all of which are of equidistant projection design that does not accommodate the fall-off of optical brightness away from the center toward the edge of the circular image field.

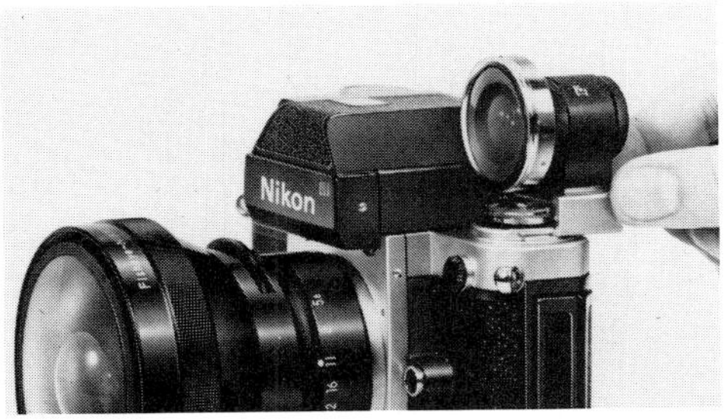

External viewfinder for 10mm *f*/5.6 OP Fisheye-Nikkor; also needed for earlier models of fixed-focus Fisheye-Nikkor lenses.

The difference between orthographic and equidistant projection formulas is expressed in the following:

Equidistant projection: $Y = c \cdot \theta$

Orthographic projection: $Y = c \cdot \sin\theta$

Y: Distance of image point from picture center

θ: Zenith angle

c: Constant

The OP Fisheye-Nikkor incorporates an aspheric front element. The designation "OP" stands for Orthographic Projection. Uniform image brightness is obtainable over the entire circular field even with the use of narrow exposure latitude color film. This property makes the OP Fisheye-Nikkor particularly useful for measuring skylight distribution, the quantitative luminance of an area or part of an area, or the effect of radiant heat. This is made possible through the ability of the lens to record a total geometrical configuration of the subject area, thereby making it possible to establish relative percentages. The OP Fisheye-Nikkor lens was designed especially to meet the needs of the urban planner and safety investigator. In high-rise construction, for example, care must be taken to avoid reducing the level of illumination, which is caused by both height and density. Planners must also consider the effects of radiant heat generated by fire on adjacent buildings in order to afford maximum safety to inhabitants. The term "configuration factor" is used to indicate or express the ratio of the area of illumination to the total area of the picture. When the light source is the sky, its percentage of the total area photographed is referred to as the "sky factor" as being synonymous with configuration factor. Uniformity of brightness or luminance recording is important when it is necessary to measure and compare densities of different parts or sections of the total area covered.

With the other Fisheye-Nikkor lenses of equidistant projection optical formulations the center of the image corresponds to the zenith in the angle of view. The distance of any point in the image from this center is directly proportional to its angle from the zenith. Equidistant formulation is shown in the diagrams included in the lens data sheets.

The Focusing Fisheye Lenses (Circular Image). The Fisheye-Nikkor Auto lenses have in common the relatively wide aperture of *f*/2.8, necessary for near-field focusing especially in dim light. Viewing

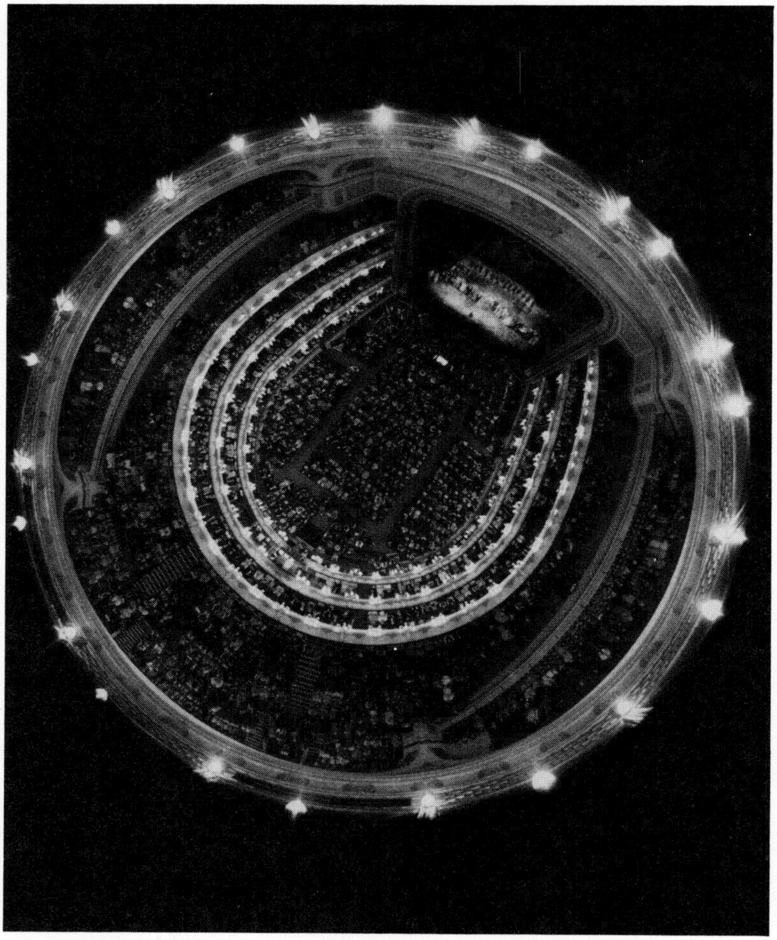

Ian Bradshaw

Royal Gala at Covent Garden, London. The fisheye lens was mounted in the roof while the exposure was made by motorized remote control. An excellent example of a naturally circular subject.

Francisco Hidalgo

When working close, magnification of foreground objects introduces additional factor in pictorial composition as with other extreme wide-angle lenses but more so because of spherical attributes. Left, 8mm *f*/2.8 lens at shortest distance, 1/30 sec., *f*/8, Kodak Plus-X. Right, 7.5mm lens, 1/30 sec., *f*/8, Kodak Plus-X.

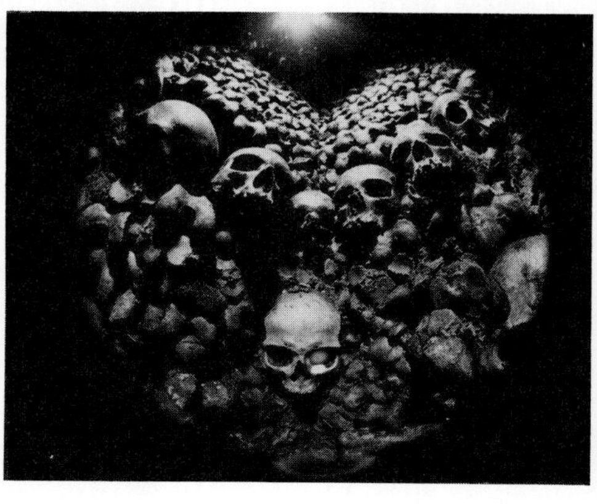

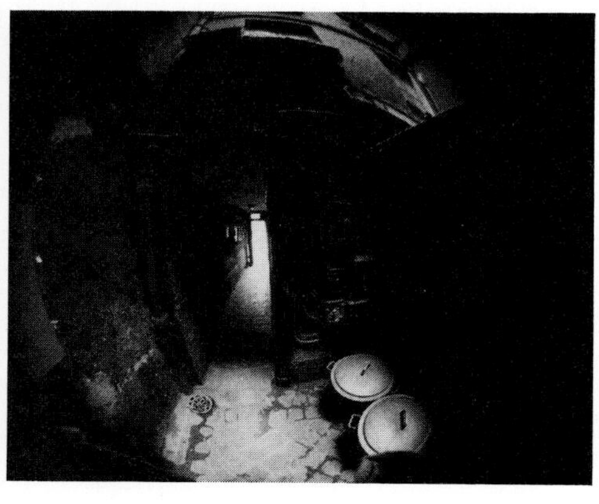

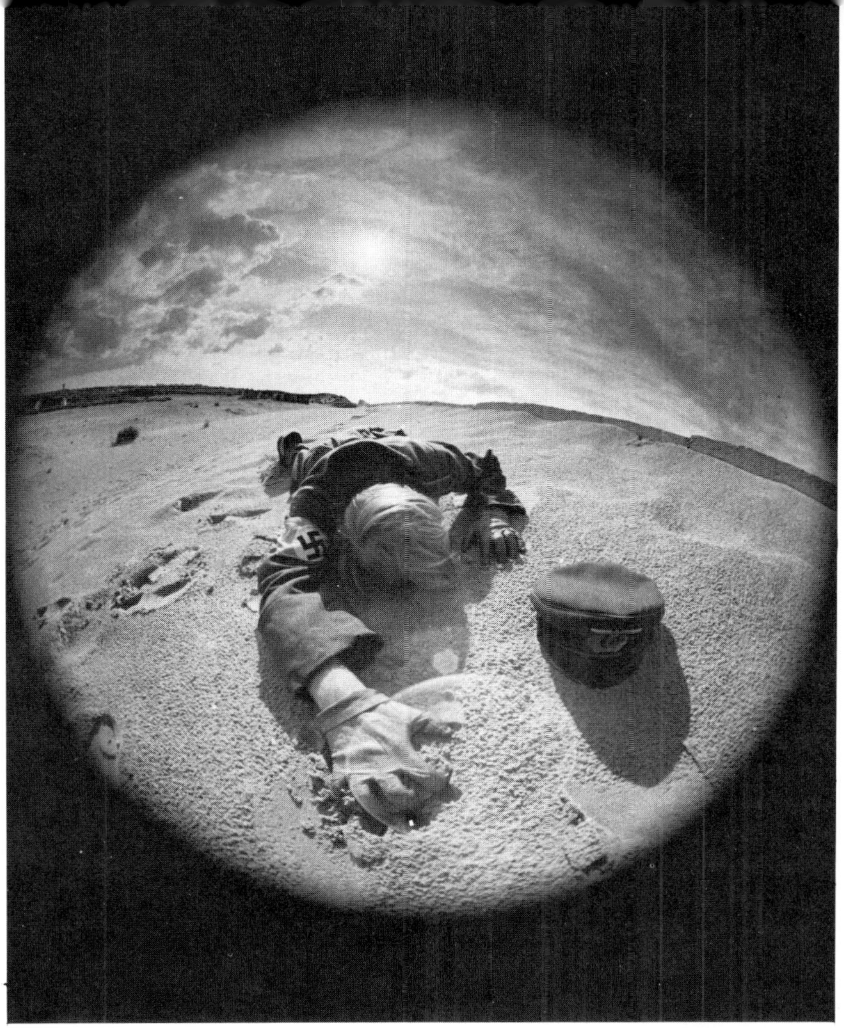

Francisco Hidalgo

A classical use of fisheye lens to create exaggerated foreground dominance. Pointing the camera downward brings out curved horizon line. Picture shot against the sun so flash used for shadow-fill. Clues to use of small aperture are in diffraction spokes emanating from sun and small hexagonal configuration of lens diaphragm reflected off a lens surface shown just beyond leading hand. Kodak Plus-X, red filter, *f*/16, 1/60 sec.

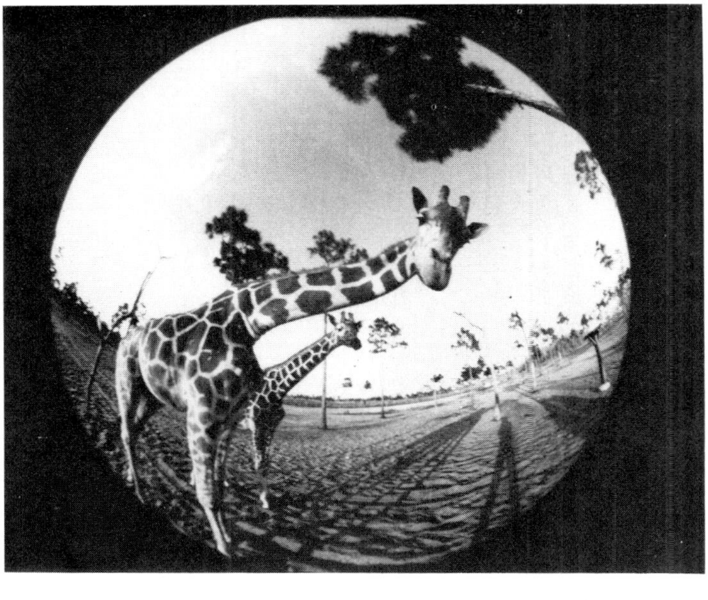

John D. Slack

Creative humor with the 8mm *f*/2.8 Fisheye Nikkor which has the advantage of viewfinder focusing. The long neck of the giraffe at Lion County Safari, West Palm Beach, Florida, is further drawn out in the foreground. Horizon curves upward due to camera tilt upward. Courtesy Nikon School.

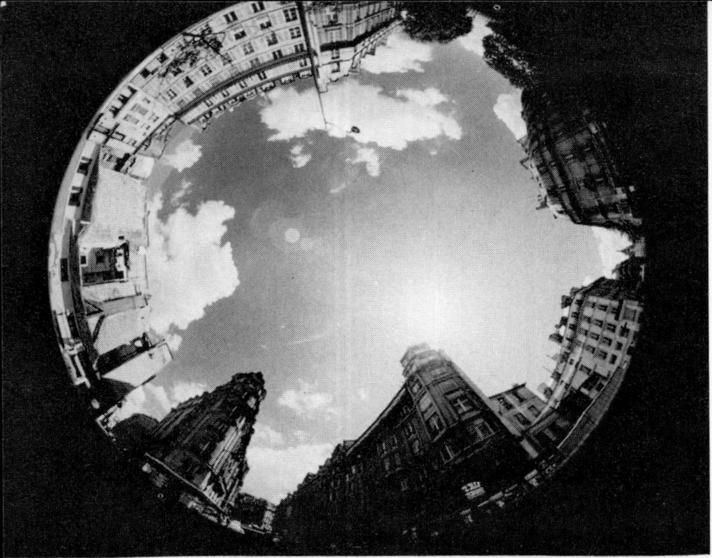

Photographer in center for peripheral composition. 8mm *f*/2.8 lens, 1/30 sec., *f*/8, orange filter, reproduced from color transparency.

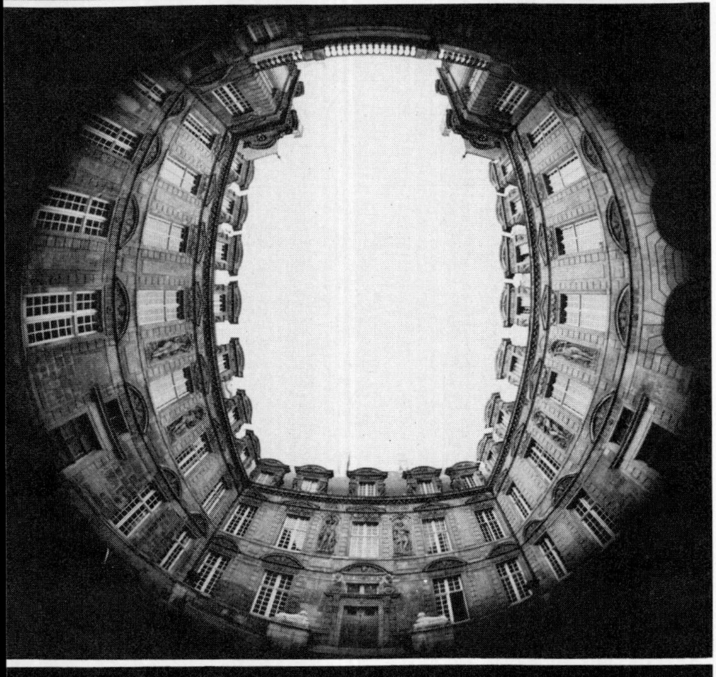

Pointing up to the sky with fisheye lenses, you get radial convergence toward optical center of sphere. If you are to retain details in ground objects, you wash out the sky. Hidalgo often uses an orange filter with both color and black-and-white films in order to darken sky and bring out clouds if present. Shooting height is a problem. If camera is held high, street-level details are lost. Otherwise, camera must be placed on ground and operated with remote control (risky if there is traffic) or one must lie on ground to get picture.

Slight shift away from center provides interesting geometric pattern while retaining parallel sides. 7.5mm *f*/5.6 lens, 1/30 sec., *f*/8, Kodak Tri-X.

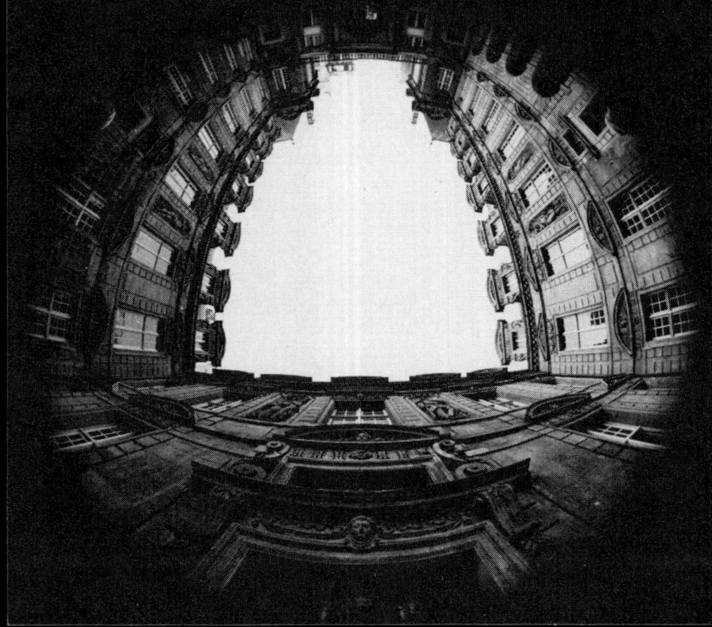

Francisco Hidalgo

Standing close to one of the building facades yields a pronounced difference in geometric form. 7.5mm *f*/5.6 lens, 1/30 sec., *f*/8 Kodak Tri-X.

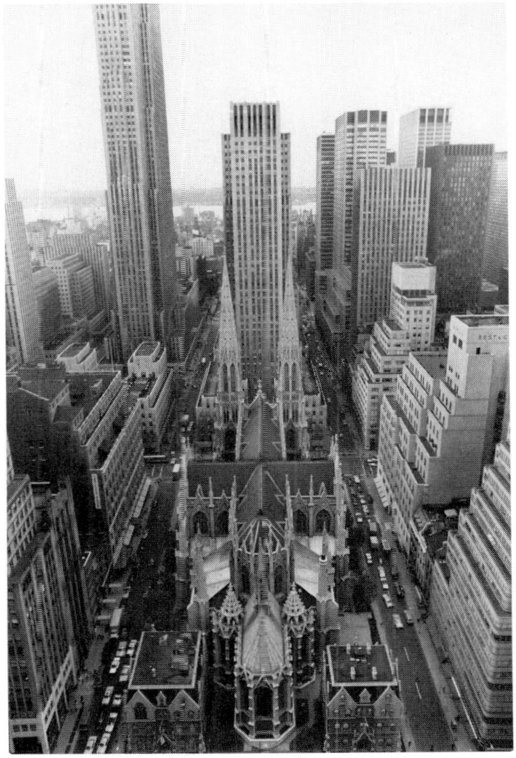

Francisco Hidalgo

The straight shot of Saint Patrick's Cathedral, New York, was made with the 28mm *f*/3.5 lens, 1/60 sec., *f*/11. The fisheye version was made with the same exposure using the 7.5mm *f*/5.6 lens, but double exposure (one-half of lens covered each time) brought out this unique configuration. E-screen used for subject alignment.

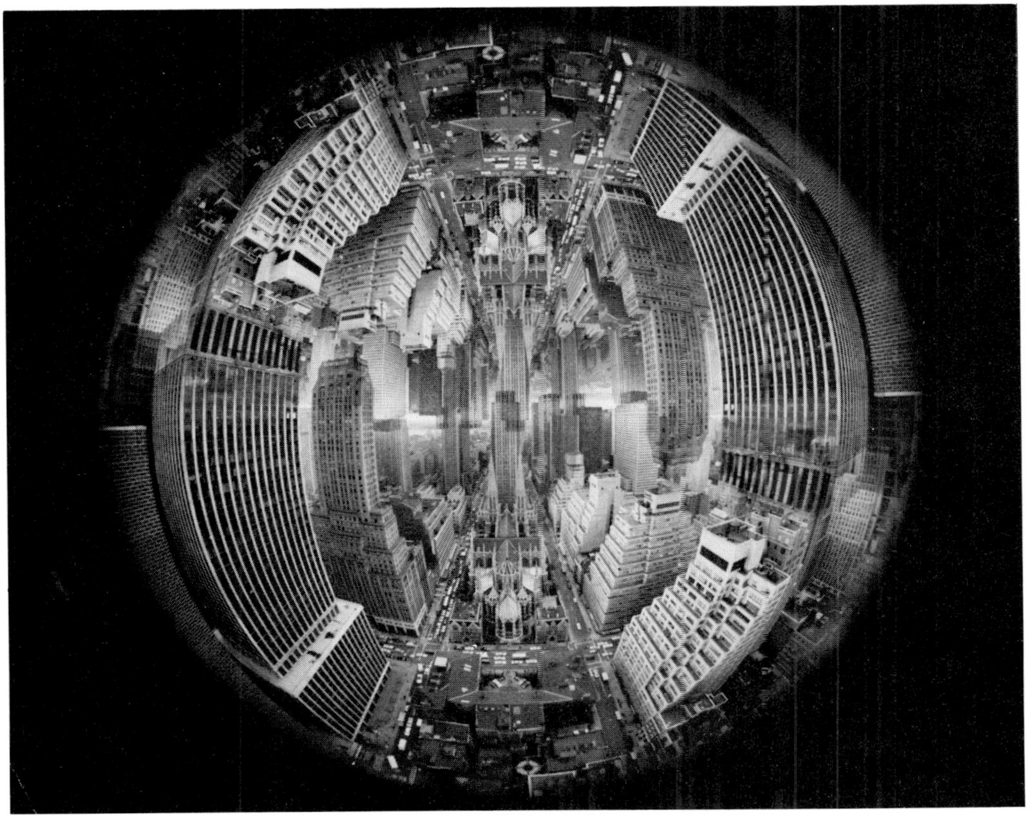

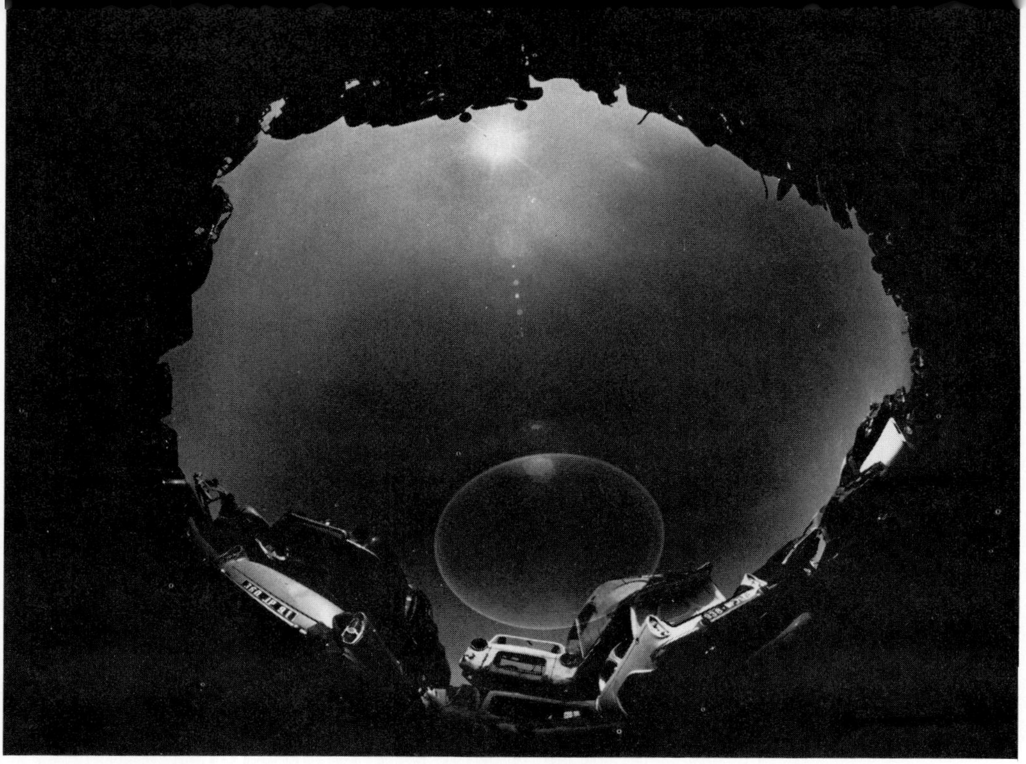

The black surrounding for the spherical image can be put to creative use in some cases where the interior of the picture is tonally compatible. The darkening of the sky in the scene above was accomplished with the orange filter while the red filter was used with the other. In both cases, an irregular natural border diminished the impression of roundness. 7.5mm *f*/5.6 Fisheye lens in both cases. Diaphragm patterns indicate use of small apertures—*f*/11 above and *f*/16 in lower picture. Kodak Plus-X.

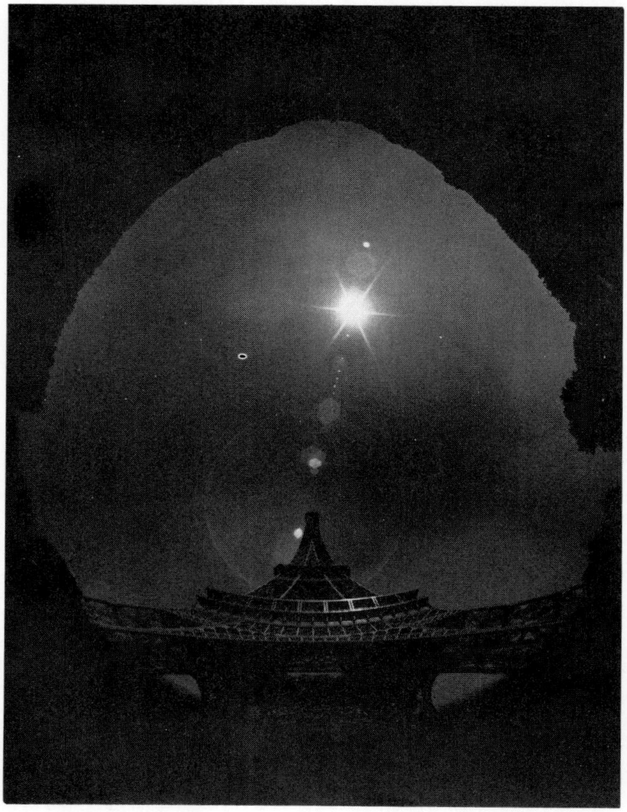

Francisco Hidalgo

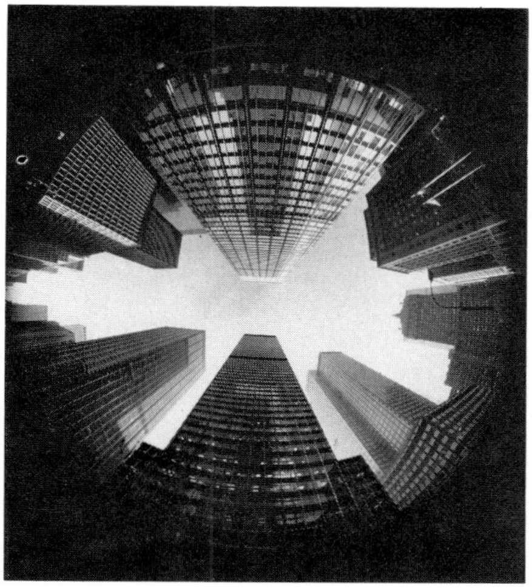

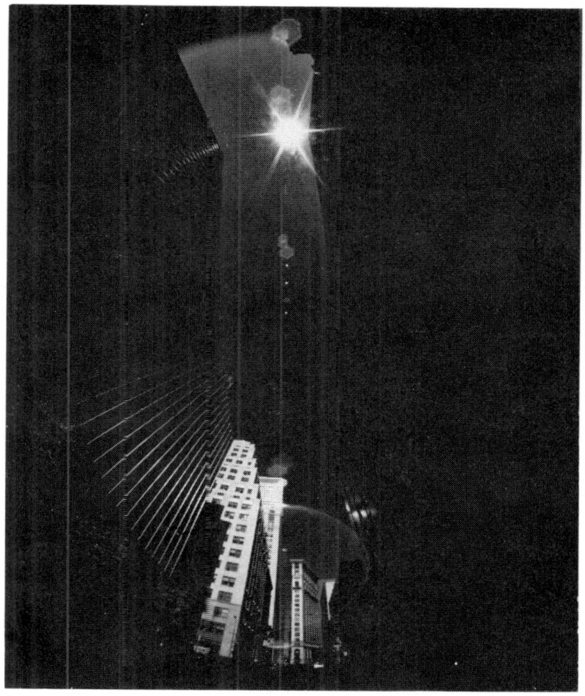

Francisco Hidalgo

Top right, illustrates how lines radiating from center are rendered as straight lines while concentric circles are observed around outer areas. Approaching the center, objects tend to be rendered in familiar geometric array.

Upper right, light and dark are elements of composition brought into spherical configuration. Lack of detail at right permits cropping. Diffraction clues indicate small aperture. 7.5mm *f*/5.6 lens, 1/250 sec., *f*/11, red filter, Kodak Plus-X. Another Wall Street, New York configuration. The tight array of buildings offers a departure from the radial effect. 7.5mm *f*/5.6,lens 1/30 sec., *f*/11 Kodak Plus-X, yellow filter.

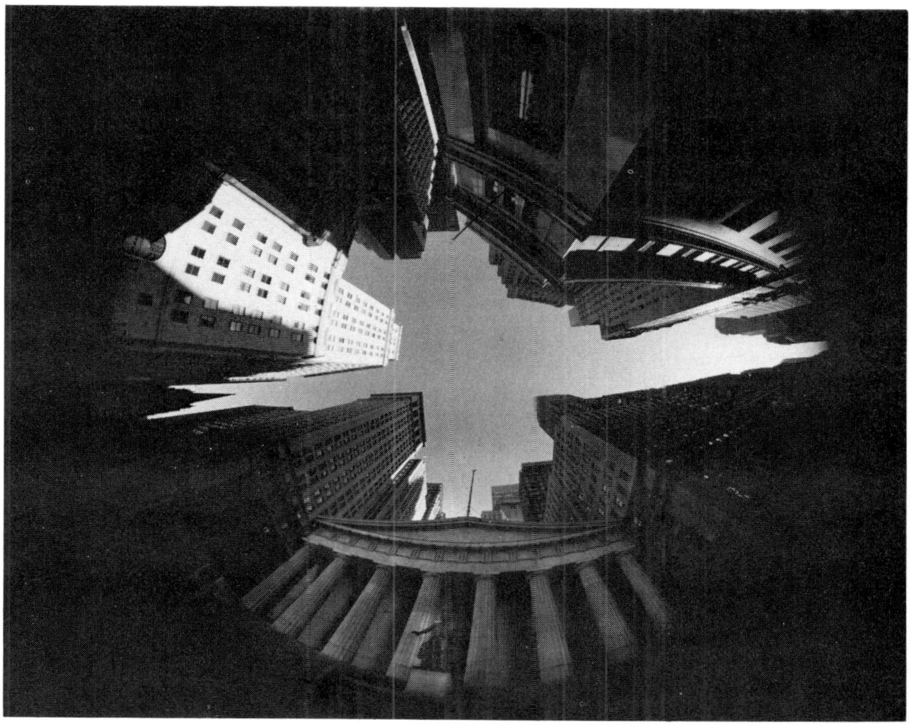

and exposure measurement are accomplished through the mirror-reflex mechanism with the mirror in normal operating mode. Both the 6mm and 8mm lenses have built-in filter sets in rear turret mounts.

For all practical purposes, except in special circumstances, the 8mm *f*/2.8 Fisheye-Nikkor Auto is probably the most commonly used lens because of its lighter weight as compared to the 6mm *f*/2.8 lens, which is also quite expensive. A comparison of the lens data sheet will show that the 6mm lens weighs five times as much as its 8mm variation.

The 8mm *f*/2.8 lens has a 180-degree angle of view. At full aperture, when focused at its near range of one foot, depth of field is about 2 inches (48mm) so that it becomes extremely convenient to have the *f*/2.8 aperture for critical focusing. As the aperture is closed down, however, depth increases substantially so that at *f*/11 and a focus setting of 2 feet, depth of field extends from slightly more than 13 inches to infinity.

The 16mm Fisheye. The 16mm Fisheye-Nikkor (full-frame fisheye) offers the imaginative photographer a wide range of practical applications in extreme wide-angle activity where linearity is not essential. The curvature attributes of this lens can also be put to creative use with interesting effects obtained when working close to objects or when the form and perspective of nongeometric configurations become spherically altered.

The total film area of 24 × 36mm utilizes only a portion of the total image projection as compared to the other fisheye lenses that project full circular images on film. The diagonal angle of view is 170 degrees—somewhat less than full hemispheric coverage. The lens is fully meter-coupled and automatic diaphragm-coupled. It focuses continuously through the mirror-reflex mechanism throughout the range of one foot (0.3 meters) to infinity.

Picture Taking With Fisheye Lenses

This section covers: (1) the characteristic curvature of fisheye lenses and effects achieved under different picture-taking conditions, (2) pictorial composition with fisheye lenses, (3) exposure problems encountered with fisheye lenses, and (4) physical management of these lenses.

Curvature Characteristics. All lenses project round images. The standard image frame of 24 × 36mm is achieved by cutting off a good part of the image area as projected by the lens and recording on film only a rectangular section that is coaxial with the image center. All of the Fisheye Nikkor lenses, with the exception of the 16mm Fisheye-Nikkor Auto, project their full images onto the film at the focal plane. The 16mm lens projects an image greater in diameter than any of the film frame dimensions so that only a portion of the projected image is recorded. With any of the fisheye lenses, other than the 16mm, the pictorial axis, with due regard to the subject matter, can be considered a diagonal drawn anywhere across the circular image. With the 16mm lens, the pictorial axis will be either a line bisecting the image vertically or horizontally within the 24 × 36mm configuration; the pictorial diagonal achieved with this lens has no significance for purposes of the succeeding discussion.

When the camera is held so that the optical axis of the lens is parallel to the ground, the image plane will then be parallel with a subject plane that is perpendicular to the ground. Under these conditions, a line of objects of the same size extending for some distance to both the right and left of the optical axis will be seen to diminish in size as recorded on film. Depending on the distance of these objects from the camera, they will taper off from some clearly discernible dimension at the center until, at the perimeter of the circular image, they are of greatly reduced size, even to the extent of being recorded as a mere dot on the edge of the circle. For objects at some distance from the camera, the rate of diminution in size from center to edge is less than for objects positioned much closer to the camera. In accordance with the ordinary rules of perspective, there is a diminution in size of objects from a position closer to the camera proceeding toward the background to pictorial infinity and beyond. The combination of these two phenomena of image size rendition accounts for the curvature characteristics of pictures made with fisheye lenses.

When objects or subjects having pictorial depth are photographed with fisheye lenses, they have a characteristic spheroid appearance. It is as though a design printed on a ball were photographed with an ordinary lens; as the surface of the ball bends away from a point on the ball closest to the lens of the camera, the details are perceived smaller and smaller in a spherical configuration.

The following performance characteristics should therefore be kept in mind as a guide for working out the best composition in a given circumstance:

1. The center of the pictorial area (or of the circle) will appear to be most normal or least distorted. This is particularly so in the absence of rectangular objects having recognizable configurations.

2. The rate of fall-off in relative size of objects from foreground to background will vary with the distance of the lens from the closest foreground objects; the closer the near objects to the lens, the greater will be the rate of fall-off. While this is characteristic of all perspective renditions, it is perceived in exaggerated form with fisheye lenses.

3. Fisheye "distortions" are most noticeable when foreground objects are very close to the camera and when there is increasing separation between foreground and background objects.

4. When the camera is held so that the optical axis extends in a downward angle, curvature patterns will also be downward. When shooting from a high elevation, as from an airplane, with the camera pointed directly downward, the earth will be seen as a huge sphere with the ground (and objects on it) curving away from the image center. When the camera is pointed upward at an angle, horizontal lines will be seen curving away from center in a bowl-like or saucer-like pattern.

Fisheye Pictorial Composition. Three main rules of pictorial management should be kept in mind. These pertain to the treatment of centrally oriented picture targets, perimeter or circumference subjects, and relationship of foreground to background. Of these three, the last is derived from ordinary rules of perspective, except that it constitutes an extreme case calling for special attention.

Prominent elements or features of a subject should be at approximately the same distance from the lens, toward the center of the field of view. Both width and depth should be minimized when this is within the photographer's control, either through pictorial choice, shift in camera viewpoint, or subject rearrangement. Thus, a subject leaning backward in his seat would have a very small head as compared to the rendered size of his hands and knees; having the subject lean forward would dramatically change the entire configuration. When two people are photographed side-by-side at the center of the field of view, fairly normal effects will be achieved. But if they are off-center, the subject closest to the perimeter will be smaller. Hence, the subject closer to the perimeter should be positioned somewhat closer to the lens than the other subject. Gross disparities in effects can be minimized through putting somewhat more distance between lens and subject; conversely, they can be enhanced or exaggerated by shortening the lens-to-subject distance. At the closest distances, gross caricaturing should be avoided—as with the human face—for purposes of good taste.

Objects at the perimeter of the circular field of view can be used as subjects in themselves or as framing for pictorial centers. A familiar example of perimeter composition is a skyscraper cluster; the camera is held pointing straight up at center in a cluster of buildings so that they are recorded on film as radials all pointing toward an open center. With non-fisheye lenses, the buildings would taper toward the center, representing perspective convergence; with fisheye lenses, this is offset by the tendency of images to taper toward the periphery of the circular field of view. Parallel objects can be used effectively to frame central subjects: most commonly, these would be pillars, posts, or other closely spaced upright verticals, but they could also be horizontally aligned objects, such as fence sections, or the top and bottom of a small window. The parallel objects at the perimeter, if close to the camera, will maintain dimension so as effectively to frame the subject.

The relationship between foreground and background objects will be governed partly by distance from the camera to the foreground object and partly by that object's separation from the background. Again, this is common to all optically recorded situations, but is uniquely true of fisheye lens phenomena. The basic rule is that objects of equal size will diminish progressively in recorded size as they recede into the background. This universal phenomenon is seen in exaggerated form with fisheye lenses because of their ability to be used at extremely close range such as to photograph a standing adult from a distance of about one foot (0.3 meters). Leaving out the problem of tapering away from the image center, discussed above, the pictorial problem here is to utilize or avoid (as the case may be) rapid fall-off in size from foreground to background. Either by moving closer to a foreground object or by separating it from its background, or by a combination of the two, an effect can be achieved in which the foreground object is dominant while the background is of desired informational size, establishing a particular relevance to the main subject. Conversely, the background can be given greater prominence either by backing away from the stationary subject or by causing the subject to move closer to the background.

The slightest shifts in camera viewpoint, apart from subject matter arrangement, can bring about noticeably different image arrangements on the film, whether they are achieved by lateral shifts of the camera, angular shifts of the lens without changing camera position, or changing the picture-taking position. Hence, it is good practice to probe the picture possibilities both before shooting a single picture and throughout the taking of a sequence.

Exposure with Fisheye Lenses. The special problem of exposure unique to fisheye lenses is that they see so much of the field of view as to often encompass the sun or artificial light sources. There is ordinarily no problem when the sun is directly behind you in a cloudless sky. A problem could arise when photographing landscapes or other open vertical areas in which large portions are put in shade by partial cloud cover. Also, there is relatively little problem under flat lighting or hazy bright illumination.

The situation changes when the sun or other source of illumination is directly within the field of view so that its rays strike directly at the lens. This will cause flare, which may or may not be objectionable, depending upon the desired pictorial effect. In some cases, interesting effects are achieved when the light patterns caused by reflections from the surfaces of the lens elements are splashed onto the film. In keeping with the modern vogue of using errors or deviations from technically correct procedures to achieve creative effects, some form of flare might be pictorially desirable. On the other hand, flare that causes objectionable image degradation is to be avoided.

One way of avoiding flare or ghost images is to create an artificial "eclipse" using a 3-inch-diameter shield attached to a thin rod or wire. The shield is held in front of the lens in such a way as to block out the direct rays of the sun. The further the shield is held away from the lens, the less conspicuous it will be in the photograph. Obviously, the longer the rod or wire, the stiffer it will have to be or it will bend. The actual diameter of a thin rod or wire would not be significantly noticeable.

Because of the possibility of wide ranges in illumination and reflectance from subject matter within the hemispheric field of view, at times it will be necessary to make selective exposure readings and determine which exposure settings to use accordingly.

The built-in filters are intended primarily for use in black-and-white photography except the L1A (skylight) filter, which is also intended for use in color photography. When exposure is calculated on the basis of ground objects, the sky ordinarily will be washed out and without detail due to overexposure. Some photographers use a yellow or orange filter with color film, with otherwise suitable subjects, to provide overall color to the sky.

Camera and Lens Operations. As already noted, viewing with the fixed-focus 6mm $f/5.6$ and 10mm $f/5.6$ fisheye lenses is by means of an accessory finder supplied with each lens. This viewfinder permits viewing a 160-degree picture field. The finder slips into the accessory shoe of Nikon cameras. With earlier Nikkormats, it is necessary to first attach the camera's accessory shoe, available as an optional accessory. It is possible, even without a viewfinder, to perceive the picture coverage. With the camera mounted on a tripod, the lens may be preliminarily sighted in the direction of the subject target. Then, refinements in targeting can be made by observing the picture coverage that is visible in the form of a reflection on the front optical surface of the lens.

The reflex mirror must be placed in the mirror lock-up position only with fixed-focus lenses.

Except at close shooting distances, critical focusing with the 8mm $f/2.8$ and the 6mm $f/2.8$ lens is not essential as the depth of field is ordinarily so great as to accommodate all sharpness requirements from near to far. For very close focusing, the image separation at full aperture is sufficiently great as to make focusing possible with the unaided eye. Where very critical focusing is needed, the use of one of the magnifying finder attachments may be helpful.

In some situations it may be desirable to take pictures without reference to a viewfinder—a technique known as "blind shooting." This method is best suited to situations in which the total subject is sufficiently continuous as to make critical viewing and framing unnecessary. It is also applicable to other situations in which a central figure occupies only a small part of the total field so that it might be positioned by manual guidance without reference to the viewfinder.

When the camera is hand-held, care must be taken to keep your feet in back of the field of view so that they will not be included in the picture. With the 180-degree lens, the field of view is delineated by the front metal ring surrounding the front lens element. With the two lenses having 220-degree coverage, your feet must be kept even further back inasmuch as the field of view extends 20 degrees on either side of the lens toward the rear. In other words, the lens will see, to some extent, in back of itself. The same precautions must be taken when using the fisheye lenses on a tripod.

THE ZOOM LENSES

The successful development of zoom lenses stems mainly from the needs of the television and motion picture industries to have lenses that can be used to alter image sizes and relationships variably and smoothly in the course of a continuous recording. It was not until the mid 1950's that the first zoom for a 35mm still camera became available—the Voigtlander Zoomar 36–82mm *f*/2.8 lens. Since then, the development of zoom lenses for still cameras has advanced remarkably. The latest zoom Nikkor lenses compare favorably with fixed prime lenses.

Nikkor Zoom lenses are of continuously variable focal length within a given range. Within the range of the particular lens, the focal length may be changed continuously and speedily and, without changing lens aperture, enable the photographer to select any desirable image size while looking through the viewfinder. Once the zoom lens is focused for a specific subject distance (by turning the focusing ring to the left or right), it remains sharply focused on that distance at all focal lengths, requiring no further adjustments unless the distance between subject and photographer changes.

The primary area of application of zoom lenses is the ability to substitute one lens for several, thereby permitting selective composing or framing of the subject, particularly one that is moving without losing time to change lenses. A collateral advantage of the zoom lens is the reduction of equipment inventory and bulk, particularly when traveling. A third advantage is the ability to obtain a variety of creative effects most conveniently, covering perspective effects as well as creative use of the mechanical attributes of these lenses, such as zooming in or out in the course of a slow exposure.

The ratio of the minimum and maximum focal lengths of a particular lens is expressed as the *zoom ratio*. Thus, the 43–86mm lens has a zoom ratio of 1:2, the 80–200mm lens has a zoom ratio of 1:2.5, and the 50–300mm lens has a zoom ratio of 1:6. These ratios can be stated conversely from longest to shortest focal lengths for any given lens, using these examples, as 2×, 2.5×, and 6×.

The maximum apertures of each of the zoom lenses are relatively wide when considered in terms of their longest focal length, but this advantage diminishes somewhat when the same lenses are zoomed to their shortest focal length. Also, the close-focusing distances for each of these lenses is relatively short, at the longest focal length, but these same close-focusing distances are maintained at the shortest focal length for each of the lenses.

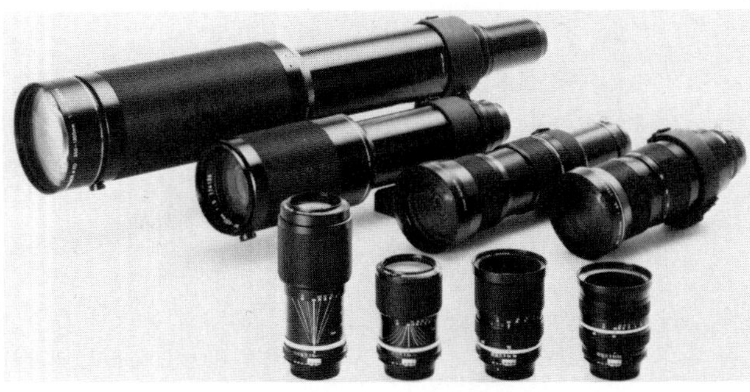

Some of the Nikkor Zooms. Top, left to right: 360—1200mm ED, 180—600mm, 50—300mm, 50—300mm ED. Bottom: 80—200mm, 43—86mm, 35—70mm, 28—45mm.

Uses of the Nikkor Zoom Lenses

The use of the zoom in selective framing—or selective magnification of the important pictorial information to fill the image area—is undoubtedly the most common of the applications of this type of equipment. We can call this *optical cropping*. Although it is a convenient technique with all films, it is most advantageous with color slide films where precise in-camera framing is desirable for projection purposes. It is so much more convenient to stand in one spot and vary the focal length than to move forward or backward or to interchange lenses of fixed focal length. When following sports or other fast-moving action, the photographer who has used a zoom lens with which to maintain comparable size of two subjects from frame to frame would not want to go back to either interchanging lenses or selecting from a battery of cameras.

The control of size relationships among objects in the foreground, middle ground, and background is a second area of versatile application. In the strictest sense, this has nothing to do with the optical characteristics of the zoom lens because perspective-governed size relationships of objects in depth are controlled solely by the distance of the camera from its subject. What makes perspective depth control particularly applicable to the zoom lenses is the convenience of being able to alter the focal length while simultaneously changing distances between camera and subject. In this way, the foreground can be selected as a constant, while the relative size of background details can be altered by moving to or from the subject while varying the focal length. Similarly, the middle ground or background can be held as constant. One limitation in this, however, is that prime lenses comparable to the shorter ends of the zoom ratios are able to be used, for perspective control purposes, at closer distances than the zooms.

The combination of a zoom with a motorized camera body is ideal, for you do not have to advance the film, which frees you to concentrate more on the zoom and focusing controls. The next step to automatic exposure control enables the photographer to concentrate even more on creative image control.

One novel technique is making slow-speed exposures while zooming the lens, starting with the longest focal length. The central image area will be sharpest while other details will be perceived as streaks radiating or bursting from the center. Suitable subjects include colorful light displays at night, bright colors against dark backgrounds, and sharp contrast in lighting. The most impressive effects are usually obtained with color films due to the interplay of color mass and tone as important elements of composition. Good results can also be achieved with black-and-white subjects, although they must be chosen with care in order to bring attention primarily to the composition rather than to the loss of image resolution more noticeable with black-and-white prints.

In making slow-speed zoom exposures the camera should be mounted on a tripod with the exposure dial set for an exposure of about ½ sec., although good results can be obtained within the range of ¼ sec. to one sec. It is a good idea to practice making exposures with particular subjects even if a few frames are wasted. In order to allow sufficient room for the "explosion" of the image from the center outward, the image must be framed quite fully at the start, at the longest focal length, so that the streaking will extend from the edges in toward the pictorial center. At night, fast films are most convenient to use because of

Joseph D. Cooper

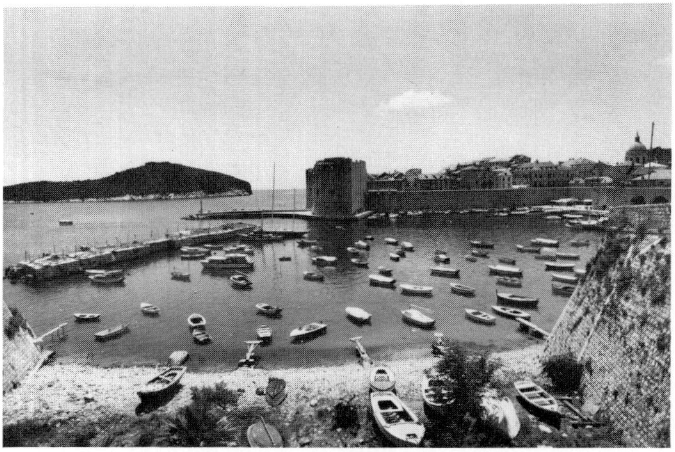

The wide view of inlet at Dubrovnik was made with 24mm lens. Other selective views were made with 80–200mm Zoom-Nikkor at different focal lengths depending on composition desired and degree of magnification. Exposure settings had to be changed for some of the pictures due to variations in scene brightness.

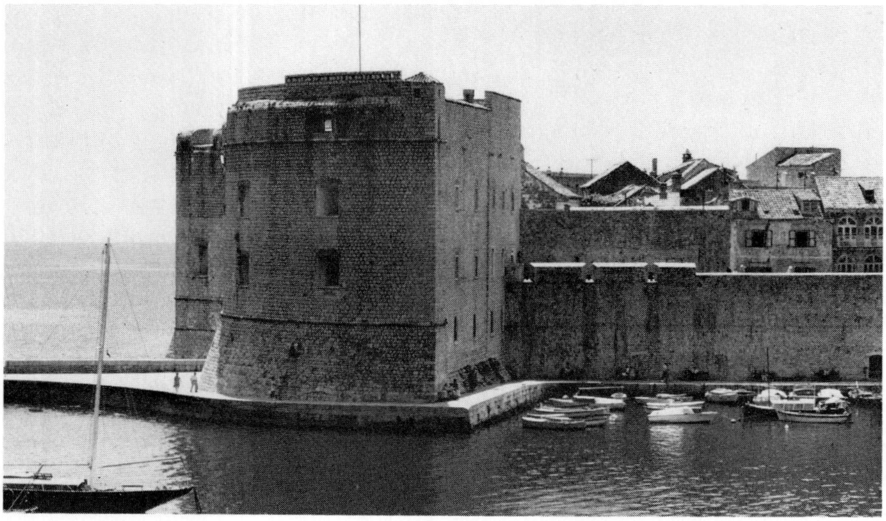

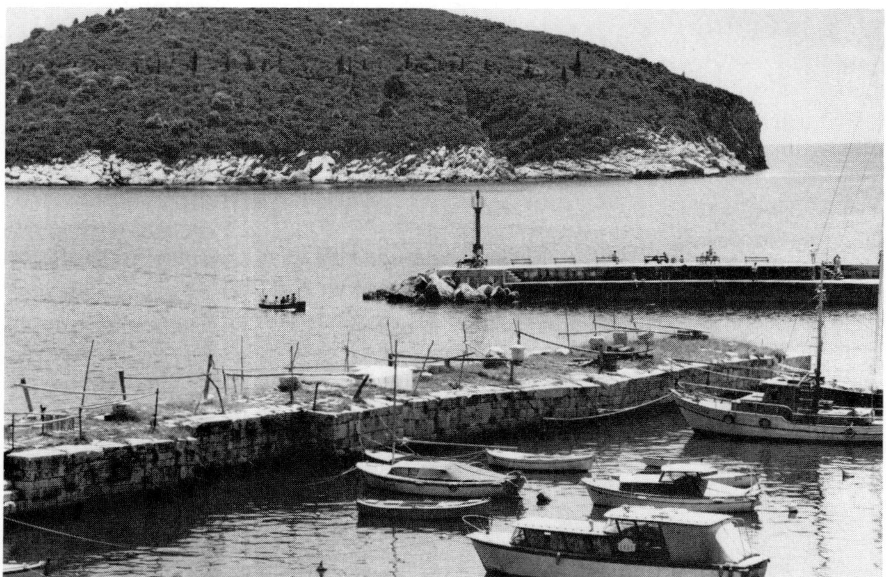

Joseph D. Cooper

Additional selective views made with 80–200mm Zoom-Nikkor from same shooting position. Compare with broad view seen top of facing page. High shooting angle against the light lends feeling of depth.

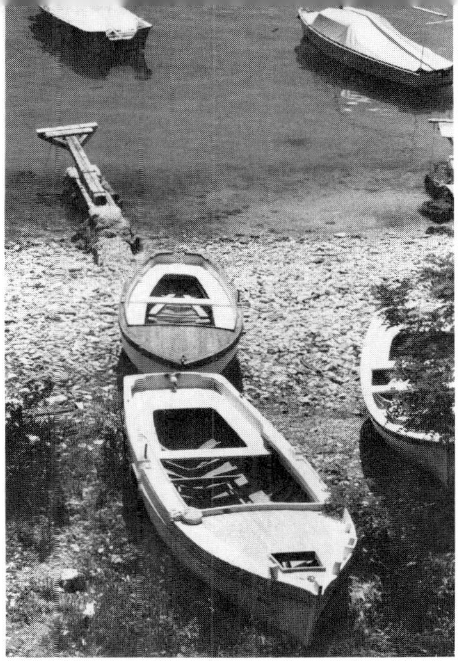

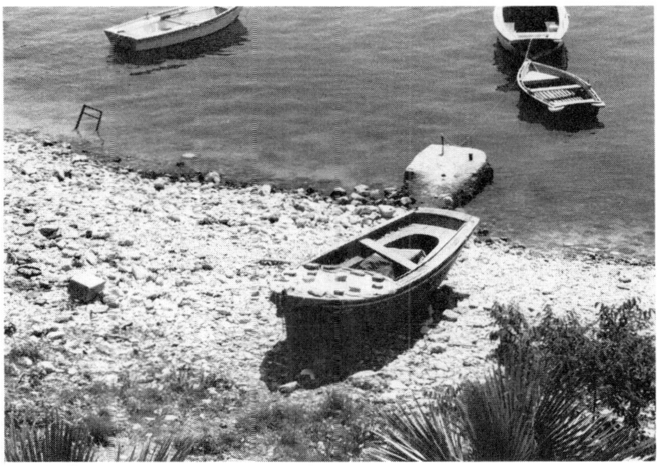

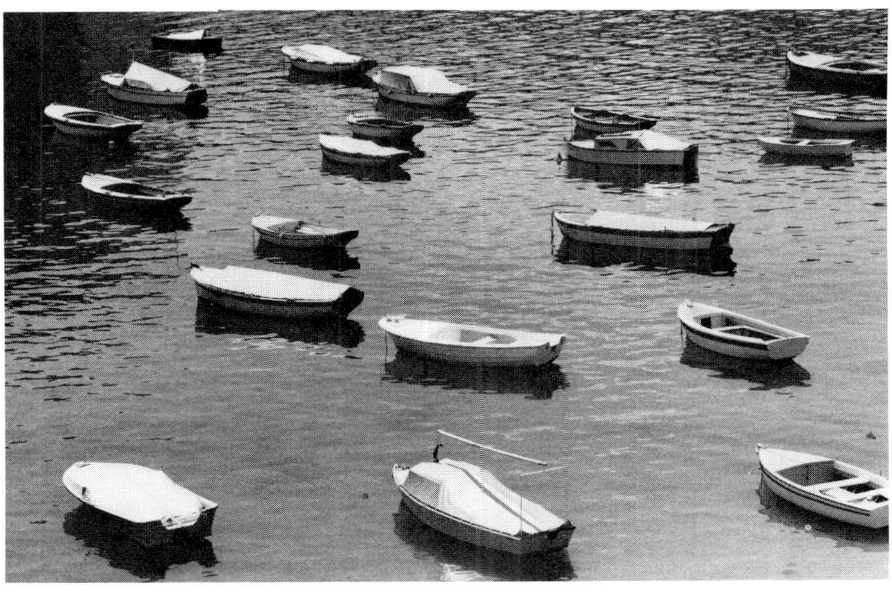

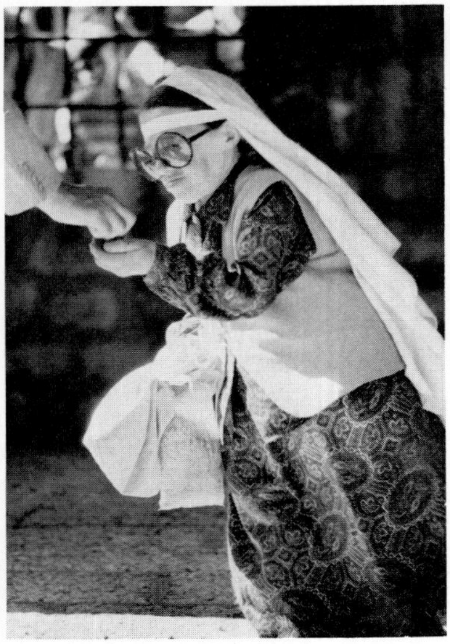

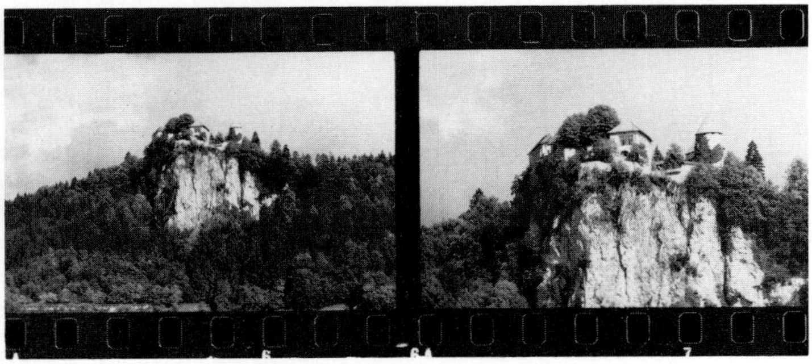

Joseph D. Cooper

For a great majority of uses, a zoom lens is used for optical cropping of the picture in the camera. While these are black-and-white shots, in-camera cropping is most important when making color slides. The 80–200mm Zoom was used for the comparison set and for the almstaker in the courtyard of a Mosque in Sarajevo.

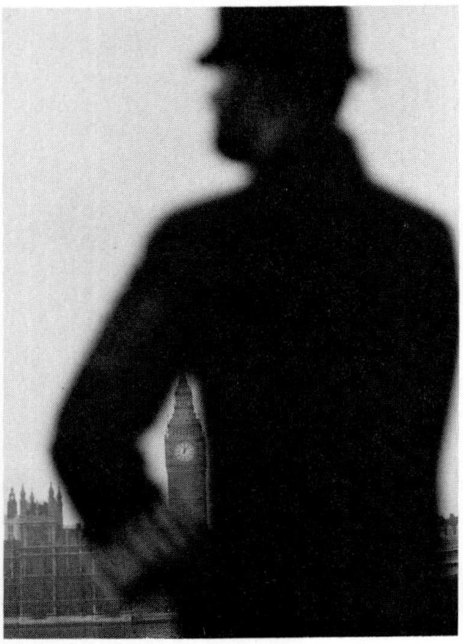

Francisco Hidalgo

Selectivity in this case meant finding just the right shooting position and image ratio that would best bring out Westminster Tower framed within the crook of the London bobby's arm. 43mm focal length of 43–86mm Zoom-Nikkor. 1/250 sec., *f*/5.6.

Gerry Cranham

For sports photographers and others who have to zoom in and out in order to display the subject sufficiently large within the viewing area, the 50–300mm Zoom-Nikkor offers great flexibility. This picture of Mary Rand, British runner, was made with the lens wide-open at 1/500 sec.

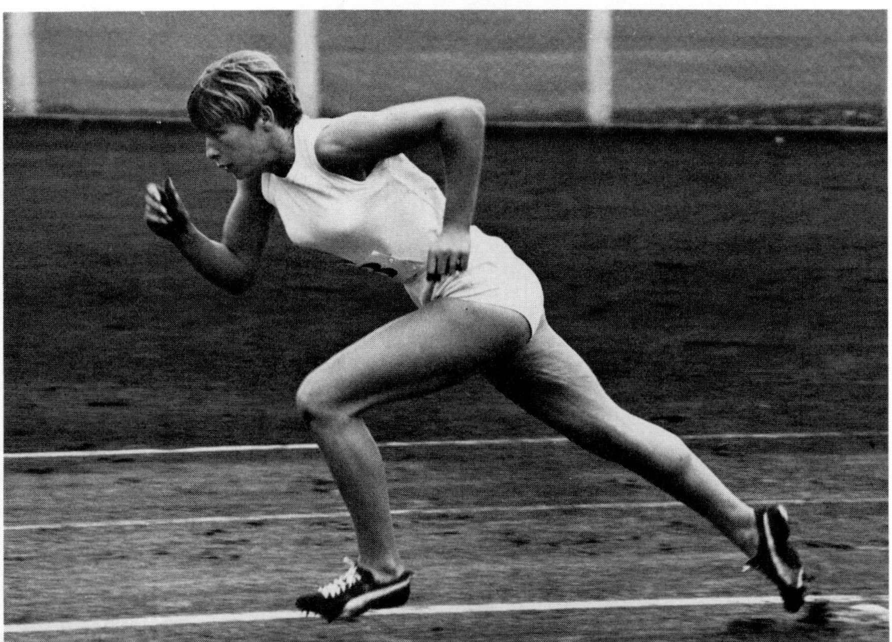

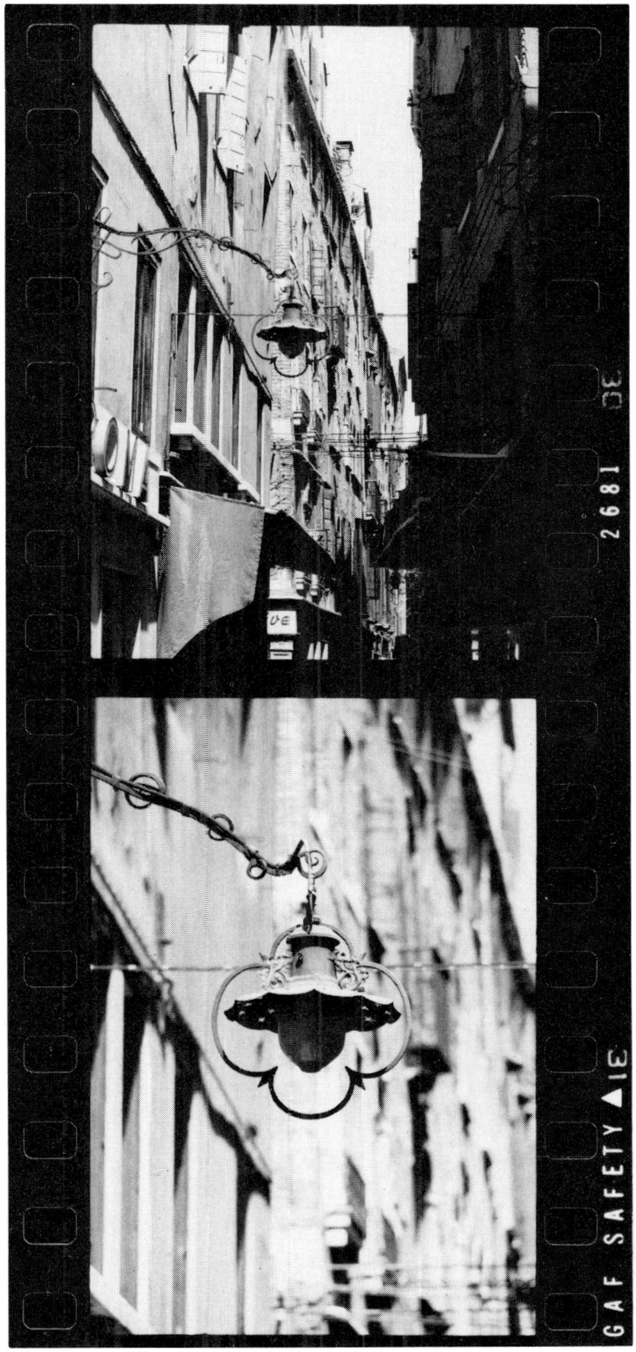

Joseph D. Cooper

A zoom lens takes on the general operating characteristics of a lens of the focal length selected. For example, the top picture, made at the 80mm focal length of the 80–200mm Zoom-Nikkor, shows much more depth of field at the same aperture than does the lower picture made with the same lens at the focal length of 200mm. Both shots were made at the same aperture. Note, however, that in the lower picture the background has gone out of focus. Sometimes different exposures are called for under the same light conditions with the same subject at different zoom focal lengths due to changes in the tonal reflection mix within the central exposure-measuring area. The zoom lens was used in this case to simplify pictorial composition.

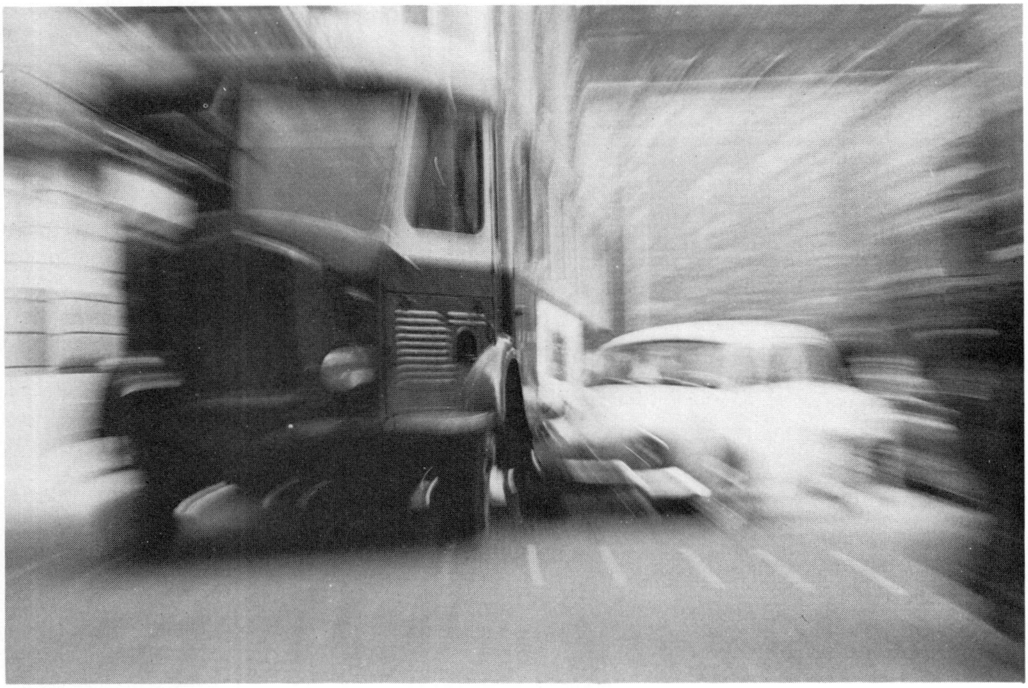

Francisco Hidalgo

Amplifying the sense of movement through slow-speed zooming. Top picture suggests forceful collision—which was not the fact. 43–86mm Zoom-Nikkor, 1/15 sec., f/8, Kodak Plus-X.

Gerry Cranham

The 6-day cycle racers at Wembley would have shown their own movement at the slow speed of 1/8 sec., but this was enhanced through slow zooming during that same interval. It was a dull day and something was needed to provide "snap."

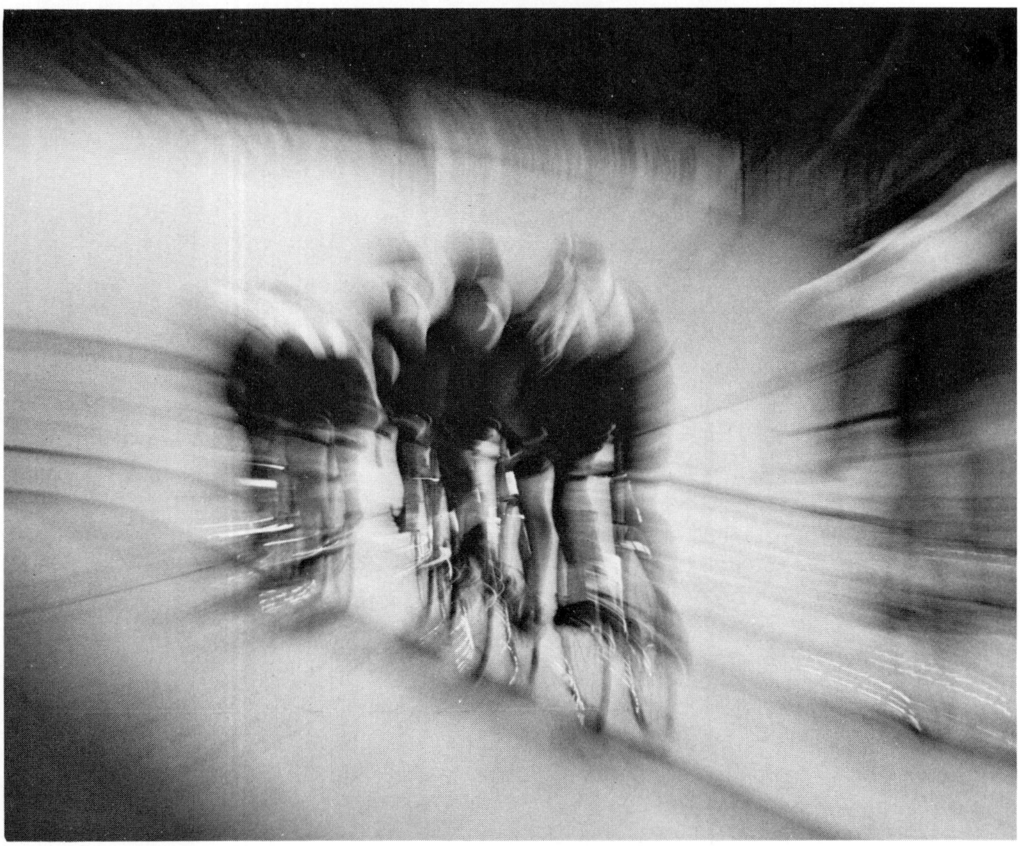

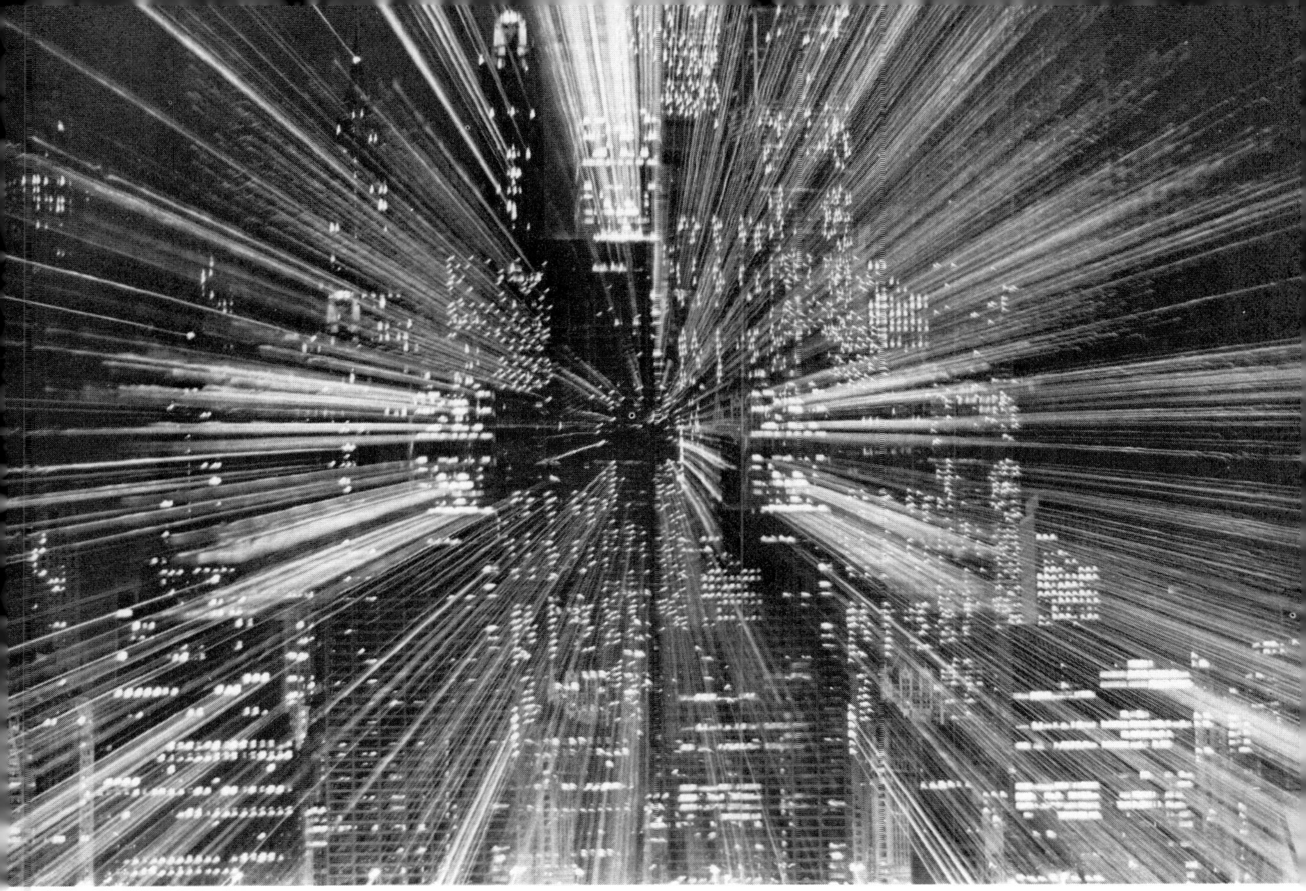

Francisco Hidalgo

Special effects achieved by holding camera on tripod during slow exposure while lens is zoomed in or out slowly. Exposure above made with 80–200mm Zoom-Nikkor f/4.5 wide-open during a 30-second exposure on tripod. Lower picture, made with 43–86mm Zoom-Nikkor, called for faster action within brief span of 1/15 sec. at f/8 because of daylight. Kodak Plus-X. Two kinds of sharp image registry can be discerned. One is at the center where zoom is least while the other is a fixed part of the scene that registers most heavily because the lens is at rest for a briefly longer duration at the beginning or end of the zoom travel. For other examples, see Chapter 16, "Special Effects."

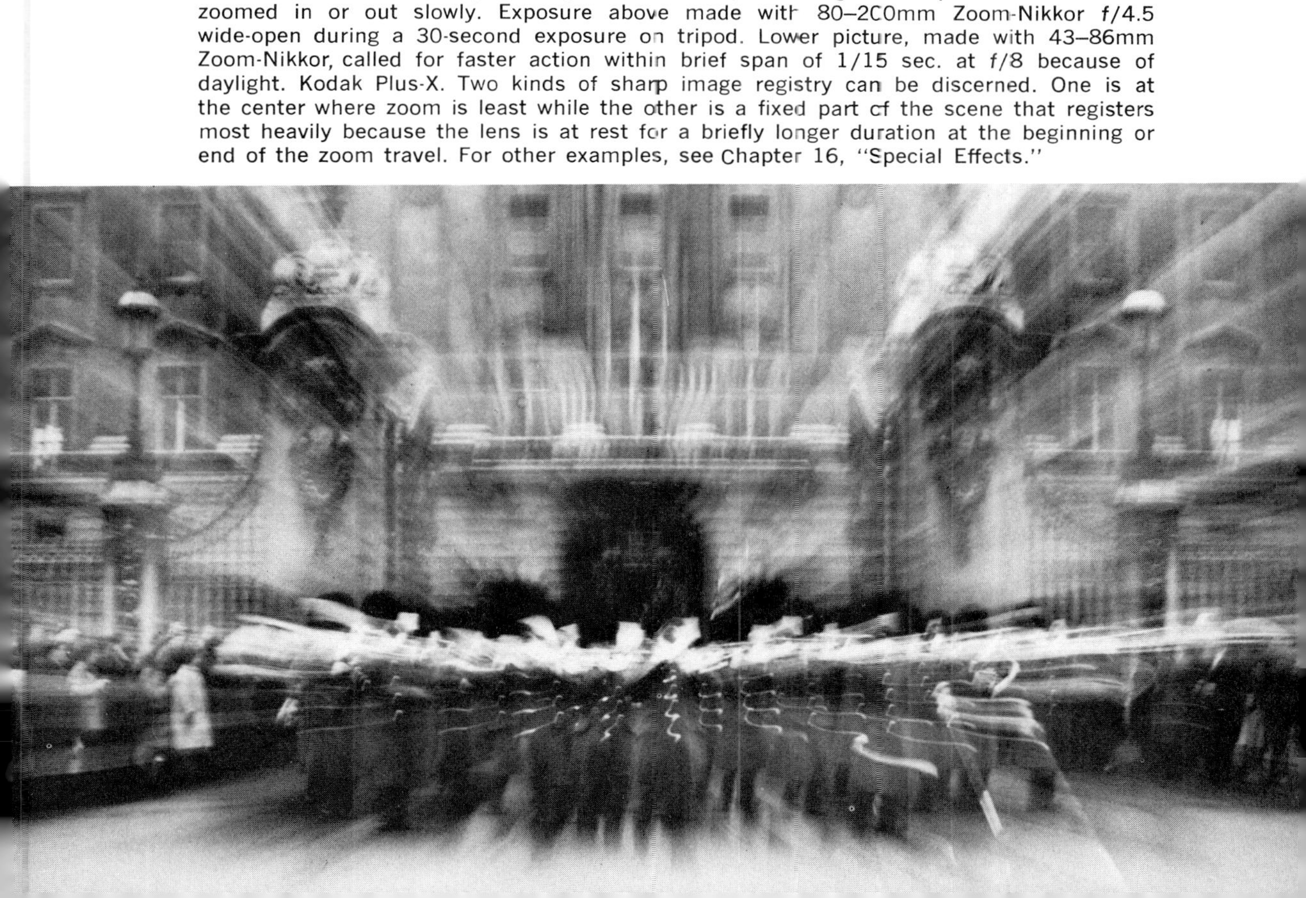

reduced light intensity. In the daytime, however, a fast film may become overexposed due to the prolonged exposure. Hence, for daylight zoom exposures a neutral density filter is necessary in order to reduce the amount of light reaching the film. An ND 2.0 filter will reduce transmitted light to 1/100th of its full strength. If you don't need that much light level reduction, you can use an ND 0.30, which passes one-half of the light, or an ND 0.60, which passes only one-quarter of the light. Obviously, the subject should be stationary or nearly so during exposure unless you are aiming for multiple effects with moving light displays.

Another creative technique is to make multiple exposures. Again, this can be done with any lens, but the advantage of the zoom is that you can gain subject size most conveniently without having to change positions. For example, you can have a display of several members of a family exposed individually in different sizes. A variance of this is to place differently scaled images of the same person overlapping each other or in different parts of the image area. A technical and creative explanation of the multiple-exposure technique is detailed in the chapters on camera operation and creative applications, respectively.

Macro close-up photography can be done conveniently and extensively using the 43–86mm lens in reverse mode. This yields an image ratio or magnification range of 1:6 to a little more than 1:1. The BR-2 Reverse Adapter Ring permits mounting the lens in reverse mode. In addition to the reverse adapter ring, you may wish to attach the Auto Ring BR-4 to the rear of the lens now brought forward. Used in conjunction with the Double Cable Release AR-4, the BR-4 ring permits automatic operation of the lens diaphragm in reverse mode A BR-3 ring will permit you to screw filters or even supplementary close-up attachment lenses to the lens.

Additionally, the No. 0 supplementary close-up lens can be used with the 43–86mm lens in order to shorten the near-focusing distance, but in this mode the lens cannot be focused at infinity. With longer zoom lenses, you can use a fractional-diopter supplementary close-up attachment lens, such as a 1/4 or a 1/2 diopter lens, not presently available from Nikon, but available through independent quality filter sources.

Operating Techniques With Zoom Lenses

Critical focusing with a standing or stationary subject is most easily achieved with the lens at its fullest extension and the depth of field is therefore at its shallowest. As long as the camera-to-subject distance is maintained, the zoom can be varied, setting it on any focal length within its range, to achieve desired image size without refocusing. However, when following a moving subject you cannot use this technique unless you can predetermine where the action will take place, for example, in car racing.

The longer zooms are best used on fairly solid tripods due to their weight. Hand-held exposures at the long end of the 50–300mm lens or at any focal length in the range of 200–600mm are not safely made because of the long focal length and the muscle stress induced by the physical size and weight of the equipment.

Exposure control is no different with zoom lenses than with other lenses, due to the constancy of aperture over the entire range of focal length. Nevertheless, when covering action situations in which you are moving about constantly, your relationship to the source of light and reflection from the subject is subject to great variation. A slight shift in direction could mean an exposure increase or decrease of one or more stops. This is no problem with a camera having automatic exposure control except where contrast ranges undergo significant change. When using equipment without automatic exposure controls, you need to check the exposure needle alignment within the viewfinder. If you are using a Nikon with a standard prism head, you need to make independent exposure verifications or modifications consistent with changes in lighting conditions. A lens hood invariably should be used since, in the course of shifting position, you may expose the front lens surface to the direct rays of the sun or other light source.

THE PERSPECTIVE CONTROL LENS

The 35mm *f*/2.8 PC-Nikkor, the 28mm *f*/4 PC-Nikkor, and the 28mm *f*/3.5 PC-Nikkor bring to the 35mm SLR camera the image control capabilities of larger format cameras, with lens carriers that shift the lens away from central axis. The PC-Nikkors have a built-in capability of being shifted off-center in any direction for a distance of 11mm. This creates an image diverging effect toward the side opposite the direction of shift. The diversion can be used to correct perspective distortions as described below.

Additionally, these wide-angle lenses of retrofocus design can be used as all-purpose lenses when maintained in normal, on-axis mode. They are manual, preset-type lenses.

General Use of the PC-Nikkor Lens

In covering large rectangular subjects, a tall building for example, the photographer may have to tilt his camera upwards to include the top of the structure, especially when working at close range. The result in the photograph is that the walls of the building appear to converge toward the top as if the building were falling over backwards, while some of the foreground is lost.

On the other hand, when using the conventional lens so that its optical axis is perpendicular to the vertical structure (thereby keeping the film in vertical plane parallel to vertical structures being photographed), there is no perspective distortion The tradeoff, however, with a tall building, is that its top is cut off while unwanted foreground is included.

The same convergence effects are achieved when tilting the camera to the side to photograph a long line of buildings. The eye accepts this type of convergence as normal because it extends into the distance with the film plane parallel to vertical structures. It is an accustomed mode of seeing. However, when the camera is tilted upwards (or downwards), the eye and brain are obliged to accommodate themselves to unaccustomed viewpoints. Thus, any perspective effects with optical axis held parallel to the ground are viewed on film or paper as normal, while any effects achieved through vertical tilt of the axis will be viewed as distortion. However, with the PC-Nikkor's shifting and rotating movements, the photographer is able to get balanced composition without tilting the camera. The film plane remains vertical while the center of the lens is placed on the line connecting the center of the subject with that of the film. The photographer is able to shift the lens horizontally, vertically, or diagonally to include the top of the building while keeping the film plane parallel to the wall surface to eliminate unwanted con-

NOMENCLATURE FOR 35mm *f*/2.8 PC-NIKKOR

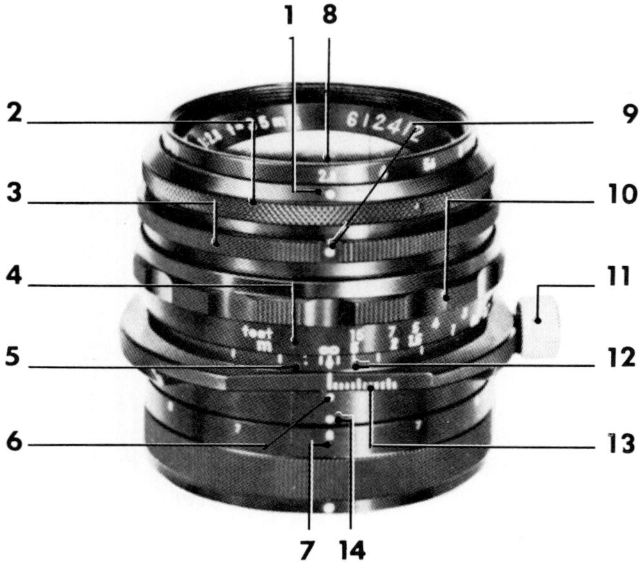

1. Aperture-Preset-Ring Index Dot
Aligns with *f*/numbers to indicate taking aperture.

2. Aperture-Preset Ring
Turns to preset the taking aperture.

3. Stop-Down Ring
Opens the lens to full aperture for focusing ease and stops down to check depth of field after presetting the aperture.

4. Distance Scale
Graduated in both feet and meters.

5. Infrared Mark
Aligns with the prefocused distance to compensate for shift in focus when using infrared film.

6. Shift-Scale Index Dot
Aligns with shift scale to indicate extent of lens shift.

7. Maximum Permissible Shift Scale
Digits indicate the maximum shift in millimeters in each direction.

8. Aperture Scale
Engraved on opposite sides of the front rim of the lens for easy reading with any rotation movement.

9. Stop-Down Ring Index Dot
Aligns with aperture-preset-ring index dot to stop down lens for shooting.

10. Focusing Ring

11. Shift Knob
Turns to shift the lens off-center

12. Depth-of-Field Scale
Color-coded lines give depth of field at different apertures.

13. Shift Scale
Graduated in millimeters

14. Maximum Permissible Shift Index Dot

verging lines. This feature is valuable when using color or monochrome reversal films that do not accommodate perspective correction in the process of enlargement.

The front part of the lens may be shifted by as much as 11mm off-center by means of a micrometer leadscrew. In addition, the entire lens mount may be rotated a full 360 degrees with click-stops at every 30 degrees. By combining the parallel movements with full-circle rotation, the lens can be shifted in any desired direction by 11mm.

To operate the PC-Nikkor, grip the camera parallel to the subject plane and shift the lens by turning the knurled shift knob while observing in the viewfinder how much of the subject is included together with its perspective correction.

The shift scale, calibrated in millimeters, shows how far the lens has been shifted. The permissible degree of shift depends on its direction. This is because the picture format is rectangular while the lens produces a circular image area. The numbers engraved on the rotating lens mount indicate the limits beyond which image deterioration occurs. But it is still possible to compensate for any image distortion by composing in such a way that unimportant background elements, such as sky or earth, are brought to the corners of the frame in the direction of the lens shift. The Type E focusing screen is recommended for use with the PC-Nikkor. The vertical and horizontal lines marked on the screen help the photographer maintain the camera parallel to the subject while framing the picture.

Some Practical Applications of the PC-Nikkor

Getting rid of unwanted elements in architectural photography. Assume that a pillar appears in the center of the viewfinder, obstructing the view of the main subject—a stone monument. The distance between the pillar and the subject is only about 2.5 meters, too short for the photographer to shoot from the front of the pillar. To get around this obstacle from behind, the photographer has to move to one side to remove the pillar from the viewing field, tilting the lens sideways to include the entire subject. With a conventional lens, this results in converging horizontal lines. By using the PC-Nikkor, the photographer is able to move his camera sideways and shift the PC-Nikkor laterally to include the whole of the monument while maintaining the film plane parallel to it.

Adding a third dimension to frontal views of cubic subjects. While it is possible to obtain the frontal view of cubic subjects, in this case a stack of books, in proper perspective with a conventional lens, the feeling of depth is lost—everything appears flat in the photograph. To add a third dimension, the photographer has to move his camera to one side, with the result of converging lines. With the PC-Nikkor, the photographer moves the camera to one side and holds it in the vertical position, shifting the lens laterally to get the three-dimensional view of the subject. Thus, he delineates depth while retaining "normal" perspective.

Correcting perspective of images on reflecting surfaces. When a painting inside a glassed picture frame is photographed directly from the front with a conventional lens, the camera itself will be reflected on the glass. Moving the camera to the side removes the camera reflection, but the horizontal lines of the painting and frame appear to converge. With the PC-Nikkor, the camera may be held parallel to the reflecting glass surface while the lens is shifted to correct perspective. This removes camera and converging lines from the picture.

Obtaining panoramic pictures without perspective distortion. When a conventional lens is used for photographing panoramic scenes by employing a two-section technique, the overlapping portions of the two exposures may not match perfectly when joined. This is because the camera has to be moved after the first exposure to get the second half of the panoramic scene, thereby giving rise to shifts in the film plane. With the PC-Nikkor, two separate exposures can be made without moving the camera. Simply shift the lens vertically or horizontally and shoot the first half of the scene. Advance the film, then rotate the lens mount a full 180 degrees, and make the second exposure. The result is a pair of frames that match perfectly.

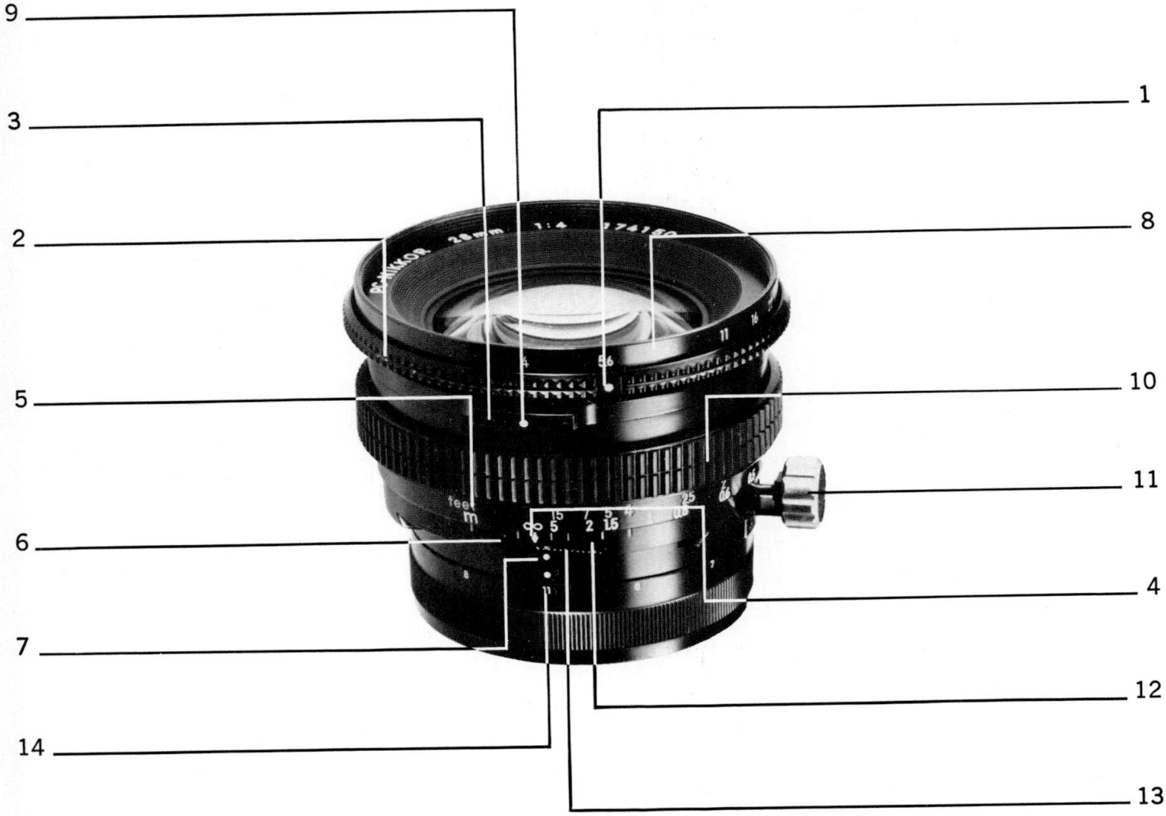

NOMENCLATURE FOR 28mm *f*/4 PC-NIKKOR

1. Preset-Ring-Alignment Index
2. Preset Ring
3. Aperture-Ring Knob
4. Distance-Scale Index
5. Distance Scale
6. Infrared Index
7. Shift-Scale Index
8. Aperture Scale
9. Aperture-Ring-Alignment Index
10. Focusing Ring
11. Shift Knob
12. Depth-of-Field Indicators
13. Shift Scale
14. Maximum Permissible Shift Values

The PC-Nikkor 28mm *f*/4 and the PC-Nikkor 28mm *f*/3.5 (the latter introduced at the 1978 Photokina) are retrofocus wide-angle lenses offering the special lens-shifting feature. As with the 35mm PC-Nikkor, the lens optics may be shifted up to 11mm off-center. The lens barrel can be rotated 360 degrees, permitting the optics to be shifted in any direction. Click stops are provided at 30-degree intervals.

The 28mm focal length of the lenses offers a wide picture angle of 74 degrees, compared with 62 degrees offered by the 35mm PC-Nikkor. When the horizontal shift is used, covering power is 92 degrees, almost that of a 20mm lens.

As with the 35mm PC-Nikkor, the 28mm lenses have a preset diaphragm which is not meter-coupled. Through-the-lens metering may be done in the stopped-down mode.

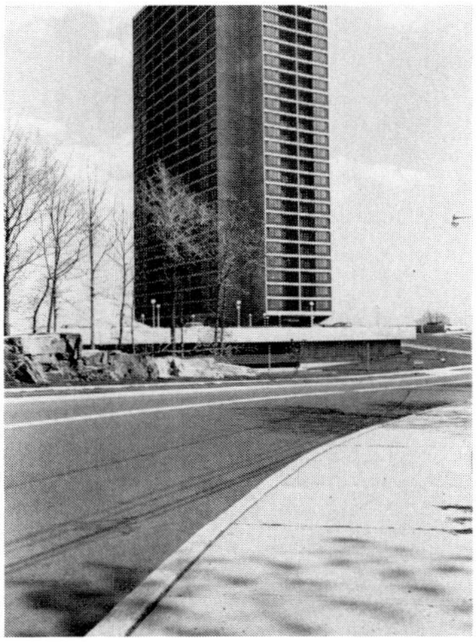

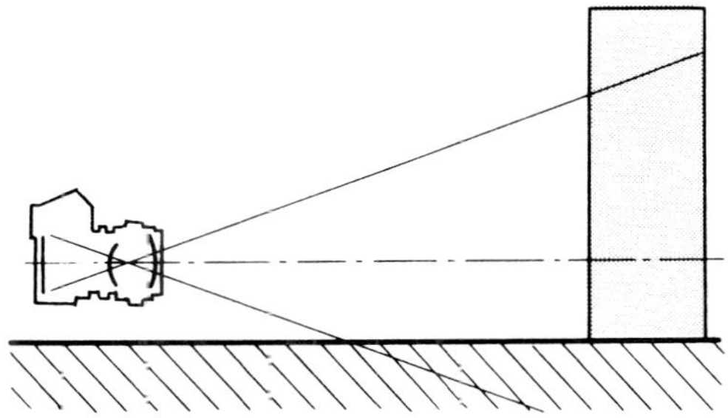

Typical problem in architectural photography, when part of subject is cut off because it falls outside of field of view of the camera mounted parallel to ground.

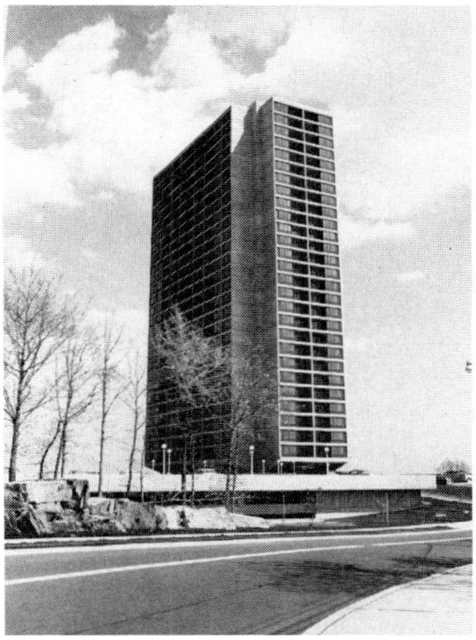

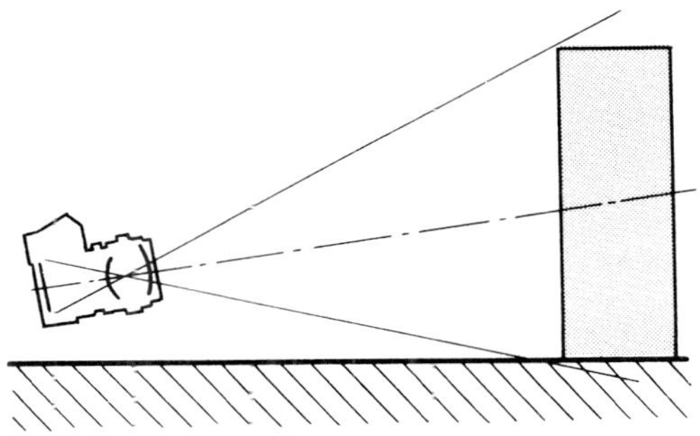

Perspective effect achieved when camera is tilted upward to embrace entire subject.

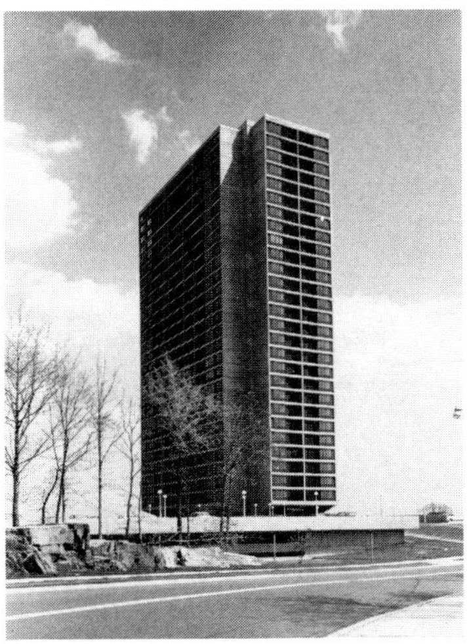

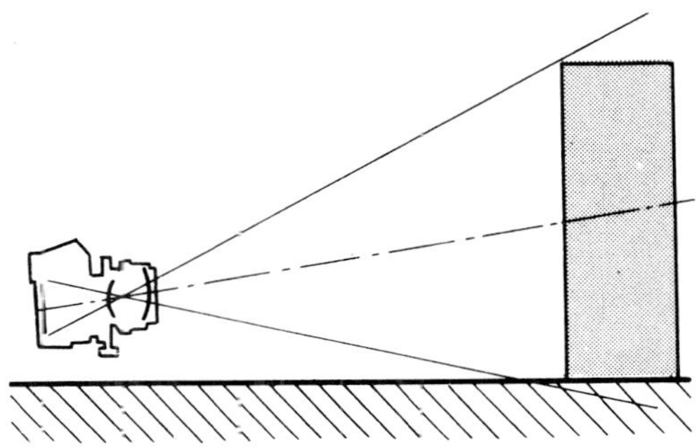

Correction achieved with PC-Nikkor through lens shift.

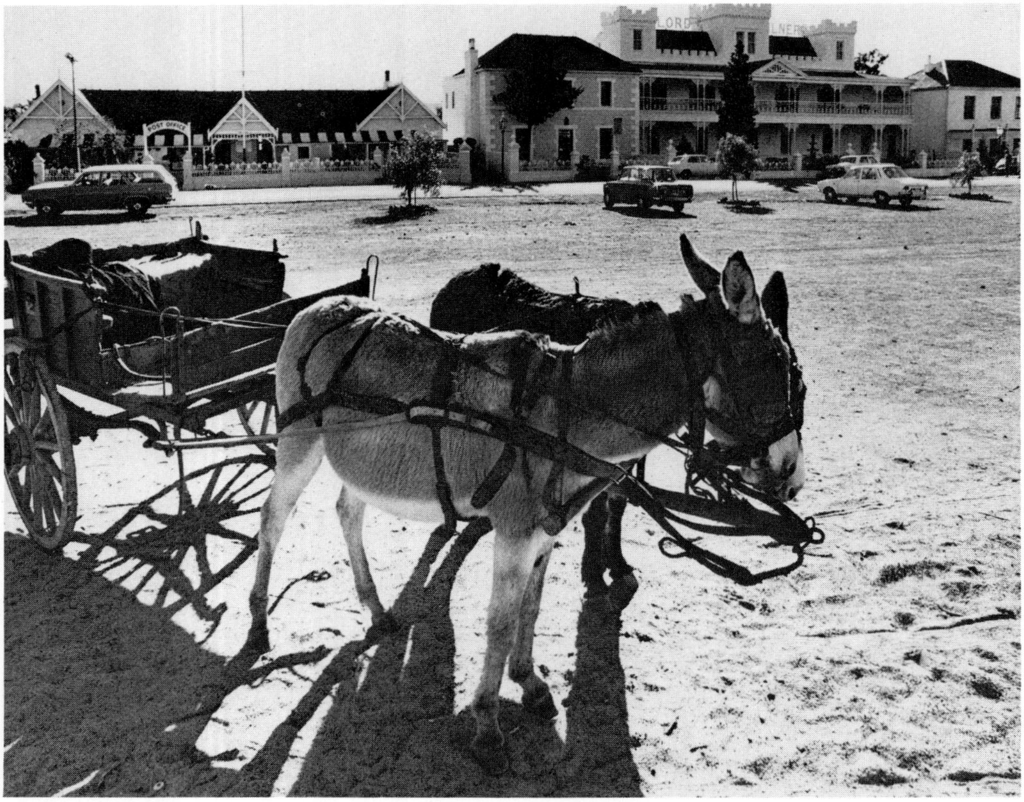

Struan Robertson

Scene at Matjesfontein, a Scottish baronial type folly built at turn of century in thinly-populated interior of Cape Province. Recently subjected to lavish restoration for the benefit of the tourist trade, it is still lacking in picturesque foreground properties. The arrival of a local black in his donkey cart (a few of which still survive) provided the foreground fill. The 35mm PC-Nikkor covered the background widely while giving dominance to foreground material—in these respects functioning as an ordinary wide-angle lens. The perspective-control feature kept the vertical building lines in parallel even though a high shooting angle was used, pointing downward somewhat, in order to separate foreground and background with open space. In the horizontal format a maximum downward shift of 11mm was possible. Lens was stopped down to *f*/32 for maximum depth of field.

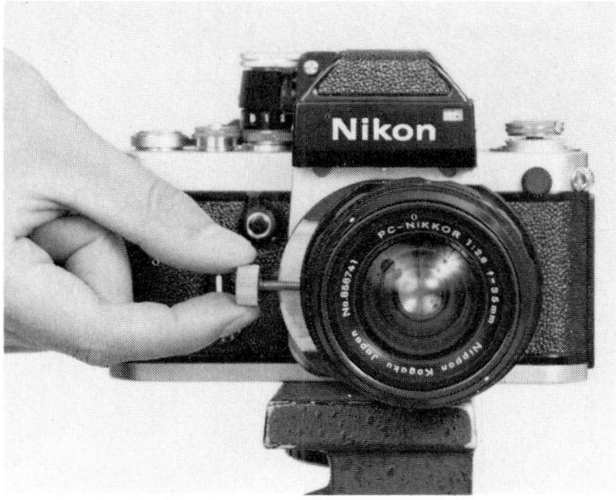

Front part of PC-Nikkor shifts up to 11mm from center in a plane parallel to film while whole lens mount rotates through a full 360 degrees. By combining parallel shift with rotation movement of lens, an infinite variety of adjustments can be made. To shift lens, turn knurled shift knob in opposite direction (top left) from that in which it is to be shifted. When shift scale is facing upward, lens can be shifted 11mm to right of center. To shift in other directions, rotate whole lens mount, stopping at one of 12 click-stop settings at 30-degree intervals. Intermediate shifts can also be made. By combining these two movements, the lens can be shifted up to 11mm from center in any direction (left center).

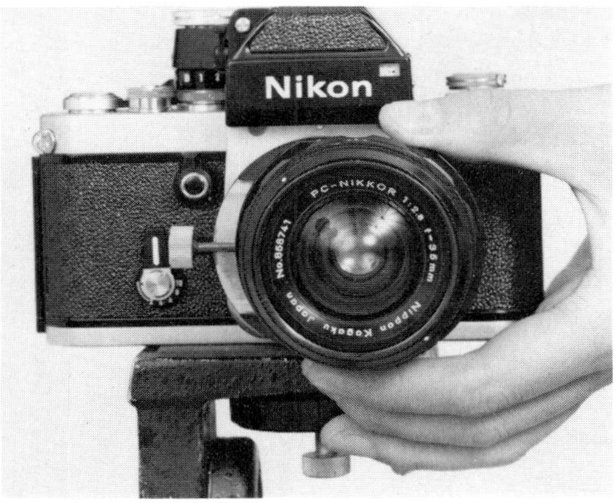

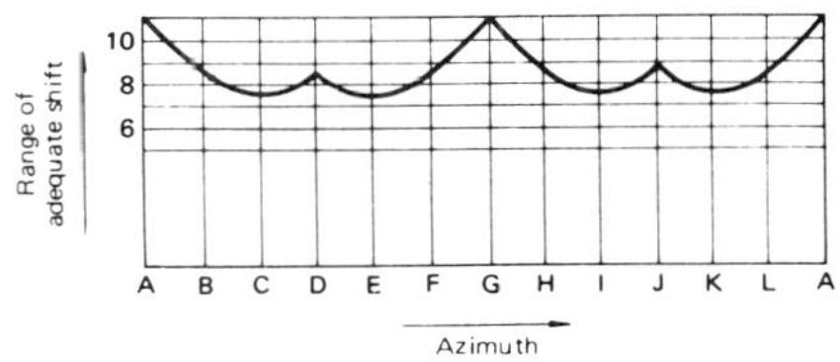

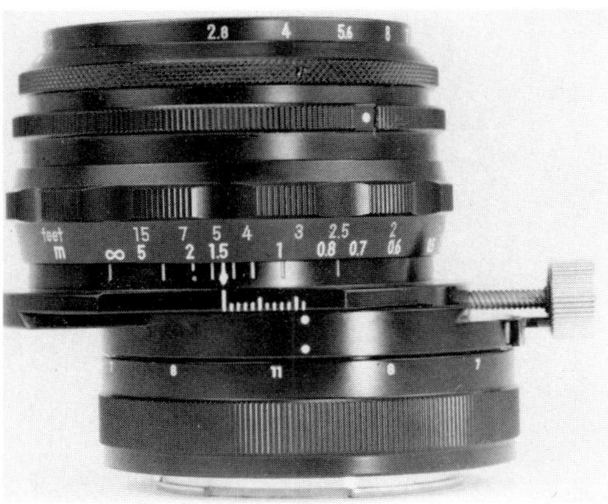

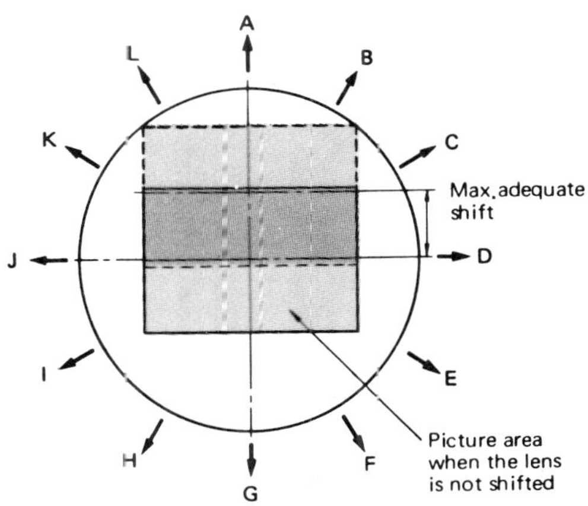

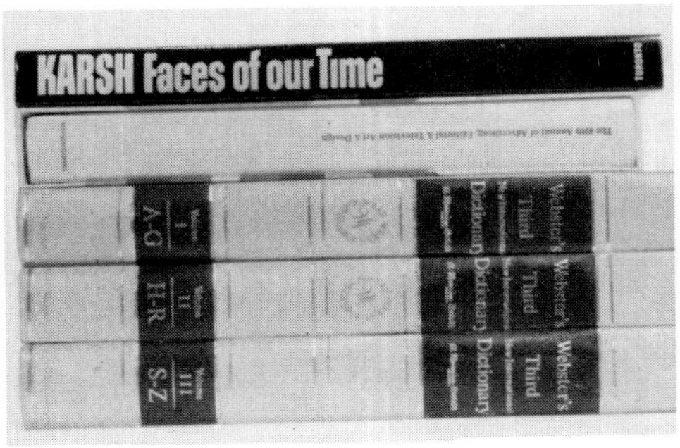

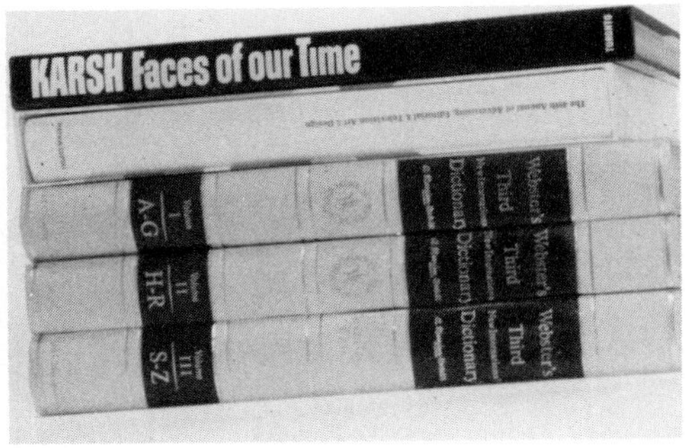

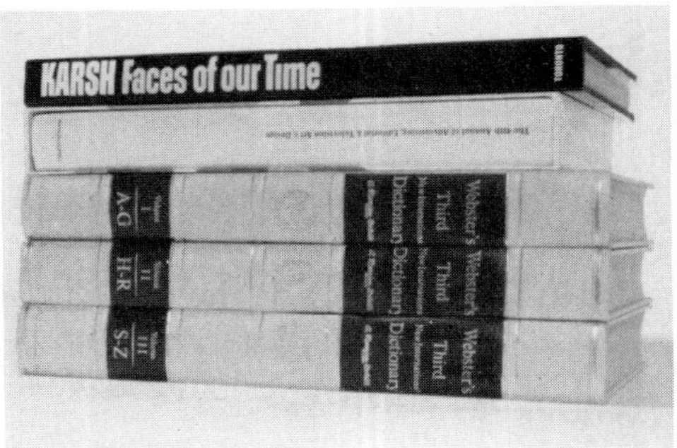

The problem here is to have a three-dimensional effect without having converging lines in front. A front view, as at top left, gives no feeling of depth. Top right view, with ordinary lens, captures depth but also records convergence. With the PC-Nikkor a slight shift of the camera to one side and a counter shift of the lens laterally will give the adjacent view.

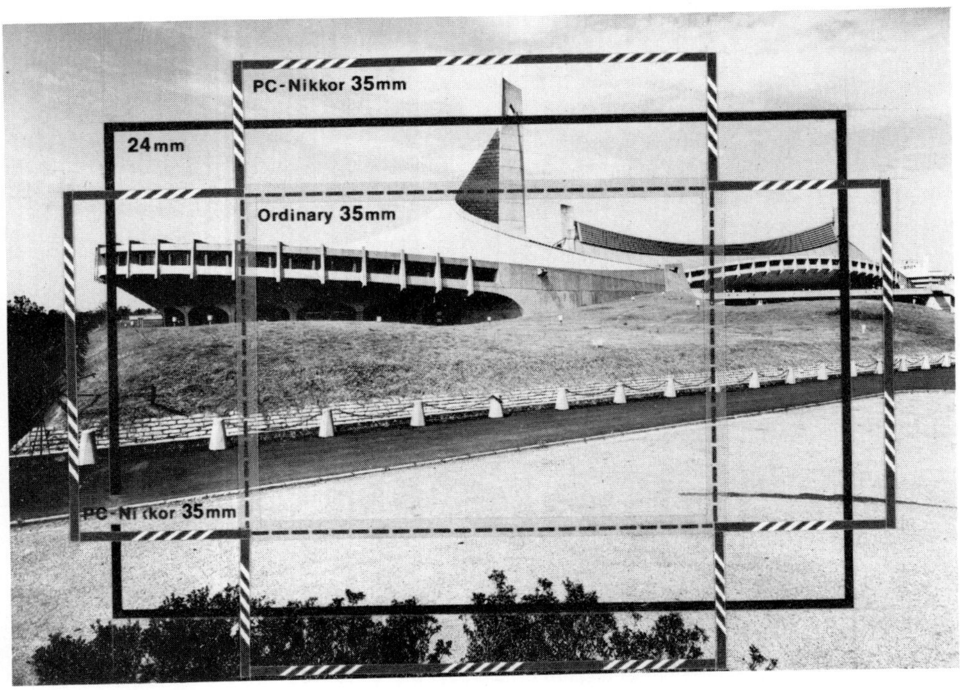

Panoramic views made with 35mm *f*/2.8 PC-Nikkor lens as compared to conventional 35mm and 24mm lenses.

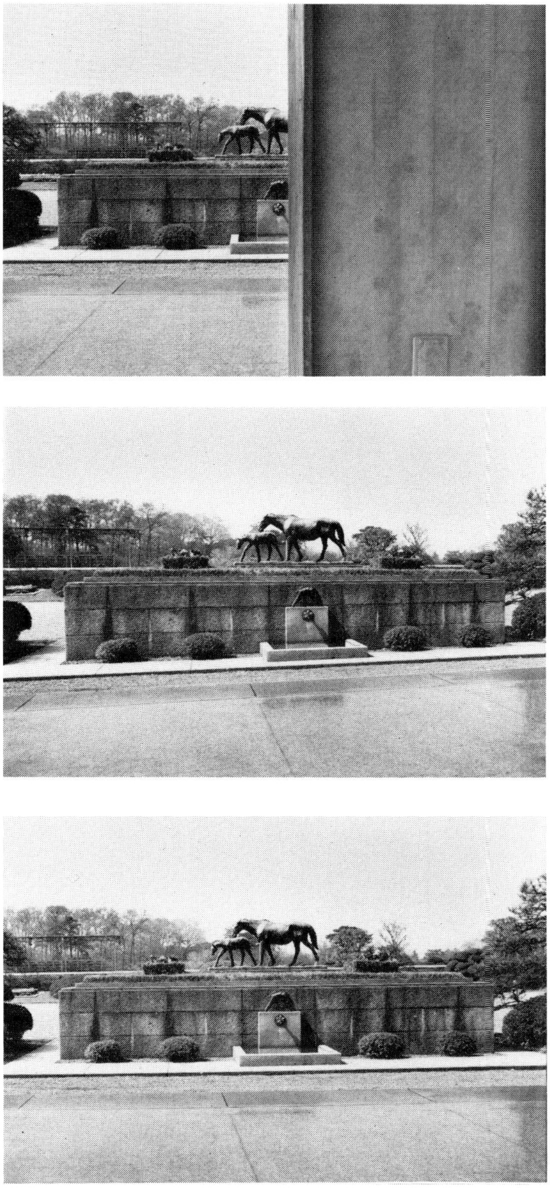

The problem is to get rid of an unwanted element in architectural photography without introducing undesired perspective effects. In this group, a stone monument is obstructed by the viewfinder. Moving to the left, you can get rid of the obstruction, but with a conventional lens the horizontal lines will converge. With the PC-Nikkor you would move to the side while shifting the lens on the camera body in the opposite direction.

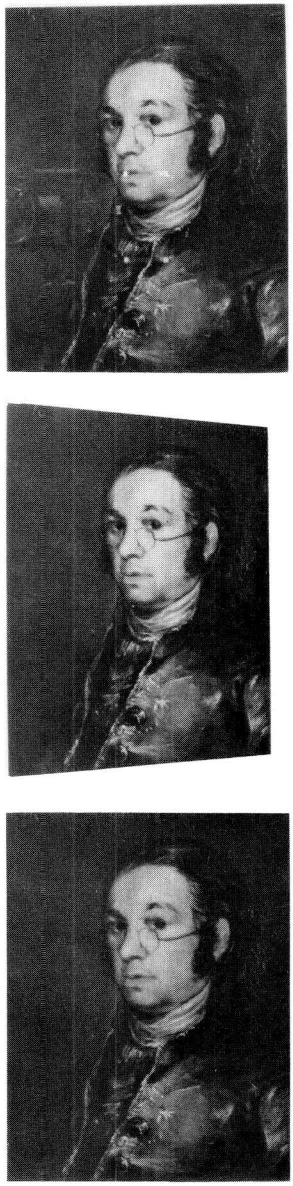

The problem is to photograph a glass-framed picture without picking up the reflections from the camera itself, as would occur with the picture at top. Shifting to the side with a conventional lens would get rid of the reflection, but would result in converging lines (middle). With the PC-Nikkor the shift of the camera to the side is accompanied by a compensatory shift of the lens to get rid of the converging lines (bottom). This technique is applicable to other frontal reflections.

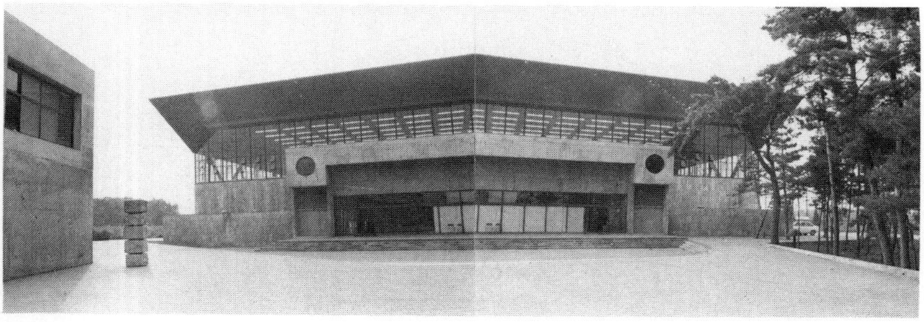

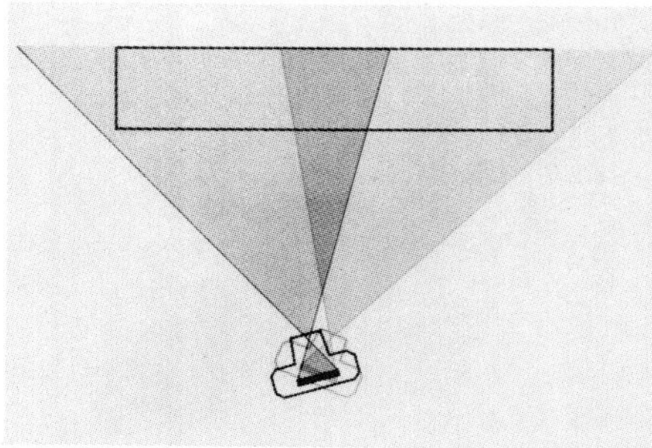

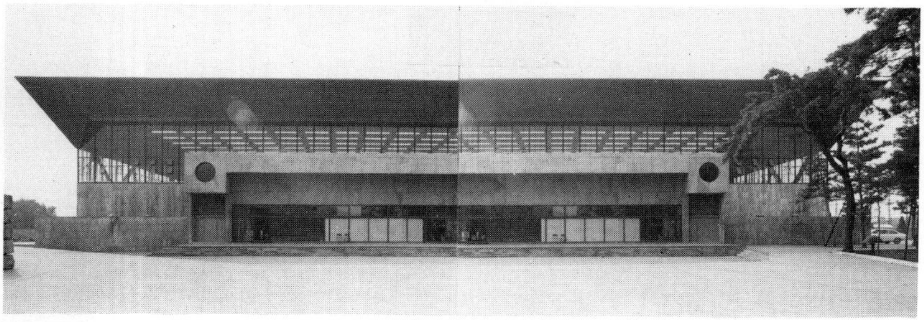

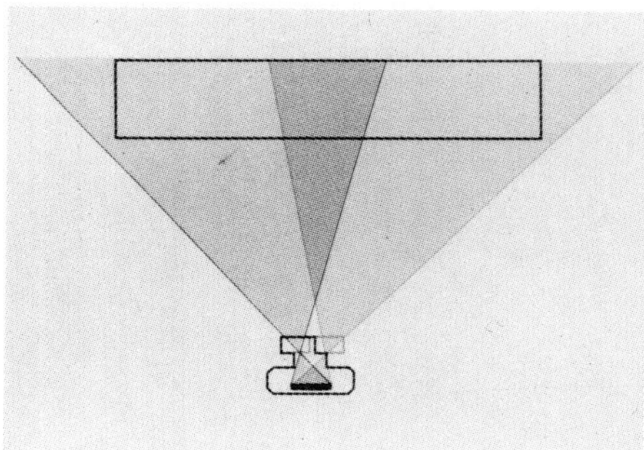

Panoramic pictures can be made through use of the PC-Nikkor shift movement. Two separate exposures are made and then overlapped after printing on paper. With a conventional lens (top photo), when two pictures are taken from the same position, the turning of the camera records a new arc of the horizon with the result that the left and right halves can never be joined perfectly. In the second example (bottom photo), the camera remains fixed in position for both pictures. The first exposure is made by shifting the lens as far to the left as possible. Then, without moving the camera, the lens mount is rotated through 180 degrees so that the shift scale faces straight down. The second exposure is then made. The geometric principles are recorded in the accompanying diagrams.

Nikkor lens		Horizontal picture angle	Vertical picture angle
20mm		83°30′	61°30′
24mm		74°	53°
28mm		64°	45°
35mm		53°	37°
28mm PC	Vertical connection	64°	79°
	Horizontal connection	92°	45°
35mm PC	Vertical connection	53°	65°
	Horizontal connection	78°	37°

Comparison of PC-Nikkor panorama picture angles with those of wide-angle lenses. Diagram below shows overlapping in horizontal and vertical shifts with the PC-Nikkors. Over lapping is least in vertical shifting.

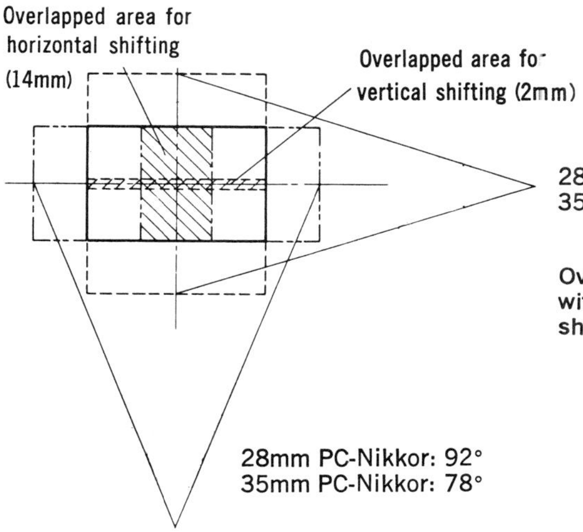

Overlapping in horizontal and vertical shifts with PC-Nikkor. Overlapping is least in vertical shifting.

45mm *f*/2.8 GN AUTO NIKKOR

The GN Auto Nikkor is designed to simplify flash photography. As its name GN (guide number) suggests, the lens employs the guide number-coupling system for automatic diaphragm adjustments.

By setting the appropriate guide number on the scale of the GN Auto Nikkor, the diaphragm ring is hooked to the focusing ring, allowing the aperture to be stopped down or opened up automatically in relation to the focused distance to give correct flash exposure. This frees the photographer from having to calculate the correct aperture and readjust the lens diaphragm. The guide number coupling may be disconnected when flash is not used.

The seven-bladed polygonal diaphragm, designed to form an almost circular aperture around the most commonly used *f*/8 setting, reduces the effects of light diffraction to the minimum. It can be stopped down to *f*/32.

Used in combination with the Nikon Speedlight Unit, the lens is particularly effective for capturing a moving subject or for candids where the photographer has no time to reset the diaphragm.

The GN Auto Nikkor may also be used as a substitute for a normal lens for general photography. It has a picture angle of 50 degrees, which makes the lens valuable for landscapes or indoor group photographs.

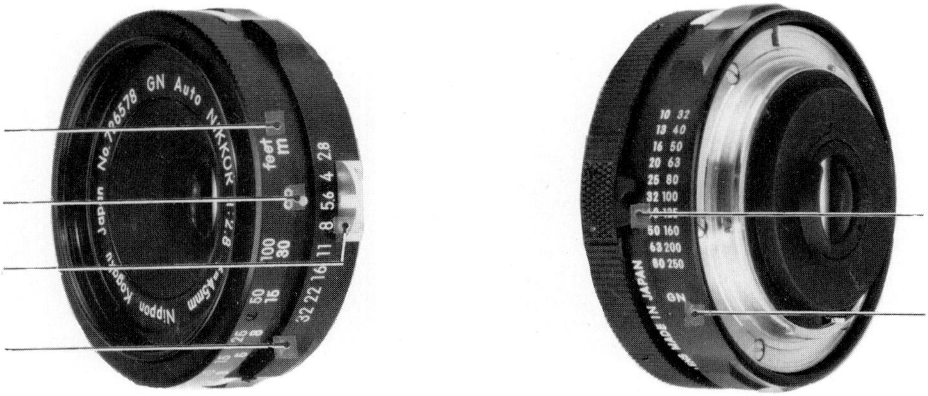

NOMENCLATURE FOR 45mm *f*/2.8 GN AUTO NIKKOR

1. Focusing Ring
2. Aperture-Indicator Dot
3. Meter-Coupling Prong
4. Aperture Ring
5. Guide-Number Scales
6. Guide-Number Coupler

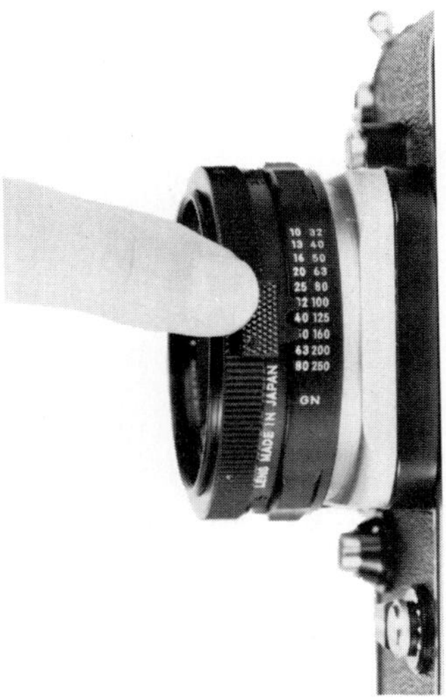

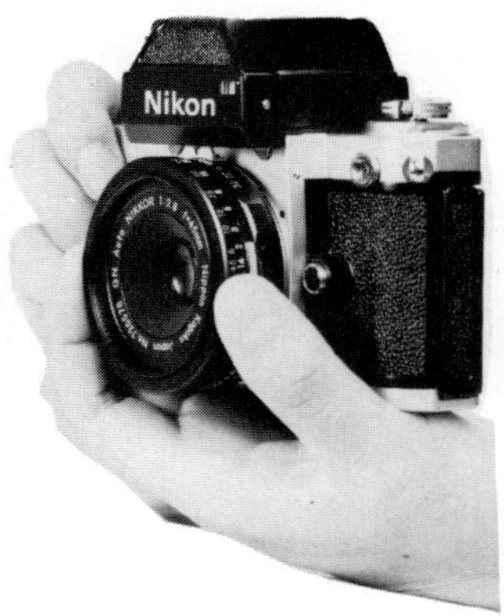

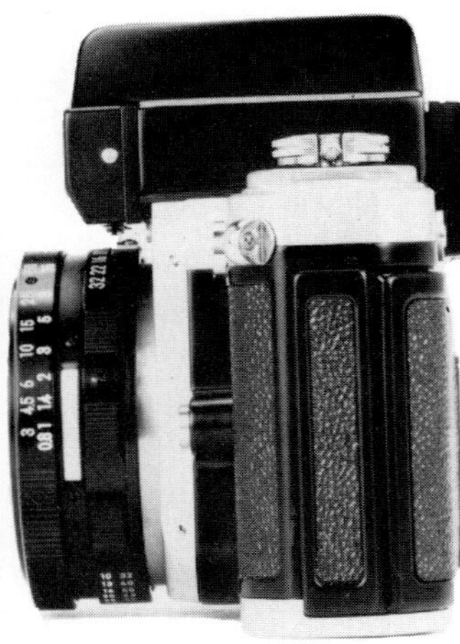

Principle of the GN Nikkor is that focusing ring and aperture ring have their separate functions interlocked and indexed to flash guide-number setting. To set lens for automatic flash, turn either the focusing ring or aperture ring until slotted pointer is opposite guide number for flash-unit/film-speed combination in use (or next nearest one). Then, push coupler in until it clicks into place. Thereafter, lens diaphragm will stop down automatically as you get closer to subject and open up as you get further away. Focusing range will be limited by flash-unit/film-speed combination. With coupler disenagaged, GN Nikkor can be used as compact normal lens.

CLOSE-UP LENSES

The main optical distinction between the close-up lenses as compared to the regular series of lenses, is that the latter are designed for best performance in the distance range of near foreground to infinity. At close macro ranges, however, ordinary lenses do not yield best edge-to-edge results.. The special close-up lenses are designed optically to yield best performance in the near ranges without incurring associated aberrations.

55mm *f*/3.5 Micro-Nikkor
105mm *f*/4 Micro-Nikkor
200mm *f*/4 Micro-Nikkor IF

Originally designed for close-up photography, these lenses feature continuous focusing from infinity to 1:2 magnification. The PK-13 ring and the PN-11 ring permit focusing in the 1:2 to 1:1 range with the 55mm and 105mm lenses, respectively. The 200mm Micro-Nikkor focuses from infinity to 1:1 when it is used with the TC-300 teleconverter.

Optimum resolving performance is at 1:10 reproduction ratio, but, since their superb resolution remains virtually unchanged throughout the entire focusing range, the lenses may be used for general photography as well. The excellent image quality, great flatness of image plane, high image contrast, and fine color rendition make these lenses especially ideal for photographing close-up subjects such as insects, flowers, and other small objects, or for critical copying of flat subjects such as documents, drawings, stamps, etc.

The 105mm and 200mm Micro-Nikkors are especially useful for close-up situations such as wildlife photography, medical photography, etc. in which greater working distance is required between camera and subject.

When an image with a reproduction ratio greater than 1:1 is desired, various close-up accessories are available for use. For example, when Bellows Focusing Attachment PB-4 is used with the 55mm Micro-Nikkor, the lens reproduction ratio extends from 1:1.3 to 3.4:1. When the lenses are used without extension or with the extension tubes which permit 1:1 focusing, the photographer may refer to reproduction ratios engraved on the lens barrel *vis-à-vis* the focused distance.

105mm *f*/4 Bellows-Nikkor

The 105mm *f*/4 Bellows Nikkor has been designed exclusively for use with the Nikon Bellows Focusing Attachments PB-4 and PB-5. It offers continuous focusing from infiinity to 1.3× reproduction ratio with the PB-4 and PB-5. The lens gives superb resolution for closeups and macrophotography.

The Bellows-Nikkor has no focusing device of its own—it is focused by the extension or contraction of the Bellows Focusing Attachment.

The manually present lens diaphragm can be stopped down to *f*/32 with one-third intermediate click-stop settings. (Black dots between the inscribed *f*/numbers indicate the two intermediate settings.)

With the long focal length of 105mm, the Bellows-Nikkor lens offers natural reproduction of perspective, while affording the photographer greater working distance for better subject handling and illumination

200mm *f*/5.6 Medical-Nikkor Auto

Incorporating a ringlight unit around its front element, the 200mm *f*/5.6 Medical-Nikkor is ideal for close-up work in the field of medicine, and has numerous other applications in science and industry. It consists of a prime lens, a set of six auxiliary lenses, and an AC or a battery power source for operating the lighting units.

The lens offers a choice of eleven different magnification ratios in combination with the six auxiliary lenses. The prime lens alone gives the reproduction ratio of 1/15× and the auxiliary lenses, attached singly or in varied combinations, provide a range of magnification ratios from 1/8× to 3×.

The Medical-Nikkor lens is self-compensating, eliminating all bothersome calculations for setting the diaphragm in relation to film speed and reproduction ratio. All that is required of the photographer is to set the lens for the ASA speed of the film used, attach the auxiliary lens or lenses in accordance with the desired magnification ratio, focus by moving the camera toward or away from the subject, and release the shutter. The automatic lens diaphragm stops down to correct aperture at the moment of exposure. Two illumination units are built into the lens: an electronic ringlight and pilot lamps—the latter is for focusing convenience.

The ringlight's color temperature of 6000 K permits the use of daylight color film. The flash duration is 1/500 sec. The Medical-Nikkor ringlight synchronizes with the Nikon F2 at 1/60 sec., with the Nikon F at 1/30 sec., and the Nikkormat at 1/60 sec. The lens also incorporates a device for printing an identification number (1 to 38) or magnification ratio (1/15× to 3×) in the lower right-hand corner of each frame by making use of a small fraction of the ringlight output or "leak" flash. The Photomic series finders function solely as viewfinders when used with the Medical-Nikkor. The self-compensating feature of the lens diaphragm eliminates the need for exposure metering.

NIKKOR ENLARGING LENSES

The finest negatives, especially color negatives, cannot be reproduced well on paper or film unless projected through quality enlarger lenses that are designed particularly for close planar projection. It makes no sense to take pictures with optically superb lenses and then to enlarge them through inferior lenses that degrade the quality of the film images.

Nikon makes two enlarging 50mm lenses for the 24 × 36mm format—the *f*/2.8 and *f*/4 El-Nikkor lenses. They provide magnifications from 2× to 20×, insuring uniform brightness and superb definition over the entire picture area. They are corrected both for visible light rays as well as for the near ultraviolet rays up to 380mm to which printing

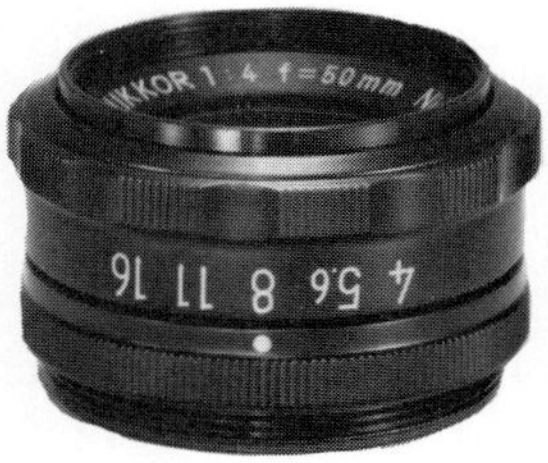

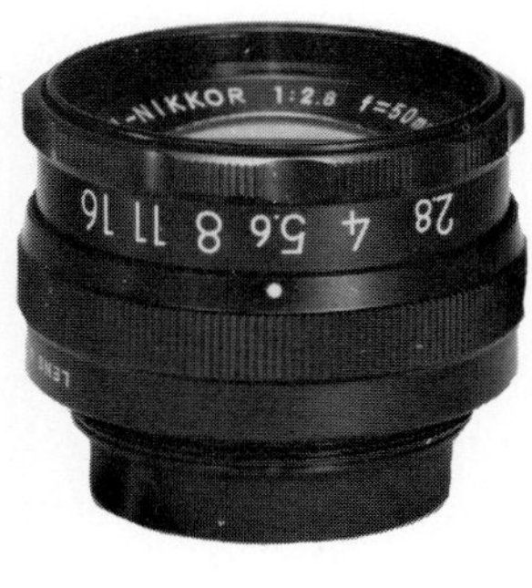

The 50mm *f*/4 and the 50mm *f*/2.8 El-Nikkors—popular enlarging lenses—are made with standard Leica male screw mount 39mm. Other El-Nikkor lenses with same screw mount are available in progressive focal lengths through 135mm. With available adapters, these lenses can also be used in photomacrography and particularly in flat copy reproduction. Note the large white numerals for convenience in darkroom dim-light reading.

papers are sensitive. They do not cause shifts in focus when their diaphragms are stopped down.

The El-Nikkor lenses come with standard Leica-thread screw mounts, click-stops, and large number *f*/stop markings to facilitate handling in the dark.

Eleven other lenses in the El-Nikkor series, for larger film formats, range from 63mm through 360mm.

50mm *f*/2.8 El-Nikkor

The 50mm *f*/2.8 El-Nikkor is reputed to be among the world's finest photo-enlarging lenses for 35mm enlargers. The lens ensures uniform image brightness over the entire picture area, with the maximum aperture of *f*/2.8 to facilitate focusing. The diameter of the front and rear lens elements is made sufficiently large to minimize vignetting. The correction covers an area slightly larger than the size of the original negative. The optimum aperture is around *f*/5.6.

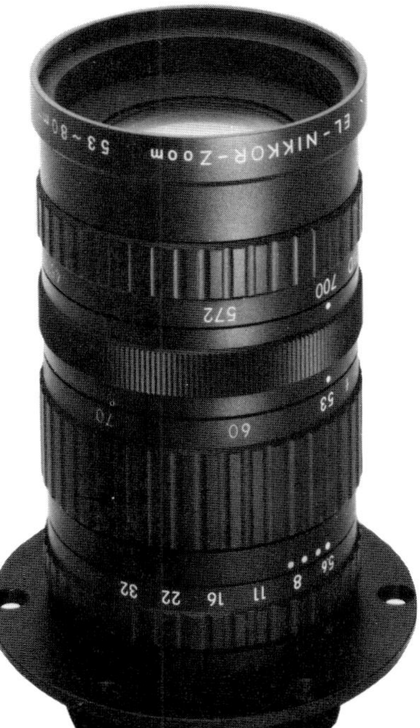

The 53 ~ 80mm *f*/5.6 E1-Zoom-Nikkor enlarging lens permits negative formats up to 6 × 6cm to be used without changing lenses. This lens and fixed focal-length E1-Nokkors starting at 150mm are equipped with service-mount flanges.

50mm *f*/4 El-Nikkor

The 50mm *f*/4 El-Nikkor is a high quality photo-enlarging lens for 35mm enlargers, specially designed for applications where brightness is not the primary requirement. It has a sufficiently large aperture and diameter in the back and front lens elements to ensure uniform image brightness over the entire picture area. Focusing is performed easily even on dense negatives or where magnification ratio is great. The aberrations of the lens have been corrected for a short focusing distance. The correction covers an area slightly larger than that of the original negative.

53 ~ 80mm *f*/5.6 E1-Zoom Nikkor

The focal length of the 53 ~ 80mm *f*/5.6 E1-Zoom-Nikkor may be changed by rotating the zooming control surrounding the lens barrel. Photographers who work in both 35mm and roll-film formats such as 6 × 6cm and 4.5cm will find this feature useful, because it eliminates the need to change lenses as different negative sizes are used. As focal length is changed, the lens' area of coverage, i.e. maximum permissible negative size, also changes as does the maximum aperture. At the 80mm setting, negatives up to 56mm square may be used; at the 53mm setting, negatives up to 24 × 36mm may be used. The maximum aperture ranges from *f*/5.6 to *f*/8.4 as focal length is changed from 53mm to 80mm.

When the lens is used with 35mm negatives, minor changes in magnification are possible by turning the zooming ring. Thus, the need to raise and lower the enlarging head is eliminated. The zooming ring has reference marks for 53, 60, 70, and 80mm.

Directory of Nikkor Lenses
Special Purpose Lenses

DISCONTINUED NIKKOR LENSES—SPECIAL PURPOSE

Lens	Smallest Aperture	Diaphragm Type	Meter Coupling	Nearest Focus	Filter Size mm ID/OD	Other
7.5mm *f*/5.6	22	Manual	No	Universal	Built-in	External finder, mirror lock-up
8mm *f*/8	22	Manual	No	Universal	Built-in	External finder, mirror lock-up
35mm *f*/3.5 PC	32	Preset	No	0.3m (1 ft.)	52	Perspective control, 11mm shift, remove Photomic finder
45mm *f*/2.8 GN	32	Auto	Yes	0.8m (3 ft)	52	
55mm *f*/4 UV	32	Auto	Yes	0.36m (1.2 ft.)	52	For use in UV range
55mm *f*/3.5 Micro-Nikkor	32	Preset	No		52	First model, continuous focusing to 1:1 without separate extension tube
105mm *f*/4 Bellows-Nikkor	32	Manual	No		52	Use with bellows
135mm *f*/4 short mount	22	Preset	No		43/46	Use with bellows
85-250mm *f*/4	16	Auto	Yes	4m (13 ft.)	Series 9	
85-250mm *f*/4-4.5 Zoom	16	Auto	Yes	4m (13 ft.)	Series 9	
200-600mm Zoom *f*/9.5-10.5	32	Auto	No	4m (13 ft.)	82/86	Aperture changes as focal length changes

6mm f/2.8 FISHEYE-NIKKOR

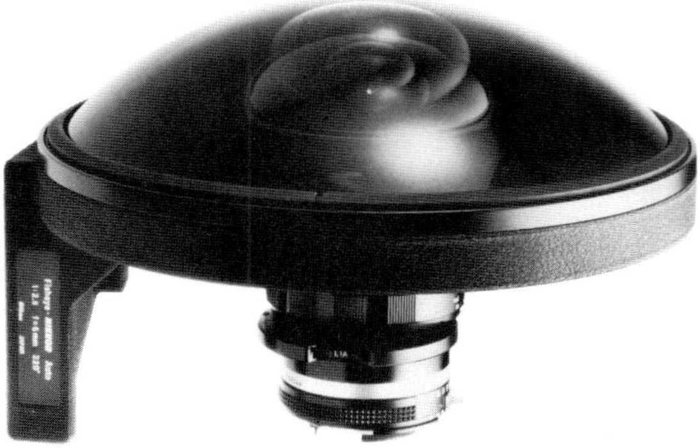

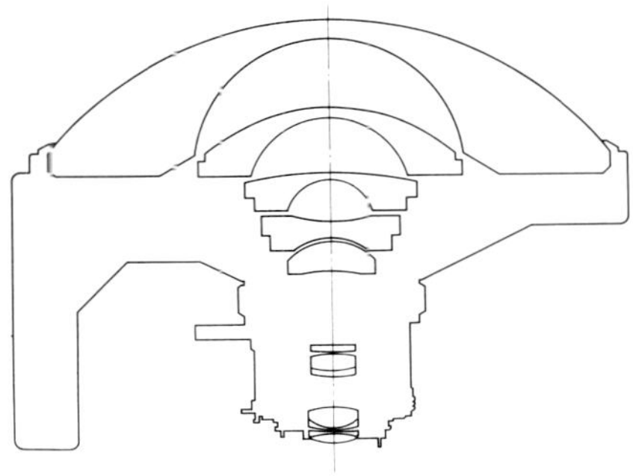

DESCRIPTION

Pictorial uses of Fisheye-Nikkor lenses include manipulation and emphasis of foreground and periphery in spherical format to yield striking effects. Originally developed for special applications in meteorological and astronomical research, applications are really limited only by imagination of user. Useful in environmental planning and control; studies of movement and concentration of large numbers of people in defined areas; and recording of interiors of pipes, boilers, conduits, cylinder bores, and other constricted areas. Used particularly in advertising photography for unusual product effects. Angle of view covers 220 degrees, requiring that the photographer be well behind the camera. The lens employs equidistant projection formula. Viewing through reflex mirror. Built-in, turret-mounted filters.

SPECIFICATIONS

Smallest aperture: 22
Nearest focus distance: 0.25m (10.8in)
Image ratio at nearest distance: 1:21.4
Image size on film: 23mm ϕ circle
Angle of view: 220° (circular image)
Ratio of image size at infinity to image of 50mm lens: 0.12:1

Filters: Built-in L1A, Y48, Y52, 056, and R60
Rear lens cap: LF-1
Front lens cap: Supplied
Lens case: Special metal case supplied
Overall size: 236mm ϕ × 171mm
Weight: 5.2 kg (11.5 lb)

DEPTH OF FIELD TABLE

Meters

m \ f/	2.8	4	5.6	8	11	16	22	Magnification
0.25	0.231–0.277	0.224–0.292	0.216–0.318	0.207–0.373	0.196–0.533	0.185–3.66	0.174–∞	1/21.4
0.3	0.266–0.354	0.255–0.389	0.242–0.458	0.228–0.647	0.212–2.60	0.196–∞	0.181–∞	1/29.5
0.4	0.327–0.553	0.306–0.684	0.283–1.09	0.260–∞	0.234–∞	0.211–∞	0.191–∞	1/45.6
0.5	0.377–0.842	0.346–1.29	0.313–8.43	0.280–∞	0.249–∞	0.221–∞	0.197–∞	1/61.7
1	0.542–∞	0.465–∞	0.395–∞	0.333–∞	0.282–∞	0.240–∞	0.208–∞	1/142
∞	0.941–∞	0.694–∞	0.525–∞	0.405–∞	0.321–∞	0.261–∞	0.219–∞	1/∞

6mm *f*/5.6 FISHEYE-NIKKOR

Requires Accessory Viewfinder

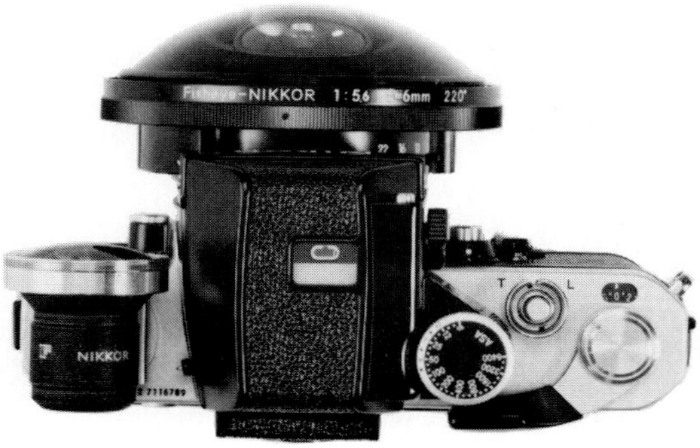

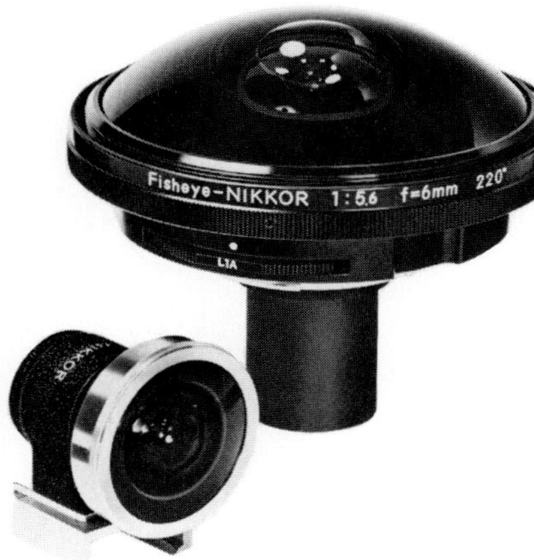

DESCRIPTION

Pictorial uses of Fisheye-Nikkor lenses include manipulation and emphasis of foreground and periphery in spherical format to yield striking effects. Originally developed for special applications in meteorological and astronomical research, applications really limited only by imagination of user. Useful in environmental planning and control, studies of movement and concentration of large numbers of people in defined areas, and recording of interiors of pipes, boilers, conduits, cylinder bores, and other constricted areas. Used particularly in advertising photography for unusual product effects. Useful in underwater applications. Angle of view is 220 degrees requiring that photographer be well behind camera. Fixed focus. Built-in, turret-mounted filters. Equidistant projection formula. Requires external viewfinder with mirror locked up.

SPECIFICATIONS

Smallest aperture: 22
Aperture diaphragm: Manual, does not couple to exposure meter
Nearest focus distance: Fixed focus
Image size on film: 21.6 mm ϕ circle
Angle of view: 220° (21.6mm ϕ image)
Attachment size (inside screw diameter): 89mm (P = 0.75)
Filters: Built-in, L1A, Y48, Y52, O57, R60, X0
Front lens cap: 89mm screw-in
Rear lens cap: LF-2
Overall size: 92mm ϕ x 81mm
Weight: 430g (15.2 oz)
Use of Nikon focusing screens: None, mirror in lock-up position; external finder used (supplied with lens)

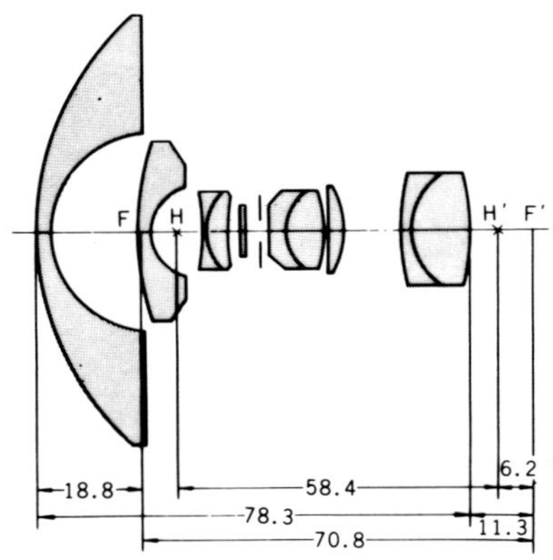

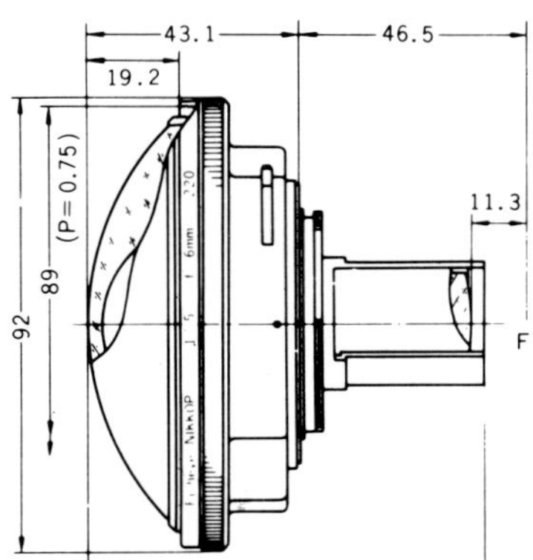

8mm *f*/2.8 FISHEYE-NIKKOR

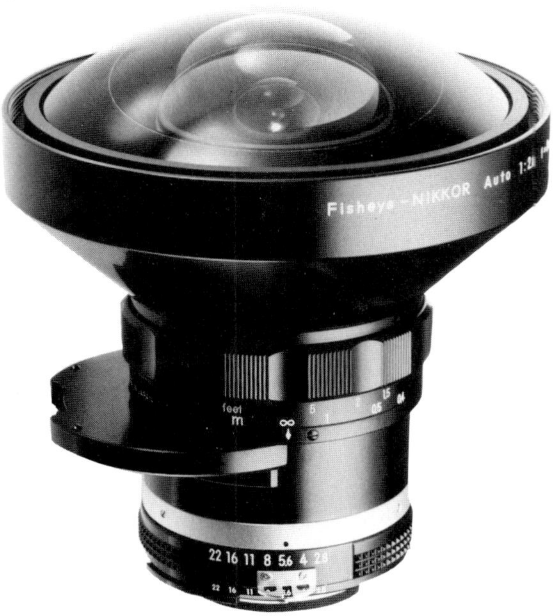

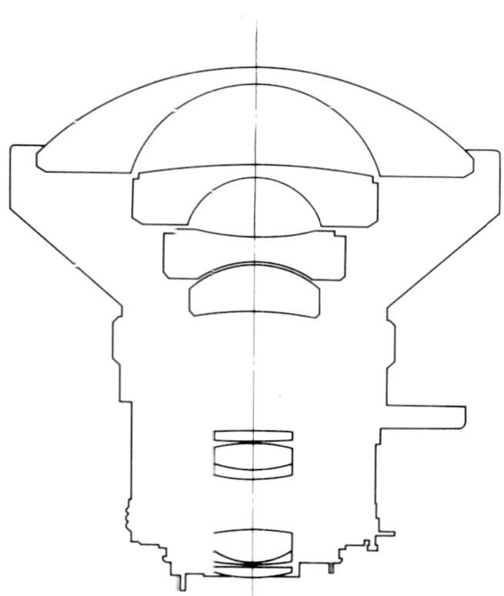

DESCRIPTION

Most versatile of Fisheye-Nikkor lenses because it optimizes wide aperture, close focusing, and physical size. Pictorial uses of Fisheye-Nikkor lenses include manipulation and emphasis of foreground and periphery in spherical format to yield striking effects. Originally developed for special applications in meteorological and astronomical research, applications are really limited only by imagination of user. Useful in environmental planning and control; studies of movement and concentration of large numbers of people in defined areas; and recording of interiors of pipes, boilers, conduits, cylinder bores, and other constricted areas. Used particularly in advertising photography for unusual product effects. Angle of view 180 degrees. Nearest focus 0.3m (1 ft). Viewing done through reflex mirror. Built-in, turret-mounted filters. Equidistant projection formula.

SPECIFICATIONS

Smallest aperture: 22
Nearest focus distance: 0.3m (1 ft)
Image ratio at nearest distance: 1:19.7
Image size on film: 23mm ϕ circle
Angle of view: 180° (circular image)
Ratio of image size at infinity to image of 50mm lens: 0.16:1
Filters: Built-in L1A, Y48, Y52, 056, and R60
Rear lens cap: LF-1
Lens case: CL-11 (supplied)
Overall size: 123mm ϕ × 140mm
Weight: 1kg (2.2 lb)

DEPTH OF FIELD TABLE

Meters

m \ f	2.8	4	5.6	8	11	16	22	Magnification
0.3	0.283–0.322	0.277–0.333	0.269–0.350	0.260–0.383	0.249–0.442	0.236–0.651	0.223–3.208	1/19.7
0.4	0.358–0.462	0.344–0.499	0.328–0.563	0.308–0.720	0.289–1.221	0.265–∞	0.244–∞	1/32.2
0.5	0.425–0.630	0.401–0.720	0.376–0.909	0.345–1.647	0.317–∞	0.284–∞	0.258–∞	1/44.7
1.0	0.668–2.473	0.593–8.945	0.521–∞	0.448–∞	0.389–∞	0.328–∞	0.286–∞	1/107.3
∞	1.513–∞	1.102–∞	0.828–∞	0.622–∞	0.491–∞	0.382–∞	0.317–∞	1/∞

10mm *f*/5.6 OP FISHEYE-NIKKOR

Requires Accessory Viewfinder

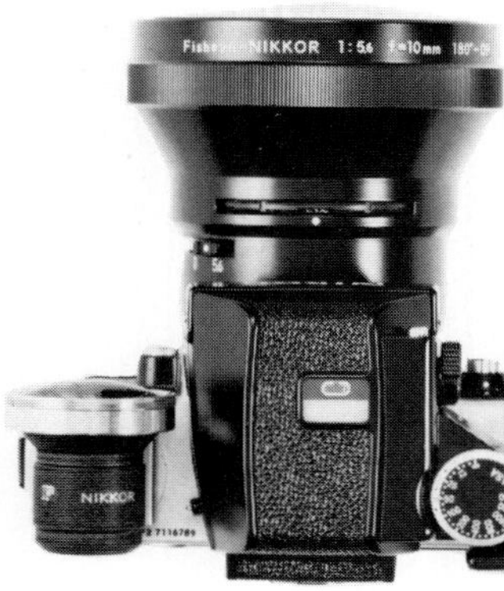

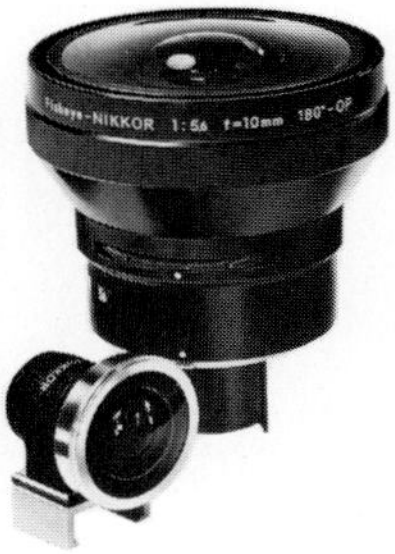

DESCRIPTION

Pictorial uses of Fisheye-Nikkor lenses include manipulation and emphasis of foreground and periphery in spherical format to yield striking effects. Originally developed for special applications in meteorological and astronomical research, applications really limited only by imagination of user. Useful in environmental planning and control, studies of movement and concentration of large numbers of people in defined areas, and recording of interiors of pipes, boilers, conduits, cylinder bores, and other constricted areas. Used primarily in advertising photography for unusual product effects. Utilizing orthographic projection formula, this version has particular application in study of sky configurations and other situations where evenly distributed exposure is important. Fixed focus, requires external viewfinder with mirror in locked-up position.

SPECIFICATIONS

Smallest aperture: 22
Aperture diaphragm: Manual, does not couple to exposure meter
Nearest focus distance: Fixed focus
Image size on film: 20mm ϕ circle
Angle of view: 180° (20mm ϕ image)
Attachment size (inside screw diameter): 79mm (P = 0.75)
Filters: Built-in, L1A, Y48, Y52, O57, R60, X0
Front lens cap: U.S. 573
Rear lens cap: LF-2
Lens case: CL-4
Overall size: 84mm ϕ x 105mm
Weight: 400g (14.1 oz)
Use of Nikon focusing screens: None; mirror in lock-up position; external finder used

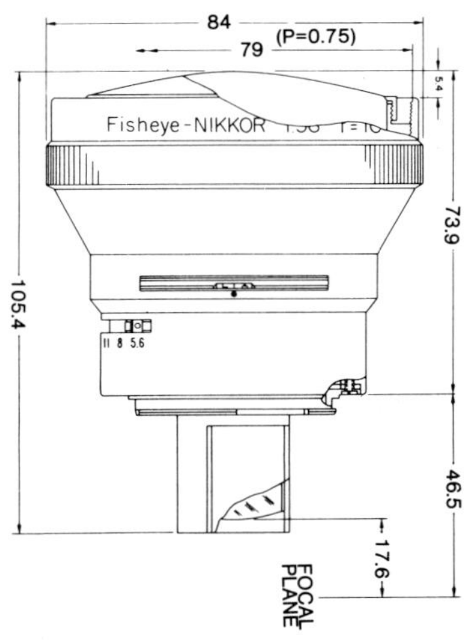

FISHEYE-NIKKOR VIEWFINDER

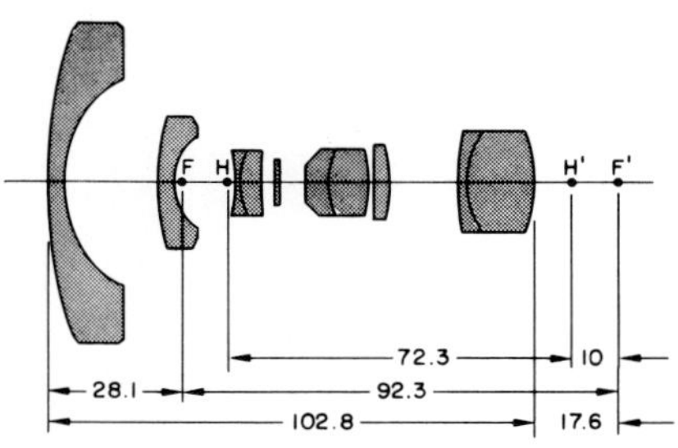

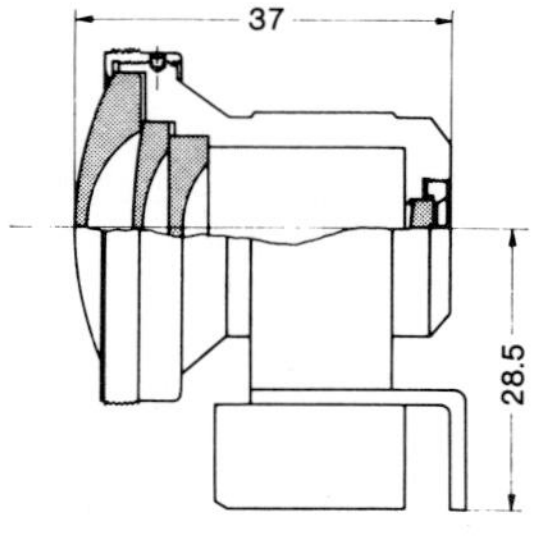

16mm *f*/2.8 FISHEYE-NIKKOR

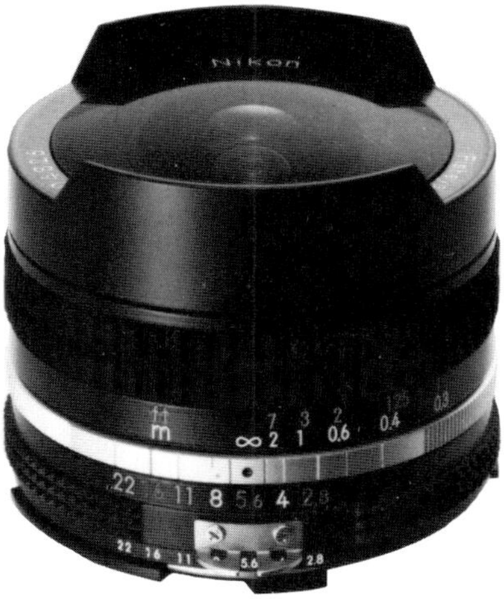

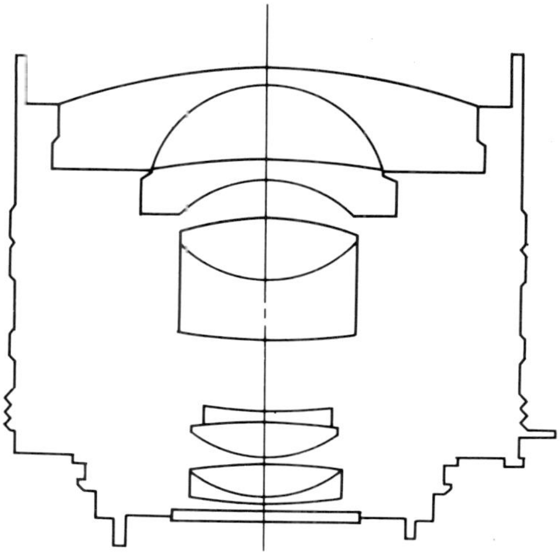

DESCRIPTION

This 16mm full-frame fisheye lens, with a diagonal angle of view of 180 degrees, is more than one-half stop faster than the 16mm *f*/3.5 resulting in a brighter image on the focusing screen Four rapid-mounting bayonet-type filters are provided as standard equipment. Although this lens offers the dramatic barrel distortion typical of fisheye lenses, the 16mm *f*/2.8 produces images which cover the entire picture format. This feature makes the lens especially useful for commercial and advertising photography. The lens focuses to 0.3m (1 ft) through the regular reflex viewing system.

SPECIFICATIONS

Smallest aperture: 22
Nearest focus distance: 0.3m (1 ft)
Subject field at nearest distance: 3.5 × 5.25cm
Image ratio at nearest distance: 1:13
Focusing distances:
One head vertical: 0.3m (1 ft) subject to distortion
Two heads horizontal: 0.3m (1 ft) subject to distortion
One to three adults standing: 0.45m (1.5 ft) subject to distortion

Angles of view:
Diagonal: 180°
Horizontal: 153°
Vertical: 106°
Ratio of image size at infinity to image of 50mm lens: 0.32:1
Filters provided: L1BC, 056, A2, and B2
Lens case: CL-31, flexible pouch 54, plastic case CP-1
Overall size: 53.5mm φ × 62.5mm
Weight: 310g (10.9 oz)

Meters

m \ f/	2.8	4	5.6	8	11	16	22	Magnification
.3	.28	.28	.27	.26	.25	.23	.21	1/13.4
	.31	.33	.34	.37	.40	.50	.73	
.4	.36	.35	.34	.32	.30	.27	.25	1/19.8
	.44	.47	.50	.57	.69	1.15	11.78	
.6	.51	.49	.45	.41	.37	.33	.29	1/32.6
	.73	.80	.94	1.28	2.47	−∞	−∞	
1.0	.76	.69	.62	.54	.47	.39	.33	1/58.1
	1.49	1.92	3.16	−∞	−∞	−∞	−∞	
2.0	1.19	1.02	.86	.71	.58	.46	.37	1/121.9
	7.21	−∞	−∞	−∞	−∞	−∞	−∞	

16mm f/3.5 FISHEYE-NIKKOR

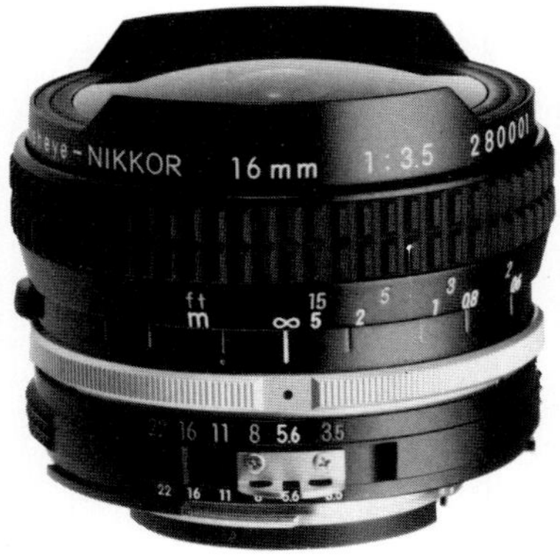

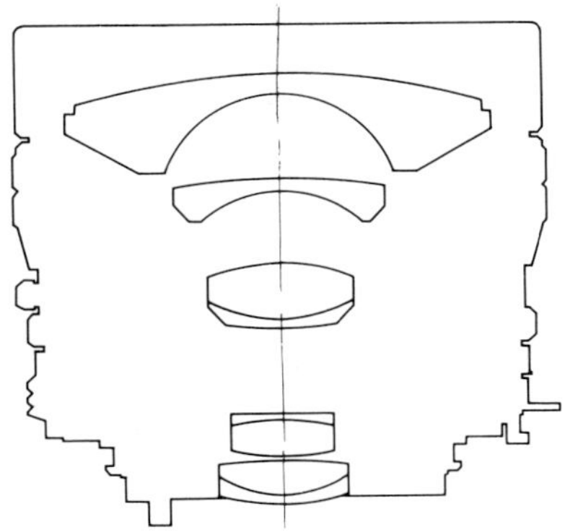

DESCRIPTION

With a near hemispheric coverage of 170 degrees, this lens has been designed to provide special effects in general photography, offering typical dramatic barrel distortion inherent in fisheye lenses. But, unlike other Fisheye-Nikkor lenses, it produces a rectangular image, filling the entire film format. Effects are most pronounced when working close to subject in foreground. The lens yields interesting panoramic effects. Color aberration is well corrected, with high-contrast images even at full aperture. Built-in, turret-mounted filters. Focuses to 0.3m (1 ft) through regular viewing system, without use of external finder.

SPECIFICATIONS

Smallest aperture: 22
Nearest focus distance: 0.3m (1 ft)
Subject field at nearest distance: 3.22 × 4.82cm
Image ratio at nearest distance: 1:13.4
Focusing distances:
- One head vertical: 0.3m (1 ft) subject to perspective distortion
- Two heads horizontal: 0.3m (1 ft) subject to perspective distortion
- One to three adults standing: 0.45m (1.5 ft) subject to perspective distortion

Angles of view:
- Diagonal: 170°
- Horizontal: 137°
- Vertical: 88°

Ratio of image size at infinity to image of 50mm lens: 1:3.2
Attachment size (inside screw diameter): Built-in filters Y48, 056, R60, and N
Lens hood: Built-in, non-removable
Front lens cap: 52mm snap-on
Lens case: CL-31, flexible pouch 54, plastic case CP-1
Overall size: 68.5mm ϕ × 60.5mm
Weight: 325g (11.5 oz)

DEPTH OF FIELD TABLE

Meters

m \ f/	3.5	4	5.6	8	11	16	22	Magnification
0.3	0.280—0.325	0.277—0.329	0.269—0.343	0.259—0.368	0.247—0.405	0.231—0.497	0.215—0.714	1/13.4
0.35	0.320—0.389	0.316—0.395	0.305—0.418	0.290—0.459	0.274—0.527	0.253—0.721	0.232—1.43	1/16.5
0.4	0.359—0.456	0.354—0.465	0.339—0.500	0.319—0.565	0.299—0.683	0.272—1.10	0.247—6.00	1/19.7
0.45	0.396—0.527	0.390—0.540	0.371—0.590	0.346—0.690	0.321—0.887	0.289—1.85	0.260—∞	1/22.8
0.5	0.432—0.601	0.424—0.620	0.401—0.690	0.372—0.838	0.342—1.17	0.304—4.12	0.271—∞	1/25.9
0.6	0.500—0.764	0.488—0.797	0.456—0.925	0.417—1.24	0.378—2.23	0.330—∞	0.289—∞	1/32.2
0.7	0.563—0.948	0.548—1.00	0.506—1.22	0.456—1.88	0.408—6.47	0.351—∞	0.304—∞	1/38.4
0.8	0.621—1.16	0.603—1.24	0.551—1.62	0.491—3.08	0.434—∞	0.368—∞	0.316—∞	1/44.7
1	0.727—1.67	0.701—1.86	0.630—2.93	0.549—30.4	0.477—∞	0.396—∞	0.334—∞	1/57.2
1.5	0.941—4.15	0.896—5.64	0.777—∞	0.653—∞	0.549—∞	0.440—∞	0.362—∞	1/88.4
2	1.10—16.0	1.04—∞	0.880—∞	0.721—∞	0.593—∞	0.466—∞	0.378—∞	1/120
5	1.60—∞	1.46—∞	1.15—∞	0.886—∞	0.694—∞	0.521—∞	0.410—∞	1/307
∞	2.28—∞	2.00—∞	1.46—∞	1.04—∞	0.783—∞	0.565—∞	0.434—∞	1/∞

25 ~ 50mm *f*/4 ZOOM-NIKKOR

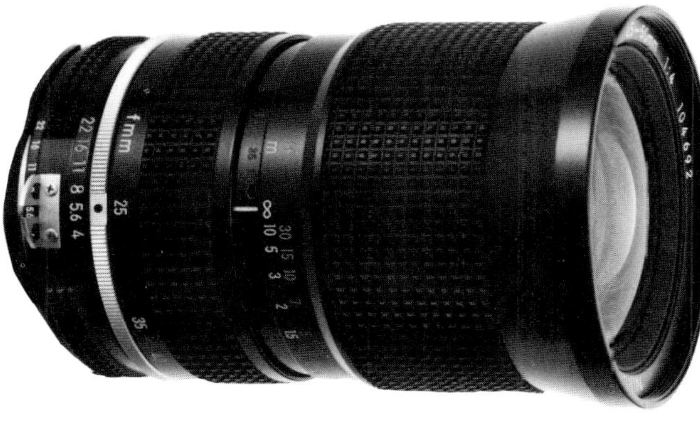

DESCRIPTION

The 25 ~ 50mm *f*/4 Zoom-Nikkor offers a wide choice of focal lengths, from a true wide-angle 25mm, to the normal 50mm, and a choice of picture angles (diagonal) from 80°40′ to 47°50′. The lens has an optical construction of 11 elements in 10 groups, consisting of diverging optics in the front group and converging optics in the rear group, that shift simultaneously during zooming. The lens design has helped to eliminate barrel distortion in the wide-angle range, previously an obstacle to the design of this type of lens. Two separate rings are used for focusing and zooming. In situations where dim light is not a problem, many photographers will choose this as the "normal" lens, kept on the camera most of the time.

SPECIFICATIONS

Smallest aperture: 22
Nearest focus distance: 0.6m (2 ft)
Zoom focal-length reference marks: 25, 35, 40, and 50mm
Angles of view:
Diagonal: 80°40′ ~ 47°50′
Horizontal: 68°30′ ~ 40°40′
Vertical: 47°40′ ~ 28°10′
Attachment size (inside screw diameter): 72mm (P = 0.75)
Overall size: 75mm ϕ × 112mm
Weight: 600g (1.3 lb)

Zoom-Nikkor 25mm-50mm f/4

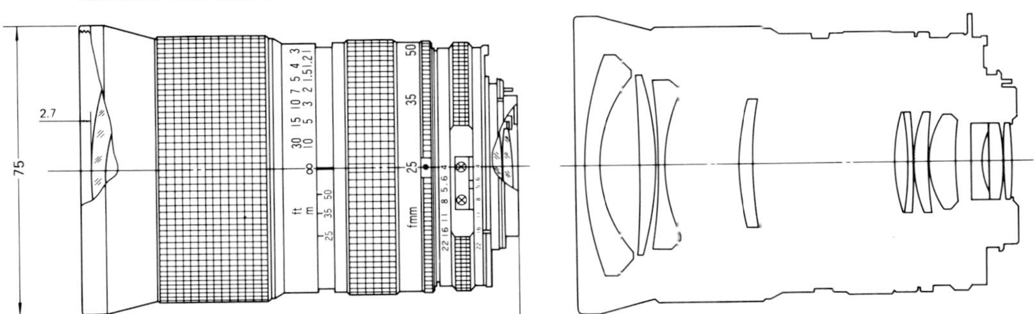

28 ~ 45mm f/4.5 ZOOM-NIKKOR

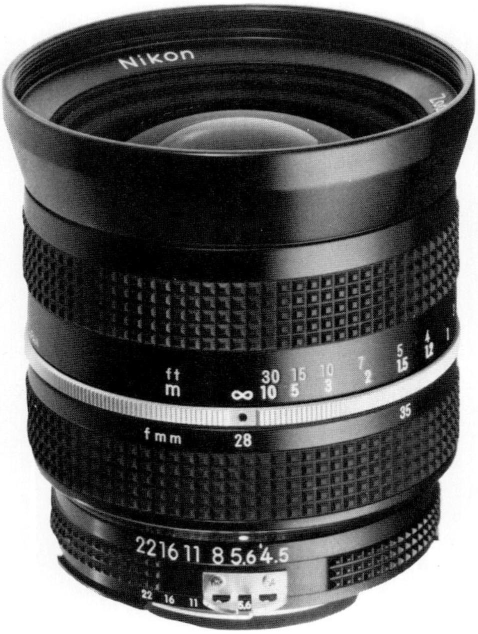

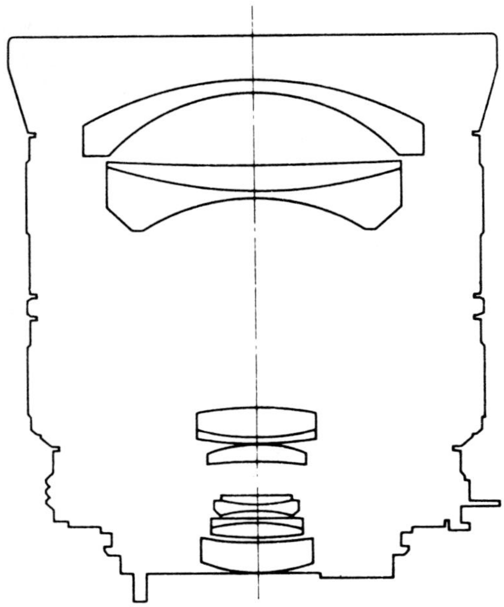

DESCRIPTION

One of the shortest of the zoom lenses available, the 28~45mm Zoom Nikkor offers a focal length range from wide-angle to about normal. Special Nikon optics ensure that the lens is well-corrected throughout the range of its focal length. The lens is well-suited for general photography such as scenics, candids, etc., when telephoto and low-light capability are not essential. The lens is also very useful for sports and press photography, where the photographer wishes to change focal lengths quickly, without having to change lenses. Zooming and focusing are done separately, via separate control rings.

SPECIFICATIONS

Smallest aperture: 22
Nearest focus distance: 0.6m (2 ft)
Zoom focal-length reference marks: 28, 35, 40, and 45mm
Angles of view:
Diagonal: 74° ~ 50°
Horizontal: 64° ~ 42°
Vertical: 45°30′ ~ 29°
Attachment size (inside screw diameter): 72mm (P = 0.75)
Lens hood: 72mm HK-1
Front lens cap: 72mm screw-in
Lens case: CL-33A, flexible pouch 55
Overall size: 75mm ϕ × 91mm
Weight: 440g (15.5 oz)

35 ~ 70mm f/3.5 ZOOM-NIKKOR

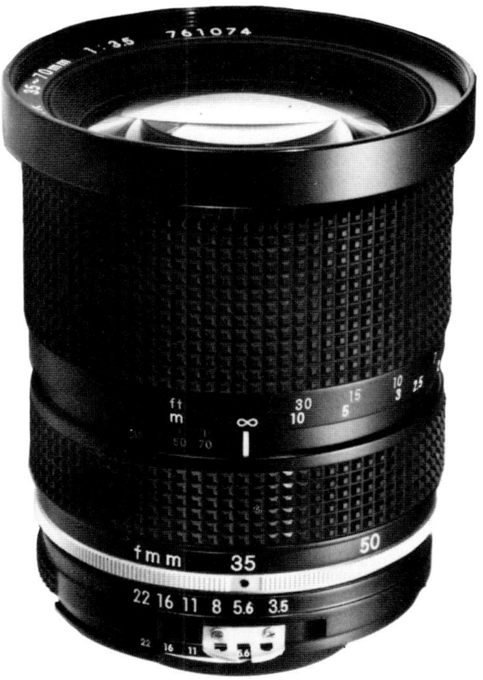

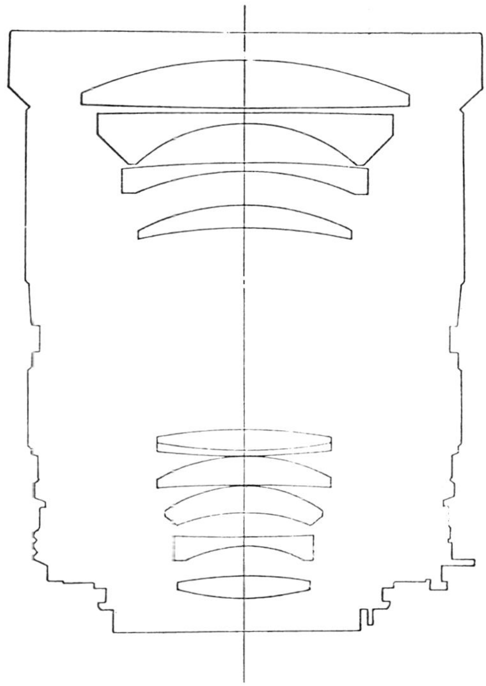

DESCRIPTION

Encompassing the moderate wide-angle, normal, and medium-telephoto ranges with its 2:1 zooming ratio, the Zoom-Nikkor 35~70mm *f*/3.5 brings increased mobility to the photographer interested in scenics, portraiture, sports and action, architectural photography, and general picture taking. The lens' ability to zoom smoothly through the 35mm to 70mm focal length enables the photographer to crop the image in the camera's viewfinder, resulting in improved picture quality when the entire negative is used to make the final print. Zooming and focusing are accomplished with separate rings. Nikon Integrated Coating is used on all lens surfaces where it is beneficial

SPECIFICATIONS

Smallest aperture: 22
Nearest focus distance: 1m (3.5 ft)
Zoom focal-length reference marks: 35mm, 50mm, 70mm
Angles of view:
Diagonal: 62° ~ 34°20′
Horizontal: 52°40′ ~ 29°10′
Vertical: 36°30′ ~ 20°20′

Attachment size (inside screw diameter): 72mm (P = 0.75)
Lens hood: Slip-on hood HK-4
Front lens cap: 72mm screw-in
Lens case: CL-33A, flexible pouch 55
Overall size: 75mm ϕ × 101mm
Weight: 540g (1 lb, 3 oz)

43 ~ 86mm f/3.5 ZOOM-NIKKOR

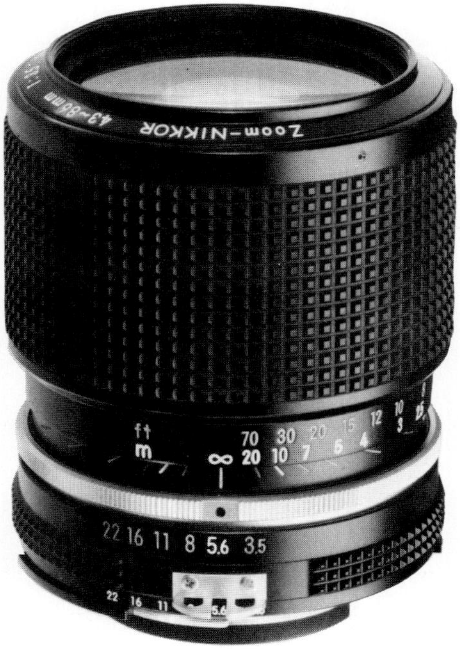

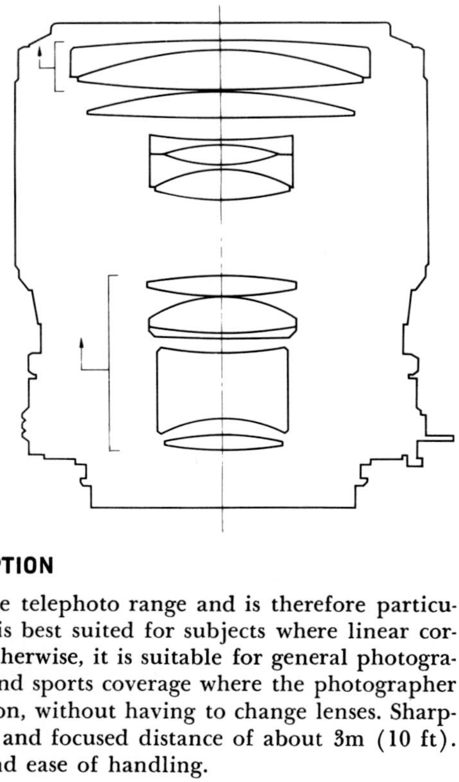

DESCRIPTION

This Zoom-Nikkor covers a normal-to-moderate telephoto range and is therefore particularly useful in working with close subjects. It is best suited for subjects where linear correction at edges and corners is not essential. Otherwise, it is suitable for general photography, including candids, landscapes, portraits, and sports coverage where the photographer wishes to change focal length in quick succession, without having to change lenses. Sharpest image is obtained at focal length of 60mm and focused distance of about 3m (10 ft). Very compact and light for utmost mobility and ease of handling.

SPECIFICATIONS

Smallest aperture: 22
Nearest focus distance: 1.2m (4 ft)
Focusing/zooming control: Via single control ring; reference marks for 43, 50, 60, 70, and 86mm are provided
Angles of view:
Diagonal: 53° ~ 28°30′
Horizontal: 45°10′ ~ 24°
Vertical: 31°30′ ~ 16°
Attachment size (inside screw diameter): 52mm (P = 0.75)
Lens hood: 52mm screw-in HN-3
Front lens cap: 52mm snap-on
Lens case: CL-32, flexible pouch 55, plastic case type CP-2
Overall size: 66.5mm ϕ × 81.5mm
Weight: 450g (15.9 oz)

50 ~ 300mm f/4.5 ZOOM-NIKKOR ED

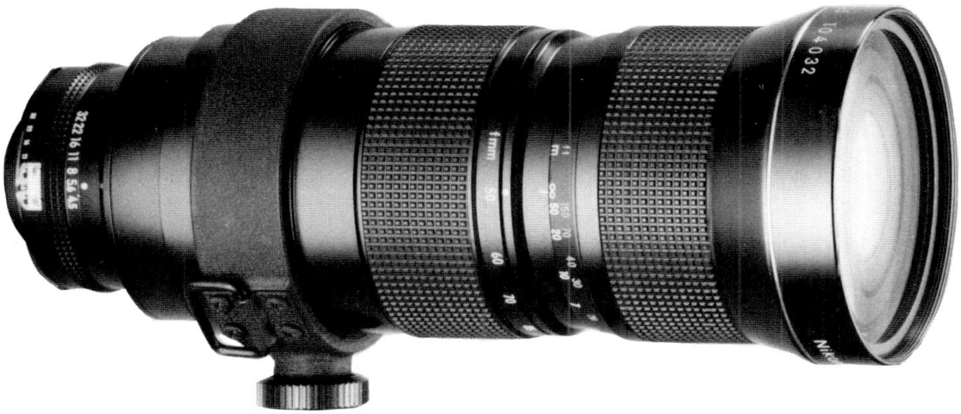

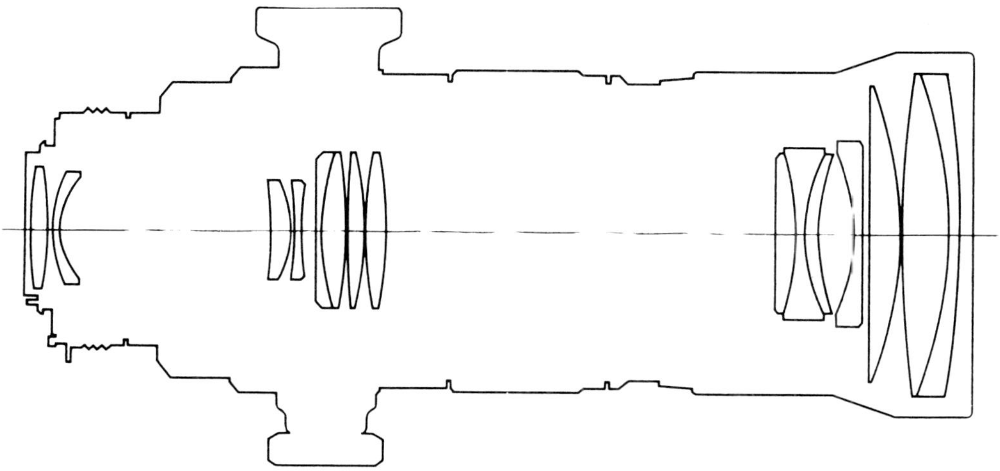

DESCRIPTION

The Zoom-Nikkor 50~300mm *f*/4.5 ED is a zoom lens with an extraordinary zooming ratio of 1:6. ED glass elements have been incorporated in its optical construction, resulting in greater compactness and outstanding correction of chromatic aberrations at longer focal lengths. Abandonment of the conventional method of zooming, using the front elements, in favor of a method using the middle elements, has also contributed to the lens' compactness. Nikon Integrated Coating on air-to-glass surfaces reduces flare and ghost. The focusing and zooming functions have separate control rings. A rotating tripod collar is provided.

SPECIFICATIONS

Smallest aperture: 32
Nearest focus distance: 2.5m (8.5 ft)
Zoom focal-length reference marks: 50, 60, 70, 85, 105, 135, 200, 250, and 300mm
Angles of view:
Diagonal: 46° ~ 8°10′
Horizontal: 39° ~ 6°5′
Vertical: 26° ~ 4°30′

Attachment size (inside screw diameter): 95mm (P = 1.00)
Lens hood: Slip-on HK-5
Front lens cap: 95mm screw-in
Lens case: Leatherette camera-lens case CE-2
Overall size: 98mm ϕ × 247mm
Weight: 2.2kg (4.8 lb)

50 ~ 300mm *f*/4.5 ZOOM-NIKKOR

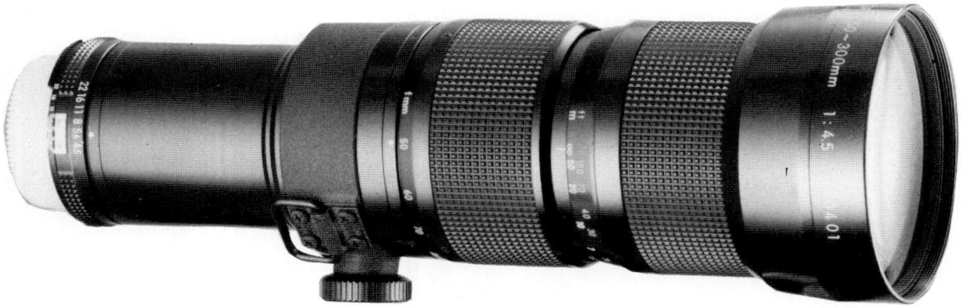

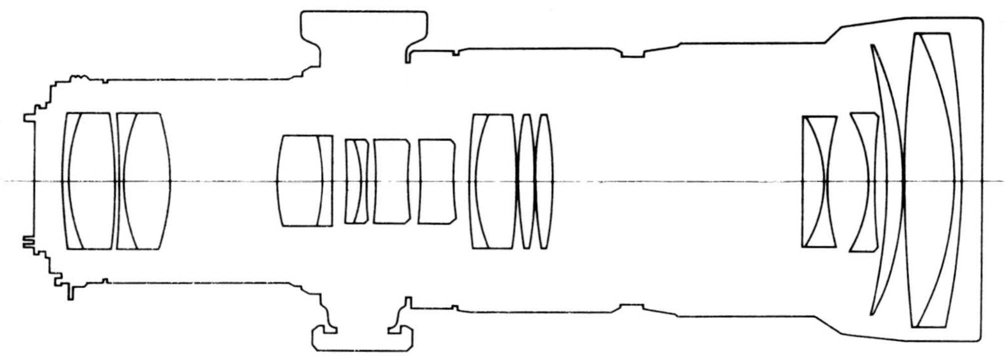

DESCRIPTION

Extraordinary zooming ratio of 6× of this zoom lens covers most frequently used focal lengths from 50mm (normal) to 300mm (telephoto). Chromatic aberrations, generally present at longer focal lengths, have been virtually eliminated, providing excellent resolution and high contrast throughout zooming range. Optimum performance is at *f*/8. Two separate rings are provided for focusing and zooming.

SPECIFICATIONS

Smallest aperture: 22
Nearest focus distance: 2.5m (8.5 ft)
Zoom focal-length reference marks: 50, 60, 70, 85, 105, 135, 200, 250, and 300mm
Angles of view:
Diagonal: 46° ~ 8°10′
Horizontal: 39° ~ 6°50′
Vertical: 26° ~ 4°30′
Attachment size (inside screw diameter): 95mm (P = 1.00)
Lens hood: 95mm screw-in HN-11
Front lens cap: 95mm screw-in
Lens case: Leatherette camera-lens case CE-2
Overall size: 98mm ϕ × 292mm
Weight: 2.3kg (5.1 lb)

80 ~ 200mm f/2.8 ZOOM-NIKKOR ED

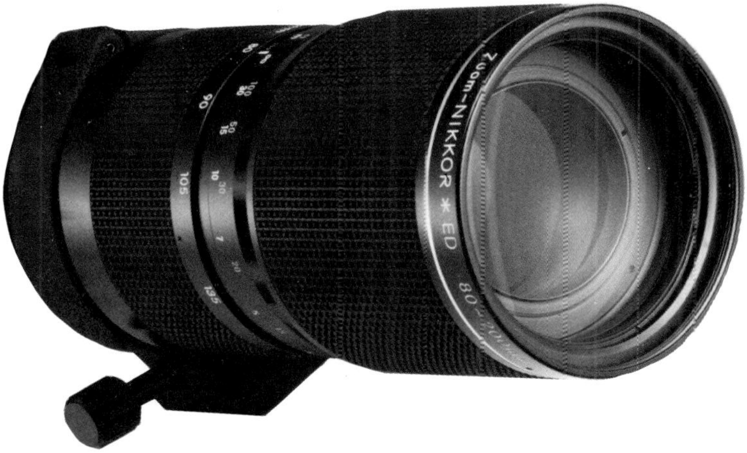

DESCRIPTION

This zoom lens is unique in that it offers a maximum aperture equivalent to that of many of the fixed focal-length lenses that fall within its zooming range. Among these lenses, only the 85mm *f*/2, the 105mm *f*/2.5, and the 135mm *f*/2 are faster. The lens design—12 elements in 9 groups—incorporates Nikon Extra Low Dispersion (ED) glass, which results in excellent correction of chromatic aberration. This degree of correction is important in a zoom lens, especially one having such a wide maximum aperture. Unlike the 80 ~ 200mm *f*/4.5, this lens has separate controls for focusing and zooming. It is also much heavier than its slower counterpart. The 80 ~ 200mm *f*/2.8 ED is especially advantageous for photojournalism, particularly in dim light, and in theatrical photography. A rotating tripod-mounting collar is provided.

SPECIFICATIONS

Smallest aperture: 32
Nearest focus distance: 2.5m (10 ft)
Zoom focal-length reference marks: 80, 90, 105, 135, and 200mm
Angles of view:
Diagonal: 30°10′ ~ 12°20′
Horizontal: 25°20′ ~ 10°20′
Vertical: 17° ~ 6°50′

Attachment size (inside screw diameter): 86mm (P = 1.00)
Lens hood: 86mm screw-in
Front lens cap: 86 mm screw-in
Overall size: 91.5mm ϕ × 204mm
Weight: 1.7 kg (3.7 lb)

Zoom-Nikkor 80mm-200mm f/2.8 ED

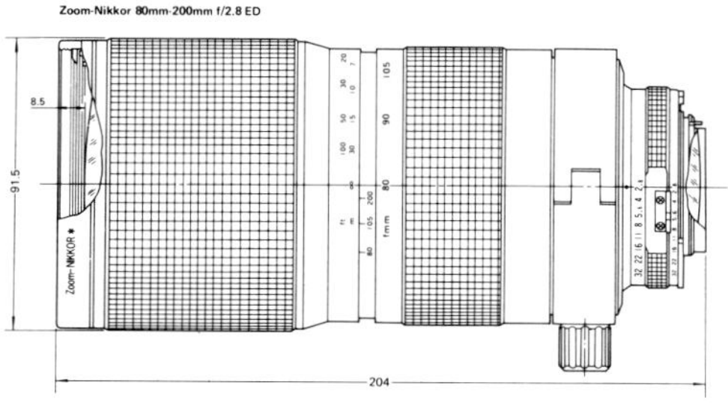

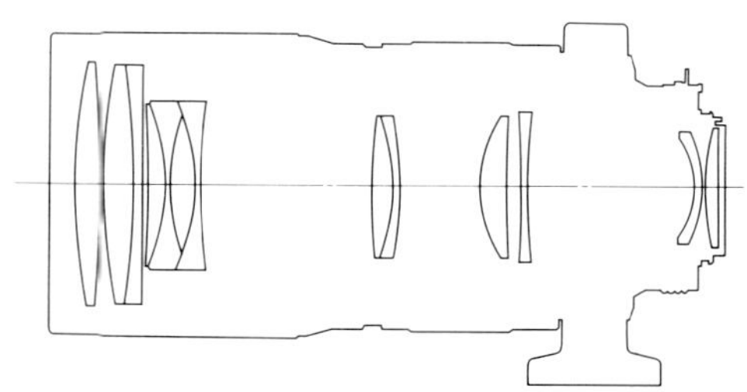

80 ~ 200mm f/4.5 ZOOM-NIKKOR (AI)

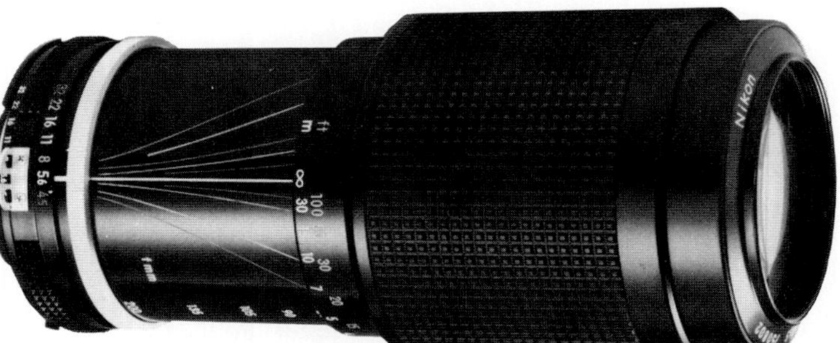

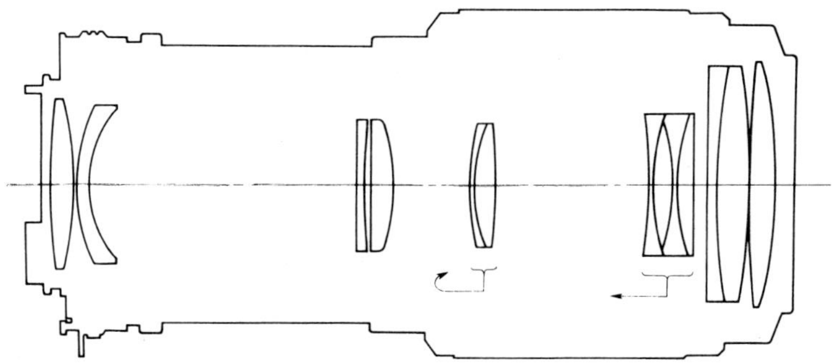

DESCRIPTION

The 2.5× zooming range of this lens covers the critical focal length of medium telephoto lenses most frequently used in photojournalism and general photography. It is often used as a substitute for the 200mm *f*/4 lens because, although heavier, it covers operating range of that lens, but also extends down to shorter focal lengths. Zooming and focusing may be accomplished singly or simultaneously with linear travel and rotation of lens sleeve. Combined with motor drive and pistol grip, this lens offers great mobility for action photographers. Optical performance is excellent even at full aperture.

SPECIFICATIONS

Smallest aperture: 32
Nearest focus distance: 1.8m (6 ft)
Zoom focal-length reference marks: 80, 90, 105, 135, and 200mm
Angles of view:
Diagonal: 30°10′ ~ 12°20′
Horizontal: 25°20′ ~ 10°20′
Vertical: 17° ~ 6°50′

Attachment size (inside screw diameter): 52mm (P = 0.75)
Lens hood: 52mm screw-in HN-7
Front lens cap: 52mm snap-on
Lens case: CL-35A, flexible pouch 56
Overall size: 75.5mm ϕ × 162mm
Weight: 820g (1.8 lb)

180 ~ 600mm *f*/8 ZOOM-NIKKOR ED

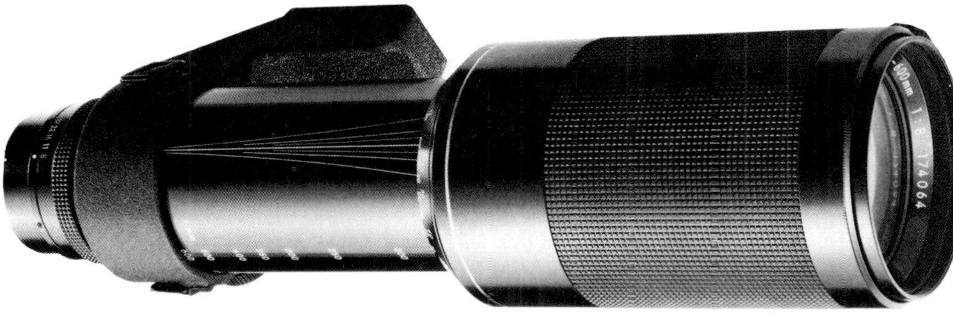

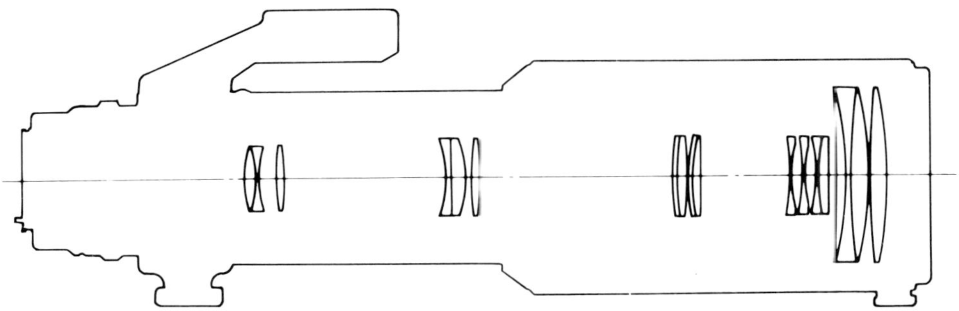

DESCRIPTION

The 180 ~ 600mm *f*/8 Zoom-Nikkor combines the advantages of ultra-telephoto magnification with the convenience of a zoom lens. Nikon ED glass is employed to provide excellent contrast and color rendition at all focal lengths. Zooming and focusing are accomplished by a single ring—making the lens especially useful for fast-changing situations such as sports events and news situations. The diaphragm is automatic, although metering must be done in the stopped-down mode. A rotating tripod collar is provided. Closest focusing distance is 2.5m (8.5 ft), which is remarkably close for a zoom lens in this focal-length range.

SPECIFICATIONS

Smallest aperture: 32
Nearest focus distance: 2.5m (8.5 ft)
Zoom focal-length reference marks: 180, 200, 250, 300, 350, 400, 500, and 600mm
Angles of view:
Diagonal: 13°40′ ~ 4°10′
Horizontal: 11°30′ ~ 3°30′
Vertical: 7°40′ ~ 2°20′

Attachment size (inside screw diameter): 95mm (P = 1.00)
Lens hood: HN-16
Front lens cap: supplied
Lens case: CZ-1860
Overall size: 105mm ϕ × 403mm
Weight: 3.4kg (7.5 lb)

200 ~ 600mm *f*/9.5 ZOOM-NIKKOR AUTO

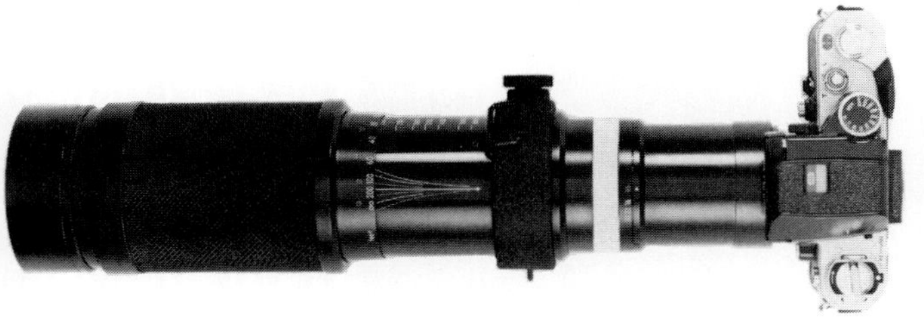

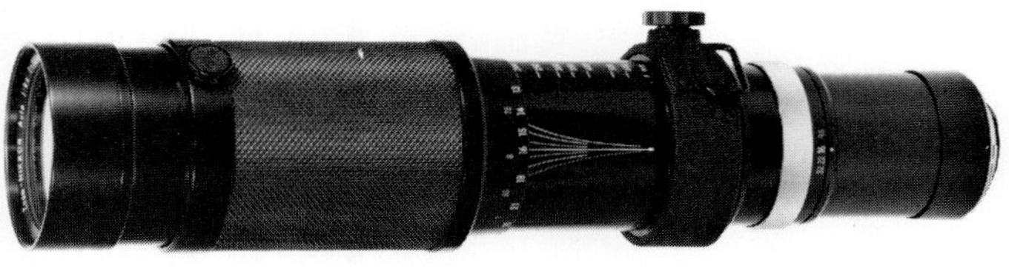

DESCRIPTION

Longest of lenses in Zoom-Nikkor range, this model has particular application in long-range situations including safaris, big, bold sports events from high elevations at great distances for best perspective effects, surveillance, space exploration, and scientific research. Single-push, in-out, rotating sleeve on lens barrel controls both zooming and focusing. Tripod socket is on rotating collar, allowing camera to be changed rapidly from vertical to horizontal.

SPECIFICATIONS

Smallest aperture: 32
Nearest focus distance: 4m (13 ft)
Zoom focal-length reference marks: 200, 250, 300, 350, 400, 500 and 600mm
Angles of view:
Diagonal: 12°20′ ~ 4°10′
Horizontal: 10°20′ ~ 3°30′
Vertical: 6°50′ ~ 2°20′

Attachment size (inside screw diameter): 82mm (P = 0.75); slip-on outer diameter: 86mm
Filter: Series 9
Lens hood: 82mm screw-in (U.S. 616)
Front lens cap: 100mm slip-on
Lens case: leatherette camera-lens case CE-3
Overall size: 89mm ϕ x 382mm
Weight: 2.3 kg (5.1 lbs)

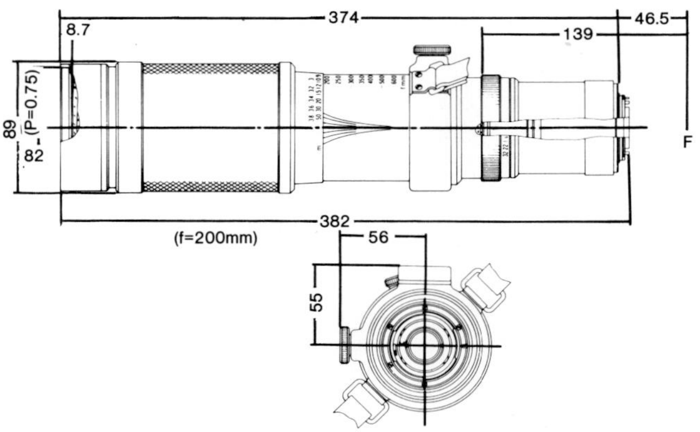

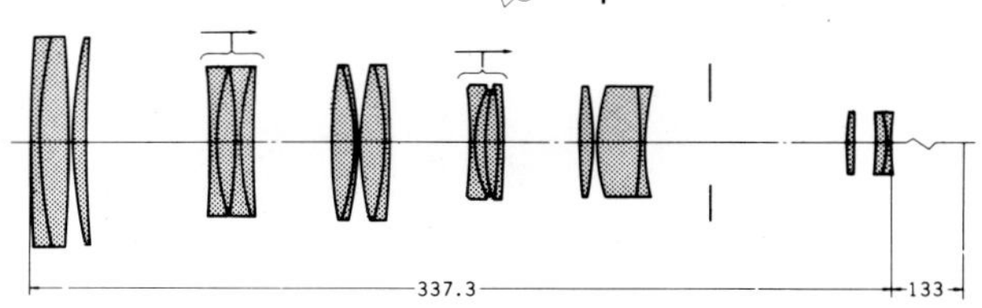

360 ~ 1200mm f/11 ZOOM-NIKKOR ED

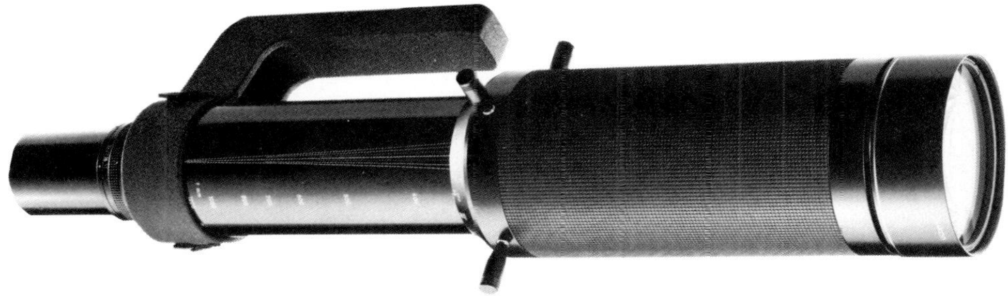

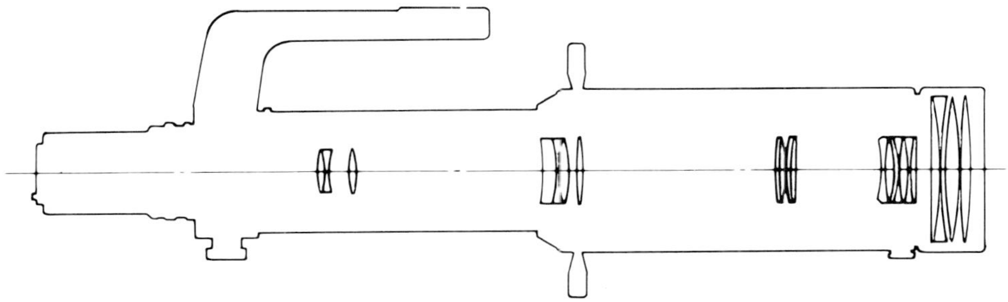

DESCRIPTION

The Zoom-Nikkor ED 360 ~ 1200mm *f*/11 is a super-telephoto lens offering the longest focal length available in a zoom lens. Nikon ED glass elements are employed to correct chromatic aberration by an approximate 90–percent reduction of the secondary spectrum across full 400– to 1000–nanometer wavelength range. The degree of correction obtained ensures exceptional image sharpness and full image contrast at all apertures, and is so complete that this lens requires no corrective refocusing for infrared photography. The wide zooming range of this lens makes it especially useful for sports, wildlife, and other types of photography which require the photographer to remain at a distance while shooting. A tripod is recommended at all times for use with this lens. Rotating tripod collar is provided. Closest focusing distance is a remarkable 6m (20 ft). Automatic diaphragm; stopped-down metering necessary.

SPECIFICATIONS

Smallest aperture: 32
Nearest focus distance: 6m (20 ft)
Zoom focal-length reference marks: 360, 400, 500, 600, 700, 800, 1000, and 1200mm
Angles of view:
Diagonal: 6°50′ ~ 2°
Horizontal: 5°50′ ~ 1°40′
Vertical: 4° ~ 1°10′
Attachment size (inside screw diameter): 122mm (P = 1.00)
Lens hood: 122mm screw-in HN-17
Front lens cap: 122mm screw-in (supplied)
Lens case: Leather lens case CZ-3612
Overall size: 125mm ϕ × 704mm
Weight: 7.1kg (15.6 lb)

28mm *f*/3.5 PC-NIKKOR

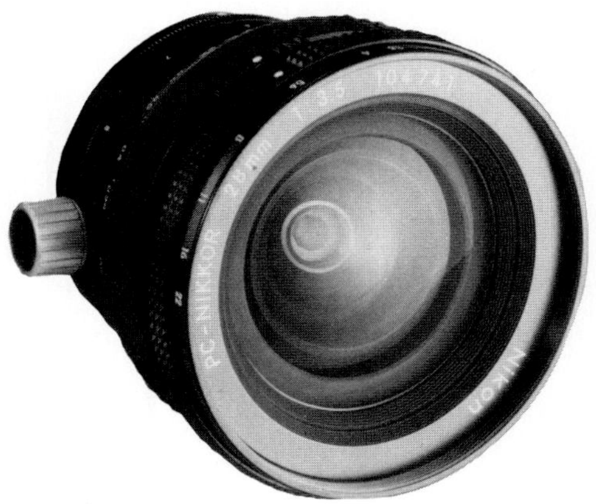

DESCRIPTION

The 28mm *f*/3.5 PC-Nikkor, introduced at the 1978 Photokina, is intended to replace the 28mm *f*/4 PC-Nikkor. Its wider aperture results in a slightly brighter image in the viewfinder. The optics of the 28mm *f*/3.5 PC-Nikkor may be shifted up to 11mm off-center. The entire lens mount may be rotated a full 360 degrees. Click stops are provided at 30-degree intervals. Thus, the shift is possible in any direction when shifting and rotation are combined. The lens may also be used as a conventional wide-angle lens, having a picture angle of 74 degrees. When two photographs made with the lens shifted in opposite horizontal directions are joined together, a panoramic picture with a 92-degree horizontal angle of view is formed. The lens is especially useful in architectural, industrial, and commercial photography. Aperture is preset; metering must be done in the stopped-down mode.

SPECIFICATIONS

Smallest aperture: 22
Nearest focus distance: 0.3m (1 ft)
Subject field at nearest distance: 17.0 × 25.6cm
Image ratio at nearest distance: 1:7.1
Focusing distances:
- One head vertical: 0.5m (1.75 ft) subject to distortion
- Two heads horizontal: 0.5m (1.75 ft) subject to distortion
- One to three adults standing: 1.7m (5.5 ft)

Angles of view:
- Diagonal: 74°
- Horizontal: 64°
- Vertical: 45°30′

Ratio of image size at infinity to image of 50mm lens: 0.56:1
Attachment size (inside screw diameter): 72mm (P = 0.75)
Lens hood: 72mm screw-in HN-9
Front lens cap: 72mm screw-in
Lens case: CL-34A
Overall size: 78mm ϕ × 68.5mm
Weight: 430g (15 oz)

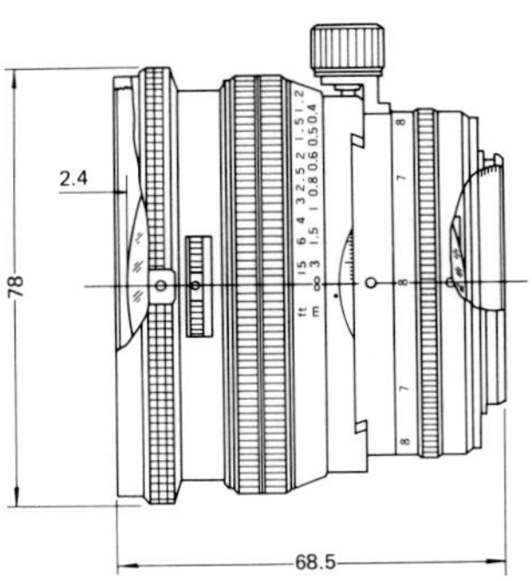

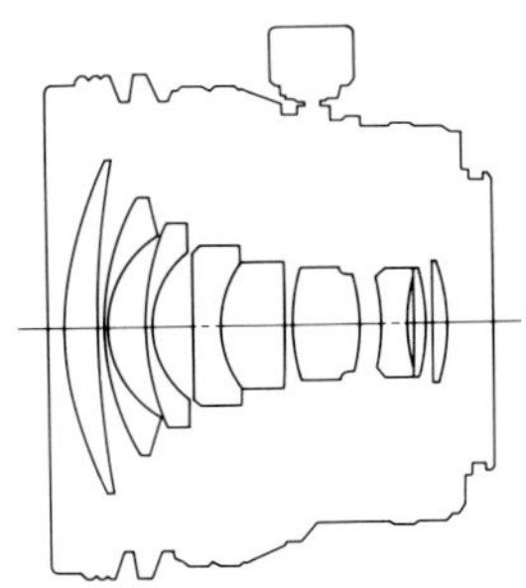

28mm f/4 PC-NIKKOR

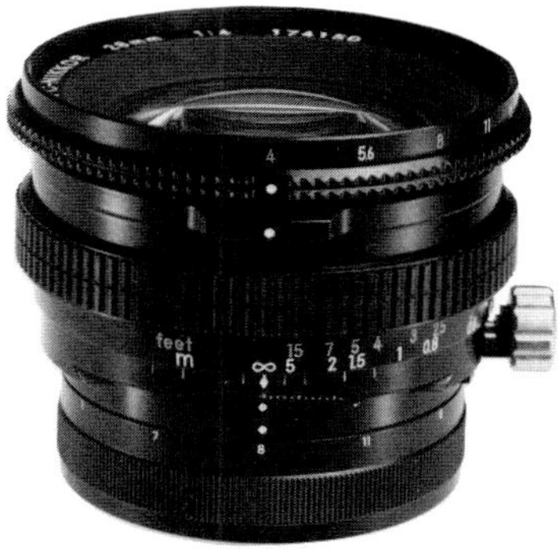

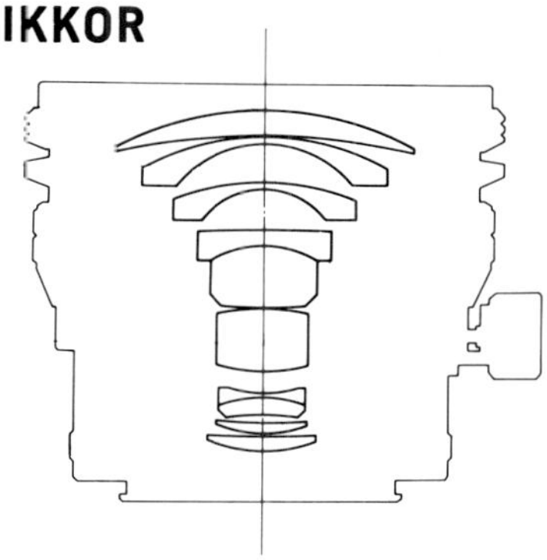

DESCRIPTION

A unique feature of this lens is its ability to shift optics as much as 11mm off-center by means of a micrometer lead-screw. This corresponds to front shift, rise, or drop of a large view or technical camera. Entire lens mount may be rotated a full 360 degrees with click-stops at 30-degree intervals. Combined shifting and rotation of the lens permits it to perform an infinite series of directional shifts. The lens can be used to produce a 92-degree (horizontal) panorama picture by placing two pictures side-by-side, with the lens shifted fully in opposite directions. It is extremely useful in architectural, industrial, and commerical photography. Permits perspective corrections on film, rather than in darkroom. Can also be used as a conventional wide-angle lens. Preset aperture; stopped-down metering necessary.

SPECIFICATIONS

Smallest aperture: 22
Nearest focus distance: 0.3m (1 ft)
Subject field at nearest distance: 17.0 × 25.6cm
Image ratio at nearest distance: 1:7.1
Focusing distances:
One head vertical: 0.5m (1.75 ft) subject to perspective distortion
Two heads horizontal: 0.5m (1.75 ft) subject to perspective distortion
One to three adults standing: 1.7m (5.5 ft)

Angles of view:
Diagonal: 74°
Horizontal: 64°
Vertical: 45°30′
Ratio of image size at infinity to image of 50mm lens: 0.56:1
Attachment size (inside screw diameter): 72mm (P = 0.75)
Lens hood: HN-9
Front lens cap: 72mm screw-in (provided)
Lens case: CL-34A
Overall size: 78mm ϕ × 67.5mm
Weight: 410g (14.5 oz)

DEPTH OF FIELD TABLE

m \ f/	4	5.6	8	11	16	22	Reproduction ratio
0.3	0.293–0.308	0.290–0.311	0.286–0.316	0.282–0.323	0.274–0.335	0.266–0.351	1/6.95
0.35	0.339–0.362	0.335–0.367	0.329–0.375	0.322–0.386	0.312–0.405	0.300–0.433	1/8.72
0.4	0.385–0.417	0.379–0.424	0.371–0.436	0.362–0.452	0.347–0.482	0.332–0.525	1/10.5
0.5	0.474–0.530	0.464–0.543	0.451–0.565	0.435–0.595	0.413–0.655	0.389–0.749	1/14.0
0.6	0.560–0.647	0.546–0.669	0.526–0.704	0.504–0.755	0.472–0.863	0.439–1.05	1/17.5
0.8	0.726–0.894	0.700–0.940	0.666–1.02	0.628–1.14	0.574–1.43	0.523–2.11	1/24.5
1	0.882–1.16	0.843–1.24	0.791–1.39	0.735–1.64	0.663–2.37	0.591–5.39	1/31.5
1.5	1.24–1.92	1.16–2.17	1.06–2.71	0.954–3.97	0.825–19.4	0.714–∞	1/48.9
2	1.55–2.87	1.42–3.48	1.27–5.18	1.12–13.7	0.942–∞	0.796–∞	1/66.3
5	2.82–24.4	2.41–∞	1.98–∞	1.63–∞	1.27–∞	1.01–∞	1/171
∞	6.27–∞	4.51–∞	3.18–∞	2.34–∞	1.64–∞	1.22–∞	1/∞

35mm *f*/2.8 PC-NIKKOR

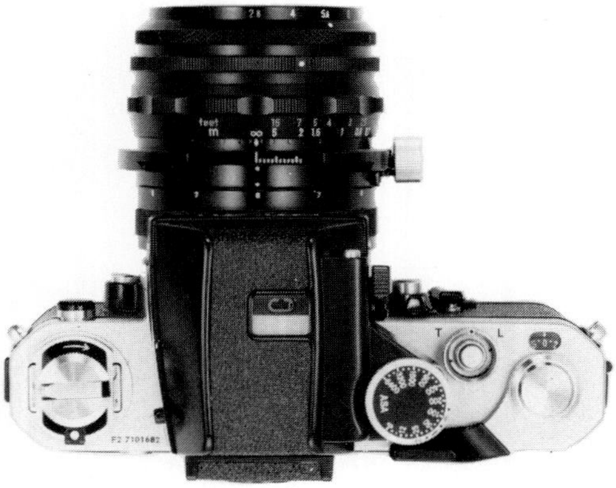

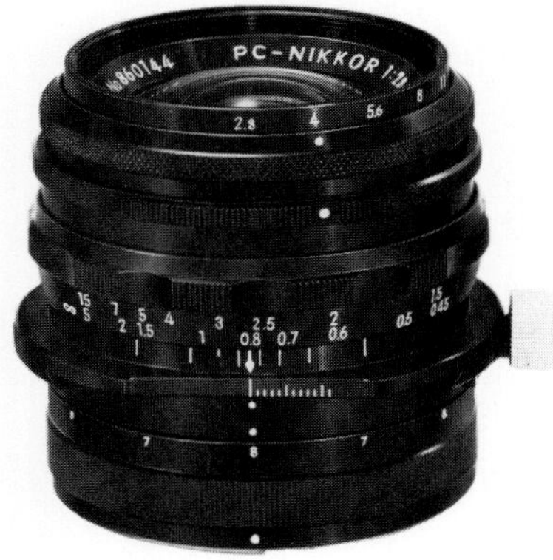

DESCRIPTION

A unique feature of this lens is ability to shift optics as much as 11mm off center by means of micrometer leadscrew. This movement corresponds to a three-inch rise on a large view camera equipped with a 9½-inch lens. Entire lens mount may also be rotated a full 360 degrees with 12 click stops positioned every 30 degrees. Combined shifting and full-circle rotation permit lens to perform an infinite series of directional shifts. Can be used to produce a 78-degree panorama picture by placing two pictures side-by-side taken separately with lens shifted to opposite direction. Extremely useful in architectural, industrial, and commercial photography to achieve perspective correction on film rather than in darkroom. Takes in tall buildings without having to tilt camera upwards. Used also as conventional intermediate wide-angle lens. Exceptionally fine optical correction, even at full aperture.

SPECIFICATIONS

Smallest aperture: 32
Aperture diaphragm: Manual preset, does not couple to exposure meter
Nearest focus distance: 0.3m (1 ft)
Subject field at nearest distance: 124.8 x 187.2
Image ratio at nearest distance: 1:5.2
Focusing distances:
- One head vertical: 0.5m (1.7 ft) subject to perspective distortion
- Two heads horizontal: 0.6m (2.1 ft) subject to perspective distortion
- One to three adults standing: 2.1m (7 ft)

Angles of view:
- Diagonal: 62°
- Horizontal: 53°
- Vertical: 37°

Ratio of image size at infinity to image of 50mm lens: .7:1
Attachment size (inside screw diameter): 52mm (P = 0.75)
Lens hood: 52mm screw-in HN-1
Front lens cap: 52mm snap-on
Lens case: CL-34, flexible pouch 51
Overall size: 70mm ϕ x 66.5
Weight: 335g (11.8 oz)

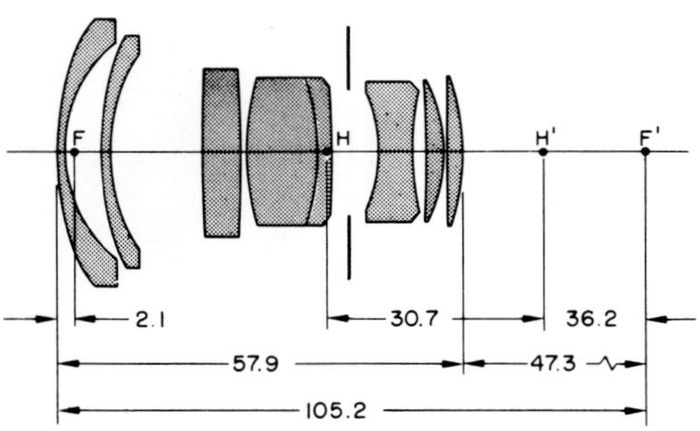

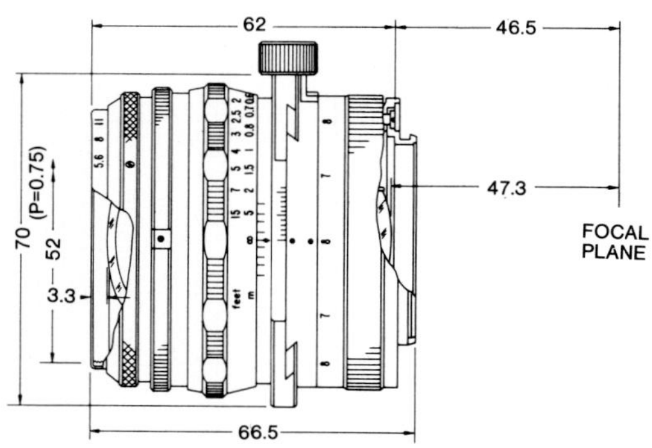

58mm *f*/1.2 NOCT-NIKKOR

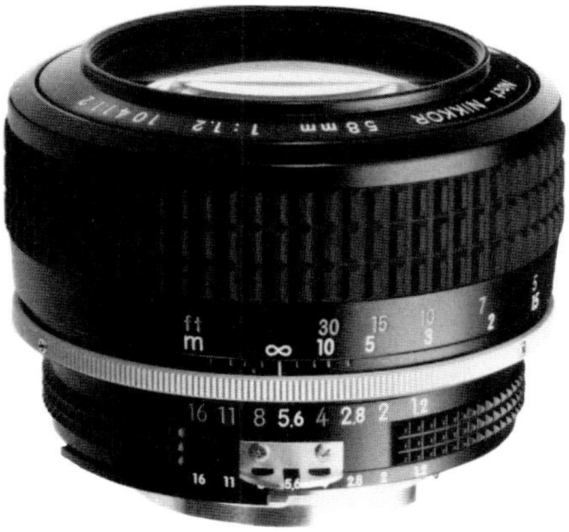

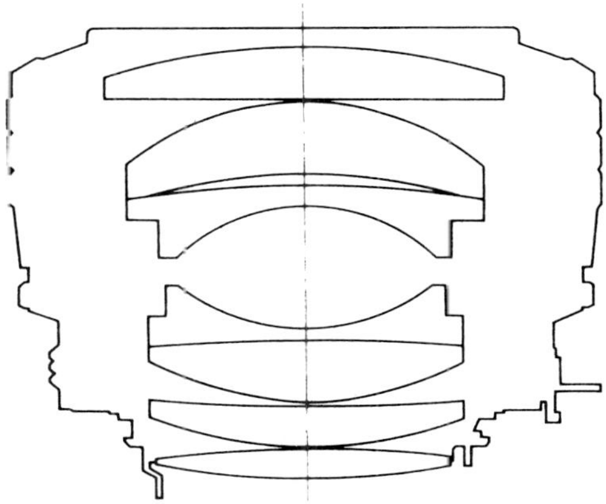

DESCRIPTION

The Noct-Nikkor *f*/1.2 is a high-speed, normal lens specially formulated for low-light photography. The lens' aspheric front element results not only in outstanding aberration corrections but also, more importantly, in significantly higher contrast—making this Nikkor one of the few high-speed lenses giving natural tonal gradation at full aperture. Nikon Integrated Coating is applied to air-glass surfaces to reduce flare and ghost, further increasing contrast and improving color rendition. This lens is well-suited for use in situations where a lens must be used with fast shutter speeds at full aperture, and great depth-of-field is not required. It is also excellent as a standard lens for general photography.

Smallest aperture: 16
Nearest focus distance: 0.5m (1.7 ft)
Subject field at nearest distance: 18.3 × 27.4cm
Image ratio at nearest distance: 1:7.6
Focusing distances:
- One head vertical: 0.7m (2.5 ft) subject to perspective distortion
- Two heads horizontal: 1m (3.3 ft) subject to perspective distortion
- One to three adults standing: 3.1m (11 ft)

Angles of view:
- Diagonal: 40°50′
- Horizontal: 34°40′
- Vertical: 24°10′

Ratio of image size at infinity to image of 50mm lens: 1.16:1
Attachment size (inside screw diameter): 52mm (P = 0.75)
Lens hood: HS-7 or HR-2
Front lens cap: 52mm snap-on
Lens case: CL-34A, flexible pouch 54, plastic case CP-1
Overall size: 74mm ϕ × 64.5mm
Weight: 480g (1.1 lb)

DEPTH OF FIELD TABLE

(ft)

Focused distance	Depth of field									Repro. ratio
	f/1.2	f/1.4	f/2	f/2.8	f/4	f/5.6	f/8	f/11	f/16	
0.5	0.498–0.502	0.498–0.502	0.497–0.503	0.495–0.505	0.493–0.507	0.491–0.510	0.487–0.514	0.482–0.520	0.474–0.530	1/6.7
0.55	0.547–0.553	0.547–0.553	0.546–0.554	0.544–0.556	0.541–0.559	0.538–0.563	0.533–0.568	0.527–0.575	0.518–0.588	1/7.6
0.6	0.597–0.603	0.596–0.604	0.595–0.605	0.593–0.608	0.590–0.611	0.585–0.615	0.579–0.622	0.572–0.631	0.561–0.647	1/8.5
0.7	0.695–0.705	0.695–0.705	0.692–0.708	0.689–0.711	0.685–0.716	0.679–0.722	0.691–0.732	0.661–0.745	0.645–0.768	1/10
0.8	0.794–0.806	0.793–0.807	0.790–0.810	0.786–0.815	0.780–0.821	0.772–0.830	0.761–0.844	0.748–0.862	0.726–0.894	1/12
0.9	0.892–0.908	0.891–0.910	0.887–0.914	0.882–0.919	0.874–0.928	0.864–0.939	0.850–0.953	0.833–0.981	0.806–1.02	1/14
1	0.990–1.01	0.988–1.01	0.983–1.02	0.977–1.02	0.967–1.04	0.955–1.05	0.937–1.07	0.916–1.10	0.883–1.16	1/15
1.2	1.19–1.22	1.18–1.22	1.18–1.23	1.17–1.24	1.15–1.25	1.13–1.27	1.11–1.31	1.08–1.36	1.03–1.45	1/19
1.5	1.48–1.52	1.47–1.53	1.46–1.54	1.45–1.56	1.42–1.59	1.40–1.62	1.36–1.68	1.31–1.76	1.24–1.92	1/24
10	8.95–11.3	8.80–11.6	8.37–12.4	7.86–13.8	7.20–16.5	6.48–22.2	5.63–47.0	4.85–∞	3.94–∞	1/171
∞	84.2–∞	72.2–∞	50.6–∞	36.1–∞	25.3–∞	18.1–∞	12.7–∞	9.28–∞	6.41–∞	1/∞

55mm *f*/3.5 MICRO-NIKKOR

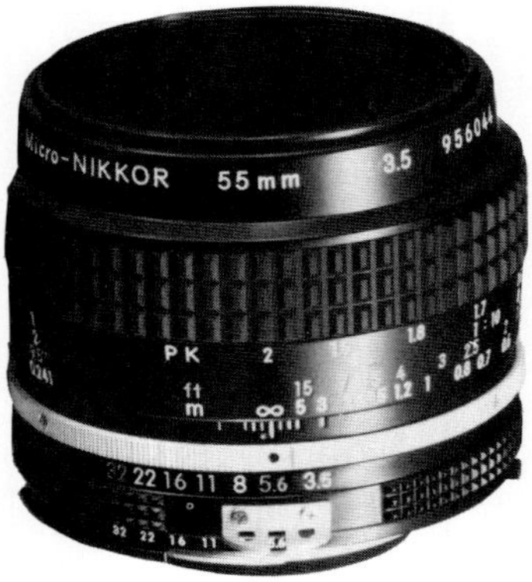

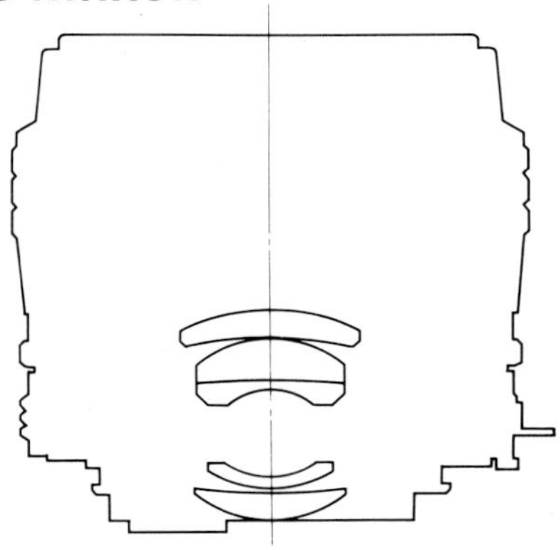

DESCRIPTION

Originally designed for close-distance photography with an image ratio range of 1:1 to infinity, this is probably the sharpest lens available for general photographic purposes, with center-to-edge resolving power exceeding that of the finest photographic emulsions. Relative to its primary purpose, the great flatness of image plane, high-image contrast, and excellent color rendition are ideal for close-up subjects. Optimum image resolution at the 1:10 image ratio, but resolution remains virtually unchanged throughout the entire focusing range. The lens by itself achieves 1:2 image ratio, but extends to 1:1 with Adapter Ring PK-13. Full diaphragm automation and meter coupling are retained when PK-13 ring is used. Image ratios are engraved on lens barrel in relation to focused distance.

SPECIFICATIONS

Smallest aperture: 32
Nearest focus distance: 24cm (9.5 in)
Subject field at nearest distance: Lens alone, 48 × 72mm; with PK-13 ring, 24 × 36mm
Image ratio at nearest distance: 1:2; with PK-13 ring, 1:1
Angles of view:
Diagonal: 43°
Horizontal: 36°10′
Vertical: 24°40′
Attachment size (inside screw diameter): 52mm (P = 0.75)
Lens hood: 52mm screw-in HN-3
Front lens cap: 52mm snap-on
Lens case: CL-33A, flexible pouch 55, plastic case CP-2
Overall size: 66mm ϕ × 64.5mm
Weight: 240g (8.5 oz)

DEPTH OF FIELD TABLE

(m)

Focused distance	Depth of Field								Reproduction ratio
	f/3.5	f/4	f/5.6	f/8	f/11	f/16	f/22	f/32	
0.241	0.240 – 0.242	0.240 – 0.242	0.240 – 0.242	0.239 – 0.243	0.239 – 0 243	0.238 – 0.244	0.237 – 0.246	0.235 – 0.248	1/2
0.25	0.249 – 0.251	0.249 – 0.251	0.249 – 0.251	0.248 – 0.252	0.248 – 0.253	0.246 – 0.254	0.245 – 0.255	0.243 – 0.258	1/2.2
0.3	0.298 – 0.302	0.298 – 0.302	0.297 – 0.303	0.296 – 0.304	0.295 – 0.305	0.293 – 0.308	0.290 – 0.311	0.286 – 0.316	1/3.3
0.35	0.347 – 0.352	0.347 – 0.353	0.346 – 0.354	0.344 – 0.356	0.342 – 0.358	0.339 – 0.362	0.335 – 0.367	0.328 – 0.376	1/4.2
0.4	0.396 – 0.404	0.396 – 0.404	0.394 – 0.406	0.392 – 0.409	0.389 – 0.412	0.384 – 0.418	0.378 – 0.425	0.369 – 0.438	1/5.2
0.5	0.493 – 0.507	0.493 – 0.508	0.490 – 0.511	0.485 – 0.516	0.480 – 0.522	0.472 – 0.533	0.462 – 0.546	0.447 – 0.570	1/7.1
0.6	0.590 – 0.611	0.588 – 0.612	0.584 – 0.617	0.577 – 0.625	0.569 – 0.634	0.557 – 0.652	0.542 – 0.673	0.520 – 0.714	1/8.9
0.7	0.686 – 0.715	0.684 – 0.717	0.677 – 0.724	0.668 – 0.736	0.657 – 0.750	0.639 – 0.775	0.619 – 0.808	0.589 – 0.870	1/11
0.8	0.781 – 0.820	0.778 – 0.823	0.769 – 0.833	0.757 – 0.848	0.742 – 0.868	0.719 – 0.904	0.693 – 0.950	0.654 – 1.041	1/13
1.0	0.968 – 1.03	0.964 – 1.04	0.951 – 1.06	0.931 – 1.08	0.907 – 1.11	0.871 – 1.18	0.831 – 1.26	0.773 – 1.44	1/16

105mm f/4 MICRO-NIKKOR

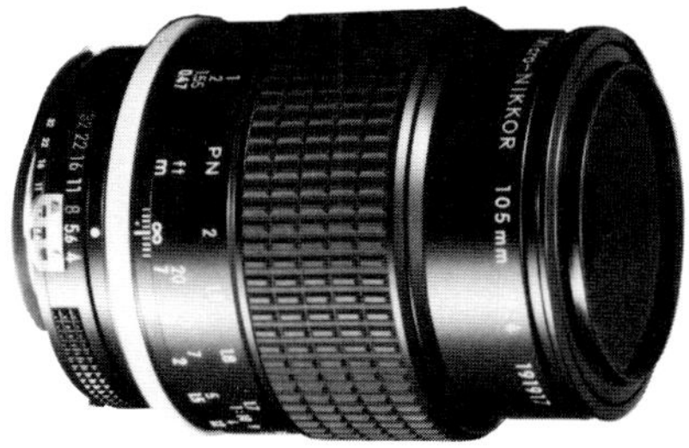

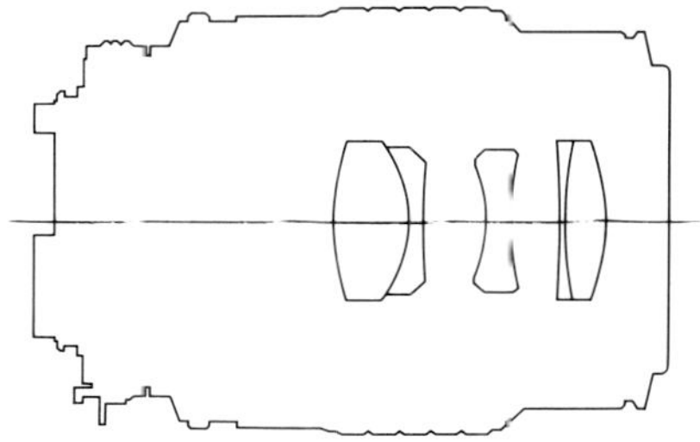

DESCRIPTION

The 105mm *f*/4 Micro-Nikkor is a special telephoto lens designed for close-up photography at high reproduction ratios. When the lens alone is mounted on the camera, focusing is possible from infinity to a reproduction ratio of 1:2. When the special Auto Extension Ring PN-11 (or PN-1, for cameras which do not feature auto-indexing) is attached between camera and lens, focusing is possible in the 1:2 to 1:1 range. Although the lens is optimized for best results at close focusing distances, resolution is excellent throughout the entire focusing range, enabling the use of this lens as a medium-length telephoto for general photography. The increased working distance between lens and subject, as compared with the 55mm Micro-Nikkor, is advantageous when lighting equipment must be accommodated or when the photographer is simply unable to get too close to the subject.

SPECIFICATIONS

Smallest aperture: 32
Nearest focus distance: 0.47 (1.55 ft)
Subject field at nearest distance: 48 × 72mm; with PN-11 Auto Ring, 24 × 36mm
Image ratio at nearest distance: 1:2; with PN-11 Auto Ring, 1:1
Focusing distances:
One head vertical: 1.5m (5.5 ft)
Two heads horizontal: 1.9m (6.3 ft)
One to three adults standing: 6.4m (21 ft)
Angles of view:
Diagonal: 23°20′
Horizontal: 19°30′
Vertical: 13°
Ratio of image size at infinity to image of 50mm lens: 2.1:1
Attachment size (inside screw diameter): 52mm (P = 0.75)
Lens hood: Built-in
Front lens cap: 52mm snap-on
Lens case: CL-35A, flexible pouch 56
Overall size: 74.5mm ϕ × 104mm
Weight: 500g (1.1 lb)

DEPTH OF FIELD TABLE

(m)

Focused distance	Depth of field							Reproduction ratio
	4	5	8	11	16	22	32	
0.47	0.469–0.471	0.469–0.471	0.468–0.472	0.468–0.472	0.467–0.473	0.466–0.474	0.464–0.477	1/1.98
0.50	0.499–0.501	0.499–0.501	0.498–0.502	0.497–0.503	0.496–0.504	0.494–0.506	0.492–0.509	1/2.35
0.55	0.549–0.552	0.548–0.552	0.547–0.553	0.546–0.554	0.544–0.556	0.542–0.559	0.538–0.563	1/2.90
0.6	0.598–0.602	0.597–0.603	0.596–0.604	0.595–0.606	0.592–0.608	0.589–0.612	0.584–0.617	1/3.43
0.7	0.697–0.703	0.696–0.704	0.694–0.707	0.691–0.709	0.687–0.713	0.683–0.719	0.675–0.727	1/4.45
0.8	0.795–0.805	0.794–0.806	0.791–0.810	0.787–0.813	0.782–0.819	0.775–0.827	0.765–0.840	1/5.45
1	0.992–1.01	0.990–1.01	0.984–1.02	0.978–1.02	0.968–1.03	0.957–1.05	0.939–1.07	1/7.40
1.2	1.19–1.21	1.18–1.22	1.17–1.23	1.17–1.24	1.15–1.25	1.13–1.28	1.11–1.31	1/9.33
1.5	1.48–1.52	1.47–1.53	1.46–1.54	1.44–1.56	1.42–1.59	1.39–1.53	1.35–1.70	1/12.2
2	1.96–2.04	1.95–2.05	1.92–2.09	1.89–2.12	1.85–2.18	1.80–2.26	1.72–2.40	1/17.0
3	2.91–3.10	2.88–3.13	2.82–3.21	2.76–3.30	2.66–3.45	2.55–3.56	2.39–4.08	1/26.5
7	6.48–7.62	6.36–7.79	6.03–8.36	5.73–9.02	5.30–10.4	4.87–12.7	4.28–20.6	1/64.7
∞	82.9–∞	66.4–∞	41.6–∞	30.3–∞	20.9–∞	15.2–∞	10.5–∞	1/∞

200mm f/4 MICRO-NIKKOR IF

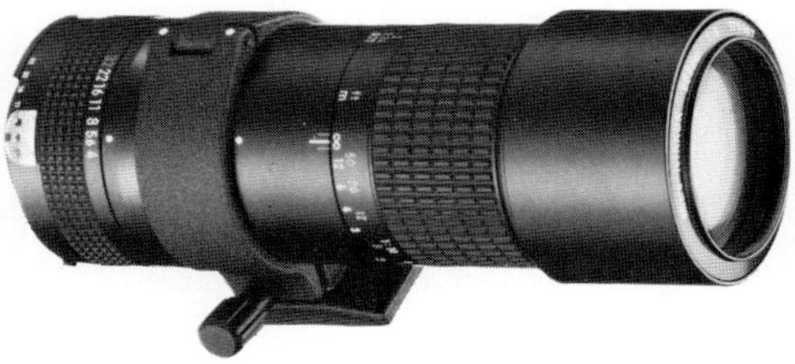

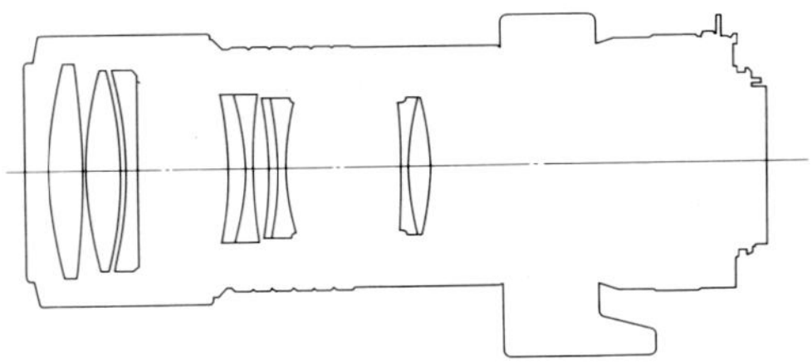

DESCRIPTION

The Micro-Nikkor 200mm *f*/4 is a close-up lens with a long focal length and a relatively wide maximum aperture. Like the Micro-Nikkors of other focal lengths, it focuses from infinity to a reproduction ratio of 1:2, with special attachments. The 200mm *f*/4 Micro-Nikkor uses the Nikon Internal Focusing (IF) system, whereby the physical length of the lens remains unchanged as focus is changed. The unique design of the lens makes it well suited for both close-up photography and general telephoto use. The long focal length permits ample working distance between lens and subject and facilitates illumination and close-up photography of elusive subjects with a natural-looking perspective. The Teleconverter TC-300 effectively doubles the focal length of the lens and enables focusing from infinity to a reproduction ratio of 1:1. A rotating tripod mounting collar is provided.

SPECIFICATIONS

Smallest aperture: 32
Nearest focus distance: 0.71m (2.34 ft)
Subject field at nearest distance: 4.8 × 7.2cm (lens alone); 2.4 × 3.6cm (with Teleconverter TC-300)
Image ratio at nearest distance: 1:2; with TC-300, 1:1
Focusing distances:
One head vertical: 2.9m (9.5 ft)
Two heads horizontal: 3.7m (12 ft)
One to three adults standing:
12.2m 40 ft)
Angles of view:
Diagonal: 12°20′
Horizontal: 10°20′
Vertical: 6°50′
Ratio of image size at infinity to image of 50mm lens: 4:1
Attachment size (inside screw diameter): 52mm (P = 0.75)
Lens hood: Built-in telescopic type
Front lens cap: 52mm snap-on
Lens case: CL-20A
Overall size: 67mm ϕ × 180mm
Weight: 640g (1.4 lb)

(m)

Focused distance	Depth of field *f*/5.6	*f*/8	*f*/11	*f*/16	*f*/22	Repro. ratio
5.5	5.49–5.51	5.48–5.52	5.48–5.52	5.47–5.53	5.45–5.55	1/8.09
6	5.99–6.01	5.98–6.02	5.97–6.03	5.96–6.04	5.94–6.06	1/8.92
7	6.98–7.02	6.97–7.03	6.96–7.04	6.94–7.06	6.92–7.08	1/10.59
8	7.97–8.03	7.96–8.04	7.94–8.06	7.92–8.08	7.89–8.11	1/12.26
10	9.95–10.05	9.94–10.06	9.91–10.09	9.87–10.13	9.82–10.18	1/15.59
12	11.93–12.07	11.90–12.10	11.87–12.13	11.81–12.19	11.74–12.26	1/18.92
15	14.89–15.11	14.85–15.15	14.79–15.21	14.69–15.31	14.58–15.42	1/23.92
20	19.81–20.19	19.72–20.28	19.62–20.38	19.45–20.55	19.24–20.76	1/32.26
30	29.55–30.45	29.36–30.64	29.12–30.88	28.72–31.28	28.24–31.76	1/48.92
70	67.51–72.49	66.44–73.56	65.10–74.90	62.87–77.13	60.2–79.2	1/115.59
∞	1929.22–∞	1350.65–∞	982.46–∞	675.65–∞	491.56–∞	1/∞

200mm *f*/5.6 MEDICAL-NIKKOR AUTO

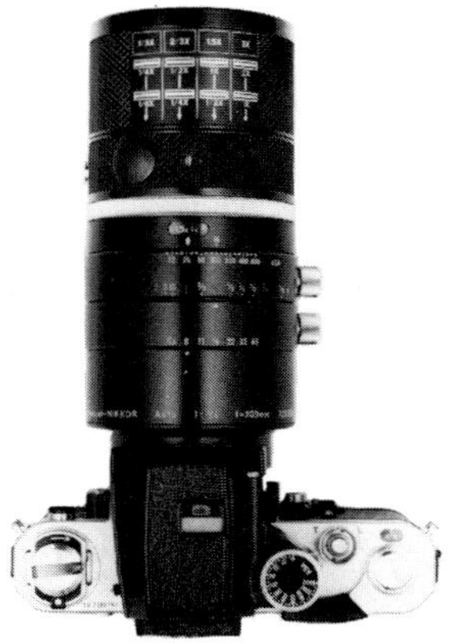

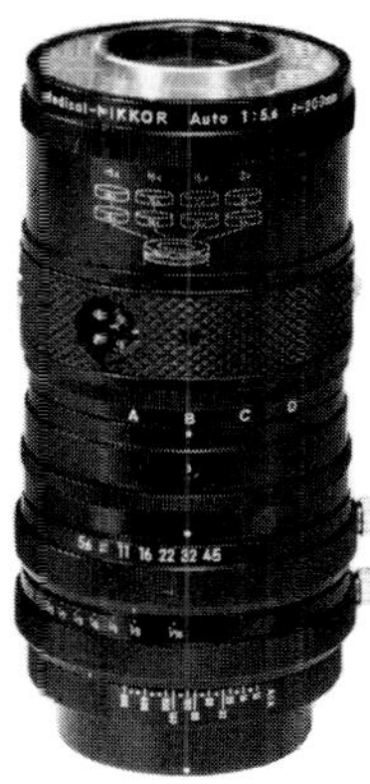

DESCRIPTION

Originally designed for close-up photography in medical fields where ample working distance and cavity illumination are required, superb definition and versatility extend range of application to nature and to commercial and industrial fields. Lens has fixed focus of 3.4m (about 11 ft.) with image ratio of 1:15, but with use of supplementary lenses singly or in combination, image ratios from 1:8 to 3 1 are achieved as diagramed on lens barrel. Focusing performed by moving camera to and from subject with focusing illumination provided by four built-in incandescent bulbs. Built-in ring flashlight (which may be disconnected for daylight photography) affords even and shadowless illumination of use in lighting cavities or recessed areas. Self-compensating feature eliminates computation in setting diaphragm in relation to film speed and image ratio. Magnification ratio from 1/15x to 3x or numerical counting from 1 to 39 can be imprinted optionally on lower right corner of each picture.

SPECIFICATIONS

Smallest aperture: 45

Subject fields: Governed by image ratios chosen through use of supplementary lenses, ranging from 1:15 (lens alone) to 1:8 to 3:1 with supplementary lenses.

Image ratio at nearest distance: 3:1

Lens fixed focus: Distance focusing with basic lens alone and with supplementary lenses is done by moving camera to and from subject until it is in focus.

Angles of view:
Diagonal: 12°20′
Horizontal: 10°20′
Vertical: 6°50′

Attachment size (inside screw diameter): 38mm (P = 0.75)

Front lens cap: 38mm screw-in

Lens case: Complete outfit case, AC: U.S. 296, battery: U.S. 297

Overall size: 80mm ϕ x 176mm

Weight: 670g (23.6 oz)

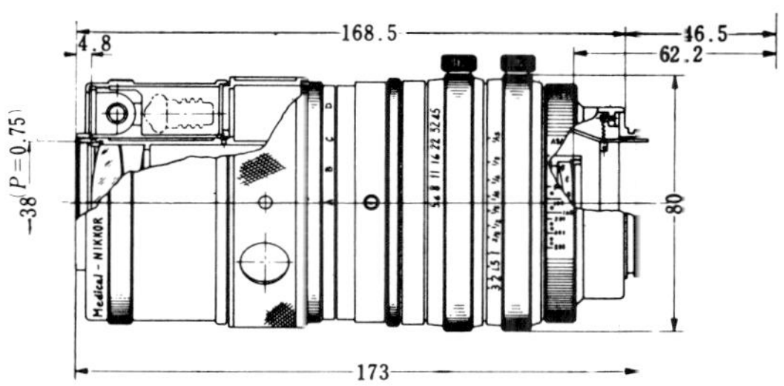

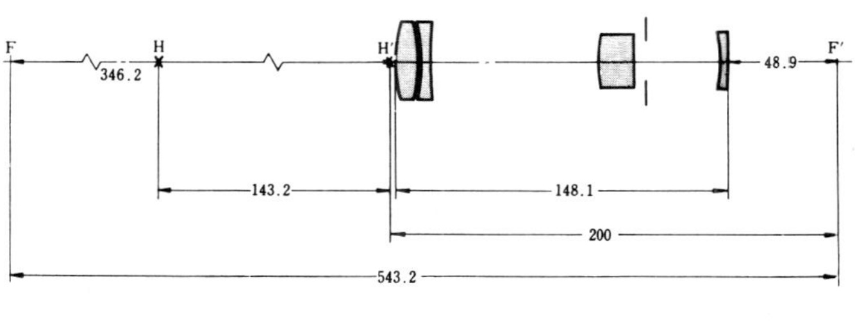

EL NIKKORS

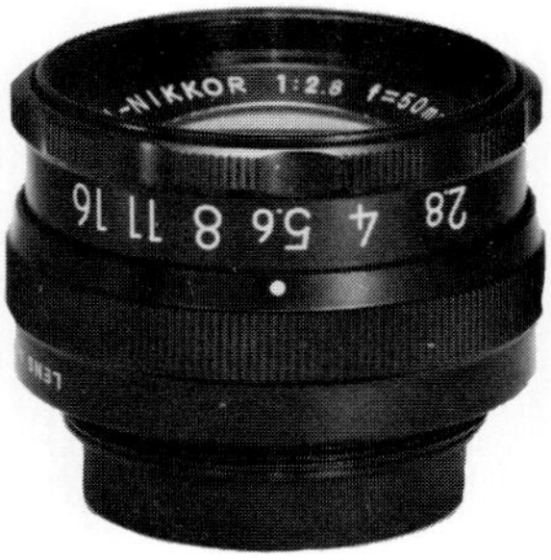

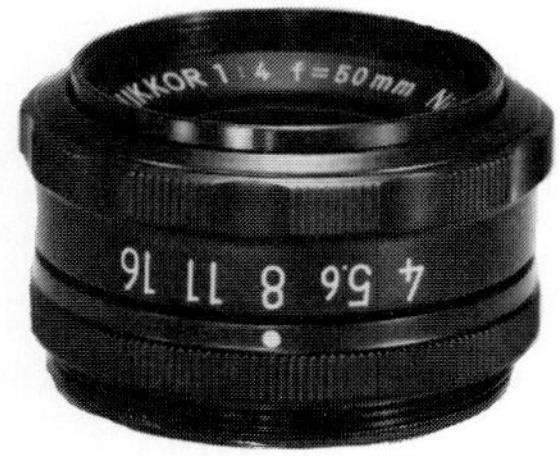

DESCRIPTION

The 50mm $f/2.8$ El-Nikkor is reputed to be among world's finest photo-enlarging lenses. Aberrations of lens are corrected specifically for near-subject distances from 2x to 20x image ratios. Image brightness is reproduced uniformly throughout entire picture area. There is no shift of focus in image plane as diaphragm is stopped down. Maximum aperture of $f/2.8$ is most convenient for focusing, but optimum aperture is around $f/5.6$. Chromatic aberrations are corrected not only for range of visible light but also for short wavelengths up to near ultraviolet 380 millimicrons. For darkroom convenience, $f/$numbers are engraved in large white figures on both sides of lens barrel together with convenient click stops.

The 50mm $f/4$ El-Nikkor is a high quality photo-enlarging lens for 35mm enlargers designed for applications where brightness is not a primary requirement. Otherwise, performance characteristics are essentially similar to those of the 50mm $f/2.8$ El-Nikkor.

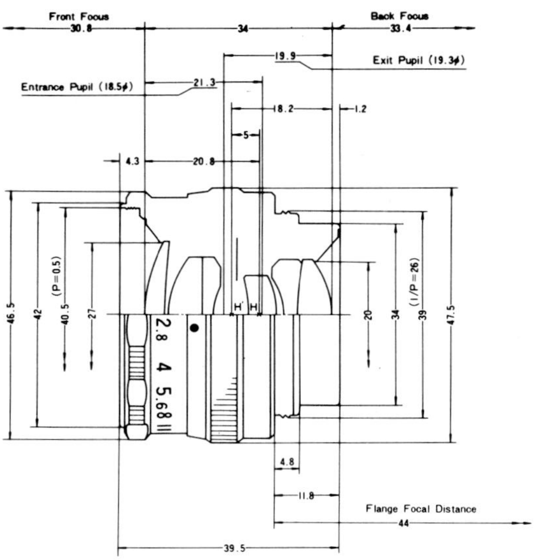

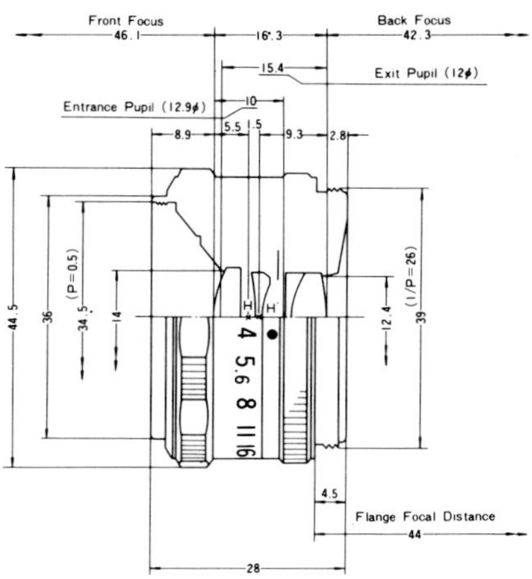

Index